FAITH AND PATRONAGE

New Directions in Irish History is a series initiated by the Royal Irish Academy National Committee for History, which showcases the work of new scholars in Irish history. The series reflects the most up-to-date research, inclusive of all historical periods and with a broad inter-disciplinary approach.

FIRST TITLES IN THIS SERIES

Seán MacEntee
A Political Life
Tom Feeney

The Glory of Being Britons
Civic Unionism in Nineteenth-Century Belfast
John Bew

The Church of Ireland and the Third Home Rule Crisis
Andrew Scholes

FAITH AND PATRONAGE

The political career of
Flaithrí Ó Maolchonaire,
c. 1560–1629

Benjamin Hazard

Ó Cléirigh Institute, University College Dublin

IRISH ACADEMIC PRESS

DUBLIN • PORTLAND, OR

First published in 2010 by Irish Academic Press

2 Brookside,
Dundrum Road,
Dublin 14, Ireland

920 NE 58th Avenue, Suite 300
Portland, Oregon,
97213-3786, USA

www.iap.ie

British Library Cataloguing-in-Publication Data
An entry can be found on request

978 0 7165 3048 0 (cloth)

Library of Congress Cataloging-in-Publication Data
An entry can be found on request

Printed in Great Britain by the MPG Books Group, Bodmin and King's Lynn

Contents

Acknowledgements

This book would not have been possible without the help of others. I began the work for it in 2001 with research into the history of Flaithrí Ó Maolchonaire's family. Since then I have accumulated many debts of gratitude. Particular thanks must go to the Irish province of the Friars Minor who provided me with essential assistance and permitted me to stay at St Isidore's College, Rome. To Thomas O'Connor who encouraged me to undertake research into the career of Flaithrí Ó Maolchonaire and carefully directed the resulting doctoral thesis. I am much obliged to Hiram Morgan, Peter Gray and Deirdre McMahon of the Royal Irish Academy Committee for Historical Sciences and to Lisa Hyde of Irish Academic Press. I wish to record my thanks to the National University of Ireland who granted me their Travelling Studentship to further my investigations overseas. My godparents John and Elena gave me a love of Spain from an early age and accommodated me during my research in Madrid. To John McCafferty and Edel Bhreathnach of the UCD Ó Cléirigh Institute for their scholarly insights, support and good humour. I have learned much from Martin Stone of the Katholieke Universiteit Leuven and am grateful for his encouragement. Craig Harline and Eddy Put generously gave their permission to reproduce the map of the Spanish Netherlands. Brian Mac Cuarta SJ drew my attention to useful source material, read through part of the book and made helpful suggestions for consideration. In Rome, I benefited from his confrère Thomas McCoog's observations on the early-modern Jesuit mission and their nuncios. Liam Chambers, Raymond Gillespie and Colm Lennon, Mícheál Mac Craith OFM, Joseph MacMahon OFM, Aonghus Meaney, Pádraig Ó Macháin and John J. Silke have read chapters and offered constructive criticism. Thanks are due to Séamas de Barra and Mícheál Ó Geallabháin for their advice on sources. I acknowledge the indispensable assistance I received from Beatrix Faerber, project manager of the Corpus of Electronic Texts. Kenneth Nicholls motivated me in the early stages of my research by sharing his knowledge of Gaelic landownership. I salute Declan Downey for his erudition and understanding of international relations. I am grateful to the authorities of the Vatican Library and Archives for permission to quote from the documents in their charge. My sincere thanks go also to Doña Isabel Aguirre and her colleagues at Simancas for their expertise and courtesy. I wish to thank the following archivists and librarians for their efficient assistance: Esther Carreño at Salamanca, Bernadette Cunningham of the Royal Irish Academy, Marco Grilli and José Antonio Yoldi SJ in Rome, Seamus Helferty and Margaret Purcell of the UCD Library and Archives, Fr Ignatius Fennessy OFM, Juan Larios de la Rosa of the Fundación Ducal de Medinaceli, Aideen Ireland at the National Archives and Penny Woods at the Russell Library, St Patrick's College,

Maynooth. I have benefited greatly from discussions and practical support from Ciaran Brady, Michael and Anne Diffley of Roscommon, David Edwards, Enrique García Hernán, Guy Holland, the Irish Pallotines at San Silvestro in Capite, Celia Kehoe, Éamonn Ó Ciardha, Gerrit Vanden Bosch, Manuel Lomas, Lanfranco Lombardi, Davide Maffi, Eduardo de Mesa Gallego, Jeroen Nilis, Seán Ó Coileáin, Vera Orschel, Ciaran O'Scea, Igor Pérez Tostado, Óscar Recio Morales, Glyn Redworth and Ana Isabel Salazar López. Closer to home, I am indebted to Seán and Noreen Hennessy. Most of all, I am deeply grateful to my mother and late father for patiently supporting me through the research and writing.

Abbreviations

AAEE	Archivo de Asuntos Exteriores de España, Madrid
FSS	Fondo Santa Sede
AConn	*Annals of Connacht*
ADM	Archivo Ducal de Medinaceli
AFM	*Annals of the Four Masters*
AGR/ARA	Archives Générales du Royaume, Brussels/Algemeen Rijksarchief, Brussel
SEG	Sécrétairerie d'État et de Guerre /Secretarie van State en Oorlog
AGS	Archivo General de Simancas
CJH	Consejo y Juntas de Hazienda
E.	Sección de Estado
ES.	Negociación de España
NP	Negocios de 'Partes'
Fl.	Negociación de Flandes
In.	Negociación de Inglaterra
R.	Negociación de Roma
GM	Secretaría de Guerra y Marina
l.	legajo (document bundle)
AHN, OOMM	Archivo Histórico Nacional, Madrid, Ordenes Militares
ALC	*Annals of Loch Cé*
An. Hib.	*Analecta Hibernica*
Archiv. Hib.	*Archivium Hibernicum*
ARSI	Archivum Romanum Societate Iesu, Rome
ASV	Archivio Segreto Vaticano, Rome
BAV	Biblioteca Apostolica Vaticana, Rome
Barb. Lat.	Codici Barberini Latini
BISCG	Biblioteca Istituto Storico della Compagnia di Gesu', Rome
BL	British Library, London
Add. MS	Additional Manuscript

BNE	Biblioteca Nacional de España, Madrid
BRB/KBB	Bibliothèque Royale Bruxelles/Koninklijke Bibliotheek van België, Brussel
Cal. Carew Mss.	*Calendar of the Carew manuscripts* (London, 1867–73)
Cal. Pat. Rolls	*Calendar of the Patent Rolls: James I*
Cal. S.P. Ire.	*Calendar of State Papers, Ireland*
Coll. Hib.	*Collectanea Hibernica*
HMC	Historical Manuscripts Commission Reports
IBL	*The Irish Book Lover: A Handbook for Irish Studies*
IER	*Irish Ecclesiastical Record*
IHS	*Irish Historical Studies*
Ir. Men of Learning	Paul Walsh, *Irish Men of Learning* ed. Colm Ó Lochlainn (Dublin: Three Candles Press, 1947)
Ir. Sword	*The Irish Sword: Journal of the Military History Society of Ireland*
Ir. Theol. Quart.	*Irish Theological Quarterly*
JCHAS	*Journal of the Cork Historical and Archaeological Society*
JGHAS	*Journal of the Galway Historical and Archaeological Society*
NAI	National Archives of Ireland, Dublin
New Hist. Ire., 3	T. W. Moody, F. X. Martin and F. J. Byrne (eds), *A New History of Ireland*, vol. 3 (Oxford: Oxford University Press, 1976)
Proc. RIA	*Proceedings of the Royal Irish Academy, section C*
RIA	Royal Irish Academy, Dublin
RBPM	Real Biblioteca de Palacio Real de Madrid
RLM	Russell Library, Maynooth
Spic. Ossor.	*Spicilegium Ossoriense [...] original letters and papers*, ed. Patrick Moran (3 vols., Dublin, 1874)
TCD Cat. Ir. Mss.	T. K. Abbott and E. J. Gwynn (eds), *Catalogue of Irish Manuscripts in Trinity College Library* (Dublin: Hodges Figgis, 1921)
TNA	National Archives, Kew
UCD-OFM	Irish Franciscan Manuscripts at University College, Dublin

Glossary of Spanish Terms

alférez – an ensign or lieutenant; i.e. second-in-command of a company.

almirante – admiral or commander of an armada, squadron or fleet.

arbitrista – Castilian economic planner and social commentator.

caballero – a knight, as distinct from a noble.

cofradía – a lay confraternity organised to conduct charitable works at parish level.

Consejo de Estado – Council of State, nominally the most important.

Consejo de Hazienda – the Council of Finance.

consulta – document of advice to the king drafted by one of his *consejos* or *juntas*.

contador – controller of accounts, or purser.

de parte – a petition made at court on behalf of an individual applicant.

ducado – the unit of account in Castile, equivalent to 375 *maravedís* or 11 *reales*. In 1623, four *ducados* were equivalent to £1.

emprezza – naval expedition.

entretenido – gentleman or gentlewoman in receipt of a retainer from the military treasury, without obligation to serve in the armed forces, although many soldiers received an extra allowance as an *entretenido*.

entretenimiento – entitlements, financial or otherwise, awarded to an *entretenido* at court.

escudo – gold coin worth 10 *reales* or 340 *maravedís*. From 1534 to 1634, despite inflation, the basic wage of a foot-soldier in the Spanish Army of Flanders was 3 escudos.[1]

florín – unit of account used in Flanders, equivalent to the *escudo*.

hábito – insignia of a knight of one of the military orders.

Junta – administrative body set up to reduce delays and bureaucracy in government.

legajo – a tied bundle of documents in a Spanish archive.

maestre de campo – colonel and captain of the first company of a *tercio*.

maravedí – copper coin current in seventeenth-century Castile in units of four, eight and sixteen.

matrícula – term used to refer to registration at university or in the forces.

merced, mercedes – favour granted by the king.

Monarquía – Spain and its empire.

patente – a captain's commission.

plaça muerte – the allowance of personnel who died or were discharged from duty, which could then be re-allocated.

procurador – an agent appointed to a member of the nobility e.g. Matha Óg Ó Maoltuile's work as secretary to Aodh Ruadh Ó Domhnaill.

prueba – official investigation by the council of military orders into the suitability of candidates proposed for knighthoods of the military orders.

real – silver coin worth 34 *maravedís;* 11 *reales* were worth one *ducado.*

reforma – disbanding of a military unit or units.

remate – payment of allowances owed.

sargento mayor – second-in-command of a *tercio;* e.g. Eoghan Ruadh's rank after the death of his first cousin Colonel Éinrí Ó Néill.

servicio – recognised service to the king.

socorro – military assistance, or part payment on account for lost or unpaid wages.

sueldo – wages.

teniente – in the early seventeenth century this referred to a cavalry lieutenant.

tercio – the characteristic *corps d'élite* of Spain's armies: divided into a variable number of companies each under the command of a captain.

vellón – alloy coinage of increasing copper content.

ventaja – bonus awarded to military personnel for exceptional service.

NOTE

1. Geoffrey Parker, *The Army of Flanders and the Spanish Road, 1567–1659: the logistics of Spanish victory and defeat in the Low Countries' wars* (Cambridge: Cambridge University Press, 1972), p. 158.

Author's Note

The number of ways that the name of Flaithrí Ó Maolchonaire (Florence Conry) was spelt during his lifetime reflects the lack of standard spelling in early seventeenth-century documents and the variety of European languages in use amongst Irish exiles. He simplified his name to 'Florencio Conrio' in Castilian and Italian sources to overcome pronunciation difficulties. In Latin he was known as 'Florentius Conrius' and in English an assortment of English derivatives were used, such as 'Florin O Mulconere'. Since this study begins with his early years, he is referred to by his Gaelic name throughout the book.[1] In the interests of consistency, a minimalist approach is applied to other Gaelic names for the most prominent protagonists such as Aodh Ruadh Ó Domhnaill (Red Hugh O'Donnell) and Aodh Ó Néill (Hugh O'Neill). Use of the definite article before the surname; e.g. the Ó Conchobhair Ruadh, denotes the leading member of the family. The word Uí denotes the plural of a family name; e.g. Uí Mhaolchonaire. Spanish terms marked with italics in the text are explained in the glossary.

The problem of dating documents from the late sixteenth to the early eighteenth centuries is, perhaps, an intractable one. All dates are left at the date of the original document. Therefore, any document from continental Europe is dated according to the New Style, Gregorian calendar introduced by Pope Gregory XIII (†1585) in March 1582. Documents written or sent from Ireland and England are dated according to the Old Style, Julian calendar which continued in use until 1752.[2]

The words Spain and Spanish are used to refer to the kingdoms of the Iberian Peninsula during the late sixteenth and early seventeenth centuries. Use of the term the 'Low Countries' refers to the whole of the Netherlands. The terms 'Spanish Flanders', the 'Southern Netherlands' and 'Spanish Netherlands' indicate that part under Spanish administration from the start of the civil wars in 1567 to the Peace of Münster in 1648[3]. Leuven and Mechelen are used when referring to the university, town and archdiocese.

NOTES

1. Tomás Ó Con Cheanainn, 'Ó Maoil Chonaire agus sloinne Shean-Phádraic', *Éigse*, 32 (2000), pp. 23–34, demonstrates why 'Ó Maoil Chonaire' is to be preferred and refers to O'Rahilly's own uncertainty on the matter.
2. George Coyne, Michael Hoskin and Olaf Pedersen (eds), *Gregorian reform of the Calendar: Proceedings of the Vatican Conference to commemorate its 400th anniversary* (Vatican City, 1983), cited by Hiram Morgan, '"The Pope's new invention": the introduction of the Gregorian calendar in Ireland, 1583–1782', a paper delivered at 'Ireland, Rome and the Holy See: history, culture and contact', a UCC History Department Symposium at the Pontifical Irish College, Rome, April 2006.
3. Gráinne Henry, *The Irish military community in Spanish Flanders, 1586–1621* (Dublin: Irish Academic Press, 1992), p. 9. See also the contributions of A. T. van Deursen and Paul Janssens in J. C. H. Blom and Emiel Lamberts (eds), *History of the Low Countries* (Oxford, 1999), pp. 143–272.

Key to Plates

Plate I: Flaithrí Ó Maolchonaire's family tree, paternal line *cf*; Paul Walsh, *Irish men of learning*, ed Colm Ó Lochlainn (Dublin: Three Candles Press, 1947), Appendix). I am grateful to Kenneth Nicholls for his help compiling this table.

Plate II: A lecture at the University of Salamanca, where Ó Maolchonaire studied in the 1590s; detail from a painting by Martín de Cervera, *c.* 1614 (Manuel Fernández Álvarez, Luis Rodíguez San Pedro, Julián Álvarez Villar, *The University of Salamanca: eight centuries of scholarship* (Salamanca: Ediciones Universidad de Salamanca, 1992) p. 71)

Plate III: Simancas Castle, now the Archivo General de Simancas, where Ó Maolchonaire attended to Aodh Ruadh Ó Domhnaill in his final days, signing his will and acting as his interpreter (courtesy of the Ministerio de Cultura, Madrid)

Plate IV: The Monastery of San Juan de los Reyes, Toledo, where Ó Maolchonaire was elected Irish minister-provincial at the Franciscan General Chapter, 1606 (reproduced by kind permission of the guardian and friars, Monasterio de San Juan de los Reyes, Toledo)

Plate V: The Southern Netherlands, 1606-29 (Craig Harline and Eddy Put, *A bishop's tale: Mathias Hovius among his flock in seventeenth-century Flanders* (New Haven: Yale University Press, 2000), p. 16, courtesy of the authors)

Plate VI: The City of Leuven (Ludovico Guicciardini, *Descrittione di tutti i Paesi Bassi* (Antwerp, 1567); John J. Murray, *Flanders and England: the influence of the Low Countries on Tudor-Stuart England* (Antwerp: Fonds Mercator, 1985), p. 65)

Plate VII: Chiesa di Santo Spirito, Rome (Giuseppe Vasi, *Delle Magnificenze di Roma Antica e Moderna,* (Roma, 1759), lib. 9, tav. 171), where Ó Maolchonaire was consecrated archbishop of Tuam in 1609; now the Sanctuary of Divine Mercy

Plate VIII: Ó Maolchonaire's Archiepiscopal seal of office, 1609-29, inscribed with the words *Florentius Conrius Archiepiscopus Tuamensis* (Archivo General de Simancas, Guerra Antigua-Servicios Militares, legajo 5, folio 78) courtesy of the Ministerio de Cultura, Madrid

Plate IX: Letter of Flaithrí Ó Maolchonaire to the guardians and friars at St

Anthony's College, February 1613, with his seal beside his signature (UCD-OFM, MS. D.01, vol. 4, p. 791), courtesy of the UCD-OFM Foundation

Plate X: Title page of Ó Maolchonaire's *Sgáthán an Chrábhaidh*, 1616, reproduced by permission of the Librarian, National University of Ireland, Maynooth, from the collections of St Patrick's College, Maynooth

Plate XI: Title page of Ó Maolchonaire's first edition of *Tractatus de statu parvulorum sine Baptismo decedentium ex hac vita: iuxta sensum B. Augustini* (Lovanii: Henrici Hastenii, 1624); reproduced by permission of the Librarian, National University of Ireland, Maynooth, from the collections of St Patrick's College, Maynooth

Plate XII: Letter of Flaithrí Ó Maolchonaire to Archbishop Jacob Boonen, Madrid, February 1627, describing his journey from the Southern Netherlands with Hugo de Burgo and pledging his loyalty to Boonen

Plate XIII: Title page of Ó Maolchonaire's first edition of *Peregrinus ierichuntinus [...]* (Parisiis: apud Claudium Calleville, 1641); reproduced by permission of the Librarian, National University of Ireland, Maynooth, from the collections of St Patrick's College, Maynooth

Plate XIV: The Convent of Jesus and Mary, and Basilica of San Francisco el Grande, Madrid, (marked 209), where Flaithrí Ó Maolchonaire died on Sunday, 18 November 1629 (Luis Miguel Aparisi Laporta, *El plano de Teixeira trescientos cincuenta años después* (Madrid: Ayuntamiento de Madrid, 2008) p. 100)

Plate XV: College of St Anthony of Padua, Leuven, founded by Flaithrí Ó Maolchonaire (from an early eighteenth-century engraving by H. Otto, in Eduard Van Even, *Louvain monumental ou description historique et artistique de tous les édifices civils et religieux de la dite ville* (Louvain: Fonteyn, 1860), p. 158)

Foreword

'the circumspection that the Irish use in their treaties in that court [of Spain], who considering that their affairs do in no way pertain to us, are wont not only curiously to conceal the same from us, but also to desire the King's ministers not to communicate them with us'

Thomas Fitzherbert, *A Defence of the Catholic cause* (Rome, 1602)

This reflection on Irish activity at the Spanish court written by an exiled English Catholic wonderfully sums up the atmosphere in which Flaithrí Ó Maolchonaire operated for roughly one half of his life. Ó Maolchonaire was himself an exile, but he was also a courtier, an intriguer, a partisan patron, a poet, a theologian, a bishop, an administrator, a militarist, a pastor, a friar. He favoured, and participated in, Spanish military intervention in Ireland, projected incorporation of the kingdom of Ireland into the Spanish *monarquía* and determined the fortunes of myriad Irish exiles and migrants to the Iberian peninsula and to Flanders. He was Franciscan provincial of Ireland, archbishop of Tuam, founder of St Anthony's college in Leuven and implacable opponent of the Jesuits. He was from a learned Gaelic family, loyal to the Ulster earls. He was at the deathbed of Aodh Ruadh Ó Domhnaill, and the Patriarch of the Indies officiated at his own requiem. He was a powerbroker, influential for long periods, sidelined for others and, above all, a man of irrepressible energy whose ambition and creativity found an outlet no matter what circumstances he found himself in. When in favour, there was high politics, when out of favour there was theological debate and publication at a distinguished level.

If Flaithrí Ó Maolchonaire had been asked to chose a single label to describe himself, he might have got no further than a shortlist composed of three words: 'Irish', 'Franciscan', 'Spanish'. But one-word summaries are a more modern passion and most of Ó Maolchonaire's interest lies in the way in which he incarnates that complex experience of dispossession, exile, acculturation and new identifications that typified Irish experiences in late sixteenth and early seventeenth century Europe. Reading this work, there are moments when Ó Maolchonaire seems to be an 'everyman' (albeit a very talented and driven one) of his compatriots and there are moments when he appears to be so idiosyncratic, so opinionated, so driven that there could be no-one else like him. Biographies of individuals from early modern Ireland are, even still, rare. When they are well-constructed and highly-researched as this monograph is they carry out a dual task of telling the reader more about the subject and simultaneously revealing rich new perspectives and seams of materials pertaining to the environment within which the protagonist operated.

Flaithrí Ó Maolchonaire has not languished in obscurity since his death in 1629. While his remains are buried still within the walls of St Anthony's at Leuven his works and influences have been widely studied. Yet because he was a man of so many parts, he has been studied in parts. You can read about Ó Maolchonaire the proto-Jansenist, you can read about Ó Maolchonaire the Machiavellian friar, you can read about Ó Maolchonaire as the translator and glossator of *Desiderius*, you can read about him as a Franciscan provincial. In this volume you can now read about all of these facets of his life and all of his immense creativity in the one place. As the list of repositories in Belgium, England, Ireland, Italy and Spain shows this is was no simple task. Flaithrí Ó Maolchonaire preferred to walk and he has left his archival footprints right across Europe. Benjamin Hazard has now essayed a full biography. Readers may judge the results for themselves. It can be said without prejudice that this work is timely. It is timely in the commemorative sense, in that it was completed soon after the 400th anniversary celebrations of his Leuven foundation and will appear during the 400th anniversary of his promotion to Tuam. In a scholarly and intellectual sense, the time is also ripe. The last decade has seen a great flowering of the long tradition of scholarship into the Irish experience on continental Europe, especially in the work and leadership provided by the 'Irish in Europe' project based at NUI Maynooth where Dr Hazard took his PhD degree. Since 2000, a partnership between the friars minor of Ireland and UCD has been expressed in the form of the Mícheál Ó Cléirigh Institute for the study of Irish history and civilisation where the papers and research materials of Ó Maolchonaire's confrères such as Luke Wadding are now being conserved, catalogued and scanned. New attitudes to ownership, use and dissemination of key archival holdings coupled with intellectual openness and keen rigorous interdisciplinarity make a study like this possible.

It is to be hoped this book will someday evoke words similar to those that Flaithrí Ó Maolchonaire used of another text published at Leuven in 1616: 'Do thaitin an leabhran-so comhór 7 sin leis gach ccrich do chum a ráinig gur cuireadh a Spáinnis, a nEadáillis, a bhFraincis, 7 a Laidin é'.

John McCafferty
Director, UCD Mícheál Ó Cléirigh Institute
July 2009

Introduction

This study deals with the political career of Flaithrí Ó Maolchonaire, a Franciscan agent of the late sixteenth and early seventeenth centuries who became Catholic archbishop of Tuam. When he was born in the early 1560s, efforts to implement Tudor state-building policies in Connacht and Ulster had just begun. He and his generation witnessed profound political and cultural changes which heralded a new order in early-modern Ireland. Within three years of building bridges over the Shannon at Athlone and Ballinasloe, the viceroy of Ireland, Sir Henry Sidney (†1586), created shires of Roscommon, Sligo, Mayo and Galway.[1] The launch of this expansion into sixteenth-century Gaelic society occurred at a time when the political power of Spain and France eclipsed that of England. Anglo-Spanish relations had become more strained after the death of Mary Tudor in 1558 and although her husband Philip II (†1598) avoided committing himself in Ireland, he identified the island as a perpetual cause of weakness to Elizabeth I who recognised the potential threat this caused.[2] Irish political approaches to Spain were made in earnest after her excommunication and Philip II eventually took steps to counter English support for the Dutch.[3] In 1588, the lord deputy reported: 'We find already that the name of the Spaniards worketh much in the hearts of the Irishry.'[4] This was particularly the case in Ireland's northern and western provinces where the people were described by the attorney general as 'dangerously affected towards the Spanish'.[5]

Flaithrí Ó Maolchonaire's direct experience of these combined developments influenced his decision to leave Ireland for Spain in the early 1590s. He entered the newly founded Irish college in Salamanca and came into contact with the local university world, especially its schools of political thought and apologetics. On returning to Ireland during the Nine Years War, Ó Maolchonaire helped realise the diplomatic and strategic possibilities that Spain offered the Ulster earls' resistance to Tudor expansion.

Despite declaring Henry VIII king of Ireland and denying papal authority, the 1541 Act for the Kingly Title promoted the idea of Ireland's sovereign status, a concept given greater legitimacy for Catholics when Pope Paul IV later created a kingdom of Ireland for Philip II and his wife Mary Tudor.[6] Flaithrí Ó Maolchonaire was among the political thinkers to develop the concept of an early-modern Irish kingdom.[7] In this context, it is vital to realise that the heterogeneous empire of the Spanish *monarquía* in Europe comprised 'a nexus of kingdoms and lordships' subject to the Habsburgs of Spain.[8] Throughout his public career Ó Maolchonaire's main priority was the defence of Gaelic political hegemony. From this perspective he considered Habsburg over-lordship preferable to that of the Tudors or Stuarts.[9]

Flaithrí Ó Maolchonaire was one of the most important Irish figures active in early-modern Europe in his role as advocate and representative of the Ulster earls and their patronage network.[10] Unlike many of his contemporaries, sufficient source material survives to document his life and works. This study traces Ó Maolchonaire's public career and assesses the strategy he developed in Spain, Rome and Flanders as an agent of the Ulster earls from the 1590s to the late 1620s. It begins with a look at the extension of Tudor influence in Connacht and Ulster from the mid-sixteenth century and explores how these changes influenced Ó Maolchonaire's relations with the Uí Dhomhnaill. It describes the circumstances of his leaving Ireland and his emergence as a key figure among the Irish abroad, from his education in Spain to his rise to political prominence as confessor to Aodh Ruadh Ó Domhnaill and the aftermath of defeat at Kinsale. Ó Maolchonaire's efforts to gain control of Irish colleges in Spanish territories and the funds provided for Irish military interests were central to his work and are considered next. Ó Maolchonaire looked on this network as crucial, not only to the renewal of Catholicism in Ireland but also to the maintenance of Uí Dhomhnaill and Uí Néill influence at home and abroad. Politicisation of his religious mission won Ó Maolchonaire many enemies not only among interests dependent on the early Stuarts but also among his Irish Catholic co-religionists.

A careful examination of Ó Maolchonaire's support of Uí Dhomhnaill and Uí Néill military and religious networks reveals his ongoing role in securing Spanish funding for his patrons. This important aspect of his career has been neglected by many historians since the nineteenth century when, sometimes for polemical or hagiographical reasons, anachronistic categories were imposed on the complexities of his political and religious preoccupations. This work seeks to re-place Ó Maolchonaire and his contemporaries in the political and religious context of the early seventeenth century. Apart from Bernadette Cunningham's work on the relevance of social and cultural change in Gaelic society to Flaithrí Ó Maolchonaire's confrères at the college he founded,[11] no concerted effort has been made to ascertain his role in the transfer of Gaelic political power and patronage to the continent.

The widespread dispersal of primary sources related to Flaithrí Ó Maolchonaire reflects the scale of religious and cultural upheaval in Ireland and abroad in the early seventeenth century.[12] From the beginning, the absence of a political biography on Ó Maolchonaire has led to repeated inaccuracies. The first contributions to the debate about his career were recorded during his lifetime and the bias to which they were prone set the precedent for a contested history.[13] Although some seventeenth-century sources did take account of the social context of Ó Maolchonaire's life, there were basic inconsistencies in details concerning his place of birth, his education, his whereabouts and his contacts.[14] Until recently, for example, Meehan's unsubstantiated claims that Flaithrí Ó Maolchonaire was born at Cloonahee, County Roscommon, entered the Franciscan order at Moyne abbey in 1584 and began his work in Madrid eight years later were widely accepted.[15] Similarly, claims that Ó Maolchonaire sailed back from Spain with the Armada of 1588 before receiving an education at Leuven, at the feet of Michael Baius, were commonplace.[16] There is no evidence to support this, nor is there substantiation for the claims that Ó Maolchonaire travelled to Brussels in 1605, was consecrated archbishop on the Salerian Road, Rome, in March 1609 before offering Hugh O'Neill's terms for a proposed reconciliation with James I later that year in Madrid, made a return voyage to Rome in 1616 and approved of negotiations for the Spanish Match.[17] These shortcomings were in large part due to the ideological conflict surrounding Ó Maolchonaire, an individual who has been glorified by devotees or vilified by adversaries in equal measure. Ó Maolchonaire's deep-seated contention with the Irish Jesuits has been attributed to an incident in the 1590s at Salamanca's Irish college but, as pointed out by Declan Downey, this dispute was nothing compared to the wrath incurred by Ó Maolchonaire when he involved himself in the University of Leuven's sanction against the Society of Jesus almost thirty years later.[18]

The diverse appeal of Ireland's early-modern political relations with the Iberian Peninsula means that historians have not ignored Flaithrí Ó Maolchonaire. At the outset, this necessitates a thorough understanding of the scholarly work conducted on the subject to date. His first modern historian was Charles Meehan, whose seminal study of the Uí Néill and the Uí Dhomhnaill was inspired, in part, by the romanticism of Irish nationalism and Gaelic revival. However, Meehan also dealt with Ó Maolchonaire as a political figure and brought many primary sources connected with him to print for the first time.[19] In the 1920s, Felim O'Brien OFM gathered together all the available material at his disposal to compile a useful series of articles on Ó Maolchonaire.[20] Although this provided a valuable resource to historians of Ó Maolchonaire and his entourage, O'Brien's work lacked a consistent chronology and, reflecting the aspirations of a newly independent Irish Free State, shied away from portraying his Franciscan confrère Ó Maolchonaire in anything other than a positive light. In a similar vein, Heaney's study of Ó Maolchonaire's theological writings in their political context was constrained by historiographical limitations and the uncompromising nature of early twentieth-century nationalism.[21]

Flaithrí Ó Maolchonaire's earliest known works and his most recognised published text, *Sgáthán an Chrábhaidh*, were written in Irish. Vincent Morley has observed that many historians have hitherto failed 'either to utilise the vernacular sources or to assimilate the findings of scholars who publish in Irish'.[22] As this assertion readily applies to Ó Maolchonaire's family background and some of his writings, it would be an oversight not to refer to relevant works written by Irish language scholars since the first half of the twentieth century.

In bringing to print the fiants relating to the families of Irish poets, historians, and judges in Tudor and Stuart times, Thomas F. O'Rahilly's work for the Royal Irish Academy in the early 1920s contextualised the culture and politics of Ó Maolchonaire's times.[23] O'Rahilly's edition of *Sgáthán an Chrábhaidh* followed two decades later.[24] With it came a concise summary of Ó Maolchonaire's family setting in Connacht which, by O'Rahilly's own admission, was limited by the lack of access to pertinent archives and information.[25] In 1947, Colm Ó Lochlainn published Paul Walsh's excellent study of the Uí Mhaoilchonaire and,[26] three years later, Brian Ó Cuív edited Ó Maolchonaire's Irish language catechism, *Teagasc Críostaí*, from an extant manuscript at the Royal Irish Academy.[27] In making this catechism accessible to a wider readership, Ó Cuív's work for the journal *Celtica* served as a catalyst for future publications.[28] In common with his peers, Ó Maolchonaire's use of such writings in Irish to inculcate Catholic reform has been identified by Breandán Ó Buachalla as a key phase in the development of political thought among Irish scholars up to the end of the eighteenth century.[29] In the immediate term, however, Archbishop Ó Maolchonaire's failure to return to Ireland after his appointment prevented him from disseminating his writings in person and his absence attracted trenchant criticism from the Catholic primate, Peter Lombard. Pádraig A. Breatnach's analysis of a Gaelic chronology and a genealogy attributed to Ó Maolchonaire attests the early-modern endurance of Gaelic kinship interconnected with the medieval tradition which traced their descent to the Iberian Peninsula.[30]Although this offers an accurate reflection of Irish custom and popular belief for the period, Ó Maolchonaire emphasised the services and losses of Irish families in his appeals to Philip III and Philip IV on their behalf.

The interests of Killiney-based Franciscan historians in the 1940s and 1950s encouraged more work on Ó Maolchonaire and his associates. The pioneering Brendan Jennings advocated the value of a source-based, critical history, with the publication of a large quantity of primary documentation from Belgian repositories.[31] His resulting article on Ó Maolchonaire's last days, for instance, is a monument to careful scholarship.[32] The same can be said for much of Ceyssens' article on Ó Maolchonaire, de Burgo and Wadding.[33] Dependable but less well-known articles based upon original archival research by recognised experts should not be overlooked either.[34] Working on behalf of the National Library of Ireland, Canice Mooney's microfilm survey of material from Simancas brought the state archives of Spain to public view in the same tradition of scientific investigation.[35] Since then Micheline Kerney Walsh dealt with the interaction between major Irish families, most notably the Uí Néill and Uí Dhomhnaill, the Spanish monarchy and the papal court.[36]

In recent decades, the history of the emergence of Irish communities in Habsburg Spain and Flanders has attracted increasing attention and provided essential context for research on Ó Maolchonaire.[37] John Silke called attention to Ireland's strategic significance to Spain and the movements of Irish exiles in mainland Europe.[38] The role of Aodh Ó Néill in this process is the subject of ongoing investigation by Hiram Morgan.[39] In 1971, Helga Hammerstein's critical overview of the Irish experience of European university education during the reign of Elizabeth Tudor placed the Irish experience in its British and Continental setting.[40] In the same decade, Thomas Morrissey SJ dealt with much material relating specifically to the Irish Jesuits in the Iberian Peninsula during the 1590s.[41] Patricia O Connell continued this theme with her studies of the colleges' origins and their Irish student populations at Santiago, Alcalá and Lisbon.[42] New primary source research under the direction of Enrique García Hernán in Madrid examines in depth how the Irish colleges functioned within the Spanish strategic system. This reveals how consistent patronage for the education of Irish clergy and their mission to Ireland formed an integral part of early-modern foreign policy objectives in Spain. The politico-religious origins of this interaction have been traced to the reign of Charles V by Declan Downey.[43] From his exploration of the converging intellectual and theological currents witnessed in the seventeenth century, he deduces that the Spanish Habsburgs were largely responsible for the effective realisation of Irish Catholic reform in its early stages.[44] In recent articles, Dr Downey has called for a complete study of Ó Maolchonaire who, despite his important role in this pastoral process and his hopes of seeing Ireland incorporated in the Habsburg *imperium*, remains 'a somewhat neglected figure'.[45] Gráinne Henry has shown the importance of the social experience of Irish soldiers and their contact with the colleges based in Spanish Flanders which, according to her work, were vital to maintaining political morale at home.[46] Throughout his work, Ó Maolchonaire succeeded in helping to establish Irish soldiers in military careers.

From the viewpoint of economic history, research has scarcely started on the commercial networks that provided the military, economic and ideological migrants with a passage through European ports to the Habsburg, Bourbon and papal territories. Although much remains to be done, Hugh Kearney's influential study of early seventeenth-century Irish trade and Karin Schüller's more recent work on Hispano-Irish mercantile links have revealed the complex economic context for the colleges and the Irish military.[47] Intriguingly, newfound evidence from the second decade of the seventeenth century points to Flaithrí Ó Maolchonaire's interest in economic matters.

The fourth centenary of events from the Battle of Kinsale to the Flight of the Earls afforded the opportunity for an extensive historical reappraisal of the period with the publication of conference proceedings from Madrid, Kinsale and Salamanca. This veritable historiographical renaissance concerning the migrant Irish has provided an appropriate background to studies into Ó Maolchonaire and his times by facilitating significant progress in the study of early-modern religious renewal, diplomacy, education and military history.[48] In the last ten years, further advances have been made in the study of Irish migration to the European mainland in the early seventeenth century.[49] Recent research findings by Brian Jackson cast new light on the ethnic background of the Society of Jesus in Ireland and the prominent part that individuals such as William Allen played in founding seminaries abroad.[50] The following study of Flaithrí Ó Maolchonaire refracts the cultural and political tensions among Irish exiles which complicated the diplomatic sensitivities involved in Spanish support for Irish causes.

By revealing the paper trails deliberately created at court by individuals seeking advancement, Ciaran O'Scea's work, particularly on Irish dealings with Castilian protocol and its labyrinth of official procedure, ably demonstrates how an Irish socio-cultural *mentalité* developed in early-modern Spain.[51] Collaborative studies between historians from Ireland and Spain continue to till fertile soil for the late sixteenth and early seventeenth centuries. Enrique García Hernán has concentrated on the reign of Philip II, [52] Óscar Recio Morales on Philip III and his son Philip IV respectively. In distinct studies they have examined the impact of the migrant Irish on Habsburg foreign policy, offering new insights on the reception of Irish arrivals in the political, religious and military circles of early-modern Spain.[53] The ground-breaking proceedings of their first

Madrid conference appeared in 2002 and, more recently, the presence of Irish soldiers in Spanish armies has received special attention.[54] The primary sources highlighted by Óscar Recio in *Archivium Hibernicum* about plans for a military assault on Ireland in 1627 bear witness to a bellicose consistency in Ó Maolchonaire's politics not displayed by his Irish rivals at court in Spain, Rome and the Southern Netherlands.[55] Valid points made by Tomás Ó Fiaich in his analysis of Ó Maolchonaire's accompanying proposals for an early-modern republic under Spanish aegis were lost amid the troubles of the early 1970s.[56] Igor Pérez Tostado shows that Irish exiles were one among many political interest groups from across Europe competing to make their voice heard at the courts of the Spanish Habsburgs, especially during the 1640s.[57] Two decades earlier, rather than being a solidly uniform bloc, Irish Catholics at home and abroad were well-established enough to confidently espouse differing views on a range of topics.[58] Mícheál Mac Craith has illustrated the subtleties of Irish political thinking for the period by comparing Ó Maolchonaire's mindset with that of Aodh Mac Aingil, fellow Franciscans.[59] Since Jerrold Casway's identification of Gaelic Maccabean philosophy with Ó Maolchonaire and his ally Eóghan Mag Mathghamhna, Mac Craith has detected clear parallels with the imagery used by Lughaidh Ó Cléirigh in *Beatha Aodha Ruaidh Uí Dhomhnaill*.[60] In a related study, Joop Leerssen has touched upon Ó Maolchonaire's role in 'the vindication of Irish civility' and the complex development of Irish nationality.[61]

Flaithrí Ó Maolchonaire's theological accomplishments have been dealt with by Thomas O'Connor in his evaluation of Irish Jansenist intrigues.[62] In the pages of *Seanchas Ard Mhacha* a few years ago,[63] O'Connor identified the need to deal exclusively with Ó Maolchonaire's political work. My research on the subject began under his supervision shortly afterwards. To overcome the paucity of early-modern historical evidence in Ireland, David Edwards and Brian Donovan recognised the need to look further afield.[64] This methodology has a bearing upon Flaithrí Ó Maolchonaire because state papers and related materials written in English often reflect the anxiety and sometimes paranoia felt in London and Dublin towards his collaborators. Resorting to such evidence on a repeated basis in the past has only added to the inertia of two irreconcilable traditions of Irish historiography and highlights the need to provide as balanced an account of Ó Maolchonaire's career as possible. The principal sources for this study are, there-fore, Flaithrí Ó Maolchonaire's own dispatches, letters and papers now preserved at Simancas, at the Vatican Library and Archive, and in Brussels. These manuscript sources are indispensable to the study of Irish relations with Spain and Rome. As already noted, the turbulent times in which he lived led to the scattering of primary source material relevant to his public career. Consequently, few of Ó Maolchonaire's sources have, up to now, been studied in their entirety or presented to the public. Nevertheless, they must be used with a certain degree of caution because of Ó Maolchonaire's recourse to rhetoric, so typical for his times. In addi-tion, I have made use of documents from the Archivo Histórico Nacional, Madrid, at the Sección Nobleza, Toledo, and some useful material relating to Ó Maolchonaire's family at the National Archives, Dublin.

Ó Maolchonaire's religious, social and cultural experiences are illustrative of a generation of Irish migrants during the first half of the seventeenth century. Chapter 1 deals with his upbringing to demonstrate that expropriation of his family's property and his education as a hereditary Gaelic chronicler and poet caused considerable dislocation in his life and influenced his public career. Evidence for his brother Maoilechlainn's response to the same events helps to illuminate Flaithrí Ó Maolchonaire's character.

Chapter 2 shows how Ó Maolchonaire's role as Ó Domhnaill's 'perfect ally' in the latter stages of the Nine Years War led him to establish close diplomatic contacts with the Spanish councils of state and war. After his election as minister-provincial of the Irish Franciscans in 1606, Ó Maolchonaire made his way to Spanish Flanders where with the support of the Habsburgs he founded St Anthony's College, Leuven. This period concluded with his role in the Ulster earls' departure from Ireland and their arrival in Rome.[65]

Ó Maolchonaire's political mission to Madrid from 1609 to 1618 is examined in Chapter 3, drawing attention to the difficulties he confronted after his appointment as Catholic archbishop of Tuam and the fierce opposition he faced from some of his fellow exiles. Significantly, before moving back to Leuven, he presented a case against the Spanish Match which sought to consolidate stable trade relations between his Irish allies and Spain. Chapter 4 studies Ó Maolchonaire's return to the Irish Franciscans' new stronghold, the college he had founded at Leuven which preceded his political decline at court in Madrid and his death in 1629. By connecting the late medieval with the early-modern, the following account of his career seeks to provide an accurate representation of the period in which he lived, thereby revealing him to be an Irish agent of continuity and change.

NOTES

1. Jon Crawford, *Anglicizing the government of Ireland: the Irish Privy Council and the expansion of Tudor rule, 1556–1578* (Dublin: Irish Academic Press, 1993), pp. 280–281.
2. Charles Petrie, 'Ireland in Spanish and French strategy, 1558–1815', in Thomas Bartlett (ed.), *Irishmen in war from the crusades to 1798: essays from The Irish Sword* (Dublin: Irish Academic Press, 2006), pp. 192–203. See also Enrique García Hernán, *Ireland and Spain in the reign of Phillip II* (Dublin: Four Courts Press, 2009).
3. Declan Downey, 'Irish-European integration: the legacy of Charles V', in Howard Clarke and Judith Devlin (eds), *European encounters: essays in memory of Albert Lovett* (Dublin: University College Dublin Press, 2003), Chapter 6.
4. William Fitzwilliam to the Privy Council, 28 Oct. 1588 (*Cal. S. P. Ire., Elizabeth,* cxxxvi, 45).
5. Sir John Popham to Burghley (*Cal. S. P. Ire., Elizabeth,* cxxxvi, 34, cited by Caoimhín Ó Danachair, 'Armada losses on the Irish coast', in Bartlett (ed.), *Irishmen in war,* p. 57).
6. See Brendan Bradshaw, *The Irish constitutional revolution of the sixteenth century* (Cambridge: Cambridge University Press, 1979), p. 265; John McCafferty, *The reconstruction of the Church of Ireland: Bishop Bramhall and the Laudian reforms, 1633–1641* (Cambridge: Cambridge University Press, 2007), pp. 5–6.
7. Bernadette Cunningham, 'Sources: Geoffrey Keating's *Foras Feasa ar Éirinn*', History Ireland (Spring, 2001), pp. 14–17.
8. Antonio Domínguez Ortiz, *The golden age of Spain, 1516–1659* (London: Weidenfeld & Nicholson, 1971), pp. 5–9. See also John H. Elliott, *Spain and its world, 1500-1700* (New Haven: Yale University Press, 1989), p. 170.
9. Downey, 'Irish-European integration: the legacy of Charles V', p. 101.
10. Oxford New DNB.

11. See Kenneth Nicholls, *Gaelic and gaelicised Ireland* (repr. Dublin: Lilliput Press, 2003); Bernadette Cunningham, 'Native culture and political change' in Ciarán Brady and Raymond Gillespie (eds.), *Natives and newcomers: the makings of Irish colonial society, 1534–1641* (Dublin: Irish Academic Press, 1986), pp. 148–70; idem, 'The culture and ideology of Irish Franciscan historians at Louvain' in Brady and Gillespie (eds.), *Ideology and the historians* (Dublin, 1991), pp. 11–30.

12. Thomas O'Connor, 'Introduction', in idem (ed.), *The Irish in Europe, 1580-1815* (Dublin: Four Courts Press, 2001), p. 26.

13. See Donnchadh Ó Maonaigh, *Brevis synopsis provinciae Hiberniae FF. minorum*, (Brussels MS. 3,947; *An. Hib.*, 5 (1934); and John Lynch, *De praesulibus Hib.*, ii, p. 246.

14. Luke Wadding, *Scriptores Ordinis Minorum*, (Rome, 1906), pp. 75–6; James Ware, *The writers of Ireland* (Dublin, 1704), p. 27. Internal evidence in these texts suggests that Wadding was Ware's source.

15. Charles Meehan, *The fate and fortunes of Hugh O'Neill, earl of Tyrone, and Rory O'Donel, earl of Tyrconnell* (Dublin: Duffy, 1886), p. 108.

16. James Neary, 'Florence Conry, archbishop of Tuam: 1608-1629', *J.G.H.A.S.* 7 (1912), pp 193–204.

17. These claims have been made repeatedly since Felim O'Brien, 'Florence Conry, archbishop of Tuam' in *Irish Rosary*, 32 (1928), p. 457 and Lucian Ceyssens, 'Florence Conry, Hugh de Burgo, Luke Wadding, and Jansenism', in Franciscan Fathers (eds), *Father Luke Wadding: commemorative volume* (Dublin: Clonmore Reynolds, 1957), pp. 295–404.

18. Declan Downey, 'A Salamancan who evaded the Inquisition: Florence Conry, pro-Habsburg archbishop, diplomat and controversial theologian (*c.*1560–1629)', in idem and Julio Crespo MacLennan (eds), *Spanish-Irish relations through the ages* (Dublin: Four Courts Press, 2008), p. 96.

19. Meehan, *The fate and fortunes of Hugh O'Neill, earl of Tyrone, and Rory O'Donel, earl of Tyrconnel*. For nineteenth-century work on the archives at Simancas and Loyola, see Denis Murphy, *The life of Hugh Roe O'Donnell, prince of Tirconnell (1586–1602)*, by Lughaidh O Clery (Dublin: Folens, 1893).

20. Felim O'Brien, 'Florence Conry, archbishop of Tuam' in *Irish Rosary*, 31–2 (1927–8), pp. 843–7, 896–904, 346–51, 454–60, 839–46.

21. C. Heaney, *The theology of Florence Conry* (Drogheda: Drogheda Independent, 1935).

22. Vincent Morley, *Irish opinion and the American Revolution: 1760–83* (Cambridge: Cambridge University Press, 2002), p. 3.

23. Thomas F. O'Rahilly (ed.), 'Irish poets, historians, and judges in English documents, 1538-1615' in *R.I.A. Proc.* (C.), 36 (1921–24), pp. 86–163; Benjamin Hazard, 'Gaelic political scripture: Uí Mhaoil Chonaire scribes and the *Book of Mac Murchadha Caomhánach*' in *Proceedings of the Harvard Celtic Colloquium, 2003* (Harvard University Press, 2009), pp. 149–64.

24. O'Rahilly (ed.), *Desiderius: Sgáthán an Chrábhaidh* (Dublin: Dublin Institute for Advanced Studies, 1941; repr. 1955, 1975). For Ó Maolchonaire's crisp contribution to *Iomarbhágh na bhFileadh*, see O'Rahilly (ed.), *Dánfhocail: Irish epigrams in verse* (Dublin, 1921), p. 31.

25. O'Rahilly, 'Introduction', *Desiderius: Sgáthán an Chrábhaidh*, pp. viii–xlvi.

26. Paul Walsh, *Ir. men of learning*, ed. Colm O Lochlainn (Dublin: Three Candles Press, 1947), pp. 34–48.

27. Brian Ó Cuív (ed.), 'Flaithrí Ó Maolchonaire's catechism of Christian doctrine', *Celtica*, 1 (1950), pp. 161–209.

28. See, for instance, Cathal Ó Háinle, 'An Phaidir: Ó Maolchonaire agus Ó hEodhasa', *Celtica*, 24 (2003), pp. 239–51; Salvador Ryan, 'Bonaventura Ó hEoghusa's *An Teagasg Críosdaidhe*: a reassessment' in *Archiv. Hib.*, 58 (2004) pp. 259–67.

29. Breandán Ó Buachalla, *Aisling ghéar: na Stíobhartaigh agus an taos léinn, 1603–1788* (Baile Átha Cliath: An Clóchomhar, 1996), pp. 23-30. See also Tadhg Ó Dúshláine, *An Eoraip agus litríocht na Gaeilge, 1600–1650: gnéithe den bharócachas Eorpach i litríocht na Gaeilge* (Baile Átha Cliath: An Clóchomhar, 1987), pp. 8, 82, 190.

30. Pádraig Breatnach, *Téamaí taighde nua-Ghaeilge* (Maigh Nuad: An Sagart, 1997), pp. 150–52.

31. Brendan Jennings (ed.), *Wadding Papers: 1614–1638* (Dublin: Irish Manuscripts Commission, 1953); idem (ed.), *Wild Geese in Spanish Flanders, 1582–1700: documents relating chiefly to Irish regiments, from the Archives Générales du Royaume, Bruxelles, and other sources* (Dublin: Irish Manuscripts Commission, 1964); idem (ed.), *Louvain Papers: 1606–1827* (Dublin: Irish Manuscripts Commission, 1968).

32. Jennings, 'Florence Conry, archbishop of Tuam: his death and the transfer of his remains' in *JGHAS*, 27 (1949), pp. 83–92.

33. Lucian Ceyssens, 'Florence Conry, Hugh de Burgo, Luke Wadding, and Jansenism' in Franciscan Fathers (eds.), *Father Luke Wadding: commemorative volume*, pp. 295-404.

34. See, for instance, Brendan Jennings, 'The career of Hugh, son of Rory O'Donnell, earl of Tirconnel,

in the Low Countries, 1607-1642', in *Studies*, 30 (1941), pp. 219–234; Patrick McBride (ed.), 'Some unpublished letters of Mateo de Oviedo, archbishop of Dublin' in *Repertorium Novum*, 1 (1955–6); Brian Ó Cuív (ed.), 'An appeal to Philip III of Spain by Ó Súilleabháin Béirre', *Éigse*, 30 (1997), pp. 18–26.

35. *National Library of Ireland Report of the Council of Trustees for 1950–1951* (Dublin: N.L.I., 1952).

36. For example: *The O'Neills in Spain* (Dublin, 1957); *Destruction by peace* (Monaghan: Seanchas Ard Mhacha, 1986). Her substantial contribution to the UCD Overseas Archive founded by Professor Patrick McBride has been donated to the Cardinal Ó Fiaich Library and Archive, Armagh.

37. See Thomas O'Connor (ed.), *The Irish in Europe, 1580–1815* (Dublin: Four Courts Press, 2001); idem and Mary Ann Lyons (eds.), *Irish migrants in Europe after Kinsale, 1602–1820* (Dublin: Four Courts Press, 2003).

38. J. J. Silke, *Ireland and Europe, 1559–1607* (Dundalk, 1966); idem, *Kinsale: the Spanish intervention in Ireland at the end of the Elizabethan wars* (New York: Fordham University Press, 1970); idem, 'Irish scholarship and the Renaissance, 1580-1675', *Studies in the Renaissance*, 21 (1973), pp. 169–205.

39. Hiram Morgan, *Tyrone's rebellion: The outbreak of the Nine Years War in Tudor Ireland* (Woodbridge: Boydell & Brewer, 1993).

40. Helga Hammerstein, 'Aspects of the continental education of Irish students in the reign of Elizabeth I' in *Historical Studies*, 8 (1971), pp. 137–153.

41. Thomas Morrissey, 'Some Jesuit contributions to Irish education' (Ph.D. thesis, 2 vols., University College, Cork, 1975).

42. Patricia O Connell, *The Irish college at Alcalá de Henares* (Dublin, 1997); idem, 'The early-modern Irish college network in Iberia, 1590–1800', in O'Connor (ed.), *The Irish in Europe, 1580-1815*, pp. 49–64.

43. Declan Downey, 'The Spanish Habsburg dimension in the Irish Counter-Reformation movement, *c.*1529–*c.*1629' (Ph.D. thesis, Cambridge University, 1994); idem, 'Augustinians and Scotists: the Irish contribution to Counter-Reformation theology in continental Europe', in Brendan Bradshaw and Dáire Keogh (eds), *Christianity in Ireland: revisiting the story* (Dublin: Columba, 2002), pp. 96–108.

44. Idem, 'A Castilian-Regalist cradling: Spanish-Habsburg formation of the early Irish Counter Reformation', in Howard Clarke and J.R.S. Phillips (eds), *A turbulent priest: essays in memory of Professor F.X. Martin OSA* (Dublin: University College Dublin Press, 2006), pp. 296–306.

45. Idem, 'Catholicism, Milesianism and monarchism: the facilitators of Irish identification with Habsburg Spain', in Enrique García Hernán and Óscar Recio Morales (eds.), *Extranjeros en el Ejército. Militares irlandeses en la sociedad Española, 1580–1818* (Madrid: Ministerio de Defensa, 2007), pp. 167–78; idem 'A Salamancan who evaded the Inquisition: Florence Conry, pro-Habsburg archbishop, diplomat and controversial theologian', pp. 88–9.

46. Gráinne Henry, *The Irish military community in Spanish Flanders: 1586–1621* (Dublin: Irish Academic Press, 1992).

47. Hugh Kearney, 'The Irish wine trade, 1614–1615', in *I.H.S.*, 9 (1955), pp. 400–42; Karin Schüller, 'Special conditions of the Irish-Iberian trade during the Spanish-English war (1585–1604)' in García Hernán, de Bunes, Recio Morales and García García (eds.), *Irlanda y la monarquía hispánica* (Madrid: Consejo Superior de Investigaciones Científicas, 2002), pp. 447–68.

48. Enrique García Hernán et al. (eds), *Irlanda y la monarquía hispánica: Kinsale 1601–2001. Guerra, política, exilio y religión* (Madrid, 2002); Hiram Morgan (ed.), *The battle of Kinsale* (Wicklow: Wordwell, 2004); Declan Downey and Julio Crespo MacLennan (eds), *Spanish-Irish relations through the ages* (Dublin: Four Courts Press, 2008).

49. Thomas O'Connor and Mary Ann Lyons, 'Introduction', in idem (eds), *Irish communities in early-modern Europe* (Dublin: Four Courts Press, 2006), p. 5.

50. Brian Jackson, 'The role and influence of the Irish missions of the Society of Jesus on the implementation of a Counter-Reformation among the Old English in Ireland, 1542–1633', (Ph.D. thesis, Dublin University, 2007).

51. Ciaran O'Scea, 'Irish wills from Galicia, 1592-1666' in *Archiv. Hib.*, 56 (2002), pp. 73-131; idem, 'The significance and legacy of Spanish intervention in west Munster during the battle of Kinsale', in Thomas O'Connor and Mary Ann Lyons (eds), *Irish migrants in Europe after Kinsale*, pp. 32-63; idem, 'Irish emigration to Castile in the opening years of the seventeenth century' in Patrick Duffy (ed.), *To and from Ireland: planned migration schemes c. 1600–2000* (Dublin: Geography Publications, 2004), pp. 17–38.

52. Enrique García Hernán, *Irlanda y el rey prudente* (2 vols, Madrid: Laberinto, 2000-2003); 'Obispos irlandeses y la Monarquía hispánica durante el siglo XVI' in María Begoña Villar García, Pilar Pezzi Cristóbal (eds), *Los extranjeros en la España Moderna* (2 vols, Universidad de Málaga, 2003) pp. 275–80; idem, 'Philip II's forgotten armada' in Morgan (ed.), The Battle of Kinsale, pp. 45–58; idem,

'Irish clerics in Madrid, 1598–1665' in O'Connor and Lyons (eds) Irish communities in early-modern Europe, pp. 267–293.

53. Óscar Recio Morales, *El socorro de Irlanda en 1601 y la contribución del ejército a la integración social de los irlandeses en España* (Madrid: Ministerio de Defensa, 2002); idem, *España y la pérdida del Ulster: Irlanda en la estrategia política de la monarquía hispánica, 1602–1649* (Madrid: Laberinto, 2003).

54. Enrique García Hernán, Ángel de Bunes, Oscar Recio Morales and Bernardo García García (eds), *Irlanda y la Monarquía hispánica: Kinsale 1601–2001. Guerra, política, exilio y religion* (Madrid: CSIC, 2002); Recio Morales and García Hernán, *La nación irlandesa en el ejército y la sociedad española, 1580–1818* (Madrid: Ministerio de Defensa, 2007).

55. Óscar Recio Morales, 'Florence Conry's memorandum for a military assault on Ulster, 1627', in *Archiv. Hib.*, 56 (2002), pp. 65–72.

56. Tomás Ó Fiaich, 'Republicanism and separatism in the seventeenth-century', in *Léachtaí Cholm Cille*, 2 (1971), pp. 74–87.

57. Igor Pérez Tostado, *Irish influence at the court of Spain in the seventeenth century* (Dublin: Four Courts Press, 2008).

58. Brian Jackson, 'Sectarianism: division and dissent in Irish Catholicism', in Alan Ford and John McCafferty (eds), *The origins of sectarianism in early-modern Ireland* (Cambridge: Cambridge University Press, 2005), pp. 203–15.

59. Mícheál Mac Craith, 'The political and religious thought of Florence Conry and Hugh McCaughwell' in Ford and McCafferty (eds), *The origins of sectarianism in early-modern Ireland*, pp. 183–202.

60. Jerrold Casway, 'Gaelic Maccabeanism: the politics of reconciliation' in Jane Ohlmeyer (ed.), *Political thought in seventeenth-century Ireland: kingdom or colony* (Cambridge: Cambridge University Press, 2000), pp. 176–88; Mac Craith, 'The *Beatha* in the context of the literature of the Renaissance', in Pádraig Ó Riain (ed.), *Beatha Aodha Ruaidh: the life of Red Hugh O'Donnell, historical and literary contexts* (Dublin: Irish Texts Society, 2002), pp. 36–53. See also Marc Caball, 'Faith, culture and sovereignty, 1558–1625', in Brendan Bradshaw and Peter Roberts (eds), *British consciousness and identity* (Cambridge: Cambridge University Press,1998), pp. 112–39.

61. Joop Leerssen, *Mere Irish and Fíor-Ghael: studies in the idea of Irish nationality, its development and literary expression prior to the nineteenth century* (Cork: Cork University Press, 1996), pp. 197–8, 260.

62. Thomas O'Connor, *Irish Jansenists, 1600–70: religion and politics in Flanders, France, Ireland and Rome* (Dublin: Four Courts Press, 2008).

63. Idem, '"Perfidious machiavellian friar": Florence Conry's campaign for Catholic restoration in Ireland, 1592–1616', *Seanchas Ard Mhacha*, 19 (2002), pp. 91–105.

64. Brian Donovan and David Edwards, *British sources for Irish history, 1485–1641: a guide to manuscripts in local, regional and specialised repositories in England, Scotland and Wales* (Dublin, Irish Manuscripts Commission, 1997), p. xi.

65. See Charles Meehan, *The fate and fortunes of the earls of Tyrone and Tyrconnell;* Richard Bagwell, *Ireland under the Stuarts* (3 vols, London: Longman, 1909), vol. 1, pp. 17–62; Canice Mooney, 'A noble shipload' in *Ir. Sword,* 2 (1954–6), pp. 195–204; Nicholas Canny, 'The flight of the earls' in *I.H.S.,* 17 (1970–1); Micheline Kerney Walsh, *Destruction by peace: Hugh O'Neill after Kinsale* (Monaghan: Seanchas Ard Mhacha, 1986), pp. 37–79; Hiram Morgan, 'The end of Gaelic Ulster: a thematic interpretation of events between 1534 and 1610' in *I.H.S.,* 26 (1988), pp. 8–32; Marc Caball, 'Providence and exile in early seventeenth-century Ireland', *I.H.S.,* 29 (1994) pp. 174–88; John McCavitt, *The flight of the earls* (Dublin: Gill & Macmillan, 1999), pp. 92–174; Jonathan Bardon, *A history of Ulster* (Belfast: Linen Press, 2001), pp. 115–30; J. J. Silke, 'Outward bound from Portnamurray' in Enrique García Hernán et al. (eds), *Irlanda y la monarquía hispánica* (Madrid, 2002), pp. 423–45; Nollaig Ó Muraíle (eag.), *Turas na dTaoiseach nUltach tar Sáile: from Ráth Maoláin to Rome—Tadhg Ó Cianáin's contemporary narrative of the journey into exile of the Ulster chieftains and their followers, 1607–8* (Rome: Four Courts Press, 2007). See also 'Éire agus Eoraip sa 17ú hAois', *Léachtaí Cholm Cille*, 38 (2008).

1

Upbringing and Family Background, *c.* 1560–90

In the sworn testimony he made in support of Fadrique Plunkett's application to join the military order of Santiago in 1626, Flaithrí Ó Maolchonaire stated that he was a native of Figh in Connacht.[1] According to the records for the registration of his studies at the University of Salamanca, Ó Maolchonaire was from County Roscommon and the diocese of Elphin.[2] The townland of Figh is in the civil parish of Tibohine, barony of Frenchpark, County Roscommon. Contrary to secondary sources written since the seventeenth century,[3] this is thirty miles west of his family's hereditary lands at Cluain na hOídhche.[4] Flaithrí Ó Maolchonaire's secretary, Hugh de Burgo OFM, and Nicholas Aylmer's epitaph at St Anthony's College, Leuven, recorded 1629 as the year that Ó Maolchonaire died, stating that he was sixty-nine years old which indicates that he was born in 1560/1.[5] O'Ferrall's *Linea Antigua* genealogies, the annals, and poetry by Fearghal Óg Mac an Bháird reveal the identity of Ó Maolchonaire's parents as Fítheal and Onóra.[6] Ó Maolchonaire had brother called Maoilechlainn Modartha (†1626) who either owned or wrote the source to a series of Fenagh poems transcribed by Mícheál Ó Cléirigh (†1643)[7]

The family of Flaithrí Ó Maolchonaire were historians to the *Síol Muireadhaigh*, the shared title for Uí Chonchobhair dynastic rulers and their kinsmen.[8] The first extant reference to the Uí Mhaoilchonaire occurs in the annals attributed to Tighearnach which record the death of Néidhe Úa Mael Conaire, *in senchaidh*, in 1136.[9] The *seanchaidh*, or chronicler and genealogist, memorised and recorded information on land ownership, maintaining the social, legal and political status of their patrons.[10] Sir John Davies' contemporary tract *Lawes of Irelande* refers to the 'Chronicler' and 'Rimer' as 'principall officers [of] the chief lord'.[11] The learned families often 'developed out of the laicised and largely hereditary personnel of the pre-reform monastic schools [...] officials who maintained possession of the old monastic termons after the monasteries themselves had been superseded'.[12] The Uí Mhaoilchonaire offer an example of this link between traditional ecclesiastical office and the function of learned intermediaries in Gaelic society. Certain professionals, such as the Uí Mhaoilchonaire, obtained land for their service to local rulers.[13] Regarded as sacrosanct in Gaelic law, their privileges had included exemptions from tribute and military service.[14]

As custodians of this literary and cultural landscape, the Uí Mhaoilchonaire were responsible for the preservation of the past. At the great assemblies held at

Ráth Cruachan and Carn Fraích the annals record that at their inauguration Uí
Chonchobhair rulers of Connacht were 'proclaimed in the style as royal, as
lordly and as public as any of his race'.[15] At these ceremonies, it was the Ó
Maolchonaire who was 'entitled to give the rod of kingship into the hands of
O'Conor'.[16] In return for his family's services to the ruling lineages of Connacht,
extensive tracts of land were granted to Mael Eóin Bodhar Ó Maolchonaire in
1232.[17] An obit from the previous year refers to Duindín Ó Maolchonaire as
ollamh, the highest office of native Irish learning.[18] A further five members of the
family are described as *ollamhain* into the sixteenth century.[19]

Ó Maolchonaire family lands were located in baronies historically under the
influence of the Uí Chonchobhair but the political authority exercised by the
Gaelic families of Ulster and Connacht was changing rapidly.[20] According to
Flaithrí Ó Maolchonaire and Aodh Ruadh Ó Domhnaill, due to the continual
wars which afflicted these regions in the late 1500s, there were 'neither the
means nor the occasion to study'.[21] Between 1587 and 1591, Tadhg Óg Ó
Conchobhair Ruadh was 'attainted high treason and felony, [was] seised of
lands, claims recorded and his rights to captaincy'.[22] By 1590, the Ó Conchobhair
Donn had allied himself to the Binghams hoping, perhaps, to help preserve his
property and status.

These changes had important implications for the patronage available to Uí
Mhaoilchonaire historians. They had, for example, been involved in the
compilation of several of Connacht's most significant annalistic collections.[23] In
the midst of an intensifying contest for control of the western province,[24] the Uí
Dhomhnaill of Tír Chonaill had both the political motivation and the means to
seek the services of families like the Uí Mhaoilchonaire. Benevolence was
regarded as a moral duty in Gaelic society where patrons directed their surplus
wealth towards feasting and poetry.[25]

The activities of Flaithrí's grandfather, the historian Muirghius Ó
Maolchonaire, reveal the increasing influence of the Uí Dhomhnaill and their
allies over Connacht. The copy of the old Book of Fenagh made by Muirghius in
1516 reflects patronage ambitious for advancement and represents an important
turning point in the region's politics during this period. It also gives an indication
of how Muirghius maintained the family's links to ecclesiastical office, in that he
compiled the work for the hereditary comharb of Fenagh, Tadhg Ó Rodaighe.[26]
Though deference is shown towards the Uí Chonchobhair, the Uí Dhomhnaill
take precedence with the honours, lands, privileges, immunities and rights of
sanctuary attaching to the office of abbot. It also includes Bréifne lore of interest
to the Ó Ruairc, a close ally of Ó Domhnaill in Cavan and Leitrim.[27] This link to
Bréifne was continued into the seventeenth century with Peadar Ó Maolchonaire
writing poetry for the comharbs of Fenagh.[28]

The scholarly families of Connacht and Ulster closely collaborated with one
another. Evidence of significant help offered to the Uí Mhaoilchonaire by the
Mac an Bhaird family, hereditary poets to the Uí Dhomhnaill, is provided in
early seventeenth-century poetry by Fearghal Óg Mac an Bháird. The historian
Muirghius Ó Maolchonaire wished to be accepted as a master of poetry, but met
with opposition to his claim.[29] On the strength of other sources, professional

poets may have resented Muirghius' ambitions.[30] His family was already recognised as belonging to 'the honourable and legal profession of chroniclers'.[31] Mac an Bháird's family, from the Donegal school of the *Clann an Bhaird*, ensured the success of his claim by endorsing his status at a gathering in Connacht.[32] This enabled Muirghius to use another source of income to safeguard his family's social status. The Four Masters recorded Muirghius' obit in an entry for 1543:

> A man learned in history and poetry, a man of wealth and affluence, a learned scribe, by whom many books had been transcribed, and by whom many poems and lays had been composed, and who had kept many schools, superintending and learning, several of which he had constantly kept in his own house.[33]

In a later plaintive call to his friend, Fearghal Óg Mac an Bháird recounted how he and Flaithrí Ó Maolchonaire were educated in the same school, recalling times when his friend was *ollamh* in poetry.[34] John Lynch (†1673) confirmed this statement with the following: 'Florentius Conrius, Hibernice Flathri [...] professione antiquarius in patriis chronicis'.[35] The highest office of native Irish learning, *ollamhnacht*, could only be awarded with the consent of a local ruler.[36] Legal commentaries show that a master of poetry with the accumulation of seven years' knowledge, *Filidheacht*, commanded sufficient fees to purchase property.[37] In turn this implies that Ó Maolchonaire had been entitled to hold land free of tribute. In 1616, Ó Maolchonaire alluded to his first formal writings in Ireland.[38] Extant Gaelic manuscripts identify his work as the source for a chronology of kings and their respective ancestors, *Réim Ríoghraidhe Shíl Éireamhóin*, and a genealogy tracing Ireland's saints to the Milesians, *Naoimhsheanchas Naomh Inse Fáil*.[39] The same sources refer to Ó Maolchonaire as 'priomhsheanchaidh na nEirionnach san aimsir dheigheanaidhsi'.[40] In other words he had shown sufficient promise to be classed among the leading Gaelic scholars of his time. Both of his earliest known works indicate prevailing concerns with kinship and hereditary claims in a traditional patronage-based society.[41] The first, *Réim Ríoghraidhe Shíl Éireamhóin*, traditionally accompanied transcripts of *Lebor Gabála*, a standard text of the schools of poetry.[42] Otherwise known as *The Book of Invasions*, this late eleventh-century source provided the Gaelic-Irish with their Milesian origin legend.[43] In this context, it is interesting to note that his grandfather Muirghius Ó Maolchonaire composed a recension of *Lebor Gabála* from the twelfth-century *Lebor na hUidre* which he had in his possession.[44]

As the sixteenth century progressed the Uí Mhaoilchonaire and poets educated in their schools looked to the Ó Domhnaill, his allies and their kinsmen for patronage and protection.[45] The strengthening Uí Mhaoilchonaire connection with the Uí Dhomhnaill crystallised in the close links between Flaithrí Ó Maolchonaire and Aodh Ruadh Ó Domhnaill, for whom he acted as spiritual director, advisor and executor.

HEREDITARY TENANTS

The administrative and economic organisation of the Church in the Pale, *Ecclesia inter Anglos*, differed greatly from the unique systems followed in the Gaelic regions of Ireland, *Ecclesia inter Hibernos*, 'the like whereof', the English lawyer Davies commented in 1606, 'are not to be found in any other part of Christendom'.[46] The seventeenth-century genealogist Tuileagna Ó Maolchonaire informed the Spanish council of military orders that, as well as being chroniclers to the nobility of Ireland, his family occupied parts of their territory as hereditary tenants of Church property.[47] These hereditary tenants were known as *airchinnigh*, or erenaghs – laymen who represented an essential part of parish organisation in Gaelic areas. They farmed the lands and often ran schools.[48] The Uí Mhaoilchonaire estates included Patrician sites, such as those at Kilmore, Clooncraff and Kiltrustan.[49] Accounts of St Patrick's itinerary in Connacht included visits to these lands and his fifth-century Christian foundations were located beside royal residences, inauguration sites and ancestral cemeteries.[50] At the close of the sixteenth century, the erenaghs 'are accounted as clergymen and do most of them speak Latin [...] but were always married'.[51] The term 'erenagh' came to mean the head of a family possessing Church lands under the bishop and was also used to mean archdeacon.[52] Clarus Ó Maolchonaire (†1251) and Tomás Ó Maolchonaire (†1266) held Church office as archdeacons of Elphin and Tuam respectively.[53] The former, the son of an erenagh, founded Holy Trinity on Loch Cé for the Premonstratensian canons,[54] evidence for the link between the Ó Maolchonaire family and the ecclesiastical hierarchy. Clarus subsequently established daughter houses to Loch Cé at Tuam, Roscommon and Cavan.[55]

A tithe was usually paid by the erenagh to the local bishop who also claimed 'noxials' or refections, the value of which might amount to many times the annual rent. These consisted of a night's lodging and entertainment for the bishop and his retinue several times a year.[56] If, like a secular lord, the bishop did not wish to take them in person he might receive a payment in money or provisions instead. In addition, erenagh families were expected to provide hospitality to those in need and provided for the upkeep of the chuch buildings. By the sixteenth century, one finds the descendants of some of the old ecclesiastical families as freeholders under the bishop.[57] The attachment between ecclesiastical and lay scholarly families and personnel 'added stability to the conduct of relations between Church and secular administration'.[58]

CHANGES IN LANDHOLDING PRACTICES

Decisive social and cultural change occurred in the western province during the early childhood of Flaithrí Ó Maolchonaire. Following the appointment of Henry Sidney (†1586) as viceroy of Ireland in 1565, bridges were built over the Shannon at Athlone and Ballinasloe.[59] This construction programme facilitated the movement of troops and undermined the authority exercised by the Uí Chonchobhair, thus enabling Sidney to create shires of Roscommon, Sligo, Mayo and Galway.[60] In 1569, Sir Edward Fyton (†1606) was named first president of Connacht.[61] The castle at Roscommon was garrisoned in 1571 and 'quickly became part of the defensive network of strongholds guarding the Pale' but the introduction of martial law by the new government in the province led to serious local unrest the following year.[62]

In ecclesiastical affairs, after the death of Archbishop Christopher Bodkin in 1572, bishops of both the Roman Catholic and the newly established state Church were appointed to western sees.[63] Three years later, sheriffs in the western province began to enforce legislation against the Mass and members of the clergy were viewed with suspicion as potential agents of Spain and Rome.[64] Priests who refused to use the Book of Common Prayer were gaoled after a third offence.[65] Since the 1530s, a large number of Connacht's friaries, abbeys and priories remained in the hands of the clergy or were held by 'papally provided commendators'.[66] As the new state Church was established, this changed. Tudor officials held inquisitions to ascertain a claimant's property and gradually took possession of ecclesiastical lands and tithes which came under the remit of the inquisitions as they were discovered.[67] In 1568, for example, Elizabeth issued John Crofton with a lease for the Trinity Abbey of Loch Cé.[68] This supplanted the Mac Diarmada, who had been the most important *oireacht*, sub-king, to the Ó Conchobhair Donn and signalled a significant change in Gaelic landholding practices. 'A Rentall of Mounster and Connaugh' of 1577 indicates that the trend continued apace. In that year, the Cistercian priory *de Innocentia* of the monks of Athlone, valued at £44 13 shillings and 4 pence sterling, was 'in the tenure of Sir Edwarde Fiton, knt',[69] first president of Connacht. Certain local lords, most notably the de Burgo, are also mentioned in the same document. The next entry tells us that Richard de Burgo, 'now Earle of Clanyrycarde [was] graunted in fee farme the Priorie of Aghrim O Manny in O Kelleis country'.[70]

These developments had an important impact upon Flaithrí Ó Maolchonaire and his family. On 24 January 1584, according to an inquisition taken at Roscommon, four quarters of land which constituted the 'Grange of the Mulchonry' were recorded as belonging 'to the queen'.[71] The term 'Grange' applied to a monastic estate and that of the Uí Mhaoilchonaire was located in the baronies of Ballintober north and Roscommon. It was sheltered by the Curlew hills to the north, benefitting from freshwater lakes, the river Shannon and its tributaries.[72] According to a survey of Roscommon's baronies in the 1580s, each quarter consisted of 120 acres.[73] The term 'quarter' was used as an assessment unit to refer, not to the size of acreage, however, but the value of specific lands. The Grange was a sought after location strategically, positioned between Athlone and Sligo. Civil strife had erupted in 1555 among the Mac Diarmada and the sons of Eoghan Mac Diarmada, leading to the burning of Boyle abbey and the capture of its abbot. Mutually destructive conflict ensued among the local Irish ruling classes.[74]

Sir Richard Bingham (†1599) was appointed governor of Connacht in 1584 following the death of his predecessor Sir Nicholas Malbie.[75] He enforced martial law in the province and quickly became known for the harshness of his rule.[76] Indeed, the lord deputy went so far as to express the view that: 'There will never be peace in Connaught under Sir Richard.'[77] From the vantage point of

Boyle abbey which he turned into 'his fortified dwelling' and with the aid of local rulers in Connacht, Bingham was able to reduce the province to submission by the early 1590s.[78] Boyle's direct proximity to the family of Ó Maolchonaire is shown in an inquisition taken in 1607, which found that 'the abbey of Boyle was possessed of the Grange of Lyshenshall near Clonpluckan.'[79] A sixteenth-century Uí Mhaoilchonaire manuscript clearly identifies *Cluain Plocáin* as the family's seat.[80] Further, the compilation of the Cottonian annals of Boyle was closely connected with Holy Trinity abbey on Loch Cé.[81] As stated above, Clarus Ó Maolchonaire had originally established this monastic settlement for the Premonstratensian canons.[82]

These fundamental changes in landholding practices occurred before those implemented in 1585 by Lord Deputy Perrott (†1592) in the *Compossicion of Conought*. The latter granted tenure, under English law, to Irish nobles of the province.[83] Smaller landowners – freeholders – were not named in the 1585 composition, thereby facilitating the endorsement of newcomers' claims.[84] According to the terms of the *Compossicion*, 'a certain portion of the lands indentured belong to Her Majesty, in right of abbeys and bishopricks.'[85] This formalised the decision reached at the inquisition taken on the 'Grange of the Mulconry' the previous January. For these reasons, therefore, the Ó Maolchonaire family were not among the names included in the agreement which followed.

The battle of the Curlews in August 1599 highlighted the strategic importance of Uí Mhaoilchonaire lands to the governor of Connacht. Moreover, information later provided to Philip III by the Conde de Puñonrostro strongly suggests that Flaithrí Ó Maolchonaire was at the battle, serving as a military chaplain.[86] After completing his studies and joining the Franciscans, Ó Maolchonaire went back to Ireland 'to the Catholic camp of Ó Néill and Ó Domhnaill staying to help in every way possible, hearing confessions and preaching'.[87] This is a source to which I return in the next chapter.

Fleeing the field after the death of their general at the hands of Aodh Ruadh Ó Domhnaill and the Mac Diarmada, 1,500 of Sir Conyers Clifford's troops retreated to the garrison at Boyle abbey. Subsequent efforts by the forces of Aodh Ruadh to capture the abbey were successfully parried by the English, an indication of how extensive and well-fortified the abbey was. Of Clifford, the annals say, his death was 'much lamented' in Connacht and 'it was grievous that he came to this tragic end.'[88] As a sign of his respect for the governor, Mac Diarmada returned the general's remains wrapped in 'a good shroud' to Loch Cé and the constable of Boyle in order to secure the release of captives and 'on account of his distinction' to ensure that Clifford was 'honourably buried'.[89] The Cistercian abbey at Boyle had previously been held by the Mac Diarmada as a function of hereditary office in conjunction with the kingship of Magh-Luirg, although as stated above, after the death of Ruaidhri Mac Diarmada, the queen granted a lease for Trinity Abbey of Loch Cé to John Crofton, clerk of the council of Connacht. By the time of the battle of the Curlews, the lands associated with this monastic foundation 'had so entirely passed away from his possession' that Mac Diarmada had to hand over Sir Conyers Clifford's torso for burial at Loch Cé.[90]

THE EXTENSION OF TUDOR ADMINISTRATION IN CONNACHT: THE FIANTS

Steven Ellis has written at length about how English common law was effectively administered in the Pale and of how crown revenues grew during the early Tudor period.[91] In Connacht and Ulster, however, the gradual acceptance of English common law by the chief lords during the late sixteenth century made it more difficult to maintain Gaelic practices in the northern and western provinces of Ireland.[92] The increasing pressures placed by the Dublin administration on the Uí Mhaoilchonaire and other professional families further eroded traditional relations and alliances. The provincial presidencies of Munster and Connacht established in the 1560s and 1570s, and the composition agreements to finance them, were signs of an increasing and unprecedented Tudor presence outside the Pale.[93] As Mary O'Dowd has shown, Dublin Castle did not recognise the growth of Uí Dhomhnaill influence over Connacht.[94] The examples of Niall Garbh, Domhnall Ó Domhnaill and Cathaoir Ó Dochartaigh show that Aodh Ruadh faced considerable opposition from within Tír Chonaill.[95] Consequently, he pursued a consistent policy of territorial expansion to avert internal strife. As is well known, the Gaelic political system was, by its nature, uncentralised. This facilitated defence against external aggression and helped to sustain success by avoiding overall control of the country.[96] Thus, the only real source of political resistance to the extension of Tudor administration in Connacht came from beyond the western province.[97] 'Returned to his own' after captivity and inaugurated at the age of twenty, Ó Domhnaill operated freely in the western province, inaugurating subordinates and making numerous raids from Tír Chonaill.[98] Soon afterwards, the Mag Mathghamhna, Ó Ruairc and Mag Uidhir formed an alliance and in 1593 Aodh Ruadh initiated contact with Spain.[99] Recognising their loyalty, he restored to power both Ó Ruairc and Mac Diarmada two years later.[100] Spanish sources for the same period reveal that 'Maguidhir, Macsuybhne [and] Oruairk' were based at Killybegs, County Donegal.[101]

With specific regard to the learned families, fines noted in the state papers further indicate a sense of animosity felt by the administration towards 'rymors and chroniklers' at the close of the sixteenth century.[102] Edmund Spenser complained that:

> Whomsoever they finde to be most lycentious or lief, most bolde and lawles in his doinges, most dangerous and desperate in all partes of disobedience and rebellious disposicion, him they set up and glorifie in theire rymes, him they prayse to the people, and to younge men make an example to followe.[103]

A series of recorded pardons reveal that Flaithrí Ó Maolchonaire and members of his family were subject to Elizabethan fiants, an indication of their part in the changing political culture in late sixteenth-century Connacht and Ulster. Indeed, this period has been identified as a 'point of eclipse' for the 'politically enfranchised *literati* [who] were being eliminated in Ireland'.[104] Irish fiants were the essential preliminary warrants directed to the lord deputy's chancery office for letters patent. The term is derived from the opening word of the usual formula,

Fiant lettere patentes: 'Let letters patent be made.' In the case of those letters granting pardons, the timing of the granting of the pardon was significant. A pardon issued after conviction could lead to seizure of the recipient's lands.[105] Recent research by K. J. Kesselring reveals how, 'in an effort to legitimise the authority of the Tudor state, pardons were exchanged for deference to the crown.'[106] These complex sources have been defined as a strategy of rule to assert and reinforce royal authority; a pardon 'had no intrinsic meaning' but recipients were required 'to show humility, repentance, and above all, submission'.[107]

The fiants concerning Flaithrí Ó Maolchonaire's family were general pardons usually issued before conviction. They were compiled from schedules sent to the provincial council in Connacht.[108] At the close of the sixteenth century, cases brought in Connacht were of a varied character and only a small proportion had to do with religious matters. The first of the letters patent warranted to the Uí Mhaoilchonaire deals with five members of the family in the early 1580s including 'Gelernuve Keighe O Mulconre of Clonpluckane, rimor', who was charged 'at Sir Nicholas Malbie's suit'.[109] He was later pardoned of these offences, but not of those 'committed during the government of the present Deputy [Perrot]'.[110] On the same date, 'Uline O Mulconry of Clonhy, a gentleman, rimor, Ferfesse O Muckory, Paidine oge O Mulcony, of same, rimor' were pardoned.[111]

The placenames referred to here are identifiable anglicised forms of Uí Mhaoilchonaire hereditary lands. 'Clonhy' corresponds to *Cluain na hOídhche*, in the barony of Roscommon, the home of Flaithrí Ó Maolchonaire's forefathers. This area remained in Uí Mhaoilchonaire hands during the early seventeenth century, most notably through claims lodged by his brother Maoilechlainn. 'Clonpluckane' or 'Clonplocan' clearly refer to *Cluain Plocáin*. These lands were known locally as Baile Uí Maelconaire from the late fifteenth century onwards.[112] The same term was still used in English derivations, such as Ballymulconry, after the Confederate war of 1641–52.[113] 'Gales O Mulconry, of Corlesconyll, gent.' received fiant of pardon on 9 December 1585.[114] The accompanying placename, *Cuirr Lessa Conaill* in Irish, was the site of an early sixteenth-century Uí Mhaoilchonaire school in the parish of Kilmore, barony of Ballintober north.[115]

In 1590, Fítheal and Maoilechlainn Ó Maolchonaire of *Baile in Chuimine* were named in another pardon.[116] As the accompanying genealogical tree shows, Maoilechlainn was one of Flaithrí Ó Maolchonaire's two brothers. Fítheal was the name of his father and of his first cousin. Gaelic scholars identified *Baile in Chuimine* as the site of a house belonging to the Uí Mhaoilchonaire in north county Roscommon.[117] Originally part of a Patrician site and subsequently land of the archbishops of Tuam, *Baile in Chuimine* was located in the old parish of Eachdruim, diocese of Elphin.[118] It is to be found on the Roscommon side of Loch Bó Deirge on the River Shannon.[119]

'INTRUSIONS INTO CROWN LANDS AND DEBTS TO THE CROWN EXCEPTED'

The earliest known reference to Flaithrí Ó Maolchonaire occurs in this same *Baile in Chuimine* fiant. Issued to 'Flarin O Molconnere' on 10 July,[120] it shows that Ó Maolchonaire did not leave Ireland before 1590 and only entered the Franciscan order after doing so. His fiant of pardon was warranted for all offences except 'intrusions into crown lands, and debts to the crown'.[121] S. C. Lomas' survey of the Egmont Papers states that 'small encroachments on land and raids on cattle, not infrequently accompanied by a free flight, were common enough throughout Ireland [...] and where the parties were found guilty, justice was usually satisfied by the payment of a fine.'[122] The fiant of Flaithrí Ó Maolchonaire was warranted by the provincial council of Connacht on condition that:

> [He] appear and submit before the justices at Assizes in that county at the next sessions, and be sufficiently bound with sureties to keep the peace and answer at sessions, when summoned, the just demands of all subjects.[123]

Fiants took up to eighteen months to be executed. Since the departure of Flaithrí Ó Maolchonaire from Ireland seems to have occurred after pardon, the fiant was not unrelated to his leaving. During his absence from Ireland, the repercussions of these and other decrees continued to be felt. Regular inspections of the family's claims followed and his brother Maoilechlainn, in particular, had to adapt to the exigencies of new landholding practices in his lifetime.[124]

In these fiants and edicts, the term 'riot' applied to anything from trespass to seizure of cattle or assault on individuals. 'Intrusions into crown lands' was often interpreted to mean occupancy.[125] In the case in question it may relate to the 'Grange of the Mulconry', which had been declared forfeit to Elizabeth six years earlier. Another explanation does present itself, however. Ó Maolchonaire's fiant was a general pardon, granted to 169 recipients. The first person named in the document is 'Donnell O Rourke, of Loghdoncorre', County Leitrim.[126] This is Domhnall (mac Tadhg) Ó Ruairc who, we learn from the annals, had been named lord over Lower Connacht by his kinsmen in 1584.[127] Three years later, up to seven others, including Cedach Ó Ruairc and Mathghamhain Mac Caba, were killed.[128] Other members of the Mac Caba family are listed in the same letter patent of pardon issued to Domhnall, his relatives and to 'Flarin O Molconnere'.[129] A close ally of the Ó Domhnaill, prince of Tír Chonaill, Brian na Murtha Ó Ruairc had poetry written in his honour by Seán Ó Maolchonaire.[130]

According to Flaithrí Ó Maolchonaire, after the destruction of the Armada in the winter of 1588, Brian na Murtha Ó Ruairc found himself at war with the English for sheltering Spaniards shipwrecked on his territories rather than delivering them to Elizabeth's ministers in Ireland.[131] The loss of twenty-six Spanish vessels and the death of approximately 5,000 men on the Atlantic coastline elicited strong sympathy for Spain in Connacht.[132] The alarm caused by these events further destabilised the region and led to an outbreak of local insurgency in 1589.[133]

Lord Deputy Fitzwilliam wrote to William Cecil telling him that the Spaniards were 'so favoured and succoured by the country people, as it will be hard to hunt them out, but with long time and great labour'.[134] Governor Bingham reacted by carrying out raids, driving local inhabitants and their cattle onto crown lands. Terms of peace were subsequently concluded. Afterwards, the governor of Connacht recorded that 'Brian of the bulwarks', as he was known in English, was 'so impoverished every way and his country so wasted, as he will not be able to rise again in haste'.[135] Domhnall Ó Ruairc then assisted in expelling Brian Ó Ruairc from Leitrim.[136]

Flaithrí Ó Maolchonaire later explained that, following these great hardships and losses, Brian na Murtha Ó Ruairc was forced to flee to Scotland. Instead of finding refuge at the court of James VI, however, the king of Scotland imprisoned Ó Ruairc before having him taken away to London where he was condemned to death.[137] He was tried at Westminster and beheaded at Tyburn in 1591.[138] The supression of his rebellion is said to have 'afforded the English their first opportunity to make inroads in Ulster'.[139] Ó Maolchonaire, on the other hand, maintained that it only heralded further political and religious instability in Ireland.[140]

Considering his family's close links with Ó Ruairc and Ó Domhnaill kinsmen in late sixteenth-century Connacht, Flaithrí Ó Maolchonaire appears to have been caught up in the post-Armada conflict. Thus, Ó Ruairc's exclusion disrupted interaction between the Uí Mhaoilchonaire and the Bréifne patron. Having already had to look beyond their traditional source of security in Roscommon, they now found themselves unable to rely upon former patrons for either their safety or material well-being. These circumstances led them to turn to the strongest Gaelic advocate available, namely the Ó Domhnaill. Reaching an understanding to the mutual benefit of both parties would also have suited Tír Chonaill with its ever-increasing ambitions. The potential for positive political propaganda from historians and poets as prominent as the Uí Mhaoilchonaire of Connacht was not to be underestimated.

Corroborative evidence suggests that Flaithrí Ó Maolchonaire left for Spain before September 1590. The best times of the year to set sail occur between the spring and autumn equinox when, during Elizabeth's reign, more than six hundred Spanish craft 'swarmed through Irish waters' thereby offering the opportunity for safe passage to Spain.[141] Irish mariners, merchants and agents had already established themselves in the ports of Galicia as Ireland became the base for clandestine shipment of English goods to Spain and Spanish exports to England.[142] The influence of Spain in Ireland was most strongly felt in Galway where the inhabitants were said 'to fetch great stores of wine and other wares'.[143]

Faced with the destruction of his patron's dynasty from the end of the six-teenth century, the O'Reilly's own chronicler described it as 'the age of catastro-phe'.[144] Due to his family's changing experience of land ownership and patronage, Flaithrí Ó Maolchonaire had felt the increasing pressure exerted by Tudor administration upon social and cultural institutions in Connacht and Ulster. Members of the Gaelic scholarly classes valued 'place, prestige and dignity [more than] land and property for itself'.[145] Those who made their way to Spain had, in the words of Ó Maolchonaire, 'lost their properties for the faith and have no means of obtaining the advantages possessed by others'.[146] As the next chapter shows, the Spanish Habsburgs were set to provide Ó Maolchonaire with a passport to prominence.

NOTES

1. Madrid, 30 Jul. 1626 Archivo Histórico Nacional (AHN), Madrid, Ordenes Militares, Pruebas de Caballeros de Santiago, expediente 6536, p. 2); 'Padre Don fray Florencio Conrrio Arçobispo Tuamense en Irlanda natural de la villa de Riegen en la provincia de Conassia y avia lo jurado en verbo sacerdotis prometto dezir verdad'.

2. 'Matriculacion: artistas y filosofos. Florencio Conrio, ne de Roscoman, Diec. de Olfin de al 3 año', Salamanca, 10 Dec. 1594; Ranson Papers, Cuaderno v, 29; cited by Ignatius Fennessy (ed.), 'Two letters from Boethius (Augustine) MacEgan, OFM, on the death of Archbishop Florence Conry, OFM, 1629', Coll. Hib., 43 (2001), pp. 7–12.

3. Lynch, De Praesulibus Hib., ii, p. 278.

4. General alphabetical index to the towns, townlands, baronies and parishes in Ireland (Dublin, 1851, repr. 1984); Ordnance Survey name books, co. Roscommon (Dublin: NLI, 1932), p. 170. The word Figh means woodland. See Kenneth Nicholls, 'Woodland cover in pre-modern Ireland', in Patrick Duffy, David Edwards and Elizabeth Fitzpatrick (eds), Gaelic Ireland, c. 1250–1650: land, lordship and settlement (Dublin: Four Courts Press, 2001), pp. 181–206.

5. Brendan Jennings, 'Florence Conry, archbishop of Tuam: his death, and the transfer of his remains', JGHAS, 3–4 (1949), pp. 83–92.

6. Pádraig Breatnach, Téamaí taighde nua-Ghaeilge (Maigh Nuad: An Sagart, 1997), pp. 150–2; Fennessy (ed.), 'Two letters from Boethius (Augustine) MacEgan', pp. 7–12; Thomas O'Connor, 'Conry's campaign for a Catholic restoration in Ireland', Seanchas Ard Mhacha, 19 (2002), p. 91; Pádraig Ó Macháin, 'Poems of Fearghal Óg Mac An Bhaird', Celtica, 24 (2003), pp. 252–63. The names Fítheal and Flaithrí recall those of Cormac Mac Airt's chief jurist and his son. See Osborn Bergin (ed.), Irish bardic poetry (Dublin: Dublin Institute for Advanced Studies, 1970), p. 296; Myles Dillon, Early Irish literature (repr. Dublin: Four Courts Press, 1994), pp. 77, 110–12.

7. Paul Walsh, Ir. men of learning, pp. 61–2. See also Walsh, Irish leaders and learning through the ages: essays collected edited and introduced by Nollaig Ó Muraíle (Dublin: Four Courts Press, 2003), p. 355.

8. Tomás Ó Con Cheanainn, 'Ó Maoil Chonaire agus sloinnte Shean-Phádraic', Éigse, 32 (2000), pp. 23–34.

9. Walsh, Ir. men of learning, p. 35; see also AFM, vol. 2, pp. 1054–5.

10. Fergus Kelly, Early Irish Farming (Dublin: Dublin Institute for Advanced Studies, 1998), pp. 411–12; Nollaig Ó Muraíle, The celebrated antiquary: life, lineage and learning (Maynooth: An Sagart, 1996), p. 172.

11. Hiram Morgan (ed.), 'Sir John Davies' Lawes of Irelande', The Irish Jurist, 31 (1995–6) pp. 307–12.

12. Proinsias Mac Cana, 'The rise of the later schools of filidheacht', Ériu, 25 (1984), p. 133.

13. Kelly, Early Irish Farming, pp. 403–12.

14. Eugene O'Curry, Lectures on the manuscript materials of ancient Irish history (Dublin, 1861), p. 2. On the family's social obligations, see Catherine O'Sullivan, Hospitality in medieval Ireland, 900–1500 (Dublin: Four Courts Press, 2004), pp. 161–2.

15. Myles Dillon (ed.), 'The Inauguration of O'Conor', in Med. studies presented to A. Gwynn (Dublin, 1961), pp. 186–202.

16. Dillon (ed.), 'The Inauguration of O'Conor', p. 187. On the persistence of these practices, see Elizabeth Fitzpatrick, 'Assembly and inauguration places of the Burkes in late medieval Connacht', in Duffy, Edwards and Fitzpatrick (eds), Gaelic Ireland, c. 1250–1650, pp. 357–74.

17. Ann.Conn., 1232.10, pp. 44–5. See Edmund Hogan, Onomasticon Goedelicum: locorum et tribuum Hiberniae et Scotiae (repr. Dublin, 2000), pp. 255, 269, 602, 675.

18. AFM, vol. 3, pp. 258–9.

19. Ann. Conn. 1404.17, pp. 390–1; Ann. Conn. 1441.2, pp. 482–3; Ann. Conn. 1468.11, pp. 540–1; London, British Library, Egerton Ms 1,782, f. 43b; Ann. Conn. 1519.9, pp. 636–7.

20. Ó Muraíle, The celebrated antiquary, p. 172.

21. 'Un memorial de la parte del collegio de Salamanca que ha dado el Conde Odonel, a 22 de mayo del año 1602' (Edmund Hogan, Ibernia Ignatiana (Dublin: Society of Jesus, 1880), pp. 106–8): 'por las guerras continuas no tienen modo ni aparato para estudiar'.

22. National Archives of Ireland, Dublin (NAI), Repertories to Inquisitions (Exchequer), County Roscommon, Elizabeth, 9/15.

23. Mac Niocaill, The medieval Irish annals, p. 35; William Hennessy, 'Introduction', in idem (ed.), The Annals of Loch Cé (Dublin: Irish Manuscripts Commission, 1939), p. liv. See also Daniel McCarthy, The Irish Annals: their genesis, evolution and history (Dublin: Four Courts Press,

2008), pp. 256–7.

24. Mary O'Dowd, *Power, politics and land: early-modern Sligo, 1568–1688* (Belfast: The Institute of Irish Studies, 1991), pp. 22–3.

25. Katherine Simms, 'Guesting and feasting in Gaelic Ireland', *Journal of the Royal Society of Antiquaries of Ireland*, 108 (1978), pp. 67–100.

26. *Bk. Fen.*, pp. 311, 391–2; 279–81. See also Bernadette Cunningham and Raymond Gillespie, *Stories from Gaelic Ireland* (Dublin: Four Courts Press, 2003), pp. 104, 128, 167.

27. *RIA cat. Ir. MSS*, p. 479.

28. H. R. McAdoo, 'Three poems by Peadar Ó Maolchonaire', *Éigse*, 1 (1939), pp. 160–6.

29. Katherine Simms, 'The poetic Brehon lawyers of early sixteenth-century Ireland', *Ériu*, 57 (2007), pp. 121–32.

30. See Robin Flower, 'The bardic heritage', in idem (ed.), *The Irish tradition* (Oxford: Oxford University Press, 1947), pp. 97–8.

31. 'Letter from Conaire Ó Maolconaire', in John Fraser, Paul Grosjean and J. G. O'Keefe (eds), *Irish Texts*, 4 (London, 1934), pp. 113–18.

32. Simms, 'The poetic Brehon lawyers of early sixteenth-century Ireland', pp. 121–32.

33. *AFM*, vol. 5, pp. 1482–3. See also *AConn*, pp. 730–1; *ALC*, vol. 2, pp. 339–41.

34. Ó Macháin, 'Poems of Fearghal Óg Mac An Bhaird', pp. 252–63. The poems are entitled *Éisd rem éagnach a fhir ghráidh* and *Fuarus iongnadh a fhir chumainn*. See *Dán Na mBráthar Mionúr*, eag. Cuthbert Mhág Craith (Baile Átha Cliath: Institiúid Árd-Léinn Bhaile Átha Cliath, 1967), pp. 117–21; Bergin (ed.), *Irish bardic poetry*, pp. 41–4.

35. Lynch, *De Praesulibus Hib.*, ii, p. 278.

36. Máire Ní Dhonnchadha, 'An address to a student of law', in Donnchadh Ó Corráin and Kim McCone (eds), *Sages, saints and storytellers: Celtic Studies in honour of Professor James Carney* (Maynooth, 1989) pp. 168–70.

37. Kelly, *Early Irish Farming*, pp. 419–24.

38. Flaithrí Ó Maolchonaire, *Sgáthán an Chrábhaidh*, ed. T. F. O'Rahilly (repr. Dublin: Dublin Institute for Advanced Studies, 1975), p. ix.

39. Breatnach, *Téamaí taighde nua-Ghaeilge*, pp. 150–2.

40. *Dán Na mBráthar Mionúr*, pp. 117–21.

41. Following the foundation of St Anthony's College for Irish Franciscans at Louvain, later copies of these works became indispensable to the studies of Colgan. See Canice Mooney, 'Father John Colgan OFM: His work and times and literary milieu', in Terence O'Donnell (ed.), *Father John Colgan OFM, 1592–1658: essays in commemoration of the third centenary of his death* (Dublin: Assisi Press, 1959), pp. 7–40.

42. Douglas Hyde, *A literary history of Ireland: from earliest times to the present day* (New York: Scribner & Sons, 1901), p. 576.

43. Bernadette Cunningham, 'Native culture and political change', in Raymond Gillespie and Ciarán Brady (eds), *Natives and newcomers: the makings of Irish colonial society, 1534–1641* (Dublin: Irish Academic Press, 1986), pp. 148–70.

44. Brian Ó Cuív, 'The Irish language in the early modern period', *New hist. Ire.*, 3, p. 517.

45. For Giolla Riabach Ó Cléirigh, Cúconnacht Comharb Mag Uidhir and Brian na Murtha Ó Ruairc, see Paul Walsh, 'The O'Clerys of Tirconnell', *Studies* (1929), pp. 247–53; idem, *Ir. men of learning*, pp. 173–4; James Hardiman, *Irish minstrelsy: bardic remains of Ireland* (2 vols, London: Joseph Robins, 1831), vol. 2, pp. 287–305; Tomás Ó Cléirigh, 'A poembook of the O'Donnells', *Éigse*, 1 (1939), pp. 51–61; 97–9; 130–42.

46. Canice Mooney, 'The Church in Gaelic Ireland', in Patrick Corish (ed.), *A history of Irish Catholicism* (Dublin: Gill & Macmillan, 1969), vol. 2, part 5, p. 10.

47. Madrid, 16 Jul. 1662 (Archivo Histórico Nacional, Madrid, Ordenes Militares, Calatrava, expediente 1834); Micheline Kerney Walsh (ed.), *Spanish knights of Irish origin: documents from the Archivo Histórico Nacional, Madrid and the Archivo General de Simancas* (4 vols, Dublin: Irish Manuscripts Commission, 1960), vol. 4, pp. 111–12.

48. *Inquisitionum in Officio Rotulorum Cancellariae Hiberniae Asservatarum Repertorium* (2 vols, Dublin, 1826–9), cited by Kieran Devlin, 'The beatified martyrs of Ireland', *Ir. Theol. Quart.*, 65 (2000), pp. 266–80. See also Henry Jefferies, 'Erenaghs in pre-plantation Ulster: an early seventeenth-century account', *Archiv. Hib.*, 53 (1999), pp. 16–19.

49. Canice Mooney, 'Elphin', *Dictionnaire d'histoire et de geographie ecclésiastiques*, 15 (1963), pp. 269–92; Kenneth Nicholls, 'Some Patrician sites of eastern Connacht', *Dinnseanchas*, 5 (1973), pp. 114–18.

50. *Vita Tripartita*, ed. Whitley Stokes, Rolls Ser. 8vo (London, 1887), vol. 1, pp. 93–4; vol. 2, p. 311.
51. Kenneth Nicholls, *Gaelic and gaelicised Ireland* (2nd ed., Dublin: Lilliput Press, 2003), pp. 111–13.
52. Ibid.
53. Lynch, *De Praesulibus Hib.*, ii, p. 278. For the obit of *Tomáss Ó Maoil Chonaire: airchidechain Tuama, quieuit in Cristo*, see *AConn.*, p. 149.
54. See London, British Library, MS Cotton, Titus A. xxv (early fourteenth century); as identified by Robin Flower, 'Ireland and medieval Europe', *Proceedings of the British Academy*, 13 (1927), p. 31.
55. Francis Burke, *Loch Cé and its annals: north Roscommon and the diocese of Elphin in times of old* (Dublin: Hodges Figgis, 1895), p. 88.
56. Noxiale to the Bishop of Elphin, 14 Jul. 1579, cited by Kenneth Nicholls, *An. Hib.*, 26 (1970), pp. 103–29.
57. Nicholls, *Gaelic and gaelicised Ireland*, pp. 185–6.
58. Colm Lennon, *Sixteenth-century Ireland: the incomplete conquest* (Dublin: Gill & Macmillan, 1994), pp. 63–4.
59. John Bradley, 'Sir Henry Sidney's bridge at Athlone, 1566–7', in Thomas Herron and Michael Potterton (eds), *Ireland and the Renaissance, c. 1540–1660* (Dublin: Four Courts Press, 2007), pp. 173–94.
60. Ciarán Brady, *The chief governors: the rise and fall of reform government in Tudor Ireland, 1536–1588* (Cambridge: Cambridge University Press, 1994), pp. 245–91.
61. Crawford, *Anglicizing the government of Ireland*, p. 455.
62. Ibid., pp. 276, 314–15.
63. Hubert Knox, *Notes on the early history of the dioceses of Tuam, Killala and Achonry* (Dublin: Hodges Figgis, 1904), pp. 124–5.
64. Ibid.
65. T. G. Connors, 'Surviving the Reformation in Ireland (1534–80): Christopher Bodkin, archbishop of Tuam, and Roland Burke, bishop of Clonfert', *Sixteenth Century Journal*, 32 (2001), pp. 335–55.
66. Kenneth Nicholls, 'A list of the monasteries in Connacht, 1577', *JGHAS*, 33 (1972–3), p. 28.
67. Knox, *Notes on the early history of the dioceses*, pp. 124–5, 289.
68. Nicholls, 'A list of the monasteries in Connacht, 1577', p. 29. On taking up his post as Escheator General in Ireland, Crofton became involved in the land tenure inquisitions. *ALC*, vol. 2, pp. 367–8; Francis Burke, *Loch Cé and its annals*, pp. 66–8. The abbey was granted outright to his son, Edward Crofton, in 1605.
69. Nicholls, 'A list of the monasteries in Connacht, 1577', p. 30.
70. Ibid; i.e. Aughrim, County Galway. At this point it is important to say that, like Ulster in the early seventeenth century, Connacht had previously been under-populated. See Kenneth Nicholls, 'Review of R. R. Davies, *Domination and conquest: the experience of Ireland, Scotland and Wales*', *Scottish Economic and Social History*, 12 (1992), pp. 82–3.
71. NAI, Repertories to Inquisitions (Exchequer), County Roscommon, Elizabeth, 9/15, 4. The term denoting a quarter of land (*ceathrú cuid*) was anglicised as carrow, carhoo, carucate or kerroo. See Richard Simmington, 'Introduction', in *Bks survey & Dist.* (3 vols, Dublin, 1949–67), vol. 1, *County of Roscommon*, p. xxxviii. See also the appendix to John O'Donovan (ed.), *The genealogies, tribes, and customs of Hy-Fiachrach: commonly called O'Dowda's Country, by Duald Mac Firbis* (Dublin: Irish Archaeological Society, 1844).
72. R. Lloyd Praeger, 'Topography', in George Fletcher (ed.), *Connaught* (Cambridge: Cambridge University Press, 1922), pp. 33–6: 'An inland, low-lying area (98% of the surface being beneath 500 ft elevation) formed almost entirely of drift-covered limestone [...] drained by the Shannon and the Suck, the first forming the eastern boundary, the second much of the western.'
73. *Government of Ireland under Sir John Perrot, knt* (London, 1626), p. 80, cited by Charles Owen O'Conor Don, *The O'Conors of Connaught* (Dublin: Hodges Figgis, 1891), p. 195.
74. *ALC*, vol. 2, pp. 368–402.
75. On Malbie, the 'strict but impartial judge, commended by natives for his fairness', see Crawford, *Anglicizing the government of Ireland*, pp. 107–8, 460–1.
76. Captain Thomas Wodehouse to Secretary Fenton, 1586 (*Cal. S. P. Ire., 1586–8*, p. 161).
77. Sir William Fitzwilliam to Lord Burghley, Dublin, Sept. 1589 (*Cal. S. P. Ire., 1588–92*).
78. *Beatha Aodha Ruaidh*, pp. 110–11.
79. Mervyn Archdall, *Monasticon Hibernicum*, p. 605.
80. Benjamin Hazard, 'Gaelic political scripture: Uí Mhaoil Chonaire scribes and the *Book of Mac Murchadha Caomhánach*', in *Proceedings of the Harvard Celtic Colloquium, 2003* (Cambridge, MA: Harvard University Press, 2009), pp. 149–64.

81. Gearóid Mac Niocaill, *The medieval Irish annals* (Dublin: Dublin Institute for Advanced Studies, 1975), p. 35.
82. Robin Flower, 'Ireland and medieval Europe', p. 31.
83. *ALC*, vol. 2, pp. 466–7.
84. Bernadette Cunningham, 'The composition of Connacht in the lordships of Clanricard and Thomond, 1577–1641', *IHS*, 24 (1984), pp. 1–14.
85. *Compossicion Booke of Conought*, ed. A. Martin Freeman (Dublin: Irish Manuscripts Commission, 1936).
86. Conde de Puñonrostro to Philip III, Madrid, 28 Nov. 1606 (AGS, Estado, legajo 1797); see Micheline Kerney Walsh, *Destruction by peace* (Monaghan: Seanchas Ard Mhacha, 1986), p. 176.
87. Puñonrostro to Philip III, 28 Nov. 1606, 'fue luego al campo catholico de los condes Onel y Odonel donde despues quedo con ellos ayudandolos en todo lo que pudo, confessando y predicando'.
88. *AFM*, vol. 6, pp. 2132–3.
89. Mac Diarmada to the Constable of Boyle, 15 Aug. 1599; cited by Denis Murphy, SJ, *The life of Hugh Roe O'Donnell, prince of Tirconnell (1586–1602), by Lughaidh O'Clery* (Dublin: Folens, 1895), pp. ci–civ.
90. Francis Burke, *Loch Cé and its annals*, pp. 66–8.
91. Steven Ellis, *Tudor Ireland: crown, community and the conflict of cultures, 1470–1603* (London: Longman, 1985).
92. *Cf.* Morgan, *Tyrone's rebellion: The outbreak of the Nine Years War in Tudor Ireland*, pp. 62–5.
93. Bernadette Cunningham, 'The Composition of Connacht in the lordships of Clanricard and Thomond: 1577–1641', *IHS*, 24 (1984), pp. 1–14.
94. O'Dowd, *Power, politics and land*, p. 34.
95. See Morgan, *Tyrone's rebellion*, p. 135.
96. O'Dowd, *Power, politics and land*, pp. 34–6.
97. For references to Aodh Ruadh as king of the Suca in Roscommon, prince of Galway and king of the fortress of Sligo, see Bergin (ed.), *Irish bardic poetry*, pp. 31, 222.
98. The birth of Aodh Ruadh can be pinpointed to Saturday 29 October 1572. See *TCD Cat. Ir. MSS.* (1921), p. 1293, entry AD1602.1; Paul Walsh, 'Short Annals of Tír Chonaill', *IBL*, 22 (1934). *Cal. S. P. Ire., 1588–92*, p. 462; Bingham to Burghley, 'Hugh Roe raids Connaught', *Cal. S. P. Ire., 1592–6*, p. 303.
99. J. J. Silke, 'The Irish appeal of 1593 to Spain: some light on the genesis of the Nine Years' War', *IER*, 92 (1959), pp. 279–90, 362–71.
100. *Beatha Aodha Ruaidh*, pp. 118–20.
101. Ó Domhnaill to Philip III, 26 May 1596 (AGS, E. Ingl., l. 839).
102. O'Rahilly (ed.), 'Irish poets, historians and judges in English documents, 1538–1615', *RIA Proc.* (C.), 36 (1921–4), pp. 86–163.
103. Spenser, *A Veue of The Present State of Ireland*, pp. 117–18.
104. David Gardiner, '"These are not the thinges men live by now a days": Sir John Harington's visit to the O'Neill, 1599', *Cahiers Élisabéthains*, 55 (1999), pp. 1–17.
105. Kenneth Nicholls, 'Introduction', *The Irish fiants of the Tudor sovereigns* (4 vols, Dublin: De Burca, 1994), vol. 1, pp. v–xi.
106. K. J. Kesselring, *Mercy and authority in the Tudor state* (Cambridge: Cambridge University Press, 2003), pp. 206–8. I am grateful to Dr David Edwards for his advice on this point.
107. Ibid., p. 2.
108. Nicholls, 'Introduction', *The Irish fiants of the Tudor sovereigns*, pp. v–xi.
109. *Irish fiants*, vol. 3, 6577 and 3941.
110. Ibid., 4678.
111. Ibid. For the pardon granted in 1583 to 'Brian O Mulconre, of Clonplocan [and] Moylonn McShane McPaidin, of same', see *Irish fiants*, vol. 3, 4240.
112. Two quatrains opening, 'Cuadhus la co Cluain Plucain', are to be found in UCD–OFM, Ms A. 7, f. 4 b. m., for which see Canice Mooney et al. (eds), *Catalogue of Irish manuscripts in the Franciscan Library, Killiney* (Dublin: Institute for Advanced Studies, 1969), pp. 14–15; Walsh, *Ir. men of learning*, p. 46; Robert Simmington (ed.), *Bks survey & Dist., Roscommon* (Dublin: Irish Manuscripts Commission, 1944); O'Rahilly, 'Irish poets, historians, and judges, 1538–1615', pp. 86–164.
113. M. J. Connellan, 'Ballymulconry and the Mulconrys', *IER*, 90 (1958), pp. 322–30.
114. *Irish fiants*, vol. 3, 4800.
115. Walsh, *Ir. men of learning*, p. 47.

116. For 'Melaughlen' and 'Feel O Molconnere […] of Ballekillecomin', see O'Rahilly (ed.), 'Irish poets, historians, and judges', p. 93. See also *AFM*, vol. 6, pp. 2290–1.
117. R. I. Best (ed.), *Facsimiles in the collotype of Irish manuscripts VI: Ms 23N10 (formerly Betham 145), in the Library of the Royal Irish Academy with descriptive Introduction* (Dublin: Irish Manuscripts Commission, 1954), p. viii.
118. Francis Beirne (ed.), *The diocese of Elphin: people, places and pilgrimage* (Dublin: Columba, 2004), pp. 196–9.
119. Ordnance Survey, Roscommon, sheet 18 and *General Alphabetical Index to the Townlands and Towns of Ireland* (Dublin, 1851, repr. 1984).
120. *Irish fiants*, vol. 3, 5439.
121. For the provisions and security see *Irish fiants*, entries 4943 and 5382.
122. *HMC Egmont*, vol. 1, part 1 (London: Historical Manuscripts Commission, 1905), p. lxvii.
123. *Irish fiants*, vol. 3, 107–8.
124. See, for instance, 'Inspection by jurors', Roscommon, 5 Jun. 1591 (NAI, Repertories to Inquisitions (Exchequer), County Roscommon, Elizabeth, 9/15). Ó Maolchonaire's brother subsequently conducted work on behalf of Sir Richard Lane (Maoilechlainn Modartha Ó Maolchonaire, 7 Aug. 1612; NAI, Chancery Master Exhibits, unsorted collection, C.106/104, box 2). I owe this reference to Kenneth Nicholls.
125. *HMC Egmont*, vol. 1, part 1, p. lxvii.
126. Ibid.
127. *ALC*, vol. 2, pp. 456–7.
128. Ibid, pp. 480–1. On the role of one Maoilechlainn Mac Cába in the winter of 1588, see Colin Martin, *Full fathom five: wrecks of the Spanish Armada* (London: Chatto & Windus, 1975), p. 201.
129. *Irish fiants*, vol. 3, 5439.
130. Hardiman, *Irish minstrelsy: bardic remains of Ireland*, vol. 2, pp. 287–305.
131. Special report on the kingdom of Ireland, Valladolid, 7 Nov. 1605 (AHL, FH/Lerma t. I/c. 27): 'Y en la guerra que ha hecho el Señor O'Roque contra los Yngleses por no entregar a los Ministros de la Reina a varios Españoles de la Armada de 1588 a quienes arrojo en tierra de este caballero el naufragio.'
132. Garrett Mattingly, *The defeat of the Spanish Armada* (London: Jonathan Cape, 1959), pp. 307–11; Robert Milne-Tyte, *Armada: the planning, the battle and after* (London: Wordsworth Military Library, 1988), pp. 133–45.
133. O'Dowd, *Power, politics and land*, p. 37. On the subject of attacks against survivors of the Armada, see Hiram Morgan, '"Slán Dé fút go hóiche": Hugh O'Neill's murders', in David Edwards, Clodagh Tait and Pádraig Lenihan (eds), *Age of atrocity: violence and political conflict in early-modern Ireland* (Dublin: Four Courts Press, 2007), pp. 95–118.
134. *Cal. S. P. Ire., Elizabeth*, cxxxviii, 29; cited by Charles Petrie, *Philip II of Spain* (London: Eyre & Spottiswoode, 1964), p. 287.
135. Fitzwilliam Papers, Oxford, Bodleian Library, Carte 55–7, 10501 (574–95); Bingham to Walsingham, 1590; cited by O'Conor Don, *The O'Conors of Connaught*, p. 206.
136. *AFM*, vol. 6, pp. 1186–7.
137. Special report on the kingdom of Ireland, 7 Nov. 1605: 'Fue forsoso despues de grandes trabajos y perdidas, huir a Escocia donde fue preso y llevandole a Londres le condenaron a ser degollado.'
138. Hardiman, *Irish minstrelsy: bardic remains of Ireland*, vol. 2, pp. 426–9. See also Hiram Morgan, 'Extradition and treason-trial of a Gaelic lord: the case of Brian O'Rourke', *Irish Jurist*, 22 (1987), pp. 285–301.
139. William Palmer, *The problem of Ireland in Tudor foreign policy, 1485–1603* (Woodbridge: Boydell & Brewer, 1994), p. 127.
140. Special report on the kingdom of Ireland, 7 Nov. 1605: 'Largo seria enumerar las otras muchas guerras que por defender la fe catholica y contra los enemigos de España han hecho.'
141. John Dee, *The perfecte arte of navigation (1577)* (repr. Amsterdam, 1968), pp. 23–4; G. A. Davies, 'Crosscurrents, commercial, cultural and religious in Hispano-Welsh relations, 1480–1630', *Transactions of the Honourable Society of Cymmrodorion* (1985), pp. 147–85.
142. G. A. Davies, 'The Irish college in Santiago de Compostela: two documents about its early days', in Margaret Rees (ed.), *Catholic tastes and times: essays in honour of Michael E. Williams* (Leeds: Trinity and All Saints College, 1987), pp. 81–126; Karin Schüller, 'Special conditions of the Irish–Iberian trade during the Spanish–English war (1585–1604)', in Enrique García Hernán et al. (eds), *Irlanda y la monarquía hispánica: Kinsale 1601–2001. Guerra, política, exilio y religión* (Madrid: Consejo Superior de Investigaciones Científicas, 2002), pp. 447–68.

143. Gerard Boate, *A natural history of Ireland* (London: John Wright, 1652); quoted by A. E. Murray, *A history of the commercial and financial relations* (London: King, 1907), p. 18.
144. Ciarán Brady, 'The end of the O'Reilly lordship, 1584–1610', in David Edwards (ed.), *Regions and rulers in Ireland, 1100–1650* (Dublin: Four Courts Press, 2004), pp.174–200.
145. James Carney, *The Irish bardic poet* (Dublin: Dublin Institute for Advanced Studies, 1958), p. 137.
146. Valladolid, 22 May 1602; quoted by Charles Meehan, *The fate and fortunes of the earls of Tyrone and Tyrconnell* (Dublin: Duffy, 1864), p. 492.

2

The Rise to Prominence, 1592–1609

In an interesting letter written at the end of the Nine Years War in Ireland, General Pedro de Zubiaur defined the Irish in Spanish territories in the following terms: 'Some will go for the cause of religion, others for vengeance and others for winning plunder, for they are people inclined to novelty.'[1] This observation provides a useful parallel with Flaithrí Ó Maolchonaire's early career in Spain. At the University of Salamanca in the early 1590s he came into contact with the Society of Jesus, joined the Franciscan province of Santiago and returned to Ireland at war before his emergence at the court of Philip III (†1621) as leader of the Irish Friars Minor. During this period Ó Maolchonaire's activities were varied. He directed patronage towards Irish exiles newly arrived in Habsburg dominions, facilitated the organisation of new Irish military units in the Southern Netherlands where he helped to provide his religious order with a new college and, having assisted Aodh Ó Néill to Rome, was appointed archbishop of Tuam in 1609.

THE UNIVERSITY OF SALAMANCA: 'THE MOST FLOURISHING OF THE WORLD'

Spain had represented both a safe haven and a potential source of patronage to Irish Catholics since the earl of Desmond's approach to Charles V in 1527.[2] Less than three decades later, Philip II (†1598) and his wife Mary Tudor (†1558) succeeded in persuading Pope Paul IV (†1559) to declare Ireland a kingdom.[3] In 1575, Flaithrí Ó Maolchonaire's kinsman Aodh wrote, 'By my God's doom, pitiful is the tale' on hearing that James Fitzmaurice and his family had to flee to the court of Philip II for their protection.[4] Following the execution of his fiant, discussed earlier, Flaithrí Ó Maolchonaire left Ireland. According to the Archduchess Isabel, Ó Maolchonaire told her that his work for the nobles of Ireland began during the reign of Philip II in 1592.[5] During the same decade, Irish migrants made regular journeys to and from mainland Europe often drawn by the prospect of employment from April to September, when sea travel was easiest.[6]

Ó Maolchonaire was among the first students to enter the Irish college at Salamanca after its foundation in 1592.[7] Encouraged by Robert Persons SJ (†1610), Thomas White of Clonmel (†1622) had taken a group of Irish students from Valladolid to Salamanca, where he received an endowment from Philip II to open a college.[8] Thomas White had entered the Jesuit noviciate by 1592.[9] Thus, as was the case with many of Spain's educational institutions,[10] control of the Irish college at Salamanca was entrusted to the Society of Jesus. At this time, there were approximately a dozen students at the college with an Irish Jesuit 'always in residence' while confrères moved between Spain, Portugal and Ireland.[11]

On Ó Maolchonaire's arrival in the early 1590s, the exiled Irish community was well established in Spain.[12] He wrote of the University of Salamanca as 'the most flourishing of the world' where one could pursue all types of studies.[13] In the words of the royal cosmographer of Spain, Pedro de Medina (†1567), scholars from many other countries flocked there, 'as though to a fair of letters and of all virtues'.[14] Salamanca was attractive due to good teaching and the comparatively low cost of living.[15] Intellectual life in the Iberian Peninsula had been expanding throughout the century and the burgeoning state bureaucracy relied upon the universities to provide trained personnel. The massive growth of university activity did, however, have its drawbacks, turning out 'an intellectual proletariat' of far more graduates than could ever hope to find professional employment.[16]

Flaithrí Ó Maolchonaire first studied the liberal arts and philosophy.[17] In late sixteenth-century Castile, this necessitated a good command of Latin and was regarded as essential for the acquisition of the religious sciences.[18] Antonio de Nebrija's Introductiones Latinae of 1481 became the standard text in the study of Latin in Spain. During his sojourn in Ireland, St Edmund Campion SJ (†1581) attested the native Irish proficiency for speaking Latin, 'almost as fluently as their vernacular language'.[19] Francisco Sánchez, 'El Brocense', (†1600), was professor of grammar at Salamanca and is still considered an authority on the subject. An independent thinker, his efforts to advance classical scholarship at the university came to the attention of the local inquisition[20] Latin and Aristotelian philosophy were taught at Salamanca's faculty of arts.[21] The university's late sixteenth-century statutes stipulated that Aristotle's Ethics was to be read in alternation with the Politics and Economics in a three-year cycle. David A. Lines notes that 'several teachers of the course were regulars [who] served for lengthy periods [and] tended not to teach other subjects concurrently.'[22] During Ó Maolchonaire's studies at Salamanca, the philosophy curriculum was regulated 'by the statutes of Pope Martin V issued in 1422, the statutes of the B.A. course prescribed a first year studying logic (Vetera and Nova), a second year studying logic and natural philosophy and a third studying natural philosophy and moral philosophy.'[23] Interestingly, Salamanca never set the study of metaphysics 'for either its arts or its theology students'.[24]

On 10 December 1594, Ó Maolchonaire was in the third year of his studies at Salamanca.[25] The following year, he registered at the Irish college as a first year student of theology.[26] The 'Prime Lecture' in theology lasted an hour and a half and began at eight o'clock in the morning and at seven in the morning from Easter until the end of term.[27] Throughout the sixteenth century, the university was a focal point for the study of St Thomas Aquinas. Following the return of Francisco de Vitoria OP (†1546) to Spain in 1523, Salamanca housed 'the most creative Dominican logicians, political theorists, and theologians in the Catholic world', renowned for their commentaries on Summa theologiae, 'especially the Prima secundae and Secunda secundae'.[28] These included Domingo Bañez (†1604) who held the cathedra de prima at the university during Ó Maolchonaire's stay at Salamanca.

Several members of the Salamanca theology faculty were sympathetic to the Irish student population at this time.[29] Of these, Francisco Zumel (†1607), superior general of the Order of Mercy, was dean of the faculty and professor of physics and moral philosophy.[30] The Dominicans Pedro de Ledesma (†1616) and Pedro de Herrera (†1622) held the university's chairs of Thomism and Scotism respectively.[31] The humanist scholar and Thomist, Juan Alfonso de Curiel OSB, served as professor of divinity until his death in 1609.[32] Though less well known, Martín Peraça, the Carmelite theologian, was also regarded as an ally of the Irish at Salamanca. In February 1603, all of the aforementioned names joined with members of Valladolid's faculty of theology to express their support, in print, for Aodh Ó Néill (†1616) and his war against Elizabeth Tudor.[33] Even so, the timing of their intervention was questionable since it occurred after the withdrawal of Irish and Spanish forces at Kinsale.

While the university was renowned for its neo-scholasticism, Flaithrí Ó Maolchonaire was strongly influenced by Augustinian currents in the university, particularly in the areas of political thought and apologetics.[34] There are signs that he considered a religious vocation on arriving at Salamanca. Among the Franciscan lectors in theology at that time were Fernando del Campo, who subsequently became a bishop, Francisco de Herrera, later procurator general of the order, and Juan de Rada, later procurator general and bishop. All three participated in the *de Auxiliis* debate concerning divine grace and free will. [35]

While Aodh Ruadh Ó Domhnaill (†1602) was instigating contact with Spain from Donegal,[36] Ó Maolchonaire translated into Gaelic a short Castilian catechism, two years after its original composition by Jerónimo de Ripalda SJ (†1618). It represents the earliest of the devotional texts translated by an Irish Franciscan.[37] In his opening lines, Ó Maolchonaire wrote that 'it was for the welfare of the soul of the Irish and his own soul's welfare that he started this work.'[38] Preparing this catechetical text, he endorsed the contemporary view that it was insufficient simply to encourage people to believe as the Church believes.[39] In-depth instruction was also needed. Ó Maolchonaire's catechism owes much to the work of the Jesuits Peter Canisius (†1597) and Robert Bellarmine (†1621), especially the latter.[40] It opens with a discourse on Christ, followed by a short explanation of the creed, the main prayers of the Catholic Church and the Ten Commandments. The text concludes with instruction on the seven sacraments, an outline of the virtues and vices, and the powers of the soul.[41] In most places, the catechism in Ireland was taught in Irish, especially on Sundays and feastdays.[42] A second, shorter text preserved in the same manuscript has also been ascribed to Ó Maolchonaire. In simple, early-modern Irish, it briefly advises the reader how to prepare for annual confession, receive communion and win salvation.[43]

Ó MAOLCHONAIRE'S RIVALRY WITH THE JESUITS AND HIS EARLY YEARS AS A FRANCISCAN

In the 1600s, a disagreement emerged at court in Valladolid between Ó Maolchonaire and the Irish Jesuits running the Salamanca College. A report lodged with the Council of Spain by the Irish Jesuit mission declared that, before entering religion, Ó Maolchonaire studied for five years at the college. During this time 'he was punished on several occasions by his superior [who] corrected his faults.'[44] It is worth noting, however, that Ó Maolchonaire arrived at Salamanca in his early thirties and his superiors were no older than he. Thomas White, for instance, was born in 1558.[45] Ó Maolchonaire may have had difficulty in submitting to the authority of those whom he regarded only as his equals or less. In his own words, he subsequently 'left the college of his own free will'.[46] He then entered the religious life at the Franciscan convent of Salamanca where he received the habit.[47]

In accordance with the university's statutes mentioned above, the local Franciscan guardian held a seat on a permanent tribunal established in 1243 to ensure the settlement of disputes arising on campus.[48] This tribunal long anticipated the need to resolve collegian conflicts. Indeed, in 1592/3 the friars had objected to the construction of a new building by the Society of Jesus, the windows of which overlooked the friary.[49] The Franciscan guardian at Salamanca from 1594 to 1598 was fray Hernando de Campo. Despite any possible intercession on his part, however, the peace restored between White and Ó Maolchonaire was to prove short-lived. This is dealt with further on in the chapter.

The seventeenth-century chronicler Gaspar Martínez described the Salamanca convent as the most important Franciscan foundation in the Iberian Peninsula.[50] The Friars Minor at Salamanca were independent of the university's structures during the sixteenth century. Nevertheless, they taught the same *studium generale* curriculum as the university where, for instance, Mateo de Oviedo OFM (†1610) had studied.[51] Flaithrí Ó Maolchonaire is recorded as 'compañero de noviciado' to Aodh Mac Aingil (†1626), a tutor to the sons of Aodh Ó Néill.[52] They and nine of their peers in the Franciscan province of Santiago were later raised to the episco-pacy.[53] According to Wadding, this had never before happened in the history of the order and was unlikely ever to repeat itself.[54]

Throughout his career, Ó Maolchonaire subsequently showed his antagonism towards the Society. This was connected with the ethnic composition of the Irish Jesuits who tended to recruit from Munster and Leinster families loyal to the Tudors. Ó Maolchonaire alleged that Catholics from these provinces were more inclined to religious schism.[55] In his own province of Connacht, three pupils from the Tuam school of the Protestant preacher Isaac Lally joined the Jesuits at Salamanca from 1615 to 1622.[56]

Ó Maolchonaire may also have been stung by the anti-Gaelic attitudes shared by members of the Society of Jesus and the Old English community. Works such as Campion's *Two bokes of the histories of Ireland* included a somewhat derogatory view of Gaelic society and later formed the basis of *De Rebus in Hibernia Gestis* by Richard Stanihurst (†1618).[57] Moreover, Stanihurst's *Harmonia, seu catena dialectica in Porphyrianas institutiones* advocated the need for social and political reform in Connacht and Ulster.[58] Stanihurst was on close terms with Secretary of State Cecil. His confrère William Bathe (†1614), author of the *Janua Linguarum*, had been selected by Viceroy Perrott to visit the court of Elizabeth (†1603) 'with some matters of importance'.[59] Ó Maolchonaire's difficulties with the Jesuits were by no means uncommon in early-modern Catholicism. Dominicans and

Franciscans, for example, shared an aversion towards the Jesuits who had begun to replace them as confessors to the prominent and powerful.[60] This was a Europe-wide phenomenon.[61] Don Juan of Austria (†1578) had attributed much of his success to his Franciscan chaplains whereas the Marqués Spínola (†1630), Philip III's commander-in-chief in Spanish Flanders, looked towards his Jesuit spiritual directors.[62] The works of the great Spanish dramatists of the age, such as Calderón and Lope de Vega, were influenced by their Jesuit education.[63] It is possible, but difficult to demonstrate, that Ó Maolchonaire's preference for Augustine was itself influenced by his difficulties with the more Thomist-leaning Society of Jesus.[64]

It would be misleading, however, to assume that nothing more than animosity towards certain Irish Jesuits led Flaithrí Ó Maolchonaire to join the Friars Minor. His experience of moving from the Society's sphere of influence to that of the Franciscans was not exceptional among Irish exiles. At Lisbon, for instance, the Jesuits taught Peter Lombard's kinsman, Luke Wadding (†1657), before he joined the Franciscan noviciate at a convent near Oporto.[65]

According to a Franciscan tradition, the first friars arrived in Ireland from Galicia during the lifetime of St Francis.[66] There were up to 850 Franciscan convents in sixteenth-century Spain, providing a long-standing network of support for the Irish Franciscan province. The convent at Toro near Zamora, for instance, served as a stopover point between the Iberian Peninsula and Ireland.[67] Mateo de Oviedo OFM emerged as the key figure in developing these links. He was from Segovia and, like Ó Maolchonaire, had received the habit from the province of Santiago at Salamanca's Franciscan convent. Fray Mateo became definitor of the same province and guardian of the convent of St Francis at Santiago de Compostela.[68] The papal nuncio to Spain sent him with James Fitzmaurice on his ill-fated expedition of July 1579. Oviedo's repeated journeys to and from Ireland over a quarter of a century and his representations on behalf of Aodh Ó Néill at the Spanish court led to his promotion to the archbishopric of Dublin in 1600.

Up to ten Franciscan convents of the Santiago province were located along the Galician coast.[69] At the port of La Coruña, the friars were well established at the convent of San Francisco de La Coruña.[70] Their chaplains confessed soldiers based in the port during Lent and at times of illness, and celebrated Mass in the fort of St Anthony on Sundays and feastdays.[71] Ships with 'cargoes of pilgrims' on their way from Ireland to Santiago de Compostela landed at La Coruña and, in the seventeenth century, thousands of Irish migrants settled in the harbour.[72] Flaithrí Ó Maolchonaire may well have arrived there[73] The Franciscans' ethos and the theological tradition of Duns Scotus (†1308) clearly appealed to him.[74] In early-modern Spain, 'the shaping flow of Franciscan currents' helped to form the religious culture of literate people.[75]

The order had a long-held reputation for learning.[76] Their collection of books at Assisi is said to have rivalled those of the Sorbonne and the Pontifical Library at Avignon.[77] Since medieval times, Irish Franciscans studied and taught in Paris, Oxford, Cambridge, Bologna, Cologne and Strasbourg. Lectors and schools of theology are mentioned at the convents of Nenagh, Limerick, Ennis, Ardfert, Armagh, Galway and Drogheda. Before the suppression of the religious houses in the early sixteenth century, it was intended that these should form the nucleus of the theological faculty in Dublin.[78] Recent research reveals the role of the Friars Minor in networks of Gaelic scholarship and patronage at this time.[79]

Mooney comments that 'on the eve of the Reformation, the Franciscans had over sixty houses' in Ireland.[80] Of the entire Third Order of St Francis, the second most populous province was to be found in Ireland.[81] Near Ó Maolchonaire's home, the Franciscans once had houses in Elphin and Roscommon,[82] while the Third Order had friaries at Caldragh and Knockviccary, Taemara, Toberely and Clonroghan.[83] Observant reform had spread rapidly among the Franciscans in Connacht and Ulster.[84] Commenting on the condition of the Irish Church in 1515, an observer said:

> Ther is no archebysshop, nor bysshop, abbot ne pryor, parson ne vycar, ne any other person of the Churche, highe or lowe, greate or smalle, Englyshe or Iryshe, that useyth to preache the wordde of Godde, saveing the poor fryers beggers.[85]

During the Reformation which followed, 'it was the canons regular, the monks, friars and nuns who largely sustained the religious ideals and satisfied the spiritual needs of the people.'[86] For these reasons it is unsurprising that a comparatively new religious order, such as the Jesuits, could be seen as a political and cultural interloper more suited to Leinster and parts of Munster. As observant or reformed friars operating within Gaelic kin-groups, the Franciscans became an early source of resistance to Protestant Reformation, all of which helped make their move to an independent mission relatively untroubled.[87] The Jesuits had had limited successes in Connacht and Ulster, whereas the benefit of experience made the Franciscan order better suited to conditions on the ground.[88]

RETURNING TO IRELAND AT THE HEIGHT OF THE NINE YEARS WAR

Aodh Ruadh Ó Domhnaill made political overtures in 1593 to Philip II in the context of his ambitions in the north of Ireland. Philip waited another two years before intervening actively in the Irish conflict.[89] In a letter to his successor, Philip III, approximately nine years after Flaithrí Ó Maolchonaire's ordination, the Conde de Puñonrostro stated that, 'due to his wish to serve God and your Majesty and to see that kingdom free of tyranny', Ó Maolchonaire had returned to Ireland as a Franciscan priest.[90] According to the Jesuit superiors at the Irish college in Salamanca, Ó Maolchonaire spent five years studying there followed by six months at the Franciscan convent before returning to Ireland.[91] This implies that Ó Maolchonaire arrived back in April 1598, after the ceasefire declared the previous year.[92] His sailing from the Tagus means that he left for Ireland from the port of Lisbon.[93]

Mateo de Oviedo was actively involved in persuading the northern confederates to take up the fight again, motivated with the promise of arms and money from the Spanish Habsburgs.[94] Ó Maolchonaire 'stayed to help in every way he could at the Catholic military camp of the earls Ó Néill and Ó Domhnaill […] hearing confessions, preaching and supporting those demoralised by the sufferings of war'.[95] To some extent, this echoes Bernadino de Mendoza's (†1604) efforts as Spanish envoy at the siege of Paris, 'the last defence against the chaos which must inevitably follow if heresy and Protestantism should prevail'.[96] War chaplains suffered similar hardships to the soldiers they served, 'journeying from place to place saying Mass [...] in the fields and by the roadside, exposed to the inclemency of the weather'.[97] They routinely accompanied into battle the armies they catechised, anointing soldiers before combat and staying with them under enemy fire.[98]

It was during the Nine Years War that Flaithrí Ó Maolchonaire became Aodh Ruadh Ó Domhnaill's 'confessor, adviser and favourite'.[99] The only known copy of Ó Maolchonaire's translation of the Ripalda catechism was sent back to Ireland in 1598.[100] This corresponds to Ó Maolchonaire's stay and he may, therefore, have been in Ulster and Connacht for the battles of the Yellow Ford and of the Curlews, accompanying Aodh Ruadh to the siege of Collooney castle in Sligo.[101] Although *Beatha Aodha Ruaidh Uí Dhomhnaill* must be treated with caution as a historical source, its account of Ó Domhnaill's exhortation to his troops at the Curlews is replete with the same Maccabean ideology advocated at regular intervals by his confessor Flaithrí Ó Maolchonaire.[102]

Thus, the claims of Wadding and Ó Maonaigh that Ó Maolchonaire was commissioned by Clement VIII (†1605) to go to Ireland with Don Juan del Águila (†1602) raise important questions.[103] Leaving the safety of Spanish forces at Kinsale to join up with Ó Néill and Ó Domhnaill would have been a precarious and complicated exercise.[104] Evidence to the contrary, that Ó Maolchonaire was already in Ireland and that he took part in the march south from Ulster, occurs in the Puñonrostro memorial which affirms that 'he went with the earls on their mission to aid Don Juan del Águila at Kinsale.'[105]

Ó Maolchonaire may have returned to Ireland with his confrère Mateo de Oviedo in the spring of 1600 to announce the departure of the expedition which eventually landed at Kinsale. It is known, for instance, that a ship from Spain arrived at Killybegs harbour that year and those on board proceeded to stay, under Ó Domhnaill protection, at the Donegal Franciscan friary before he and Aodh Ó Néill received the ship's Spanish envoy.[106] During the war, Ó Maolchonaire had spent his time:

> Working hard to maintain accord between the nobles of the Catholic Confederacy against the foe, [and] he achieved a great deal due to the love and respect which all those noblemen held for him and continued the above mentioned services.[107]

Letters in his hand offer further support for Flaithrí Ó Maolchonaire's work for the Catholic Confederacy at the height of the Nine Years War. At the end of March 1600, he wrote hurriedly to Clement VIII on behalf of Aodh Ó Néill and his allies James, earl of Desmond (†1607), Florence MacCarthy More (†1640) and his brother Dermot Maol MacCarthy.[108] Comparing their war to a Christian crusade, they asked for indulgences to be granted to those fighting with them. They then appealed to the pope for appointments to Munster's vacant bishoprics and for benefices in Ireland.[109] Combined with Peter Lombard's representations at the papal court, this led Clement VIII to issue a Bull of Indulgence to Ó Néill the following month.[110] Acknowledging that 'you have long struggled to recover and preserve your liberty', the papacy granted 'plenary pardon, and remission of all sins' for all who supported Aodh Ó Néill, 'styled earl of Tyrone, baron of Dungannon, and captain-general of the Catholic army in Ireland'. This indulgence corresponded to those 'usually granted to those setting out to the war against the Turk for the recovery of the Holy Land'. It was issued on condition that all involved 'truly repent and confess, and if possible receive Holy Communion'.[111]

In another letter composed by Ó Maolchonaire, Ó Néill complained to Cardinal Aldobrandini (†1621) at the numbers of Irish fighting on the opposing side and asked for the excommunication of those who failed to support the confederates at war. He declared that he had turned down offers of peace because freedom of worship was not included among the concessions and requested support for the Irish colleges in Spain, Portugal and the Low Countries.[112] The next day, Ó Maolchonaire drafted a progress report to Clement VIII, signed by Ó Néill, stating that the earl of Ormond, Thomas Butler, had been captured. Referring to Lombard's agency for him in Rome, Ó Néill requested more help from the papacy.[113]

Recognising Flaithrí Ó Maolchonaire's efforts on their behalf, Ó Néill and Ó Domhnaill wrote to Philip III from Donegal in January 1601, nominating him for the Irish episcopacy.[114] Describing Ó Maolchonaire as 'a consummate theologian and preacher of the order of Saint Francis of the Observance', they recounted that he had been 'a student of the seminary raised in Salamanca with the great kindness of your most invincible father'.[115] They then proposed him 'for the archbishopric of Tuam or for the bishopric of Elphin, although we would prefer him to receive the archbishopric'.[116] Their recommendation appears among a collection of autograph letters in Latin and Castilian by seven leaders of the Irish 'Catholic League', which report on the course of events in the Nine Years War.

This, the first known call for ecclesiastical promotion made on Ó Maolchonaire's behalf, was made in conjunction with the Catholic confederates' appeal for a bull of excommunication for those who refused to support the war in Ireland. The king of Spain responded favourably, giving Ó Maolchonaire his approbation in a letter to the Duque de Sessa, ambassador to the Holy See.[117] According to Philip III's representative at Brussels, Baltasar de Zúñiga, Sessa made arrangements to forward a papal brief in reply to Ó Néill, stating that it had been entrusted to an Irish gentleman along with a letter from Archduke Albert.[118] The said gentleman may well have been Ensign Thomas Stanihurst, brother of the historian and scientist Richard, who served as a messenger between Ó Néill and the archducal couple at this time.[119] Hopes for a bull of excommunication against Irish troops in the service of Elizabeth Tudor were frustrated, however, and in its place Ó Néill received an 'exhortation to continue that war in defence of the Catholic religion'.[120]

Before the arrival of Don Juan del Águila at Kinsale, the most significant event of the year for Aodh Ruadh and Flaithrí Ó Maolchonaire, his confessor, was the destruction of the Franciscans' Donegal foundation. Ó Domhnaill's rival kinsman, Niall Garbh (†1626), seized control of this 'secure fortress' with support from English troops until powder kegs stored there exploded and wrecked the friary at the end of September. On hearing that the Spanish fleet had landed at Kinsale, Ó Domhnaill raised his siege of Niall Garbh and immediately prepared to muster his forces from Ulster and Connacht.[121] He began 'his celebrated and swift march south' from Ballymote, County Sligo, on 23 October 1601 and had joined forces with Aodh Ó Néill west of Inishannon, County Cork, by 15 December.[122] The combined Irish infantry numbered approximately 6,000, three times that of Lord Deputy Mountjoy (†1606).

Fighting began at dawn on 24 December according to English sources, 3 January 1602 according to the Gregorian calendar.[123] The army of Ó Néill and Ó Domhnaill approached Kinsale with reinforcements under the command of Don Alonso del Campo.[124] In the vanguard were Captain Richard Tyrell, the Munster Irish under Ó Súilleabháin Béarra, and 200 Spaniards.[125] Coming to raise the siege of the town, the Irish and Spanish were overthrown near Kinsale by Mountjoy and part of Elizabeth's forces. Ó Néill's infantry division was first to break and the Irish cavalry scattered after repelling an initial attack. The Irish foot 'fought a short, sharp fight [until] broken in upon by the English horse'. Tyrell's division of 600 infantry had failed to reach their meeting point with Águila. Caught in the flank, they were attacked and 'thrown into disorder'.[126] Delayed by a mist that morning, Ó Domhnaill's rearguard formation of 4,000 infantry witnessed the rout and withdrew from the battle.[127] Ninety of the Spanish troops with Tyrell died on the field and a further fifty were taken prisoner by Mountjoy.[128] Flaithrí Ó Maolchonaire was caught up in the fray and after the defeat a contemporary source described him as *per Anglos proscriptus*.[129]

THE IMMEDIATE AFTERMATH: RENEWED CALLS FOR MILITARY INTERVENTION

General Pedro de Zubiaur (†1605) commanded seven ships laden with ammunition and supplies for the Spanish expedition of 1601.[130] Following their defeat, he 'encouraged all [the Irish] and told them that God and your Majesty will send them help'.[131] From Kinsale, Aodh Ruadh made his way to Inishannon and onto Castlehaven with Flaithrí Ó Maolchonaire, 'hart broken, and in great difficultie'.[132] Despite attempts by Zubiaur and others to persuade Aodh Ruadh to stay and offer encouragement to his followers, 'The poor lord, so ruined over so many years, did not wish to remain under any circumstances and neither did his men.'[133] Ó Domhnaill decided that 'he was going to take his chance and, if he escaped, he would try to get to Scotland or France.' As a result, on 6 January, Zubiaur decided to set sail with them in a Scottish ship bound for Spain. Caught up in a severe sea storm, the general reported that he 'had great difficulty in saving our lives'.[134] Also on board were Raymond de Burgo, Hugh Mostian 'and nine gentlemen more'.[135] Unlike Ó Néill's forces, Ó Domhnaill had not been routed at Kinsale but the opposition he faced from within Tír Chonaill made the prospect of his return home extremely difficult.[136]

After almost a week at sea, Zubiaur landed at the harbour of Luarca in Asturias. From there Aodh Ruadh took with him only Flaithrí Ó Maolchonaire and Matha Óg Ó Maoltuile (†1610), his secretary, planning to go directly to Philip III. Zubiaur opted to take 'all the others with me to La Coruña'. Ó Maoltuile carried with him a full account of 'everything that had happened'.[137] Ó Domhnaill reconsidered his earlier decision, choosing instead to travel over land 'to La Coruña and await your Majesty's orders'.[138] On the way, Ó Maolchonaire took him to see the Tower of Brigantia, from where it was believed the sons of Milesius had first come to Ireland.[139] On 21 January 1602, the small party arrived with Zubiaur in the city, where they were warmly welcomed by the Conde de Caracena (†1626), captain general of Galicia.[140] Caracena remained a staunch ally and patron of the Irish in Spain.[141]

A week later, with a force of almost 3,500 the Irish at Kinsale were described by Mateo de Oviedo as 'well disposed as ever'.[142] Carew, meanwhile, was struggling to maintain an army of 2,000–3,000 in Munster, only 10 per cent of which were English born.[143] Renewed military action to overturn the defeat remained a realistic prospect. To this end, after discussions with the Irish, Zubiaur proposed landing at Limerick before proceeding onto Galway. He subsequently sent instructions on fitting out another fleet.[144] From La Coruña, Ó Domhnaill and Ó Maolchonaire immediately dispatched letters to Philip III appealing for further military and financial support.[145] Having waited a short time in Galicia, Ó Domhnaill travelled south to meet Philip III at court in Zamora.[146] Flaithrí Ó Maolchonaire accompanied the young Ó Domhnaill 'in order to assist with his business and to translate his correspondence'.[147] Ó Domhnaill relied upon Ó Maolchonaire in unfamiliar surroundings where the system of roads was 'chaotic and communications between the centre and periphery of the peninsula were well nigh non-existent'.[148]

The king responded favourably to Ó Domhnaill's requests for a new army and recognition of his authority in Ireland, whereupon he was told to return to La Coruña and wait there until everything was ready.[149] A ship was promised to take Ó Domhnaill home but no further aid was actually forthcoming. Compelled by his 'obligation to serve Our Lord Jesus Christ [and] his desire to see our Catholic king lord of Ireland and the entire world', Flaithrí Ó Maolchonaire wrote in person to Philip's favourite, the duke of Lerma (†1625).[150] Commenting on the single vessel promised to Ó Domhnaill, Ó Maolchonaire advised that it was dangerous to send a lone vessel into hostile waters. Ó Domhnaill deserved better, Ó Maolchonaire asserted. There was, he affirmed, no-one more important or noble in Ireland that had done his majesty such great service.[151] Sending him back without the assistance he needed would end Irish hopes, thereby doing more harm than good.[152] Instead, Ó Maolchonaire proposed that a force of up to 3,000 should be raised for a return to Ireland at the earliest opportunity. Easter was fast approaching and, with it, the best time of the year to set sail. Otherwise Ó Domhnaill would be forced to leave, thereby placing himself at risk of death in exile.[153] Considering Lerma's obsession with *Reputación*, despite the letter's abject ending,[154] this plea was clearly intended to appeal to Castilian pride. Ó Maolchonaire's proposal was put to the council of state on the grounds that it could draw Elizabeth's forces away from the Low Countries, but doubts were raised as to whether the resources were available.[155]

The presence at court of one James Blake of Galway threatened to jeopardise matters for Aodh Ruadh and his confessor. Captain Blake was a merchant who, early in 1602, made his way to Philip III hoping to convince the king that he should fund an invasion of Galway.[156] Moreover, Flaithrí Ó Maolchonaire held Blake 'under grave suspicion of being an English spy'.[157] A letter from Captain Thomas Lee (†1601) to Blake gives detailed advice on how the latter could kill Ó Domhnaill.[158] From Sir George Carew's (†1612) cipher notes in a letter to Mountjoy, it seems likely that Blake, probably working under orders from the president of Munster, intended to do so.[159] Lee reminded Cecil of a letter from James Blake, and also of an offer of service by MacWilliam de Burgo (†1604) to Lee. 'Blackaddell', that is Blake, countersigned this offer. A warrant was issued to Blake to meet Mac William Burke, with whom he devised a scheme 'to cut off O Donell, or take him prisoner and send him to her majesty or to any appointed by her'.[160] Elizabeth and Sir Robert Cecil approved the offer.[161]

Protected by the queen, Blake revealed these plans to the president of Munster, Sir George Carew, before departing for Spain. He landed at Lisbon in May 1602.[162] Making his way to Valladolid, he presented proposals for an invasion of Galway to Ludovico Mansoni SJ, papal nuncio to Ireland. In a letter to Rome on 30 August, Mansoni noted that Blake then discussed this projected invasion with the Spanish council of state. While at La Coruña, Ó Domhnaill learnt of Blake's presence at court. In response, he sent Ó Maolchonaire to make representations accusing the captain of espionage.[163]

In June 1602, Flaithrí Ó Maolchonaire attempted to get approval for Ó Domhnaill to meet Philip III in person but Aodh Ruadh continued to be kept at arm's length by the court.[164] His hopes for another assault on Ireland fell foul of the bureaucratic 'labyrinth creeks' where Lerma manipulated appointments to the secretariat and controlled access to the king.[165] Ó Domhnaill was alarmed by competing plans to acquire Spanish aid and by the delay in sending support to Ireland. He travelled to Simancas to appeal in person to Philip III but, alienated and despondent at having to wait so long for a response, he became seriously ill.[166] Along with Muiris Ultach OFM and Matha Óg Ó Maoltuile, Ó Maolchonaire attended to Aodh Ruadh in his final days, signing the earl's will and acting as his interpreter.[167]

Repeating the calls he and Ó Néill made the previous year, Ó Domhnaill requested a bishopric for Flaithrí Ó Maolchonaire in recognition of his diligence, commending his sound judgment on Irish affairs.[168] In his last hours Aodh Ruadh 'made his confession without reserve' receiving Holy Communion from Ó Maolchonaire and Ultach, who anointed him before he died.[169] Writing to Rome, Ludovico Mansoni recorded the day of the earl's death as 9 September, informing the papal secretary of state that after sixteen days' illness Ó Domhnaill died from a tapeworm.[170] In keeping with his patronage and protection of the order in Ireland, Aodh Ruadh was buried in a friar's habit at the chapter house of Valladolid's Franciscan convent.[171]

Following the earl's death, Flaithrí Ó Maolchonaire and Matha Óg Ó Maoltuile reiterated their allegations that James Blake was a spy. The evidence they had to offer did not persuade the nuncio, who was advised on these matters

by Raymond de Burgo, the baron of Leitrim: 'It was Blake's opposition to Ó
Domhnaill claims to the governance of Connacht that had set Blake at odds with
the deceased lord of Tyrconnell.'[172] Worried that this challenge would damage his
chances of Philip III recognising his claims to the western province, Aodh Ruadh
and Flaithrí Ó Maolchonaire sought to deny James Blake any influence by conspiring against him. For his own protection, it seems, Blake eventually handed
himself over to be imprisoned by the Spanish.[173]

THWARTING NUNCIO MANSONI: Ó MAOLCHONAIRE'S SALAMANCA
LETTER OF PROTEST

On 19 May 1601, Clement VIII had made an Italian Jesuit, Ludovico Mansoni,
nuncio to Ireland.[174] This was contrary to the wishes of Aodh Ó Néill and his
allies who expressed the view that Mateo de Oviedo OFM should be appointed
to the role.[175] The previous year, as a pledge of his loyalty to Philip III, Ó Néill
had sent his second eldest son to Spain.[176] Éinrí (†1610), whose mother was Aodh
Ruadh's sister, stayed at the Franciscan convent in Salamanca while completing
his studies at the university and held the friars in such high regard that he had to
be dissuaded from joining the order.[177] Aware of his father's views on the nunciature, Éinrí travelled to court in Valladolid.[178] In the meantime Aodh Ó Néill, Éinrí
reported, had written to Rome asking for Mansoni's departure to be delayed at
least. Sending him would only scandalise Ireland, 'a land filled with heresies and
the greatest of wars, and without many churches capable of supporting the said
nuncio'.[179]

Ludovico Mansoni, however, sailed from Genoa and stayed with the Duque
de Feria in Barcelona before making his way to Valladolid.[180] Éinrí asked the papal
secretary of state to persuade Clement VIII to overturn the decision to favour
Mansoni. Then Philip III could order Mansoni to return to Italy. With his experience
of the Irish wars, Mateo de Oviedo was, Éinrí asserted, more qualified than his
counterpart.[181] The letter closes with a request for one Edmond MacDonnell, a priest
whose family had lost all their property in support of Ó Néill. Éinrí asked
Aldobrandini to advance MacDonnell's career, possibly with a view to making him
archbishop of Armagh, something Aodh Ó Néill had proposed to Clement VIII in
January 1601.[182] MacDonnell was not the only candidate, however. Since his arrival
at the papal court in 1600, Peter Lombard's diligent efforts to justify the war had set
him apart from his rivals for the Catholic primacy of Ireland, which was granted to
him on 14 December the following year.[183] Ó Néill and his confederates, according
to Lombard, were 'engaged in a struggle for the vindication of the Catholic religion,
the glory of God, the liberty of their country and their own security'.[184]

Meanwhile, Claudio Aquaviva (†1615), superior-general of the Society of
Jesus, selected William Bathe SJ of Dublin to accompany Mansoni on his mission
to Ireland.[185] Arriving at the court in Valladolid, Mansoni reported that Thomas
White, rector of the Irish college in Salamanca, approached him seeking to priori-
tise liberty of conscience for Catholics in Ireland.[186] White and his supporters were
not opposed to Aodh Ó Néill *per se* but their main concerns were far less inter-
ventionist than those of Flaithrí Ó Maolchonaire. The latter held out hopes of

armed support from Philip III to continue the war in Ireland. In this regard, the Jesuits reflected the more moderate approach to European affairs of Clement VIII which emerged after his absolution of Henry IV on 17 September 1595, thereby revealing an effort to free the papacy from its traditional dependence on Spain by allying the Holy See with France.[187]

According to the Irish province of the Society, Flaithrí Ó Maolchonaire now hindered the Jesuit nuncio's journey on to Ireland.[188] His work with Ó Domhnaill as 'confessor, adviser and favourite' enabled him to make an official complaint against the Jesuit superiors of the Irish college at Salamanca.[189] Setting forth their objections on both spiritual and temporal grounds, Ó Maolchonaire and Ó Domhnaill accused Thomas White of excluding entrants from Connacht and Ulster families. In so doing, they argued, White encouraged obedience to the English monarchy, partiality towards schismatic religious interests and a disregard for use of the Irish language among the student body. Echoing his own difficulties at Salamanca almost a decade earlier, Ó Maolchonaire alleged that White, 'even should he be compelled by force to receive them, he will treat them in a way that will be impossible to be endured.'[190] Moreover, Ó Maolchonaire believed, preference was shown towards the sons of merchants. He specifically states that Muiris Ultach and Edmond MacDonnell, followers of Ó Domhnaill and Ó Néill respectively, were denied entry on financial grounds.[191] This appears to confirm early-modern Jesuit practice whereby instruction and administration were provided chiefly to 'those few wealthy students who boarded within the college'.[192]

Mansoni became embroiled in the case at court where he tried to settle matters.[193] Above all he was concerned with the repeated Gaelic calls, outlined above, for the pope to excommunicate those in Ireland who refused support to the war.[194] An earlier request by Ó Néill, Ó Domhnaill, MacWilliam de Burgo and Ó Ruairc for 'adhesion to the confederacy' had gone unheeded in Munster.[195] Even after Don Juan del Águila's arrival, Catholic loyalists remained reticent about entering the conflict and Mateo de Oviedo was perturbed to find priests preaching against the Spaniards and their allies.[196] Responding in 1604, Old English lords and gentlemen vehemently defended themselves against accusations of disloyalty to Catholicism by describing the religious persecution suffered in Leinster and Munster.[197] Concurrently, the Jesuits argued that Ó Maolchonaire's letter of protest was inspired by 'indiscreet zeal, or passion, or ignorance'. Their defence differentiated between the wars of the Geraldines and those of Ó Néill, describing Flaithrí Ó Maolchonaire's 'imprudent' claims against Irish merchant families as idle fears.[198] It would, though, be an oversight to ignore the fact that the lack of assistance given to Ó Néill in the towns of those regions during the recent wars fuelled the grievances of some Gaelic leaders. Apart from notable exceptions such as James Archer,[199] the Jesuits 'had been in no hurry to participate' while others had waited until March 1602 before declaring their encouragement.[200]

Faced with calls at court for Spain to change its policies towards Ireland, Ó Maolchonaire was aware that the patronage vital to military intervention and to the education of their followers came from the same sources. For instance, on taking holy orders in Spain, Irish students were then paid *viaticum* for their return to Ireland.[201] The college, Ó Maolchonaire argued, received funds from the Ulster earls' allies in Spain, such as Caracena, the bishops of Segovia and Salamanca, and many of Galicia's monasteries.[202]

Despite Mansoni and Bathe's arrival at court, Philip III remained 'totally noncommittal', they were forced to wait six months for a royal audience and once peace was concluded with England their journey to Ireland was no longer necessary.[203] Instead, the nuncio remained in Valladolid where he corresponded with the papal secretary of state, Pietro Aldobrandini, archbishop of Ravenna and nephew of Clement VIII.[204] Bathe, meanwhile, was consulted as an adviser at court together with his brother John.[205]

The *regulae* at Salamanca's Irish college were drawn up in 1604. These stipulated that students over twenty-five were ineligible for entry.[206] Memories of Ó Maolchonaire may have had a bearing upon this condition of entry. Obedience to the Jesuit rector was compulsory in all matters and it was he who decided who was suitable for the higher stream of studies in logic, controversy, conscience, philosophy and theology.[207] Three Spanish rectors, including Antonio de Padilla SJ, replaced White as rector from 1605 until 1608.[208]

THE ABANDONED EXPEDITION TO IRELAND OF 1603

With help from Matha Óg Ó Maoltuile, Flaithrí Ó Maolchonaire continued to press for action after the death of Ó Domhnaill. At the Escorial palace, his confessor presented a report on Irish affairs to the council of state.[209] Ó Maolchonaire averred that after nine years, the war in Ireland was sustained more by miracles than physical strength.[210] 'Worn-out and weary of unfulfilled promises from Spain, to overcome their doubts, they had sent their best messenger, the young Ó Domhnaill, to represent the needs of the Irish to the king and to ask for his assistance.'[211] Without further help from Spain, the friar warned, Kinsale and its aftermath created the conditions for an English policy of divide and rule.[212] 'In the event that the principal lords of Ireland still have some forces, they will only come to general agreements but if they lack forces and are in great difficulty, the enemy will freely offer excellent terms to each lord separately'.[213] Isolated as a result, they would be powerless to resist any further. Regardless of infinite works in the service of the king, the Irish nation would, therefore, be lost to Spain.[214] 'Seeing this pitiful event and the wretched spectacle of Ireland's destruction for the lack of aid from Spain', Ó Maolchonaire declared, other nations would never place their trust in its promises again.[215]

All this could be averted, he claimed, by sending forthwith the help that Ó Domhnaill had requested for Connacht and Ulster. Realising that the Spanish were reluctant to commit large numbers of troops to an Irish expeditionary force, Ó Maolchonaire proposed that, rather than sending up to 12,000 to Cork or Limerick, approximately 2,000 could make their way north to Donegal and Sligo.[216] Were 3,000 soldiers provided, they could take Galway and join up with the Aodh Ó Néill and his brother. Galway would offer itself up within days and Lord Deputy Mountjoy would be unable to relieve the city by land or by sea.[217] With this in mind, Ó Domhnaill had brought to Spain the baron of Leitrim,

Raymond de Burgo, whose lands were in that region.[218] As Galway was almost an island, the Franciscan asserted that it would be easy to cut 'an insuperable trench' at the narrow point that joined it to the land. By raising a bastion on that part of the river and placing two pieces of artillery on it, he continued, one could prevent enemy ships from entering the port.[219] Ó Maolchonaire concluded this proposal with the following description:

> Connacht is enclosed by a great river called the Shannon that flows from the earls' lands. It has only two crossings, one at Limerick and the other at Athlone. Sixteen miles of forest enclose the first where neither horses nor artillery can pass. For the other, there are four miles of forest and two of marshes with a pathway of stone and logs that, once destroyed, is impossible to pass.[220]

Philip III expressed his hopes that substantial assistance could be provided,[221] but the Irishman's proposal was delayed at court. Early in 1603, he reiterated his call 'to send some support to encourage the Catholics of Ireland and prevent them giving way to despair on hearing of the earl's death'.[222] The previous October, the council of state had resolved to intervene with money, arms and munitions.[223] However, Ó Maolchonaire's hopes of returning home proved unfounded when the 50,000 ducados failed to appear.[224] Blaming the lack of help on his sins, those of Ireland and Spain, the friar told Philip that his ministers had asked for another four reports to be submitted.[225] Seven months passed before his proposal was finally referred to the president of finance.[226] Ó Maolchonaire reported that, in spite of setbacks, the Catholic confederacy had 'gained considerable victories as will be confirmed from many quarters'.[227] Events in Ireland had quietened down since, he added, encouraging Philip to give orders to 'despatch [the Irish] speedily'. In the event that the king decided against further intervention, the Franciscan begged him to inform them 'so that they may be able to make the best terms they can'.[228] The figures for a new expedition were amended to 30,000 ducados but the money remained unpaid.[229] Ó Maolchonaire and Ó Maoltuile were then obliged to spend on their stay the money that was given to them for the voyage.[230] The council of state insisted with the president of finance that they should be provided for immediately from any available source, 'so that they may be sent at once'.[231] Two ships, the *Santiago* and the *Trinidad*, to be commanded by Don Martín de la Cerdá, were fitted out at La Coruña.[232] He was already well acquainted with Irish affairs. After accompanying Mateo de Oviedo to Donegal during the Nine Years War, Don Martín prepared a detailed report on conditions in Ireland for Philip III.[233]

The new mission, however, never landed in Ireland. Three years later, the Conde de Puñonrostro glossed over the total failure of this 1603 expedition.[234] He stated that Philip III had sent Flaithrí Ó Maolchonaire to serve as translator to 'assist the Catholics of Ireland'. On hearing that events had forced Ó Néill to sue for peace at Mellifont, Ó Maolchonaire went back to Spain without putting ashore in Ireland.[235]

The Irish blamed Don Martín de la Cerdá for this farce.[236] Ó Domhnaill's former secretary, Matha Óg Ó Maoltuile, and Roibeard Mac Artúir accompanied Ó

Maolchonaire on the voyage. Mac Artúir had studied at Salamanca before his ordination in 1599 and subsequently became an influential cleric in Madrid.[237] Don Martín had been driven by ambition, Mac Artúir said, and showed 'neither prudence nor discretion in his actions'.[238] Two days into the voyage, Don Martín had asked Ó Maoltuile why he had presented Caracena with a request for embarkation. The governor of Galicia, Caracena, had nothing to do with the ships under de la Cerdá's command who stated that his orders had come from Philip III.[239] Ó Maoltuile responded by saying he thought Caracena should have a say in these matters. Don Martín replied that if Ó Maoltuile didn't shut up he would live to regret it.[240] Mac Artúir argued that, due to the favour and benevolence that Caracena had always shown the Irish, it was essential they maintain contact with him.[241] Don Martín, however, accused them of disloyalty for approaching Caracena with a request to send more followers of the Ulster earls with the mission.[242] After that, Ó Maoltuile and Mac Artúir claimed, instead of trusting their advice and that of Ó Maolchonaire, Don Martín relied upon his own opinion and on 'servants of the enemy'.[243]

The resulting lack of consultation between captains assigned to the expedition and the Irish led to a fatal breakdown in communication. To make matters worse, Ó Maoltuile and Mac Artúir contended that, off the coast of Ireland, Don Martín had handed over letters intended for Aodh Ó Néill to the English.[244] Less than fifty miles from Donegal by sea, Matha Óg Ó Maoltuile took a boat to go ashore with a merchant. Don Martín was enraged at this and accused him of taking letters to Ó Domhnaill.[245] Mac Artúir, described here as tutor to Aodh Ó Néill's son, vouched for Ó Maoltuile and wrote to inform Tyrone of developments.[246] In a letter to the earls' ally Caracena, Ó Maoltuile expected that Flaithrí Ó Maolchonaire would give an account of events.[247]

Don Martín de la Cerdá sailed back to La Coruña, returning to the paymaster the 30,000 ducados and supplies intended for Aodh Ó Néill. In an attempt to salvage Philip's support for his cause, Ó Néill sent MacWilliam de Burgo to Spain with Ó Maolchonaire and de la Cerdá as a pledge of his loyalty to the king.[248] On their arrival, Ó Maolchonaire acted as translator for MacWilliam de Burgo.[249] Awaiting permission to go to court they approached the governor of Galicia, Caracena, who provided for their expenses. In early July 1603, Caracena relayed the news to Philip III that Ó Néill and his followers had been driven, for the present, to accept their enemies' wishes. Nevertheless, with the necessary help from Spain they would continue to offer service to the king.[250] Flaithrí Ó Maolchonaire wished to return to Ireland again but was instructed by Philip III to stay in Spain to offer advice on Irish affairs.[251] By now, the king had extended his felicitations to Elizabeth Tudor's successor, James I (†1625), thereby paving the way to open negotiations for peace with England.[252]

After the debacle at sea, Roibeard Mac Artúir and Matha Óg Ó Maoltuile went along with Ó Néill and Ó Domhnaill to meet James I in London. On his return to Spain, Mac Artúir gave Ó Maolchonaire an account of the outcome for the Catholic confederacy.[253] Somewhat ambiguously, Ó Maolchonaire stated that, even though James I had shown the earls favour on their visit, he would not grant them liberty of conscience but ordered that they not be harassed in matters of religion.[254] The king of England was 'also unwilling to withdraw English garrisons from fortifications located on the earls' estates'.[255] 'With that,' Ó Maolchonaire continued in his report to Caracena, Ó Néill and Ó Domhnaill 'travelled back to Ireland dispossessed of the great lords they had previously for vassals'.[256] Ó Ruairc of West Bréifne was the most helpless of all. Nobody knew of his whereabouts and James I did not want to pardon him before he gave Ó Ruairc's lands to his brother.[257] The friar reported that Florence MacCarthy More and the earl of Desmond remained in the Tower of London, where the former was kept in solitary confinement.[258] The earl of Bearhaven who was in London but had been given 'neither pardon nor licence to return to his lands', therefore urged Mac Artúir to ask Caracena to help him flee to Spain.[259] These combined events had a direct bearing upon the earls' flight from Ireland three years later, of which more anon.

Ó MAOLCHONAIRE, THE KING'S CONFESSOR AND
THE CONDE DE PUÑONROSTRO

On account of their Spanish contacts Irish nobles and dependants who suffered loss during the Nine Years War and its aftermath looked to the Spanish crown for compensation.[260] From January 1601 to June 1606, the court of Philip III resided at Valladolid where the arrival of Irish petitioners in ever larger numbers caused growing concern. Bureaucratic obstacles were raised to stem the flow. Flaithrí Ó Maolchonaire quickly learned of the rigorous procedures required by Spanish bureaucracy before granting documentation to Irish migrants for rights and emoluments in Spain. Trained as a chronicler and genealogist, Ó Maolchonaire was, perhaps, well suited to his new role as intermediary at the Spanish court for the incoming Irish. According to the late seventeenth-century historian John Lynch, the Franciscan was gifted with 'a singular power of intuition', which enabled him to duly consider 'the ability and industry of men'.[261]

Ó Maolchonaire was to spend the next three years working with Philip III's confessor and the Spanish councils of state and war to accommodate Irish military migrants and their dependants in Spain.[262] The friar's first task was to assess payments to the Irish as part of the discretionary spending conducted by fray Gaspar de Cordova (†1604), the royal confessor. At the courts of the Habsburgs, confessors enjoyed prestige among government ministers and council members of the crown.[263] Generosity to exiled Irish soldiers made amends for sins of omission, such as the capitulation of Spanish forces at Kinsale and the surrender of Irish castles on the coast of west Cork.[264] Be that as it may, the inclusion of early Irish appeals with those from Spanish, Flemish, French and Italian soldiers also indicates that the authorities in Spain initially underestimated the numbers arriving from Ireland.[265]

The Irishman's name occurs repeatedly in the accompanying reports on compensation for Irish military service and losses incurred during the late 1590s, verifying appeals from 1603 onwards. The first of these refers to one Conor McMorris, an ensign officer wishing to serve in Spanish Flanders who was granted 50 ducados assistance, 'in consideration for the many years of service to his Majesty and to the princes of Ireland'.[266] An ensign, or lieutenant, was second-in-command of a company who, among other duties, carried the colours of the company.[267] McMorris had already served in Spanish Flanders and Brittany. At the end of his letter, the president of finance states that 'Friar Florencio, confessor of the Conde Ó Domhnaill, officially confirms it.'[268] In document bundles for 1603/4, Ó Maolchonaire attests a further twenty-five requests made by Irish petitioners. The amount of money awarded to them varied. This enabled Ó Maolchonaire to use his newfound role with discretion to favour some applicants more than others. These decisions reflect both his ecclesiastical background and the strength of his political conviction.

In September, four of Ó Domhnaill's followers appealed for funds to return to Ireland. Earlier that year they had been sick with fever and, therefore, unable to join the failed expedition to assist the Ulster earls.[269] Their names were Hugh Gallagher, Donagh MacSweeney, Didicus Crawford and Nicholas Collins. MacWilliam de Burgo endorsed these petitions in view of their immediate needs and for Aodh Ruadh's service to Philip III.[270] Accepting that 'Friar Florencio says that it is as they describe it', fray Gaspar wrote to the president of finance instructing him to award them alms of 200 reales each.[271] In return for fighting alongside Captain Tyrell, Antoine Ó Domhnaill received 200 reales for his journey home to Ireland.[272] The following month, the king's confessor recommended that Ó Maolchonaire receive 300 ducados for his own use and a further 300 to be allocated to Aodh Ruadh's relatives.[273] At the close of 1603, the Irish Franciscan appealed on behalf of former Uí Dhomhnaill page, Simon O'Shea. Despite being included as a legatee in the late earl's will, he had not received any financial support since his arrival in Spain. O'Shea wished to return to Ireland due to continued ill-health, a request which fray Gaspar recommended to Philip III's first minister, Lerma, who ordered that O'Shea be given 300 reales before his departure.[274] Tadhg O'Hey and David Roche, described respectively as an Irish gentleman[275] and the son of an Irish nobleman,[276] each received 300 reales for serving in the war in Ireland, while Irish clerical student Daniel Manin was granted 400 reales for his education.[277] Fernando Hagan, an Irish priest who administered to the needs of the holy clergy, was awarded 500 reales.[278] A once-off payment of 300 ducados was made to Elena and Honora O'Driscoll, sisters of the lord of Castlehaven. Ó Maolchonaire described them as 'poor women' deserving of support since they were in their forties and therefore unlikely to marry.[279]

Other Irish appeals for patronage from the same sources are more detailed in their assessment of claims. Denis Kelly, 'an Irish gentleman', was recommended for 400 reales. Again Ó Maolchonaire vouched for his record. After five years' service at war in Ireland he had been forced to flee with his wife and children and wished to travel on to Flanders.[280] Ó Maolchonaire stated that Dominic Barrett's father Albert helped the Spanish by providing them with the use of his family home and, in return, he received 500 reales.[281] The cases of Kelly and Barrett came up again in 1604.[282] The same amount of money was provided to Conor O'Brien. A similar account was given for Daniel Conry who, we are told, lost his lands to the English after placing them at the disposal of the Spanish.[283]

As stated above, those who had defended the castles at Dunboy, Baltimore and Bearhaven during the Kinsale expedition were treated well by the Spanish.[284] Maurice O'Donovan was granted 1,000 reales. Having arrived in Valladolid with Donagh O'Driscoll, Morgan Macfynin found himself destitute. Flaithrí Ó Maolchonaire communicated this to fray Gaspar, who arranged for the soldier to receive immediate alms followed by a later instalment of 300 reales.[285] Daniel Regan is described as another of O'Driscoll's followers who also served with the earl of Desmond and his brother John Fitzgerald for three years. Accordingly, fray Gaspar advised the council of finance to award the soldier 200 reales.[286] John O'Carroll, a native of Kinsale, had arrived at court with his wife, three sons and two daughters after losing his lands in Cork. Expressing compassion for their plight, fray Gaspar advised that they should receive 400 reales.[287]

An indication of worsening conditions in Ireland came in January 1604 with the arrival at court of followers of Aodh Ó Néill. Richard O'Brien received 500 reales in consideration of six years' military service and the loss of his property. Terence O'Hagan had been wounded in Flanders after the war in Ireland and obtained 100 ducados with help from Florence Conry. Andrew French, who had lost all his property after assisting priests during the war, received alms of 200 reales.[288]

Another document deals with both Raymond de Burgo and Eóghan Mag Mathghamhna (†1623). The latter was a close ally of Aodh Ó Néill who later served as archbishop of Dublin from 1611 to 1623. He wished to buy some books and vestments. Fray Gaspar provided 600 reales for his use in Salamanca, 'to help the Catholics of his country'.[289] On this occasion, baron of Leitrim, Raymond de Burgo, only obtained 400 reales. The baron's grant was described as a single amount to pay off some of his debts and defray the costs of his planned journey to Ireland. Raymond de Burgo had informed Ludovico Mansoni of James Blake's opposition to Ó Domhnaill claims to Connacht. As stated above, this set Blake against Aodh Ruadh. Concerned that this could ruin his hopes of Philip III declaring him overlord of the western province, Ó Domhnaill and Ó Maolchonaire conspired against Blake until, it seems, he handed himself over to the Spanish.[290]

Flaithrí Ó Maolchonaire knew that military followers were maintained at the expense of their leader. Ó Maolchonaire's deft use of his contact with fray Gaspar enabled him to keep Raymond de Burgo in check. In 1607, afraid that his cavalry company would be unable to reform in Flanders, de Burgo felt compelled to write to the Spanish secretary of state, Andrés de Prada (†1611), pleading for Philip III to support him.[291] This represented a reversal of fortune for the baron of Leitrim. The previous September the Spanish council of war judged him a 'noble person of much confidence, quality and service'.[292]

In the midst of all these changes, therefore, old rivalries continued to exist among Irish exiles in Spain and Flanders. Evidence of James Archer's efforts on behalf of certain applicants appear in appeals from the first half of 1603.[293] The previous year he had received 700 ducados as part of a 22,000 ducado payment to twenty Irish signatories.[294] Crucially, however, he was deprived of the role granted to Flaithrí Ó Maolchonaire and from this point on, the Franciscan gained the edge on his old adversary in helping to direct funds towards preferred candidates and causes. As shall be seen later, their rivalry resurfaced before Ó Maolchonaire left Castile in late 1606. James Archer had joined the Jesuits in 1581. As the Nine Years War intensified, he arrived at Waterford from Spain under the name of 'Bowman'.[295] Ó Maolchonaire's differences of opinion with Archer reflected those of Mateo Oviedo OFM, archbishop of Dublin, with the same individual. The Oviedo–Archer dispute at sea led to complaints by Don Juan del Águila and hampered the Kinsale expedition.[296]

Fray Gaspar died in office in June 1604, throwing Ó Néill's hopes of obtaining an annual retainer from the Spanish court into suspense.[297] The importance of fray Gaspar's role in helping Irish exiles is not to be underestimated. After his death, Flaithrí Ó Maolchonaire referred to the Dominican as 'their dear father and patron who had been constant in his support of the Irish'.[298] By then, according to Captain Edward Fitzgerald, there were more than 600 Irish refugees at court.[299] Within the same decade, claims from Irish petitioners rose to approximately 1,200 per month. Few spoke Spanish and this contributed to significant delays in the settlement of their cases.[300] The increase of claims appears to have convinced Lerma of the need for an interim policy to deal with the problem. To this end, Francisco Arias Dávila y Bobadilla (†1610), the Conde de Puñonrostro, was made protector of the Irish. Flaithrí Ó Maolchonaire was appointed to serve as his adviser, thereby consolidating his position at court in Valladolid.[301] As a first step, the council of state notified the inquisitor general that Ó Maolchonaire was to ensure all of the Irish arriving at court received confession and communion in accordance with their Lenten observances.[302]

Puñonrostro had sat on the council of war for five years, and was in Valladolid from August 1602 to May 1605 to participate in enquiries concerning the expedition to Kinsale.[303] The Spanish Habsburgs were concerned about the wellbeing of English Catholics. As part of his work, Puñonrostro corresponded with Joseph Creswell SJ (†1623) and merchants from England.[304] Philip III showed genuine concern for English Catholics and, in the early 1600s, wished to grant them the same favours as the Irish. To this end, he sought to receive into Spanish society those persecuted, while pursuing his peace settlement with London.[305] Since 1588, Spanish Jesuits had argued in favour of private toleration of Catholics in England.[306] Their English confrères subsequently espoused this idea in their work. Robert Persons SJ, for instance, held that the British Isles were to be regarded as a single pastoral entity.[307] He and Joseph Creswell argued that Elizabethan penal laws and the repression of conscience would provoke serious unrest, and the latter proposed that 'subiectes of different religions' should 'live together in dutifull obedience'.[308] The Jesuits' *officium regulae* for 1598 made no reference to either Scotland or Ireland and the latter was understood to benefit from episcopal continuity. The proposal to treat all three countries as a pastoral unit was subsequently proposed for Ludovico Mansoni's jurisdiction as nuncio.[309] This was, of course, contrary to the hopes of Aodh Ó Néill and his followers who waited for further armed support.

Although different court factions vied for control of foreign policy, support grew in Spain for peace. Following the death of Elizabeth and the succession of James I, the Conde de Villamediana (†1607) left Madrid on 3 May 1603 'to convey the customary felicitations to the sovereign'. Simultaneously, in Flanders, the Archdukes Albert and Isabella appointed the Conde de Aranberg to the same purpose. Peace talks soon proceeded between England and Habsburg Spain.[310] The following year, Juan Fernández de Velasco Tovar (†1613), constable of Castile, was sent to conclude the peace.[311] Peace with England was seen as vital to peace in Flanders, and also offered the chance to replenish Spain's coffers with the proceeds of renewed trade with England.[312] As strategic pressures caused Spanish interest in a military intervention in Ireland to ebb away, Ó Maolchonaire and its other proponents were obliged to adapt.

LAUNCHING THE Ó NÉILL *TERCIO* IN FLANDERS

Crucial to Spanish bureaucracy's attempts to deal with the inflow of Irish migrants was the proposal to form a dedicated Irish military unit in the Spanish army, preferably in Flanders. Since the 1580s, the emerging Irish military community in the Low Countries had drawn its leaders from loyalist Irish families.[313] From 1605, however, Flaithrí Ó Maolchonaire tipped the balance in favour of the Uí Néill and their allies. The ever-increasing presence of Irish soldiers in Spain had to be tackled. The councils of state and war accepted that the best answer for all concerned would be to transfer these Irish troops who arrived in Spain to serve in Flanders.

Sent to pledge Ó Néill's loyalty to Philip III, MacWilliam de Burgo had made his way with Ó Maolchonaire to Valladolid where he fell ill. There were health concerns for the newly arrived Irish too.[314] Valladolid was known for serious problems of public health and, 'locked in by the city's walls', a plague epidemic hit the area in the early 1600s.[315] MacWilliam was taken to the convent of San Francisco. Mateo de Oviedo stayed there.[316] Making calculated use of Aodh Ó Néill's principal Spanish ally in Galicia, Flaithrí Ó Maolchonaire wrote to the Conde de Caracena. He stated that MacWilliam de Burgo had suffered for a month from 'double tercian fever' and from 'melancholy at seeing peace brokered with the English'.[317] In his final three days, able to take only bread and water, he entrusted his son to the custody of Puñonrostro and died as he had lived, 'a very Christian knight'.[318] On 11 November 1604 the Marques MacWilliam de Burgo was interred in the convent chapter house, next to Aodh Ruadh Ó Domhnaill who ten years earlier had inaugurated him leader of his sept.[319]

Ó Maolchonaire told Caracena that Éinrí Ó Néill and many others had attended MacWilliam's burial with appropriate honours provided by the king of Spain.[320] Following his description of MacWilliam's reaction to news of peace with England, Ó Maolchonaire concluded his letter to Caracena by recommending Éinrí Ó Néill's promotion to colonel, *maestre de campo*, of Irish military units (*tercio*) in Flanders,[321] an idea that appealed to Éinrí.[322]

The Franciscan revealed that, on the following Tuesday, he and Puñonrostro were to give the council of state their report on approximately 250 Irish exiles.[323] He expected, 'without doubt', that Philip III would order their transfer to Galicia.[324] With two companies stationed in Lisbon and those formed by Éinrí Ó

Néill, they would then sail to Flanders. Ó Maolchonaire reported that Éinrí had already received letters from the king intended for Archduke Albert (†1621). These confirmed his promotion and a payment of 2,000 ducados for the voyage.

Considering 'the services of his father and uncle, and to clear the Irish out of Spain', it was only right, Ó Maolchonaire asserted, that Éinrí should receive the title of colonel before their departure.[325] This was more than just a pragmatic response to stemming the flow of Irish migrants. Refusing such a request after the death of MacWilliam could have contravened protocol at the Spanish court. Philip III's secretary accepted Ó Maolchonaire's request, leading to the additional payment of 200 ducados per month to the young Ó Néill, surplus to his salary.[326] While Éinrí made preparations to leave for the Spanish Netherlands, the council of war decided in favour of moving Irish soldiers from Castile to Galicia from where they could join up with the Ó Néill *tercio* in Flanders.[327] To this end, Puñonrostro and Ó Maolchonaire submitted a detailed register of the Irish and the funds given them to date. It comprises 229 people in several categories: officers maintained for service, soldiers in receipt of ordinary pay for Flanders, the poor, Irish priests and students, widows and young unmarried women. Several entries are followed by a short account of their circumstances.[238] Almost all were from Munster.

Diarmaid Ó Súilleabháin, *entretenido*, was among those earmarked for transport. He was described as the earl of Bearhaven's sixty-six-year-old uncle. Along with his wife and 'many children', he received 50 ducados per month and a further 150 for costs. Daniel MacCarthy was a distinguished knight and the lord of two castles defended against the English where munitions had been stored. He was paid 40 ducados per month and 150 to cover his expenses. Miler MacMahon, a principal gentleman, had served since the Geraldine war (1579–83) and had lost two brothers and most of his property. Living in Galicia with his wife and eight children, he was granted 25 and 150 ducados.[329]

Soldiers for service in Flanders were also included. For instance, Manuel MacSweeney, 'a courageous captain and honourable gentleman, [who] served many years against the English [and] lost much of his property and three brothers in the war', was paid 25 and 40 ducados.[330] Gillanaofa Egan had been wounded while carrying letters from Mateo de Oviedo to Don Juan del Águila. Christopher de Roquefort's father had died in the Tower of London.[331] Of twenty-nine ✗ unnamed soldiers maintained on a salary, twelve were said to have been married. All had lost their property, some their parents and siblings. A total of 1,986 ducados was shared among them.[332] Forty-seven soldiers, also unnamed, were in receipt of ordinary pay. Seventeen paupers and ten students from Ireland were found in Valladolid.[333] Twenty-nine unmarried women were also recorded. Though unnamed, they were from 'the same distinguished families'.[334]

Significantly, forty-one war widows received special mention. Recalling his work as a genealogist and chronicler in Connacht, Flaithrí Ó Maolchonaire described Jerónima O'Connor as 'a noblewoman from one of the most distinguished houses of the kingdom', who was related to MacWilliam de Burgo, Ó Ruairc and other principal lords.[335] The friar's use of the Spanish verb *calificarse* denotes proof of noble birth and descent according to law. Isabel and Leonora

MacCarthy applied for the 40 ducados allocated to them three months earlier. Twelve ducados per month and 25 for *ayuda de costa* were paid to Elena, the noble daughter of Diarmaid Ó Súilleabháin, mentioned above, whose husband had been killed at war. Sabina and Mariana MacSweeney suffered in the same way. Each received twelve and twenty ducados.[336]

A list of 'other persons' was appended to the preceding names.[337] First among these was Roibeard Mac Artúir. He, Ó Maolchonaire explained, had returned to the court a year earlier with letters from Ó Néill to Philip III. In debt after the journey, he received 300 ducados. Flaithrí Ó Maolchonaire described Fr Thomas Fitzgerald (†1610), the son of an Irish knight, as a fine theologian in need of 100 ducados to purchase a chalice and Mass vestments before travelling to Ireland.[338] Eugene O'Brien was an Ó Domhnaill chaplain who had studied in Spain and also wished to return home to preach. John de Burgo, a cousin of MacWilliam de Burgo, sought the 30 ducados paid to his deceased father. Conor Kelly had served with distinction against the English with Richard de Burgo. Having recovered his health, William Field worked at the hospitals in Esgueva and San Bartolomé. Dr John Nynan of Munster spent almost twenty years in Zaragoza and Paris. Ó Maolchonaire and Puñonrostro believed it would be 'muy conveniente' to send him to Flanders as a military physician. 'He had left Ireland about twenty years before' and was a graduate of Lerida University in Catalonia. Nynan treated Aodh Ruadh Ó Domhnaill on his deathbed but had been paid nothing in return and looked to Philip III to reimburse him.[339]

According to Flaithrí Ó Maolchonaire, Barco de Lega had served in the Armada of 1588 and at Kinsale. Based in Lisbon where he was in debt after illness, arrangements were made to pay him 50 ducados. The Irish company commanded in Lisbon by Richard de Burgo was reported to be badly equipped. The severe winter had brought with it illness and they needed financial relief. Finally, Raymond de Burgo and John Fitzgerald also intended to go to Flanders, while the earl of Bearhaven would negotiate terms in letters to Puñonrostro from Santiago.[340]

With these, Puñonrostro proposed sending fourteen Irish *entretenidos* from La Coruña to Flanders on full pay, along with those based in Lisbon. Another four were assigned to accompany the Irish troop units transferred to Galicia.[341] Among these was Conor O'Driscoll, eldest son of the lord of Baltimore and Castlehaven, who wished to serve his 'lord Harry' [Éinrí Ó Néill], colonel of roposed that the young Ó Néill could raise three companies, each with their own captains and officers.[343] The transfer to Flanders would then proceed. To ensure its prompt and safe conclusion, a 200-tonne vessel was to be prepared under the command of Don Luis da Silva while, in La Coruña, the Conde de Caracena was advised to prepare another, *El Espiritu Sancto*, for the same purpose.[344] Their plans were to be kept as secret as possible. In order to avoid being intercepted by the Dutch at Dunkirk, Puñonrostro proposed waiting until the spring, thus allowing time for the Irish to gather in La Coruña first.[345]

Before taking further action, Philip III sought the views of Juan de Tassis, conde de Villamediana, his ambassador in London, who advised that, to avoid causing James I any disquiet so early into their peace treaty, the transfer should be delayed forthwith.[346] The council of state tried to calm these fears the following year, directing the ambassador to reassure James that Irish troops would only be used in the Dutch wars.[347] This approach appears to have worked. Despite diplomatic smoke screens, the lord deputy in Dublin held the view that well-trained yet idle Irish soldiers seasoned in the Nine Years War were better out of the country.[348] Moreover, the levies paid by officers raising Irish troops for service in Spanish Flanders represented a useful source of income for James I's treasury.[349]

Flaithrí Ó Maolchonaire's role in providing for Irish soldiers arriving in Spain did not meet with approval in all quarters. More specifically, his reputation for favouring Gaelic interests stirred up the resentment of Old English troops in the Southern Netherlands who claimed that no-one from Ireland obtained an income from the Spanish Habsburgs 'but by his recommendation'.[350] Numbers of migrants from Ireland continued to make their way to ports in Galicia. By 1606, this represented a serious problem for the authorities. In response to calls for their repatriation, James Archer SJ believed that matters should be handled as subtly as possible. This, however, did not prevent him from openly accusing Flaithrí Ó Maolchonaire of misusing his position as *relator* in Valladolid. The Franciscan had, he alleged, encouraged large numbers of Irish claimants to come to court in search of money. They would remain a nuisance to Philip III and his council of state:

> [...] as long as there are those in Valladolid who will secure their interests and who will act as clerk and godfather to them, such as friar Flaithrí and others, who claim the aforementioned occupation. [351]

The English ambassador to Madrid referred to Puñonrostro as the archangel Raphael 'that offereth up the prayers of certain Irish of the best sorte sythence the conclusion of the truce'.[352] The criticisms levelled at Ó Maolchonaire appear to have taken root with some state officials in Spain. This helps to explain why the protector of the Irish wrote the following note to Caracena, the governor of Galicia:

> Father Friar Flaithrí [...] who is here as I write, begs you turn from those who make complaints who, I can say in truth, certainly have little justification in doing so. Since His Majesty made him my associate for matters relating to the Irish, he is among the best religious that I have dealt with.[353]

The increasing Irish presence described by James Archer SJ was to have damaging consequences for the Irish at court before the end of the same decade.

FROM TOLEDO TO LEUVEN: FOUNDING THE COLLEGE OF ST ANTHONY OF PADUA

Flaithrí Ó Maolchonaire's selection as minister-provincial of the Irish Friars Minor in 1606 illustrates further how, throughout this early stage, his public career spanned both the military and ecclesiastical spheres. Armed with a papal brief from Paul V (†1621) on 3 May, the apostolic nuncio, Archbishop Diego García Millino, presided over the Franciscan general chapter at the friary of San

Juan de los Reyes, Toledo. In the history of the order, it ranked 'among the most celebrated, famous and respected ever held'.[354] Philip III was present along with 2,000 friars, the princes of Savoy, Cardinal Rojas y Sandoval, and the dukes of Lerma, Alba, Medinaceli and Céa. On the first day of Easter, all in attendance processed through the streets of Toledo to the cathedral. The costs of the chapter were paid by the Conde de Chinchón. Arcángel de Mesina was appointed minister general of the order, Franciscan theses were defended during the proceedings and the order's campaign to defend the doctrine of the Immaculate Conception was launched.[355]

Several Irish friars were present at the chapter, notably Edmond Mullarkey, the former Irish provincial who served as a military chaplain in the Low Countries, Owen O'Friel, a superior or *custos* of the Irish province, and Flaithrí Ó Maolchonaire.[356] As stated above, Ó Maolchonaire's friendship with Mateo de Oviedo illustrates the well-established links between Irish and Spanish Franciscans. On 13 May 1606, the Feast of the Ascension, Ó Maolchonaire was elected Irish minister provincial despite the objections of delegates from Ireland. His appointment was exceptional. In the previous twenty years, every superior had been a novice of the Donegal friary. Never before had the election been taken out of the hands of Irish Franciscans who knew that Ó Maolchonaire was compromised in the eyes of the English and felt that their rights had been infringed. Nevertheless, the state of Ireland was given due consideration. At that time, there was no Irish provincial. Political conditions caused great difficulty in sending a commissary or official visitor into the country to hold a provincial chapter.[357] Ó Maolchonaire was regarded as the most qualified candidate by the Sicilian de Mesina and the fathers of the order. The Irishman's assimilation into Castilian life and the contacts he had made since receiving the habit in Salamanca were of considerable benefit to his confrères and successors.

The most notable act of his tenure as provincial was the founding of a new Irish college with Habsburg–Spanish patronage. The burning down of five Franciscan friaries at the end of the Nine Years War made this a practical necessity, according to Ó Maolchonaire.[358] In 1605, he drafted a description of Ireland for the Spanish king. His underlying aim was to highlight the Gaelic rift with the Society of Jesus at Salamanca.[359] The report opened with a brief topography of Ireland.[360] Quoting from Hector Boethius' (†1536) work *Scotorum Historiae a Prima Gentis Origine* and Polydor Virgil's *Anglicae Historiae Libri*, Ó Maolchonaire then stated that the sons of Milesius arrived in Ireland about 700 years before Christ.[361] He then named the major Gaelic families before moving on to St Patrick's mission, followed by a description of the sixteenth-century Irish wars. Ó Maolchonaire conveniently combined the Geraldine conflict with the Nine Years War, connecting both, in turn, with the Armada of 1588. In doing so he suggested that Philip II had persuaded the Geraldines to undertake their war of seven years before the Ó Néill and Ó Domhnaill fought for another eleven.[362] To beat them, Elizabeth had to spend money and troops which would otherwise have been used against Spain's Atlantic fleet and Spanish forces in the Netherlands.[363] Up to seven generals from the flower of the English nobility had died in a war which left Ireland empoverished, he continued.[364]

Ó Maolchonaire's Gaelic partisanship is clear. In common with his earlier protest against the Irish Jesuits at Salamanca, he singled out the Anglicised Irish, a term which would re-emerge in Gaelic petitions from 1611 onwards, accusing them of caring little for the kingdom of Ireland.[365] The noble families of Spain and Ireland had, he said, been in possession of their lands for nearly 3,000 years and had remained constant in their Catholicism for 1,200. In the case of the Irish, this was achieved despite the best efforts of the Danes and the English. Thus, there had always been great affection between Ireland and Spain.

Ó Maolchonaire reasserted the case against the rectors at Salamanca's Irish college: 'certain fathers […] of English descent' who still showed little affection for Connacht and Ulster, even though Philip III intended the college at Salamanca to benefit the whole kingdom of Ireland.[366] 'A thousand excuses, such as claims of their illegitimacy and disobedience, were used to exclude applicants from the rest of the kingdom,' he continued.[367] Since aspirant clergy from Connacht and Ulster had been disregarded, half of Ireland lacked preachers and confessors trained in moral theology.[368]

According to Ó Maolchonaire, with a perpetual grant equivalent to that of Salamanca much more could be achieved. Indeed, apart from preserving Catholicism in Ireland, he advocated that Philip III's magnitude and generosity could convert England.[369] To achieve this, though, parity of esteem had to be maintained between students from Ireland's four provinces.[370] Three weeks after his election as minister provincial, Ó Maolchonaire prevailed upon Philip III to act as patron for a new Irish college in Spanish Flanders. He introduced his petition to the king by explaining that a companion of St Francis had established the first Franciscan house in the kingdom of Ireland at Youghal followed by another four or five foundations.[371] Ever since, Ó Maolchonaire declared, the Irish province of the order had flourished as one of the best in Europe and had grown to about 140 convents throughout the country, not including nunneries.[372] It counted among its sons, he claimed, the subtle doctor Duns Scotus, master of all the Scotists, and William of Occam, master of metaphysical nominalism, earning the greatest of esteem from most of Ireland's principal families who retained Franciscan confessors and were laid to rest in their friaries.[373] The people's affection for and devotion to the friars meant that, despite the suppression of the monasteries by Henry VIII and his daughter Elizabeth, the province had endured.[374] 'Of all the religious in these last wars,' Ó Maolchonaire stated, 'only the Franciscans served your majesty from start to finish, hearing confessions and preaching to the Catholic army.'[375] As a result:

> The heretics persecuted them with so much fury that they burned and destroyed most of the convents that remained, since it was Donegal's celebrated convent which had received the weapons and silver that your majesty had dispatched to the Catholics.[376]

Rather than portray the loss of the Donegal foundation as a complete disaster, however, Ó Maolchonaire reported that 200 of the heretics inside the friary had burned in the miraculous fire which destroyed it.[377] With Philip III's benevolence, he said, students could be sent to the University of Leuven.[378] For lack of comfort, those young Irish friars who had already gone to France and the Spanish Netherlands were unable to study.[379] Those sent to Spain had found the climate so inclement that they had expired.[380]

The loss of Franciscan houses during the Nine Years War and the ongoing Irish dispute at Salamanca meant that the Southern Netherlands offered the best prospects for a new foundation. Witnessing 'the vacuum of ecclesiastical authority in the Dutch Republic', the Spanish authorities had actively encouraged a bulwark of Catholic clergy to build up in the southern states of the Netherlands.[381] The decision to open the new college at Leuven and the archdiocese of Mechelen was not clear-cut, however. Instead, Philip III's advisers and the protector of the Irish to the Holy See sought a ready-made solution to the problem – the Irish college established at Douai by Christopher Cusack.[382]

For a number of reasons, Flaithrí Ó Maolchonaire found this unacceptable. Aside from anything else, Douai had a well-established population of English Catholic exiles. Ó Maolchonaire wrote to the king to express his concern two months after his initial petition. In gratitude for Philip III's generous patronage, Ó Maolchonaire said, the Irish Franciscan province 'remains obliged to always pray to God for your Majesty'.[383] However, it was impossible to accommodate friars at the Douai seminary where more than forty members of the secular clergy already occupied twenty-five lodgings. As the Douai superior was at the court of Philip III he could confirm this point, Ó Maolchonaire added.[384] Secondly, even though space could be made available, it was unfeasible to expect secular and regular clergy to share the same college, especially with a secular priest in charge.[385] It would, Ó Maolchonaire claimed, be much less convenient to have two rectors, two sets of rules and separate ceremonies which would only disturb the peace and seclusion necessary for the exercise of virtue and learning.[386] Therefore, Ó Maolchonaire humbly begged the king to write in favour of a new Franciscan college to the papacy, the archdukes and the Marqués Spínola, Philip's commander-in-chief and president of the exchequer in the Southern Netherlands.[387]

The council of state deliberated on Ó Maolchonaire's request a fortnight later with Juan de Idiáquez, Cardinal Bernardo Sandoval y Rojas, Juan Fernández de Velasco Tovar, Condestable de Castilla, and the Conde de Olivares in attendance.[388] The following month, 'for the preservation of the Catholic religion and their holy order in Ireland', Philip III instructed Archduke Albert to provide for a new college at Leuven. A perpetual grant of 1,000 ducados, payable from military coffers, was to be overseen by Spínola.[389] Paul V issued a bull of foundation on 3 April 1607 and instructed Matthias Hovius, archbishop of Mechelen, to assist in building the new seminary. The College of St Anthony of Padua formally opened at Leuven the following month with Donnchadh Ó Maonaigh as its first superior.[390] In the same year, the archducal couple conducted an official visitation of the University of Leuven. Their tour of inspection was unprecedented in the Southern Netherlands. The consensus it helped establish between the central government and academics with regard to the programme of studies and the conferring of degrees was instrumental in the university's resurgence during the next decade.[391]

Philip III declared that his order remain 'in force and in effect from now onwards' and called for the archducal couple to provide 'annual alms during the persecution'.[392] This suggests that the initial provision of accommodation and facilities for Irish clerical students at Leuven was regarded as an interim measure until such time as Catholicism could be restored in Ireland or, at the very least, liberty of conscience.[393] In contrast to other religious orders in Ireland at the time,[394] the subsequent success of St Anthony's at Leuven ensured the continued existence of a functioning Irish province of the Friars Minor within the international order. Ó Maolchonaire's part in founding the college clearly influenced the new Catholic pastoral mission to Ireland during the seventeenth century. Moreover, St Anthony's remained pivotal to the success of the Franciscan manuscript scheme to harness Ireland's cultural legacy to serve their pastoral and sometimes their political purposes.

FLAITHRÍ Ó MAOLCHONAIRE AND THE ULSTER EARLS' DEPARTURE TO ROME, 1606–08

After completing his work at court with Puñonrostro, Flaithrí Ó Maolchonaire wished to go to Ireland to fulfil his duties as Irish Franciscan provincial.[395] The question then arises: how was Ó Maolchonaire able to resolve his proscribed status with his hopes of returning home? A possible answer may be that he was aware of plans for a renewed assault on Ireland and planned to participate. One such plot was reported in the spring of 1607 when informants to the authorities revealed designs to seize Dublin Castle and execute the lord deputy.[396]

Puñonrostro petitioned for 500 ducados to pay for Ó Maolchonaire's journey and to provide books for his homilies, stating that he had incurred debts 'during a grave illness'. The accompanying response from the council of state commended Ó Maolchonaire's dedication to his work and endorsed the 500 ducados requested.[397] However, the Irishman's application to return home was delayed until the following year. Significantly, his request was made in conjunction with a claim for an annual payment of 10,000 ducados to the Ulster earls. Matha Óg Ó Maoltuile, who was in Madrid with Ó Maolchonaire, wrote to the king implying that unless the earls received financial help, they would be forced to come to Spain.[398] Due to Ó Maolchonaire's notoriety at the English court, Ó Maoltuile also asked that, in the event that he returned to Ireland, Ó Maolchonaire should have a passport to travel overland through France as it would be too dangerous for him to sail in open seas.[399] News of his involvement with Ó Néill had reached the attorney general Sir John Davies (†1626) in Dublin by 1606.[400]

Delayed in Madrid, Ó Maolchonaire appointed Muiris Ultach vicar-provincial and sent him in his place.[401] Detained at Dublin Castle, Thomas Fitzgerald OFM said that he had 'expected the coming over of Fr Florence' that summer, but later understood that he would 'not come until some settlement or alteration'.[402] Instead, according to an Old English report from the Low Countries, Ó Maolchonaire sent two friars 'to withdraw the hands of the gentlemen of Munster from the king's obedience'.[403] Ultach arrived at Donegal friary with letters to Rudhraighe Ó Domhnaill, and Owen Groome McGrath, the guardian. Meanwhile, Rudhraighe's kinsman Niall Garbh promised to cooperate fully with Lord

Deputy Chichester by informing him of any further developments.[404]

In late December 1606, Ó Maolchonaire travelled to Spanish Flanders with David and Richard de Burgo, and Matha Óg Ó Maoltuile. On their arrival, Ó Maolchonaire enjoyed access to the court in Brussels.[405] Together with Nicholas Lynch, a Galway merchant, and Rury Albanagh, a Tyrone priest, Ó Maolchonaire was 'conversant and very great' with Aodh Ó Néill's son Éinrí, colonel of the Irish *tercio* in the Netherlands.[406]

When the college opened, Ó Maolchonaire was among the first community of friars but his mind was occupied with matters other than St Anthony's. Living in modest surroundings, they relied upon the English canonesses at St Monica's for the use of their chapel.[407] In the same month, Cú Chonnacht Mag Uidhir (†1608) presented himself to the archducal couple at Brussels where Ó Maolchonaire seems to have warned him that Ó Néill faced possible arrest in London.[408]

Nine months after Flaithrí Ó Maolchonaire's initial request, Philip III notified Spínola that he had granted the Franciscan permission to travel home, and directed him to pay 300 ducados to Ó Maolchonaire, who was 'in those states to establish the Irish friars' college'.[409] Despite this, Ó Maolchonaire abandoned his departure plans. Within weeks of his receiving permission, the Ulster earls had left Ireland. The long delay which Ó Maolchonaire experienced beforehand may have had a bearing upon their decision. Unable to use the money for its intended purpose, one wonders what happened to Ó Maolchonaire's payment. News that the earls had fled was greeted with consternation by Philip's ambassador in Rome, who told the pope of Spanish anxieties: the English would think that Spain had encouraged the earls to leave.[410]

In Ireland, statements regarding the earls' exit were submitted under oath to the lord deputy by Niall Garbh Ó Domhnaill and the baron of Howth, Christopher St Lawrence. These mooted that Ó Néill, Ó Domhnaill and Mag Uidhir 'meditated seizing the king's forts and garrisons' in a plot with the pope, the king of Spain and the Jesuits, providing the pretext for summoning them to London, where it was intended that Ó Néill would be arrested.[411] Howth and Niall Garbh probably expected recompense for their information. Their allegations, especially about the amount of money provided by Spain, were therefore prone to exaggeration. The baron claimed that he had heard about the hopes for an expedition to Ireland before making his denunciations against the earl and his followers. In the Low Countries, he said, Frs Richard Stanihurst and Christopher Cusack had told him that a plot was widespread.[412] Significantly, Howth made overt reference to the political liaisons by one 'Flarie Omulconnor' in negotiations and fund-raising:

> [...] by whom he was assured that all things were concluded, and that he himself was to go into Ireland to ascertain the lords, cities and towns of the aid promised and to conclude with them for the time.[413]

After informing Salisbury, Howth returned to the Low Countries where, he alleged, Ó Maolchonaire disclosed that Philip III had provided up to £6,000 for Tyrone's use.[414] This sum was, at the very least, exaggerated by Howth. As shown above, bureaucratic delays and faction fights at court made extracting large sums of money from state coffers problematic, often leading to the reappraisal or the rebuttal of petitions.

According to information provided to Guido Bentivoglio (†1644), the papal nuncio in Brussels, by 'un Padre di S. Francesco d'Ibernia', the principal collaborators were the Ulster earls and the Barons Delvin and Howth.[415] Howth declared that Ó Maolchonaire had been working on behalf of Ó Domhnaill from the outset. He expected nothing 'more manifest' until the arrival of 'father Florence […] when he shall contrive the matter that he shall be taken with all his letters and papers about him'.[416]

Contrary to some authorities,[417] Flaithrí Ó Maolchonaire did not travel with Cú Chonnacht Mag Uidhir to Fermanagh to meet the Ulster earls. On Monday 22 October 1607, having passed through the county of Flanders, he was at Douai with Mac Artúir to greet the earls after their two-month journey from Ulster.[418] Orations in Latin, Greek and English were delivered in tribute to the earls and their entourage.[419] At Hal, Éinrí Ó Néill guided the company to the archdukes' court at Binche where a meeting was held on 5 November with Philip III's representatives. Of these only the duke of Osuna, Don Pedro Téllez Girón, openly supported a return to war.[420] Three days later, Ambrosio Spínola, commander-in-chief and president of the exchequer in Spanish Flanders, extended a generous welcome in recognition of the earls' services to Philip III.[421]

Archbishop Lombard (†1625), Catholic primate of Ireland, wrote to the earls, to the Mag Uidhir and to Ó Maolchonaire from Rome.[422] He expressed the pope's support and his best wishes for the future. The 'most ample' of his letters was directed at 'Father Florence'. Lombard had been brought to tears by news of the earls' flight yet he was relieved to know that they had 'arrived safely upon Catholic ground'.[423]

On Sunday 25 November, the earls left Leuven with thirty horsemen.[424] Flaithrí Ó Maolchonaire accompanied them as interpreter and advisor. They had intended to meet Philip III in person but were thwarted a day into their journey south at Namur by the Marqués de Guadaleste, Spanish ambassador to Brussels.[425] Guadaleste requested that Ó Maolchonaire await news from Madrid. The Franciscan was distressed to hear Philip's decision against direct military intervention and had the unenviable task of imparting this news to the earls.[426] James I had protested at the reception offered the earls by the archducal couple and, on the observations of Albert, the Spanish king decided against granting the favours requested by Ó Néill and Ó Domhnaill.[427] Indeed, Philip III went so far as to assure the English ambassador, on oath, that he had no involvement in the earls' departure from Ireland, since doing so would place an unreasonable burden on Habsburg coffers.[428]

Spending Christmas in Leuven and faced with increasingly uncomfortable political circumstances, the earls prepared to leave for Rome. Realising that Spain was making every possible effort to send them to Rome, the nuncio had three meetings with an Irish Franciscan friar in Brussels and politely opposed the move.[429] As Philip III 'had received military service from Ó Néill,' Bentivoglio stated, 'the king must be the first to reimburse the earls.'[430] Considering his work on their behalf as interpreter and adviser, the friar referred to by the nuncio was almost certainly Flaithrí Ó Maolchonaire. On 12 January 1608, Bentivoglio wrote to the secretary of state in Rome stating that in Ireland there were two sorts of inhabitants, the ancient Irish and the English. The greatest of enmity had always existed between them, as the Nine Years War had shown, the leader of which was *il Conte Tirroni* head of the Uí Néill who were the principal family of all the ancient Irish.[431]

The nuncio anticipated that there would be one further meeting with Ó Maolchonaire.[432] Less than a week later, however, Ó Néill and Ó Domhnaill departed for Italy, hoping to sail from there to Spain.[433] Flaithrí Ó Maolchonaire accompanied them but, realising the seriousness of the situation, he delegated responsibility for St Anthony's to Aodh Mac Aingil.[434] Nuncio Bentivoglio, meanwhile, wrote on Ó Maolchonaire's behalf to the archducal couple recommending that the Irish friars receive permission to collect alms in the surrounding districts.[435] While occupied with events, Ó Maolchonaire's duties in Spain were seen to by Matha Óg Ó Maoltuile, who 'lately sent a packet of letters to a shipp of Dongarvin lyeing at Bilbowe [Bilbao], to be conveyed into Ircland'.[436]

Unable to fulfil their hopes of travelling to Madrid, Ó Néill and his allies were forced to prevaricate and regarded the prospect of staying in Rome as a temporary solution to their needs. Peter Lombard had encouraged the idea and they themselves saw consideration from the papacy 'as their hereditary prerogative'.[437] They took the relatively secure route known as the Spanish Road: the military corridor from the Southern Netherlands to Lombardy via Lorraine, the Franche-Comté and the pro-Spanish Catholic cantons of the Swiss Confederation. Writing to Lombard from Milan, the earls conveyed their unease to the primate on 2 April 1608, stating that they would go no further until receiving orders from Philip III, 'who otherwise might have an excuse for abandoning them and throwing the whole burden on the pope'.[438] After waiting in vain for news from Philip, they made their way south to Bologna and onto Rome.

Despite being deterred from Madrid, Ó Néill and Ó Domhnaill remained determined in their cause. Ó Maolchonaire continued to assist them as they explored other ways to achieve their aims. Shortly before their arrival in Rome, Cornwallis said the Irish hoped before long 'for a world better suyteing with their affections'.[439] He wrote that 'most of the gentlemen of the country and many of the towns would eyther publicquely or secretly give Tyrone and Tyrconnell assistance at their returne'. All they required was financial support: 'for the country would yield to them so many bodies, as the Englishe forces sent thither by the king should be but a breakfast.' The Irish in France and Spain, the ambassador asserted, 'were called home for that purpose'.[440]

As Nollaig Ó Muraíle's new edition of Tadhg Ó Cianáin's diary shows, Flaithrí Ó Maolchonaire's journey to Rome with the earls was harrowing. Overcome by searing Italian heat, the earl of Tyrconnell, Rudhraighe Ó Domhnaill, his brother Cathbharr and Ó Néill's young son Aodh became seriously ill during the summer of 1608. Rudhraighe and his brother died within six weeks of one another and were laid to rest in the habit of the Friars Minor at the Franciscan church of San Pietro in Montorio.[441] Meanwhile, Cú Chonnacht Mag Uidhir and Séamus Mag

Mathghamhna travelled to Genoa. Hoping to reach Spain by sea and convince the king to grant them an income, they fell prey to the same sickness and died. The Franciscan confessor who accompanied them may have been Flaithrí Ó Maolchonaire.[442] In recognition of Ó Néill's losses in the service of Catholicism and of Ó Maolchonaire's work on his behalf, the papacy and Spain offered the earl the consolation of successfully nominating Ó Maolchonaire to the archbishopric of Tuam.

Ó MAOLCHONAIRE'S APPOINTMENT TO THE SEE OF TUAM

Papers from the private collection of the Marqués de Aitona, Spanish ambassador to Rome, record that, at two successive audiences in 1608, he and Paul V had deliberated over 'the bishops of Ireland'. The exact content of the two meetings is unknown, but in all probability the decision to raise Ó Maolchonaire to the episcopacy was discussed at that time.[443] At the Quirinale palace, Rome, on 30 March 1609, Cardinal Pompeo Arrigone, protector of the Irish, submitted a request from Aodh Ó Néill to nominate Flaithrí Ó Maolchonaire for the see of Tuam.[444] The archbishopric had been vacant since the death of James Healy in 1595.[445] Pope Paul V acceded to the nomination which was sent to be dealt with by the papal chancellery at San Lorenzo in Damaso, Rome.[446] This represented the culmination of a process between the Ulster earls, the papacy and the Spanish monarchy which had begun during the Nine Years War. Following a joint proposal by Ó Néill and Ó Domhnaill in January 1601, Philip III notified his ambassador in Rome that he approved of Ó Maolchonaire's candidature.[447] This occurred before Aodh Ruadh repeated the call in his last will and testament, requesting a bishopric for Ó Maolchonaire in recognition of his diligence and sound judgment.[448]

Seven years later, Ó Néill received papal sanction to make nominations for ecclesiastical office within Ulster.[449] On Sunday 3 May 1609, Flaithrí Ó Maolchonaire was consecrated archbishop by Cardinal Maffeo Barberini (†1644), assisted by bishops Octavio Acorambono and Andrea Sorbolengo. The diocesan priests Carlos Antonio Vaccario and Antonio Maroccho witnessed events at the Chiesa Santo Spirito in Sassia.[450] Since the previous year, Aodh Ó Néill and friends had regularly been to Mass and vespers at 'the great church of Santo Spirito'.[451] Just a short distance from St Peter's Square, it was built between 1538 and 1544. During the last quarter of the sixteenth century the interior was restored in 'the style of decoration employed in a number of subsequent undertakings in Rome including that of the nave of S. Maria Maggiore and the transept of S. Giovanni in Laterano'.[452] The earls attended ceremonies at the Santo Spirito on Pentecost Sunday 1608 with Ó Maolchonaire and their followers.[453] The feastday is said to have found its 'most eloquent expression' in the same church. Here, the frescoes of Jacopo Zucchi evoke the potent, new concepts of the Counter-Reformation: 'the creation of an organised church, the institution of a priestly class and the missionary expansion of religion based on the word of God'.[454]

Established by the twelfth-century synods of Rathbreasail and Kells, Tuam subsequently absorbed two other medieval dioceses: Annaghdown and Mayo.

Geographically split north and south by Loughs Mask and Corrib, it stretches from Achill Island to Moore parish on the Shannon, a distance of 120 miles: the largest Catholic archdiocese in Ireland.[455] Rumours regarding the likelihood of Ó Maolchonaire's election did not escape the attention of Sir John Davies, who referred to him as 'the pope's titulary bishop of Tuam' in 1606.[456]

While Tyrone was denied the chance to meet the king of Spain in person, Philip III and Paul V were willing to grant Ó Néill the concession of Ó Maolchonaire's promotion. There were competing pressures on the pope in this regard. While wanting to act in the Roman interest, as a member of the pro-Spanish Borghèse family he had to consider the views of Philip III. The denouement of Ó Maolchonaire's appointment can thus been seen as one of the last vestiges of Aodh Ó Néill's influence in Madrid and in Rome where Paul V was more influenced by the Irish primate, Peter Lombard. The insistence with which the Uí Néill and Uí Dhomhnaill had pressed for Ó Maolchonaire's advancement depended upon his unequivocal support for their political aims. The rancour it subsequently stirred up among other prominent Irish political and religious figures of the early seventeenth century calls into question the advisability of such a decision in his favour.

After his consecration, Flaithrí Ó Maolchonaire chose the Red hand emblem of the Uí Néill for his coat of arms, beneath a flat, wide-brimmed episcopal hat, flanked by four rows of tassels on each side. His archbishop's cross appears between it and the red hand in the crest which is inscribed with the words *Florentius Conrius Archiepiscopus Tuamensis*. This was the mark Ó Maolchonaire subsequently used to seal his correspondence, although it seems to have survived intact on   only   a handful of documents.[457] With promotion came the authority for the new archbishop to travel to Spain on behalf of Ó Néill. Proscribed from returning to Ireland and otherwise occupied with his work in Madrid, Ó Maolchonaire was unable to return to Tuam in 1609. He selected Fr William Lynch, a Carmelite, as his vicar-general. From one of the fourteen principal families of Galway, Lynch remained in the post until Ó Maolchonaire left Madrid in 1618.[458]

CONCLUSION

Flaithrí Ó Maolchonaire's experiences at the start of the seventeenth century encapsulate the significant political transition witnessed in Ireland at that time. His work as an agent of the earls, his engagement with the Irish abroad, the Spanish monarchy and the Counter-Reformation demonstrate his involvement in the religious and temporal spheres during the two decades dealt with in this chapter. In the words of Philip III, Ó Maolchonaire 'had been raised up at Salamanca to become an eminent theologian and preacher'.[459] His cultural background and upbringing, however, led to an inexorable clash with the Irish Jesuits there in the 1590s. As the next chapters show, he had made lasting enemies who would continue to stand in the way of his political aims. The importance of kin-groups in contemporary Irish society made matters worse as extended family members involved themselves on either side of the dispute. Paradoxically, Ó Maolchonaire and the Jesuits employed the same strategy: direct participation in secular affairs to secure patronage and influence political decision-making at court, combined with the promotion of like-minded intellectual formation by obtaining funds for new and existing colleges.

On his return to Ireland during the Nine Years War, Flaithrí Ó Maolchonaire fulfilled the duties of a military chaplain, using his catechism for the formation of Catholic soldiers in the field and cooperating with officers to restore morale. Taking his place among the clergy who sided with the Catholic confederacy, Ó Maolchonaire's education at Salamanca taught him that depicting the conflict as 'defence of the true religion' was the best way to gather support from Spain and the Holy See.

Upon his arrival at court in 1602, however, the Franciscan was forced to adapt to circumstances beyond the control of the warring Irish nobles he served, underlining how dependent they were upon Philip III and his council of state. Lerma and his followers had decided that further military intervention in Ireland was not in Spain's political interests and that Philip III would be better served by stabilising trade relations in a treaty with England.[460] Following the death of Aodh Ruadh Ó Domhnaill, Ó Maolchonaire's rapport with Philip III's confessor, fray Gaspar de Cordova, ensured his success in directing Spanish funds towards his preferred causes. It was Ó Maolchonaire's personal intervention that secured the patronage of key Irish political figures at the Spanish court and made sure that the power of others was neutralised. This set the precedent for his role as adviser to Conde de Puñonrostro, protector of the Irish at court. Incorporating Irish soldiers into troop units based in Spanish Flanders was regarded as the most acceptable compromise to deal with the levels of migration from Ireland to Spanish territories. Ó Maolchonaire's involvement tilted the balance of power in Irish military units under Spanish command in favour of Gaelic leaders and their allies. Closely examining the names of those he helped most suggests that he did encourage Irish emigration to Spain and the Low Countries. This is most apparent in the funds directed to other followers of Aodh Ruadh Ó Domhnaill. Nevertheless, the failure of the 1603 expedition to bring aid directly to the Ulster earls only made matters worse in Galicia and Castile.

With regard to the Franciscans, since pressure could not be 'exerted strongly and simultaneously' in both the Gaelic and Old English regions of Ireland, the political divide in the country benefited the friars there.[461] Acting on his authority as minister-provincial, Ó Maolchonaire made the most of the organisation maintained by his order and responded to their immediate needs by providing them with a centre to train aspirant clergy at St Anthony's, Leuven. 'Fired by a keen appreciation of the Catholic reform,' he realised 'the importance of providing well-trained missionaries.'[462] In this regard his work can be seen as emblematic of the order's achievements throughout the seventeenth century.

The same cannot be said for the friars' secular patrons, the Uí Néill and Uí Dhomhnaill. Deep-seated resentment continued to fester after their failure to convince the Old English of Munster and Leinster of the Catholic confederates' case for war. The theatre of operations soon changed to Spain and the Southern Netherlands but fierce internal rivalries continued among the Irish. Assigned to advise and guide the exiled earls in liaison with Madrid and Rome, Ó Maolchonaire may have earned his appointment to the archbishopric of Tuam but his suitability for this role was soon called into question by peers, most notably Peter Lombard, who regarded him as too partisan and compromised in English eyes.

Momentous changes in Rome and London had an immediate effect upon Spanish foreign policy.[463] The death of Clement VIII in 1605 and the election of Paul V as his successor signalled the start of a new era in Irish relations with the papal court during this period. As a member of the pro-Spanish Borghèses, the new pope had to consider the opinions of Philip III and his advisers. Meanwhile, the enactment of legislation against the Catholic clergy by James I and his insistence upon 'loyalty to the tenets of the reformed religion' soon scuppered Irish hopes for his conversion and for the public practice of Catholicism in Ireland.[464] It is against this background that Ó Maolchonaire used his new position to galvanise the Gaelic campaign in the coming years and continued to propose uniting Ireland and Spain under the Spanish monarchy. It is with these changes in mind that the next chapters assess his subsequent work in Spain for Ó Néill, his return to the Southern Netherlands after arguing against the prospect of a Spanish Match and, finally, his eventual decline at court in Madrid.

NOTES

1. Zubiaur to Philip III, Castlehaven, 20 Jan. 1601: '[…] unos yran por la religion, otros por vengar, otros por hurtar, son ynclinados a novedades.' Conde de Polentinos (ed.), *Epistolario del General Zubiaur, 1568–1605* (Madrid: Consejo Superior de Investigaciones Científicas, 1946); Niall Ware, 'The letter book of General de Zubiaur', 1602 (uncatalogued Special Collections manuscript, Boole Library, University College, Cork). For a calendar of these letters, see J. Coombes and N. Ware, 'The letter book of General de Zubiaur: a calendar of the "Irish letters"', *JCHAS*, 83 (1978), pp. 50–8.
2. J. J. Silke, *Kinsale: the Spanish intervention in Ireland at the end of the Elizabethan wars* (New York: Fordham University Press, 1970), pp. 13–14; Declan Downey, 'Irish–European integration: the legacy of Emperor Charles V', in Howard Clarke and Judith Devlin (eds), *European encounters: essays in memory of Albert Lovett* (Dublin: University College Dublin Press, 2003), pp. 97–117.
3. John Hagan (ed.), 'Ireland declared a kingdom', *Archiv. Hib.*, 4 (1915), p. 217.
4. *MS 23 N 10 (formerly Betham 145) in the Library of the Royal Irish Academy, facsimiles in collotype of Irish manuscript*, 6, ed. R. I. Best (Dublin: Irish Manuscripts Commission, 1954), pp. viii, 77.
5. Archduchess Isabel to Philip IV, Brussels, 22 Oct. 1626 (AGR-ARA, EGC, reg. 195, folio 219): 'Fray Florencio Conryo Irlandes, Arçobispo Tuamense me ha representado que ha 34 años que empezo a ser empleado y diputado por los Nobles del Reyno de Yrlanda para tratar con el Rey mi Señor, y Padre que aya gloria negocios de importancia.'
6. Éamon Ó Ciosáin, 'A hundred years of Irish migration to France, 1590–1688', in Thomas O'Connor (ed.), *The Irish in Europe 1580–1815* (Dublin: Four Courts Press, 2001), pp. 93–106.
7. Denis O'Doherty, 'Students of the Irish college, Salamanca (1595–1619)', *Archiv. Hib.*, 2 (1913), p. 3. A record of the students' sworn statements at the time of their admission to the college was not kept until 1595.
8. See Thomas Morrissey's entry on White in Charles O'Neill and Joaquín María Domínguez (eds), *Diccionario histórico de la Compañia de Jesús* (4 vols, Rome, 2001), IV, p. 4031.
9. Ibid.
10. Richard Kagan, *Students and society in early-modern Spain* (Baltimore, MD: The Johns Hopkins University Press, 1974), pp. 50–4; Julián Lozano Navarro, *La Compañía de Jesús y el poder en la España de los Austrias* (Madrid: Cátedra, 2005), pp. 33–46.
11. Thomas O'Connor, 'Irish migration to Spain and the formation of an Irish college network, 1589–1800', in Luc François and Ann Katherine Isaacs (eds), *The Sea in European History* (Pisa: Edizioni Plus, 2001), pp. 109–25.
12. J. J. Silke, 'The Irish Abroad, 1534–1691', in T. W. Moody, F. X. Martin and F. J. Byrne (eds), *A New History of Ireland* (Oxford: Oxford University Press, 1976), vol. 3, pp. 587–633; Thomas Morrissey, 'The Irish student diaspora in the sixteenth century and the early years of the Irish college at

Salamanca', *Recusant History*, 14 (1978) pp. 242–60.

13. 'Siendo la universidad de Salamanca la mas florente del mundo donde esta todo genero de estudios' (RLM, S59/9/11, f. 3).

14. Pedro de Medina, *Libro de grandezas y cosas memorables en España* (Alcalá de Henares, 1548), f. 90.

15. Domínguez Ortiz, *The golden age of Spain*, pp. 232–41.

16. R. T. Davies, *The golden century of Spain, 1501–1621* (London: Macmillan, 1939), p. 280; John H. Elliott, *Imperial Spain, 1469–1716* (Harmondsworth: Penguin, 2002), p. 311, 316.

17. 'Matriculacion: artistas y filosofos. Florencio Conrio, ne de Roscoman', Salamanca, Dec. 1594 (Ranson Papers, Cuaderno v, 29; now held by Msgr James Hammell, Annacurra, County Wicklow); Fennessy (ed.), 'Two letters from Boethius (Augustine) MacEgan', pp. 7–12.

18. Kagan, *Students and society in early-modern Spain*, pp. 32–48.

19. S. P. Ó Mathúna, *William Bathe, SJ, 1564–1614: a pioneer in linguistics* (Amsterdam: John Benjamins, 1986), p. 34.

20. Eugenio Escobar Prieto, 'Francisco Sánchez, "El Brocense"', *Revista de Extremadura*, 1 (1899), pp. 38–48; Henry Kamen, *The Spanish inquisition: a historical revision* (New Haven: Yale University Press, 1997), pp. 126–8.

21. Domínguez Ortiz, *The golden age of Spain, 1516–1659*, pp. 234–8.

22. David A. Lines, 'Moral philosophy in the universities of medieval and renaissance Europe', *History of Universities*, 20 (2005) p. 51.

23. *Constituciones de la Universidad de Salamanca, 1422: edición paleográfica, prólogo y notas*, ed. Pedro Urbano González de la Calle and Amalio Huarte y Echenique (Madrid, 1927), cited by Richard Tuck, 'The institutional setting', in Daniel Garber and Michael Ayers (eds), *The Cambridge history of seventeenth-century philosophy* (Cambridge: Cambridge University Press, 1998), pp. 16–20.

24. Ibid.

25. 'Matriculacion: artistas y filosofos. Florencio Conrio, ne de Roscoman, Diec. de Olfin de al 3o año', Salamanca, 10 Dec. 1594 (Ranson Papers, Cuaderno v, 29).

26. 'Matriculacion. Florencio Conrio B.A. 1a año T[eologi]a', Salamanca, 20 Nov. 1595 (Ranson Papers, Cuaderno v, 33).

27. *The collected works of St John of the Cross*, ed. Kieran Kavanaugh and Otilio Rodríguez (Washington: Institute of Carmelite Studies, 1973), p. 18.

28. M. W. F. Stone, 'Aristotelianism and Scholasticism in early-modern philosophy', in Steven Nadler (ed.), *A companion to early-modern philosophy* (Oxford: Oxford University Press, 2002), p. 17.

29. 'Censura Doctorum Universitatum Salmanticae et Vallisoleti de praesenti Iberniae bello, et eorundem declaratio litterarum Sanctissimi domini nostri Clementis Papae octavi super eodem bello [...] Datum Salmanticae 2. Februarii anno Domini 1603' (*Cf. Commentarius Rinuccinianus*, vol. 1, pars. III, ann 1600–41, pp. 195–8).

30. Vicente Muñoz Delgado, 'Francisco Zumel y la ética en Salamanca de 1578–1607', *Cuadernos salmantinos de filosofía*, 17 (1990), pp. 143–58.

31. Fray Pedro de Herrera OP became bishop of Túy in 1622 before his death in Salamanca at eighty-two years of age. See Fermín Arana de Varflora, *Hijos de Sevilla ilustres en santidad, letras, armas, artes, Ò dignidad: dalos al publico, colocados por orden alfabetico* (Seville: Vazquez è Hidalgo, 1791), pp. 61–2.

32. Santiago Orrego (ed.), *Pedro de Ledesma: La perfección del acto de ser creado* (Pamplona, 2001); Vicente Beltrán de Heredia, 'Los manuscritos de los teólogos de la Escuela de Salamanca', *La Ciencia Tomista*, 42 (1930), p. 347; Ramón Hernández Martín, 'El teólogo Pedro de Herrera en los claustros salmantinos, 1593–1598', *Revista Española de Teología*, 34 (1974), pp. 373–92.

33. 'An extracte of the determination, and censure of the doctours of the vniversities of Salamanca and Valledolid touching the vvarres of Ireland', Salamanca, 2 Feb. 1603. See British Library, London, STC–21,595; I am grateful to Dr Hiram Morgan for this reference.

34. Declan Downey, 'Augustinians and Scotists: The Irish contribution to Counter-Reformation theology in Continental Europe', pp. 96–108.

35. Idem, 'Florence Conry, pro-Habsburg archbishop, diplomat and controversial theologian', p. 91.

36. J. J. Silke, 'The Irish appeal of 1593 to Spain: some light on the genesis of the Nine Years' War', *IER*, 92 (1959), pp. 279–90, 362–71.

37. Brian Ó Cuív (ed.), 'Flaithrí Ó Maolchonaire's catechism of Christian doctrine', *Celtica*, 1 (1950), pp. 161–209.

38. Ibid., 'les anma do na hÊirendchaibh 7 dō fēin do thionnscain sé in obair si'.

39. Salvador Ryan, 'Bonaventura Ó hEoghusa's *An Teagasg Críosdaidhe*: a reassessment', *Archiv. Hib.*, 58 (2004) pp. 259–67.

40. Cathaldus Giblin, 'The contribution of Irish Franciscans on the continent in the seventeenth century', in Michael Maher (ed.), *Irish spirituality* (Dublin: Veritas, 1981), pp. 88–104.

41. Ibid., p. 90. See also Mary O'Reilly, 'Seventeenth-century Irish catechisms: European or not?',

Archiv. Hib., 50 (1996), pp. 102–12.

42. John O'Heyne, *Epilogus chronologicus exponens succincte conventus & fundationes Sacri Ordinis Praedicatorum in Regno Hyberniae* (Louvain, 1706; repr. Dundalk, 1902), pp. xi–xiii.
43. Ó Cuív, 'Ó Maolchonaire's catechism', p. 161; Giblin, 'The contribution of Irish Franciscans', p. 90.
44. 'Respuesta breve a las acusaçiones de Fr Florencio [...]' (RLM S52/9/14, f. 1).
45. Hogan, *Distinguished Irishmen of the sixteenth century*, p. 48.
46. Ó Maolchonaire to the Jesuit minister provincial Madrid, 23 Nov. 1610 (RLM S52/9/6, f. 1): 'como yo de ally supe el salio de su propria voluntad'.
47. Conde de Puñonrostro to Philip III, 23 Nov. 1606 (AGS, E., NP, l. 1797, unfoliated); see Kerney Walsh, *Destruction by peace*, p. 176.
48. Manuel Rodríguez Pazos (ed.), *Los estudios en la provincia franciscana de Santiago: tratado histórico* (Madrid: Liceo Franciscano, 1967), p. 131. These royal letters patent of 'el Santo Rey Fernando' are the oldest extant sources at the university's archives. The bishop of Salamanca, the dean of the university, the local Dominican prior and others were among the other adjudicators.
49. Manuel de Castro, *San Francisco de Salamanca y su Studium Generale* (Santiago de Compostela: Aldecoa, 1998), pp 256–61.
50. Pazos (ed.), *Los estudios en la provincia franciscana de Santiago*, pp. 129–30.
51. Manuel de Castro, *San Francisco de Salamanca*, pp. 146–50. Mateo de Oviedo took his oath at the university on 18 Dec. 1583 and studied at the Colegio Mayor de Alba de Tormes.
52. Jacobo de Castro, *El Arbol Cronológico de la Santa Provincia de Santiago*, vol. 1, (Salamanca, 1772), pp. 107, 116–17, 156, 289–90.
53. Pazos, 'De nuestro archivo Compostelano. Religiosos irlandeses en la provincia de Santiago', *El Eco Franciscano*, 62 (1945), p. 212.
54. *Scriptores Ordinis Minorum*, pp. 75–6; quoted by Manuel de Castro, 'Wadding and the Iberian peninsula', in Franciscan Fathers (eds), *Father Luke Wadding commemorative volume* (Dublin, 1957), p. 120.
55. 'Un memorial de la parte del collegio de Salamanca que ha dado el Conde Odonel, a 22 de mayo del año 1602'; see Edmund Hogan, *Ibernia Ignatiana* (Dublin: Society of Jesus, 1880), pp. 106–8.
56. Alan Ford, *The Protestant Reformation in Ireland* (Dublin: Four Courts Press, 1995), p. 118.
57. Colm Lennon, *Richard Stanihurst the Dubliner, 1547–1618: A biography, with a Stanihurst text on Ireland's past* (Dublin: Irish Academic Press, 1981), pp. 88–105. Stanihurst was a convert to Catholicism and, after his second wife's death, he became a priest. His two sons, Peter and William, joined the Jesuits.
58. John Barry, 'Richard Stanihurst's *De Rebus in Hibernia Gestis*', *Renaissance Studies*, 18 (2004), pp. 1–18.
59. Victor Treadwell, 'Sir John Perrott and the Irish parliament of 1585–6', *PRIA*, section C, 85/10 (1985).
60. Jonathan Wright, *The Jesuits: missions, myths and histories* (London: Harper, 2004), p. 151.
61. Lozano Navarro, *La Compañía de Jesús y el poder en la España de los Austrias*, p. 118.
62. Enrique García Hernán, 'Capellanes militares y reforma católica', in idem and David Maffi (eds), *Guerra y sociedad en la monarquía hispánica: política, estrategia y cultura en la Europa moderna* (2 vols, Madrid: Consejo Superior de Investigaciones Científicas, 2006), vol. 2, pp. 709–42.
63. Margaret Wilson, *Spanish drama of the golden age* (London: Pergamon Press, 1969), pp. 17, 58, 151; Cayo González Gutiérrez, 'El teatro escolar de los Jesuitas en la Edad de Oro: su influencia en la Comedia nacional del siglo XVII', *Cuadernos para la Investigación de la Literatura Hispánica*, 18 (1993), pp.7–147.
64. Ibid., p. 24.
65. Pazos, 'De nuestro archivo Compostelano', p. 212.
66. Francesco Gonzaga, *De origine Seraphicae Religionis Franciscanae* (Rome: Basae, 1587); cited by F. J. Cotter, *The friars minor in Ireland from their arrival to 1400* (New York: Franciscan Institute, 1994), p. 12. Ó Maolchonaire's Irish confrères Donnchadh Ó Maonaigh and Francis Harold gave the same information.
67. Patrick McBride (ed.), 'Some unpublished letters of Mateo de Oviedo, archbishop of Dublin', *Repertorium Novum*, 1 (1955), p. 160.
68. Diego de Colmenares, *Historia de la insigne ciudad de Segovia y compendio de las historias de Castilla*, p. 45; Manuel Rodríguez Pazos, *El convento de San Francisco de Santiago y sus dos iglesias* (Santiago de Compostela: Estudios Compostelanos, 1979), pp. 154–6.
69. Manuel Castro, *La provincia Franciscana de Santiago. Ocho siglos de historia* (Santiago de Compostela: Liceo Franciscano, 1984), pp. 86–181.
70. Pazos, 'Cofradías piadosas y capellanías castrenses en el convento de San Francisco de La Coruña (siglos XVI–XVII)', *Boletín de la Real Academia Gallega*, 24 (1945), pp. 423–37; cited by Óscar Recio Morales, *El socorro de Irlanda en 1601 y la contribución del ejército a la integración social de los irlandeses en España* (Madrid: Adalid, 2002), p. 111.

en Saavedra Vázquez, 'Algunos rasgos del comportamiento religioso de los ñoles en época austriaca: el ejemplo de La Coruña', *Historia Moderna*, 7 (1994), pp. azos, 'Enterramientos en la iglesia de San Francisco de La Coruña, 1555–1615', *Boletín eal Academia Gallega*, 25 (1944), pp. 277–80.

ger Stalley, 'Sailing to Santiago: medieval pilgrimage to Santiago de Compostela and its artistic influence in Ireland', in John Bradley (ed.), *Settlement and society in medieval Ireland: studies presented to F. X. Martin, OSA* (Kilkenny: Boethius Press, 1988), pp. 397–420; Recio Morales, *El socorro de Irlanda en 1601*, p. 111.

73. On the subject of Irish traffic to Galicia's neighbouring ports of Biscay during the same period, see Schüller, 'Special conditions of the Irish–Iberian trade during the Spanish–English war', in García Hernán et al. (eds), *Irlanda y la monarquía hispánica*, pp. 452–3.

74. Ceyssens, 'Florence Conry, Hugh de Burgo, Luke Wadding', pp. 295–404.

75. Felipe Fernández Armesto, 'The improbable empire', in Raymond Carr (ed.), *Spain: a history* (Oxford: Oxford University Press, 2000), pp. 116–51: 142.

76. See, for instance, *Summa de casibus conscientiae (c.* 1317) by Astesanus of Asti; the *Summa Confessorum* by Johan of Erfurt (*c.* 1255–*c.* 1320) and *Liber de virtutibus et vitiis* by Servasanto da Faenza (†*c.* 1300). I am grateful to Professor Martin Stone for this reference.

77. Canice Mooney, 'Irish Franciscan libraries of the past', *IER*, 5/60 (1942), pp. 214–28.

78. Flower, 'Ireland and medieval Europe', p. 31.

79. Edel Bhreathnach, 'The friars and vernacular Irish learning', in Edel Bhreathnach, John McCafferty, Joseph MacMahon and Colmán Ó Clabaigh (eds), *The Irish Franciscans 1540–1990* (Dublin: Four Courts Press, at press).

80. Canice Mooney, 'The first impact of the Reformation', in Patrick Corish (ed.), *A history of Irish Catholicism* (Dublin: Gill & Macmillan, 1967), vol. 3, part 1, pp. 27–8.

81. *An. Hib.*, 6 (1934), pp. 102–4; Francesco Bordoni, *Historia tertii Ordinis Regularis S. Francisci* (Parma, 1658), caps. xxxiv and xl.

82. Kenneth Nicholls, 'Monasteries in Connacht, 1577', *JGAHS*, 33 (1972–3), pp. 28–43.

83. Ibid. See Inquisitions of 15 Jan. 1584; 4 Nov. 1586; and 10 May 1587 (NAI, Repertories to Inquisitions (Exchequer), County Roscommon, Elizabeth, 9/15).

84. Colmán Ó Clabaigh, *The Franciscans in Ireland 1400–1534: From reform to reformation* (Dublin: Four Courts Press, 2002), pp. 53–7.

85. *Cal. S. P. Ire., Henry VIII*, II, 15, cited by Mooney, 'The first impact of the Reformation', p. 7.

86. F. X. Martin, 'Confusion abounding: Bernard O'Higgin, bishop of Elphin, 1542–1561', in Art Cosgrove and Donal McCartney (eds), *Studies in Irish History presented to R. Dudley Edwards* (Dublin: University College Dublin Press, 1979), pp. 38–84.

87. Patrick Corish, *The Catholic community in the seventeenth and eighteenth centuries* (Dublin: Helicon, The Educational Company, 1981), p. 10.

88. Martin, 'Confusion abounding: Bernard O'Higgin, bishop of Elphin', pp. 69–71.

89. Silke, 'The Irish appeal of 1593 to Spain', *IER*, 92 (1959), pp. 279–90, 362–71.

90. Conde de Puñonrostro to Philip III, 23 Nov. 1606 (AGS, E., NP, l. 1797, unfoliated).

91. Karin Schüller, *Die beziehungen zwischen Spanien und Irland im 16. und 17. Jahrhundert: diplomatie, handel und die soziale integration katholischer exulanten* (Münster: Aschendorff, 1999), pp. 172–5.

92. *Cf.* Hiram Morgan (ed.), 'The 1597 ceasefire documents', *Dúiche Néill: Journal of the O'Néill Country Historical Society* (1997), pp. 9–33.

93. *Brevis synopsis provinciae Hiberniae FF. minorum* (Brussels MS. 3,947; *An. Hib.*, 5 (1934), p. 38).

94. McBride, 'Letters of Mateo de Oviedo', pp. 109–10.

95. Puñonrostro to Philip III, 23 Nov. 1606.

96. Delamar Jensen, *Diplomacy and dogmatism: Bernardino de Mendoza and the French Catholic League* (Cambridge, MA: Harvard University Press, 1964), p. 207.

97. O'Heyne, *Epilogus chronologicus*, pp. xi–xiii.

98. Alfred Poncelet, *Histoire de la Compagnie de Jésus dans les anciens Pays-Bas. Etablissements de la Compagnie de Jésus en Belgique et ses développements jusqu'à la fin du règne d'Albert et d'Isabelle* (2 vols, Bruxelles, Académie royale de Belgique, 1926–8), vol. 2, p. 408.

99. 'Fray Florencio Conrrio de la orden de San Francisco […] confesor, y consultor y muy privado' (RLM S52/9/15, f. 3).

100. Ó Cuív, 'Ó Maolchonaire's catechism of Christian doctrine', p. 161.

101. Darren McGettigan, *Red Hugh O'Donnell and the Nine Years War* (Dublin: Four Courts Press, 2005), p. 98.

102. Mac Craith, 'The *Beatha* in the context of the literature of the Renaissance', pp. 48, 53.

103. *Scriptores Ordinis Minorum* (Rome, 1906), pp. 75–6: 'In order that he might aid with his advice the army sent by King Philip III to relieve the Catholics': *a Clémente VIII in Hiberniam amandatus, ut*

exercitu a rege Catholico Phillippo in subsidium Catholicorum misso adesset consilio. Donnchadh Ó Maonaigh's work served as Wadding's source for this statement.

104. See Hiram Morgan, 'Missions comparable? The Lough Foyle and Kinsale landings of 1600 and 1601', in idem (ed.), *The battle of Kinsale* (Bray: Wordwell, 2004), pp. 73–90.

105. Puñonrostro to Philip III, 23 Nov. 1606 (AGS, E., NP, l. 1797): '[…] vino con los dichos Condes a la Jornada que hizieron a socorrer a Don Juan del Aguila a Quinzal'.

106. *Beatha Aodha Ruaidh Uí Dhomhnaill*, ed. Paul Walsh (2 vols, Dublin: Irish Texts Society, 1948, 1957), vol. 1, pp. 280–4.

107. Puñonrostro to Philip III, 23 Nov. 1606: '[…] travajando mucho para conserver a los señores de la liga Catholica en concordia y union contra los enemigos en lo qual hizo mucho provecho por el amor y respeto que todos aquellos señores le tenian y continuo los dichos servicios padenciendo grandes travajos'.

108. Ó Néill, James Fitzgerald, MacCarthy More and Dermot MacCarthy to Clement VIII, 30 Mar. 1600 (ASV, Fondo Borghèse III, vol. 124c, p. 15); *Archiv. Hib.*, 2 (1913), pp. 288–9.

109. Ibid.

110. 'Clemens Papa 8us universis et singulis venerabilibus fratribus Archiepiscopis, et praelatis, nec non dilectis filiis Principibus, Comitibus, Baronibus ac populis Regni Iberniae salutem et Apostolicam Benedictionem', Rome 16 Apr. 1600 (*Commentarius Rinuccinianus*, vol. 1, pars. III, ann 1600–41, pp. 194–5).

111. *Cal. Carew MSS*, vol. 3 (1589–1600), Appendix, document 5.

112. Ó Néill to the papal secretary of state, Donegal, 27 Apr. 1600 (ASV, Fondo Borghèse III, vol. 124c, p. 9); *Archiv. Hib.*, 2 (1913), pp. 290–2.

113. Ó Néill to Clement VIII, 28 Apr. 1600 (ASV, Fondo Borghèse III, vol. 124c, p. 13); *Archiv. Hib.*, 2 (1913), p. 290.

114. Ó Néill and Ó Domhnaill to Philip III, 14 Jan. 1601 (AGS, Estado, legajo 236, unfoliated).

115. Ibid., 'Florencio Conrio que en otro tiempo fue alumno del seminario erigido en Salamanca por la real liveralidad de Vuestro Imbictissimo padre y a ora es consumado theologo y predicador de la orden de Sant Francisco de la Observancia.'

116. Ibid., 'a este tal proponemos para el arcobispado Tuamense o para el obispado de Fenense aunque mas le querriamos para el arcobispado por el bien mas unibersal que de el pende'.

117. Philip III to the Duque de Sessa, Valladolid, 19 Jun. 1601 (AGS, Estado, legajo 1856, unfoliated).

118. Brussels, 25 Mar. 1601 (Kerney Walsh, *Destruction by peace*, p. 158).

119. Brussels, 15 Jun. 1600; John Hagan (ed.), 'Miscellanea Vaticano-Hibernica, 1580–1631', *Archiv. Hib.*, 3 (1914), p. 237.

120. Kerney Walsh, *Destruction by peace*, p. 158.

121. *Beatha Aodha Ruaidh Uí Dhomhnaill*, vol. 1, pp. 303–19.

122. John McGurk, 'The Kinsale campaign: siege, battle and rout', *Seanchas Ard Mhacha*, 19 (2002), pp. 59–65.

123. Silke, *Kinsale*, p. 1. For a detailed description of that day's proceedings, see Silke, *Kinsale*, pp. 140–7.

124. NLI, Stafford MS, 'Plan of battlefield at Kinsale', 24 Dec. 1601 [O.S.] (*Pacata Hibernia*, 1633), see Éamonn Ó Ciardha (ed.), *Staidéar Bunfhoinsí Imeacht na nIarlaí* (Dún na nGall, 2007), document 6.

125. Edward O'Mahony, 'West Cork and the Elizabethan wars, 1565–1603', *Irish Sword*, 96 (2004), pp. 148–50.

126. G. A. Hayes-McCoy, 'The Renaissance and the Irish wars', *Iris Hibernia*, 3 (1957) p. 50.

127. Darren McGettigan, 'Gaelic military organisation and the Nine Years War: the army of Red Hugh O'Donnell', *Irish Sword*, 98 (2005), p. 410.

128. O'Mahony, 'West Cork and the Elizabethan wars', pp. 148–9.

129. Luke Wadding, *Scriptores Ordinis Minorum*, pp. 75–6.

130. Philip O'Sullivan Beare, *Hist. Cath. Ibern.*, pp. 142–3.

131. Zubiaur to Philip III, Luarca, 15 Jan. 1602 (*Epistolario del General Zubiaur, 1585–1605*).

132. Robert Cecil, secretary of state, to Ralph Winwood, Whitehall, 20 Jan. 1601 [O.S.] (*Memorials of affairs of state in the reigns of Q. Elizabeth and K. James I collected chiefly from the original papers of the right honourable Sir Ralph Winwood, Kt. [Winwood Papers]*, ed. Edmund Sawyer (3 vols, London, 1725), vol. 1, pp. 377–9).

133. Zubiaur to Philip III, Luarca, 15 Jan. 1602. See also *AFM*, vol. 6, pp. 2292–3.

134. Zubiaur to Philip III, 15 Jan. 1602.

135. *Pacata Hibernia*, vol. 2, p. 479.

136. Hiram Morgan, 'The real Red Hugh', in Ó Riain (ed.), *Beatha Aodha Ruaidh: the life of Red Hugh O'Donnell, historical and literary contexts*, p. 32.

137. Zubiaur to Philip III, 15 Jan. 1602.

138. Ibid.

139. *Beatha Aodha Ruaidh*, vol. 1, pp. 340–1.
140. Zubiaur to Philip III, La Coruña, 21 Jan. 1602.
141. Ciarán O'Scea, 'Caracena: champion of the Irish, hunter of the Moriscos', in Morgan (ed.), *The battle of Kinsale*, pp. 229–40.
142. Oviedo to Philip III, Kinsale, 27 Jan. 1602 (AGS, GA, l. 3145); Patrick McBride, 'Some unpublished letters of Mateo de Oviedo, archbishop of Dublin', *Repertorium Novum*, 1 (1955), p. 115. See also *Beatha Aodha Ruaidh*, vol. 1, p. 337.
143. Ó Mathúna, *William Bathe, SJ, 1564–1614*, p. 54.
144. Zubiaur to Philip III, 21 Jan. 1602.
145. 'El Conde Odonel', La Coruña, 18–20 Jan. 1602 (AGS, E. Es. l. 189–91).
146. *Beatha Aodha Ruaidh*, vol. 1, pp. 342–3.
147. Puñonrostro to Philip III, 28 Nov. 1606 (AGS, E. NP, l. 1797).
148. Manuel Fernández Álvarez and Luis Enrique Rodríguez-San Pedro, *The University of Salamanca: eight centuries of scholarship* (Universidad de Salamanca, 1992), p. 51.
149. Flaithrí Ó Maolchonaire to Lerma, La Coruña, 21 Mar. 1602 (AGS, E., Es., l. 188).
150. Ibid.
151. Ibid.
152. Ibid.
153. Ibid.
154. Ibid. On *Reputación*, see Antonio Domínguez Ortiz, 'La defensa de la reputación', in VVAA (eds), *Arte y saber: la cultura en tiempos de Felipe III y Felipe IV* (Valladolid, 1999), pp. 25–54.
155. Silke, *Kinsale*, p. 166.
156. Paul Walsh, 'James Blake of Galway', *IER*, 50 (1937), pp. 382–97. This article was reprinted in *Irish leaders and learning through the ages: essays collected, edited and introduced by Nollaig Ó Muraíle*, pp. 204–16. See also McGettigan, *Red Hugh O'Donnell*, pp. 114–15.
157. F. M. Jones, 'James Blake and a projected Spanish invasion of Galway in 1602', *JGAHS*, 24 (1950–1), pp. 1–18.
158. Lee to Blake, Jun. 26 1600 (*Cal. S.P. Ire. 1600*, p. 258).
159. *Cal. Carew MSS*, vol. 4 (1601–3), pp. 350–1, 370.
160. *Cal. S.P. Ire. 1600*, pp. 100, 104–5, 415; see Walsh, 'James Blake of Galway', p. 392.
161. Ibid.
162. Jones, 'James Blake and a projected Spanish invasion of Galway', p. 4.
163. Ibid.
164. *Cal. S.P. Spain (1587–1603)*, pp. 719, 732.
165. O'Scea, 'The role of Castilian royal bureaucracy in the formation of early-modern Irish literacy', in Thomas O'Connor and Mary Ann Lyons (eds), *Irish communities in early-modern Europe*, pp. 200–39.
166. *Beatha Aodha Ruaidh*, vol. 1, pp. 344–5.
167. Canice Mooney, 'The death of Red Hugh O'Donnell', *IER*, 81 (1954), pp. 332–7.
168. J. J. Silke (ed.), 'The last will of Red Hugh O'Donnell', *Studia Hibernica*, 24 (1988), pp. 51–60.
169. *Beatha Aodha Ruaidh*, vol. 1, p. 345.
170. Mansoni to Aldobrandini, Valladolid, 11 Sept. 1602 (ASV, Particolari I, pp. 485–9).
171. *Beatha Aodha Ruaidh*, vol. 1, p. 345.
172. *Cal. S.P. Ire, 1603–06*, pp. 4, 8; see Jones, 'James Blake and a projected Spanish invasion of Galway', p. 18.
173. Ibid.
174. John Hagan (ed.), 'Papers relating to the Nine Years War', *Archiv. Hib.*, 2 (1913), p. 275. Mansoni had been Jesuit provincial of Naples and Milan. He was still active in 1613 when he translated into Italian a Portuguese life of St Francis Xavier SJ by Joao Lucena, which had been published at Lisbon in 1600. See Georg Schurhammer, 'Ein christlicher japanischer Prunkschirm des 17. Jahrhunderts', *Artibus Asiae*, 2 (1927), pp. 94–123.
175. 'Convento de Dunigal', 24 Apr. 1600 (AGS, Estado, l. 840, f. 4); see also Ó Néill's nomination of Oviedo for Dublin; AGS, E., Inglaterra, l. 2511 (1599).
176. Silke, *Kinsale*, pp. 69, 75.
177. Fray Mathieu de Caria to Aodh Ó Néill, La Coruña, 5 Jan. 1601 (*Cal. S. P. Ire., 1600–1*, p. 107); Letter of Richard Golbourne to Lord Loftus, Blois, 21 Jun. 1601: on the information of Friar Browne at Bordeaux (*Cal. S. P. Ire., 1600–1*, pp. 124, 425). See Gráinne Henry, *The Irish military community*, p. 191.
178. Éinrí Ó Néill to Cardinal Aldobrandini, Valladolid, Jan. 1602 (ASV, Particolari I, f. 391).
179. Ibid.
180. Mansoni to Aldobrandini, Valladolid, 26 Oct. 1601 (ASV, Particolari I, f. 360).
181. Éinrí Ó Néill to Cardinal Aldobrandini, Valladolid, Jan. 1602.

182. Ó Néill to Clement VIII, Donegal, 25 Jan. 1601; see John Hagan (ed.), 'Miscellanea Vaticano-Hibernica, 1580–1631', *Archiv. Hib.*, 3 (1914), p. 241.

183. Thomas O'Connor, 'Diplomatic preparations for Kinsale: Lombard's *Commentarius* (1600)', in García Hernán et al. (eds), *Irlanda y la monarquía hispánica*, pp. 137–50.

184. F. M. Jones, 'The Counter Reformation', in Patrick Corish (ed.), *A history of Irish Catholicism* (Dublin: Gill & Macmillan, 1967), vol. 3, part 2, pp. 44–8.

185. Timothy Corcoran, *Studies in the history of classical teaching, Irish and continental: 1500–1700* (Dublin: The Educational Company of Ireland, 1911), pp. 17–22; Ó Mathúna, *William Bathe, SJ, 1564–1614*, p. 53.

186. Mansoni to Aldobrandini, Valladolid, 18 Mar. 1602 (ASV, Particolari I, f. 427).

187. Richard Bonney, *The European dynastic states: 1494–1660* (Oxford: Oxford University Press, 1991), p. 176.

188. 'Fray Florencio Conrrio de la orden de San Francisco' (RLM S52/9/15, f. 3).

189. Ibid., 'confesor, y consultor y muy privado'.

190. Meehan, *Fate and fortunes*, p. 492.

191. 'Un memorial de la parte del collegio de Salamanca que ha dado el Conde Odonel', Valladolid, 22 May 1602. See Hogan, *Ibernia Ignatiana*, pp. 106–8.

192. Kagan, *Students and society in early-modern Spain*, pp. 52–3; Lozano Navarro, *La Compañía de Jesús y el poder en la España de los Austrias*, p. 47: 'Los jesuitas se encuentran cómodos junto a los nobles. Fundamentalmente, porque las granjean la influencia social que necesitan y una capacidad de intervención política nada deseñable.'

193. 'Fray Florencio Conrrio de la orden de San Francisco' (RLM S52/9/15, f. 3).

194. Ibid. See also Ó Néill to Clement VIII, Donegal, Jan. 1601 (*Archiv. Hib.*, 2 (1913), p. 241).

195. Hiram Morgan, *Tyrone's rebellion: The outbreak of the Nine Years War in Tudor Ireland* (Woodbridge: Boydell, 1993), p. 212.

196. Silke, *Kinsale*, pp. 118–19, 157.

197. See 'Informacion de los cavalleros irlandeses en septiembre de 1604', Valladolid, (RLM, S52/9/4); Hogan, *Ibernia Ignatiana*, pp. 143–4.

198. Brief response to the accusations of Friar Flaithrí Ó Maolchonaire, Irishman: 'los yerros que hizo a zelo indiscreto, a ignorancia, o pasion [...] las posteras guerras de Onel o las passadas de los Geraldinos [...] los vanos temores' (RLM, S52/9/14, ff 3–4).

199. Thomas Morrissey, *James Archer of Kilkenny: an Elizabethan Jesuit* (Dublin: Studies Publications, 1979).

200. Helga Hammerstein, 'Aspects of the continental education of Irish students in the reign of queen Elizabeth', *Historical Studies*, 8 (1971), pp. 137–53: 150. For a copy of the declaration, see Philip O'Sullivan Beare, *Hist. Cath. Ibern.*, tom iii, lib. viii, p. 204.

201. O'Doherty, 'Students of the Irish college, Salamanca', pp. 1–36.

202. RLM, S59/9/11: '... muchos titulados y prelados de España que hazen particular mercedes al dicho seminario como son el Conde de Caracena, el Obispo de Segovia y el de Mondanedo el de Salamanca, Cabildo de Santiago y casi todos los cabildos y monasterios ricos de Galicia.'

203. Ó Mathúna, *William Bathe, SJ, 1564–1614*, p. 54.

204. F. M. Jones, 'Correspondence of Father Ludovico Mansoni, SJ, papal nuncio to Ireland', *Archiv. Hib.*, 17 (1953), pp. 1–51.

205. Ó Mathúna, *William Bathe, SJ, 1564–1614*, pp. 54–7.

206. See *Collegii Hibernorum Salmantini Constitutiones*, in *Historical Manuscripts Commission, tenth report* (1885), Appendix, part 5, pp. 340–79.

207. Ibid.

208. Thomas Morrissey, 'Some Jesuit contributions to Irish education' (Ph.D. thesis, 2 vols., University College Cork, 1975), p. 42. Antonio de Padilla to Philip III, Salamanca, 30 Nov. 1610 (AGS, Estado, legajo 226).

209. Friar Flaithrí Ó Maolchonaire on Irish matters, 1602 (Archivo Histórico de Loyola, FH/Lerma t. I/c. 27, 26/9).

210. Ibid., '[...] al cabo de nueve años que sustentan los Catholicos guerra contra el enemigo ingles mas con milagros que con poder humano'.

211. Ibid.

212. Ibid.

213. Ibid., 'Si tienen aún fuerzas haran convenios generales: si carecen de ellas y estan en mucho aprieto, á cada señor en particular ofrecera el enemigo de buena voluntad excelentes partidos.'

214. Ibid., 'De esta suerte dejará aislados á los principales y sin poder resistir – Es gran lastima – que deste modo se pierda para España la nacion Irlandesa despues de los infinitos trabajos que se ha impuesto para servir a su Rey!'

215. Ibid., 'Se ha de seguir de aqui que viendo las demas naciones este lastimoso suceso y miserable espectáculo de la destrucion de Irlanda por falta de este auxilio de España, nadie querrá ponerse jamas en peligro fiado en las promesas de esta nacion.'
216. Friar Flaithrí Ó Maolchonaire on Irish matters, 1602 (Archivo Histórico de Loyola, FH/Lerma t. I/c. 27, 26/9).
217. Ibid.
218. Ibid., 'Por esto trajo el Conde de O Donell en su compañia al Baron de Letrym de quien es todo aquel pais.'
219. Ibid., 'Y siendo casi una isla con gran facilidad se puede hacer inespugnable haciendo una trinchera en la lengua que le une con la tierra, y levantando un baluarte por la parte del rio y colocando en él dos piezas de artilleria, se impide que puedan entrar en el puerto barcos enemigos.'
220. Ibid.
221. Recio Morales, *El socorro de Irlanda en 1601*, p. 86.
222. Ó Maolchonaire to Philip III, 1603 (AGS, E., Inglaterra, l. 840, ff 200–1): 'fray Florencio yrlandes confesor que era del Conde Odonel que aya de Gloria […] desde la muerte de aquel noble conde en Symancas, procurando que Vuestra Magestad embiasse algun socorro a los catholicos de Yrlanda para animarlos para que no se demayassen oyendo la muerte del conde.'
223. Ó Maolchonaire to Philip III, 1603 (AGS, E., Inglaterra, l. 840, ff 200–1): 'como el mesmo [Ó Domhnaill] suppca a Vuestra Magestad en su testamento fue la santa muerte del conde la gran christiandad y clemencia de Vuestra Magestad y Dios sobre todo servido que un mes despues fuesse resuelto en consejo de estado que se embiase socorro a Yrlanda.'
224. Council of state to Philip III, 13 Feb 1603 (AGS, E., l. 840, f. 37); *Cal. S.P. Spain (1587–1603)*, pp. 719, 732.
225. Ó Maolchonaire to Philip III, 1603 (AGS, E., Inglaterra, l. 840, ff 200–1): 'pero por mis pecados y por los de Yrlanda y de España, el socorro y todos estamos aqui aun, porque quando fue esso resuelto nos respondian los ministros que era menester haçer otro acuerdo a Vuestra Magestad y una semana despues otro acuerdo, y un mes despues otro, y un mes despues otro'.
226. Ibid., 'y assi passamos 7 meses hasta que al cabo llego el negocio dispachado al presidente de hacienda'.
227. Ibid., 'Los Catholicos estan en pie aun, y an llevado buenas victorias como consta por muchos caminos gracias a Dios.'
228. Ibid.
229. Council of state to Philip III, 13 Feb 1603 (AGS, E., l. 840, f. 37): 'El consejo dize que por consulta de 3 de março del año passado resolvio Vuestra Magestad que se embiassen al conde Oneil 50V ducados y las armas y municiones que se pudiesse y despues por otra consulta de 2 de noviembre del mismo año fue servido de mandar que fuese 30V desde principio deste año.'
230. Ó Maolchonaire to Philip III: 'Los que solicitamos este negocio como yo y el secretario del dicho conde tenemos gastado lo que nos dio Vuestra Magestad.'
231. Council of state to Philip III, 13 Feb 1603 (AGS, E., l. 840, f. 37); *Cal. S.P. Spain (1587–1603)*, pp. 719, 732.
232. Recio Morales, *El socorro de Irlanda*, p. 92. The type of vessel used, the *pataje*, was a tender or advice-boat.
233. O'Connor, 'Diplomatic preparations for Kinsale', p. 138.
234. Puñonrostro to Philip III, 28 Nov. 1606 (AGS, E. NP, l. 1797).
235. Ibid.
236. Matha Óg Ó Maoltuile to the Conde de Caracena, del Puerto del Rio, 8 Jun. 1603 (AHN, Nobleza, Frias, caja 66, d2, ff 110–111v): 'Toda esta desastre á succedio por la subervia de Don Martín que quijo haçer todas estas cosas de su cabesa.'
237. Enrique García Hernán, 'Irish clerics in Madrid, 1598–1665', in O'Connor and Lyons (eds), *Irish communities in early-modern Europe*, pp. 275–6.
238. Roibeard Mac Artúir to Caracena, De la Mar, 8 Jun. 1603 (AHN, Nobleza, Frias, caja 66, d2, ff 108–9v): 'su ambiçion no le da lugar de acertar en cosa alguna ni usar prudençia ni discreçion en sus actiones'.
239. Ó Maoltuile to Caracena, 8 Jun. 1603: 'Don Martin de la Cerda dos dias despues que partimos de la Coruña me á llamado y pregunto porque á dado un memorial en La Coruna a Vuestra Excellencia pidiendo embarcaçion […] y que Vuestra Excellencia no tenia que hacer con los navios teniendo el orden de su Majestad para venir con el despacho.'
240. Matha Óg Ó Maoltuile to the Conde de Caracena, del Puerto del Rio, 8 Jun. 1603 (AHN, Nobleza, Frias, caja 66, d2, ff 110–111v): 'y quando yo le respondi que pense que Vuestra Excellencia podia dar orden en lo que tocava a esto, Don Martin me dixo si no callasse que hiziesse accorder me del.'
241. Roibeard Mac Artúir to Caracena, De la Mar, 8 Jun. 1603 (AHN, Nobleza, Frias, caja 66, d2, ff

108–9v): 'en el accustombrado favor y benevolencia que Vuestra Excellencia siempre ha muestrado y continuamente muestra a los criados del Señor O Neill del qual soy yo indignamente criado y capillan'.

242. Ibid., '[Don Martín] dixo que eramos traydores a su Magestad por suplicar paraque diesse orden que algunos criados que traymos se embiassen para avisar a los Condes O Neill y Odonel.'

243. Ó Maoltuile to Caracena, 8 Jun. 1603: 'En llegando a estas costas Don Martin no á querido oyr una palabra mia ni de los padres Fr Florencio y Roberto Chamberlino [Roibeard Mac Artúir], y fiacca se de los criados del enimigo.'

244. Mac Artúir to Caracena, 8 Jun. 1603: 'entregaron al enemigo las cartas que escrivio al Señor O Neill'.

245. Ó Maoltuile to Caracena, 8 Jun. 1603: 'stuvo sesenta leguas por tierra del Conde O Neill donde aporto, y quinze leguas del Conde Donell por mar, jamas le a escrito [...] tomo un barco y un mercader al qual Don Martin dio tormentos para haçer le confessar si yo le mano llevar alguna carta al Conde O Donell'.

246. Ibid., 'El Licenciado Roberto [Roibeard Mac Artúir] que es ayo del hijo del Conde O Neill escriviesse al Conde O Neill'; Mac Artúir to Caracena, 8 Jun. 1603: '[...] por sospechar que Mattheo escrivole algunas cartas al Conde O Donel, las quales no ha escrito como Dios es testigo.'

247. Ó Maoltuile to Caracena, 8 Jun. 1603: 'el padre fray Florencio va alla a dar cuenta de esto'.

248. MacWilliam de Burgo to Caracena, Valladolid, 18 Sept. 1604 (AHN, Nobleza, Frias, caja 67, d. 1).

249. Puñonrostro to Philip III, 28 Nov. 1606 (AGS, E. NP, l. 1797): 'bolvio a España, y despues de interpretar otra embaxada a Vuestra Magestad que los Catholicos embiaron con el Marques Macvilliam Burk'.

250. Caracena to Philip III, La Coruña, 5 July 1603 (Kerney Walsh, *Destruction by peace*, pp. 28, 150).

251. Puñonrostro to Philip III, 28 Nov. 1606.

252. Kerney Walsh, *Destruction by peace*, p. 163.

253. Ó Maolchonaire to Caracena, Valladolid, 15 Nov. 1603 (AHN, Nobleza, Frias, caja 66, d2, f. 251).

254. Ibid., 'Aqui a llegado de Londres el Padre Roberto capellan del Conde Onel [Roibeard Mac Artúir], que viene con orden del Rey Ingles [...] a me dicho que los condes Onel y hOdonel estuvieron en Londres y que aun alli mostraron su valor y christianidad, hizo les el Rey merced, aunque no quito dar libertad de consçiençia. Pero mando que no los molestassen en materia de religion.'

255. Ibid., 'Tampoco el Rey quito sacar la guarniçion del Ingleses de las fortaleças de los estados de los Condes.'

256. Ibid., 'Y con esto se an buelto a Irlanda desposados de los mayores señores que tenian por vassallos.'

257. Ó Maolchonaire to Caracena, Valladolid, 15 Nov. 1603 (AHN, Nobleza, Frias, caja 66, d2, f. 251): 'El pobre [...] Señor O Rorq es el mas desamparado porque no se sabe a donde esta, el Rey no le quiere perdonar antes dio su estado a su hermano.'

258. Ibid., 'Don Florencio Macarte y el Conde de Desmon estan prestos en la torre de Londres y no dexan hablar a Don Florencio con nadie.'

259. Ibid., 'El Señor de Viraven esta en Londres, no le dan ni perdon ni licençia para yr a su tierra, rogo mucho al Padre Roberto [Roibeard Mac Artúir] que tratase con Vuestra Excelencia si le convendria huyrse y venir a España destar se quedo.'

260. Ciarán O'Scea, 'The significance and legacy of Spanish intervention in west Munster during the battle of Kinsale', in Thomas O'Connor and Mary Ann Lyons (eds), *Irish migrants in Europe after Kinsale, 1602–1820* (Dublin: Four Courts Press, 2003), pp. 32–63.

261. John Lynch, *Pii Antistitis Icon or the Life of Francis Kirwan, bishop of Killala* (Saint-Malo, 1669; repr. Dublin: Irish Manuscripts Commission, 1951), pp. 14–17.

262. Council of state to Flaithrí Ó Maolchonaire, the Conde de Puñonrostro and the Inquisitor General, 9 Apr. 1604 (AGS, E., Corona de Castilla, l. 198).

263. Henar Pizarro Llorente, 'El control de la consciencia regia', in José Martínez Millán (ed.), *La corte de Felipe II* (Madrid: Alianza Universidad, 1995), pp 149–88; Bernardo García García, 'El confesor Fray Luis Aliaga y la consciencia del rey', in Flavio Rurale (ed.), *I religiosi a corte: teologia, política e diplomazia in Antico Regime* (1995), pp. 159–94.

264. I am grateful to Ciarán O'Scea for making this point.

265. See AGS, Consejo y Juntas de Hazienda (CJH) 429–12 (Casa Real): 'Pagos por servicios a criados y funcionarios de Casas Reales y en obras de Alcázares; mercedes, limosnas, ayudas de costa, gajes a caballeros españoles, franceses, flamencos, irlandeses, italianos; quitaciones a continuos' (1602–3). This folder also contains appeals from an African convert to Christianity, two Greeks and a French priest. All were dealt with by fray Gaspar.

266. President of finance to the secretary of state, 8 May 1603 (AGS, CJH 431–16): 'en consideracion de los muchos años que a servido a Su Magestad y a los principes de Yrlanda.'

267. Geoffrey Parker, *The Army of Flanders and the Spanish Road: the logistics of Spanish victory and defeat in the Low Countries' Wars*, p. xv.
268. 'El presidente de Hazienda a Pedro de Contreras, secretario de Su Magestad' (AGS, CJH, 431–16): 'certificando lo asi Fraí Florencio, confesor del Conde Odoneil'.
269. 'El padre confesor al señor presidente', 13 Sept. 1603, Valladolid, (AGS, CJH 429–12): 'Quatro irlandeses criados del Conde Odonel suplican a VMD sea servido de mandarles socorrer con alguna limosna para irse a su tierra que por estar enfermos quando fue Don Martin de la Cerda no pudieron ir con el.'
270. Ibid., 'Hugo Galgher, Donato Suyn, Didico Crawford y Nicolas Collino […] certificaciones de Mac Villiam Burk […] en consideraçion de los servicios del dicho Conde y de la necessidad.'
271. Ibid.
272. Ibid., 12 Sept. 1603.
273. Ibid., 15 Oct. 1603.
274. Ibid., 8 Dec. 1603.
275. 11 Jul. 1603 (AGS, CJH 429–11).
276. Ibid., 18 Sept. 1603.
277. Ibid., 11 Aug. 1603.
278. Ibid., 4 Oct. 1603.
279. Ibid., 6 Oct. 1603: 'yrlandeses hermanas del Señor de Castelhaven'.
280. 9 Sept. 1603 (AGS, CJH 429–12).
281. Ibid., 19 Aug. 1603.
282. Report of the Irish in Spain submitted to Philip III, Valladolid, 18 Nov. 1604 (Archivo Histórico de Loyola, FH/Lerma t. I/c. 27). *Cf.* 'A list of the names of such Irish have shipped themselves for Spaine out of Munster besides divers others whose names are not known, all which set sail since December, 1601', cited by Denis Murphy, *The life of Hugh Roe O'Donnell, prince of Tirconnell (1586–1602), by Lughaidh O'Clery* (Dublin: Folens, 1893), pp. cliii–iv.
283. 'Daniel Conry yrlandes […] con su muger y dos hijas', 4 Aug. 1603 (AGS, CJH 429–12).
284. Robert Cecil to Ralph Winwood, 20 Jan. 1601 [O.S.] (*Winwood Papers*, vol. 1, pp. 377–9).
285. 30 Sep. 1603 (AGS, CJH l. 429–11).
286. 3 Sept. 1603 (AGS, CJH l. 429–11).
287. Valladolid, 13 Oct. 1603: 'estos pobrecillos' (AGS, CJH l. 429–12).
288. AGS, CJH l. 429–12.
289. 23 Jul. & 1 Aug. 1603 (AGS, CJH, l. 431–16; AGS, CJH 429–12)
290. *Cal. S.P. Ire, 1603–06*, pp. 4, 8.
291. 'Don Reymundo de Burgo baron de Letrym a Prada', 15 May 1607 (AGS, E., NP, l. 1748).
292. 'Sobre el despacho de los irlandeses', 25 Sept. 1602 (AGS, Guerra Antigua, l. 589): 'bona persona de mucha confianca, qualidad y servicio'.
293. 'Pedro Archero, hidalgo, y Roberto Nogol, soldado', 10 Aug. 1603 (AGS, CJH l. 429–11).
294. 'A Padre Archero', 28 May 1602 (AGS, E., Es., l. 188).
295. 'Do P. João Howling ao P. Geral, Lisboa, 25 de Outubro de 1597' (Arquivo Nacional da Torre do Tombo, Lisbon, Manuscritos de Anglia 31–II, fo. 699); cited by M. Gonçales da Costa, *Fontes inéditas portuguesas para a história de Irlanda* (Braga, 1981), pp. 222–3.
296. McBride, 'Letters of Mateo de Oviedo, archbishop of Dublin', pp. 114, 360–2.
297. Kerney Walsh, *Destruction by peace*, p. 384.
298. Special report on the kingdom of Ireland, Valladolid, 7 Nov. 1605 (AHL, FH/Lerma t. I/c. 27): 'su cariñoso padre y patron, y tan devoto de los Irlandeses como fue el Padre fray Gaspar'.
299. Silke, *Kinsale*, p. 174.
300. O'Scea, 'Castilian royal bureaucracy in the formation of early-modern Irish literacy', pp. 200–39.
301. 'Al Inquisidor General, Puñonrostro y fray Florencio', 3 Apr. 1604 (AGS, Corona de Castilla, l. 198); 'Consejo de Estado al obispo Inquistor general, fray Florencio y Puñonrostro', 9 Apr. 1604 (AGS, Corona de Castilla, l. 199).
302. Ibid. 'Al Obispo Inquisidor General: Por via del Consejo de Estado ha resuelto su Magestad que para que los irlandeses que andan en esta corte confiessen y comulgen y cumplan con la obligacion deste santo tiempo conforme a lo que manda la Santa Iglesia cometa VS Illma a Fray Florencio Conrrio de la orden de San Francisco que es de la misma nacion y fue confessor del Conde Odoneill el cargo de cura de todos los dichos irlandeses para este effecto, por la buena relacion que se tiene de su virtud.'
303. *Epistolario del General Pedro de Zubiaur* (1568–1605), pp. 103–10.
304. Puñonrostro to Creswell, Valladolid, 21 May 1605 (AGS, E. l. 2527); see also 'Juan Norris, mercator ingles, a Puñonrostro', 26 Aug. 1606 (AGS, E., Inglaterra, l. 2858, f. 86).
305. P. L. Willaert, 'Négociations politico-religieuses entre l'Angleterre et les Pays-Bas catholiques', *Revue d'histoire ecclésiastique*, 6 (1905), pp. 47, 566, 811; 7 (1906), p. 585; 8 (1907), p. 81.

306. Pedro de Ribadeneira SJ, *Historia ecclesiastica del scisma del reyno de Inglaterra...* (Madrid, 1588); *Segunda parte de la historia del scisma [...]* (Alcalá, 1593); cited by Albert Loomie, *English polemics at the Spanish court: Joseph Creswell's letter to the ambassador from England, 1606* (New York: Fordham University Press, 1993), p. 31.

307. 'Robertus Personius a Carolo Tancardo', Valladolid, 30 Aug. 1596: 'Instructiones pro missione classica' (AGS, E., Inglaterra, l. 839, f. 143).

308. Loomie, *English polemics at the Spanish court*, p. 31.

309. Thomas McCoog, 'Jesuit nuncios to Tudor Ireland', in García Hernán et al. (eds), *Irlanda y la monarquía hispánica*, pp. 23–38.

310. 'Sobre puntos de cartas del conde de Villamediana', 8 Nov. 1603 (AGS, E., Inglaterra, l. 2557, f. 8).

311. José Pablo Alzina, *Embajadores de España en Londres: retratos de la embajada de España* (Madrid, 2001), pp. 89–105.

312. Council of state to Philip III, 1603 (AGS, E., Inglaterra, l. 840, ff 7–8; AGS, E., Inglaterra, ll. 841–2).

313. Gráinne Henry, 'Ulster exiles in Europe, 1605–41', in Brian Mac Cuarta (ed.), *1641: aspects of the rising* (Belfast: Institute of Irish Studies, 1993), pp. 37–60.

314. MacWilliam de Burgo to Caracena, Valladolid, 18 Sept. 1604 (AHN, Nobleza, Frias, caja 67, d. 1).

315. Patrick Williams, 'Lerma, Old Castile and the travels of Philip III of Spain', *History: the Journal of the Historical Association*, 73 (1988), pp. 379–97. See also Bartolomé Bennassar, *Valladolid au siècle d'Or: une ville de Castille et sa campagne* (Paris: Mouton, 1967), p. 389.

316. Diego de Colmenares, *Historia de la insigne ciudad de Segovia y compendio de las historias de Castilla*, p. 182; cited by Silke, *Kinsale*, p. 174. María Antonia Fernández del Hoyo, *Patrimonio perdido: Conventos desparecidos de Valladolid* (Ayuntamiento de Valladolid, 1998), pp. 53–104.

317. Flaithrí Ó Maolchonaire to Caracena, Valladolid, 14 Nov. 1604 (AHN, Nobleza, Frias, caja 67, f. 675): 'despues de estar malo 30 dias de tercianas dobles y de melancolia por ver hechas las paçes de Inglaterra'.

318. Ibid., 'murio como caballero muy christiano que tal era en vida'.

319. Ibid; *Beatha Aodha Ruaidh Uí Dhomhnaill*, vol. 1, pp. 116, 344.

320. Ó Maolchonaire to Caracena, Valladolid, 14 Nov. 1604: 'que le enterrasemos muy onrradamente veniendo a que los señores Don Enrique Onel y otros muchos en su enterro Su Magestad honra mucho merced'.

321. Ó Maolchonaire to Caracena, Valladolid, 14 Nov. 1604.

322. Jerrold Casway, 'Henry O'Neill and the Irish regiment in the Netherlands, 1605', *IHS*, 18 (1972), pp. 481–8: 482. On average, in the early seventeenth century, a *tercio* consisted of 1,500 troops. See Julio Albi de la Cuesta, *De Pavía a Rocroi: los tercios de infantería española en los siglos XVI y XVII* (Madrid: Balkan Editores, 1999), p. 386.

323. Ó Maolchonaire to Caracena, Valladolid, 14 Nov. 1604: 'aqui estan a pie de 250 personas de los quales el Señor Conde Puñonrostro y yo por orden de Su Magestad daremos relaçion en consejo el martes que viene'.

324. Ibid.

325. Ibid., 'que era justo por los serbicios de su Padre y su Tio, y para limpiar España de los yrlandezes dale titulo de Coronel aqui'.

326. Andres de Prada to Archduke Albert, 16 Sept. 1605 (AGS, CJH, l. 437–26).

327. Ó Maolchonaire's report of the Irish in Spain submitted to Philip III, Valladolid, 18 Nov. 1604 (Archivo Histórico de Loyola, FH/Lerma t. I/c. 27): 'Y haciendo Vuestra Magestad merced a Don Enrique Oneill de que vaya a servir a Flandes con titulo de Coronel como el lo tiene suplicado; vendra muy a propósito el que tenga este titulo desde esta ciudad, y an podra conducir a la Coruña toda la gente que esta aquí desde donde podra con ella embarcarse para Flandes.'

328. Ó Maolchonaire's report of the Irish in Spain submitted to Philip III, Valladolid, 18 Nov. 1604 (Archivo Histórico de Loyola, FH/Lerma t. I/c. 27): 'Los irlandeses que hay en esta ciudad van dividos en entretenidos, aventajados, soldados ordinarios, pobres, sacerdotes, estudiantes, mugeres viudas y doncellas, con la calidad de cada uno y lo que parece se puede hacer en ellos segun sus meritos.'

329. Ibid.

330. Valladolid, 18 Nov. 1604 (Archivo Histórico de Loyola, FH/Lerma t. I/c. 27).

331. Ibid. The other names are: Raymond Barrett, James Cussen, Maurice Fitzgerald, Walter Power, first cousin of John Fitzgerald, Denis Kelly, Mahon O'Driscoll, Daniel Farrell, Owen O'Sullivan, Rory Kelly, Richard O'Donovan, Thomas Ring, Morgan O'Connor of Kerry, Hugo Maddy, David Gibon, Terence MacSweeney and the MacCarthy kinsmen Florence, Daniel and Dermot.

332. 'Siguen agora los que llama la lista aventajados de ellos doce casados. Todos ellos perdieron sus

haciendas, algunos sus padres y hermanos en las guerras de Irlanda. Se repartieron entre ellos 1,986 ducados.'

333. Ibid., 'Soldados de paga ordinaria son 47. Pobres en Valladolid – 17 – Estudiantes id. 10.'
334. Valladolid, 18 Nov. 1604; i.e. MacMahon, MacCarthy, MacSweeney, O'Sullivan, O'Driscoll, Kelly and O'Connor.
335. Ibid., 'Doña Jerónima Conor muger noble de una casa de las mas calificados del Reino, tiene parientes con el Señor Oroork y con el Señor Macvilliam Burk difunto y con otros .'
336. Ó Maolchonaire's report of the Irish in Spain submitted to Philip III, Valladolid, 18 Nov. 1604 (Archivo Histórico de Loyola, FH/Lerma t. I/c. 27).
337. Ibid., 'otros personajes'.
338. Ibid., 'Fr. Tomas Geraldino es hijo de un caballero de Irlanda y buen teologo. Quiere volver a predicar en Irlanda; pida para un caliz y ornamento – 100 ducados.'
339. Canice Mooney, 'The death of Red Hugh O'Donnell', *IER*, 81 (1954), pp. 328–45: 331. In a petition to return to Ireland in 1601, Nynan promised Philip III that he would 'not cure any Protestant unless he first becomes a Catholic' ('y juro como Cristiano de no curar ningun Luturano sino se combierte!').
340. Ó Maolchonaire's report of the Irish in Spain submitted to Philip III, Valladolid, 18 Nov. 1604 (Archivo Histórico de Loyola, FH/Lerma t. I/c. 27).
341. Ibid., 'de los entretenidos que estan en la Coruña podran pasar catorce a Flandes con sus entretenimientos, y lo mismo los que de esta clase estan en Lisboa. Otro cuatro podran ir con las compañias que van a la Coruña.'
342. Ibid., 'podra ir con ellos a Flandes Don Cornelio Driscol con el entretenimiento que tiene en la Coruña com el lo tiene pedido'; Conor O'Driscoll to Flaithrí Ó Maolchonaire, La Coruña, 26 Aug. 1605 (AGS, E., Inglaterra, l. 843, f. 57).
343. Ibid., ' [...] la gente de Lisboa y la Coruña podra Don Enrique Oneill formar nombrando capitanes y oficiales dando a cada jefe con igualidad la gente que le sea mas aficionada.'
344. Ibid., 'Y para que se haga con mas brevedad y securidad, sera bien dar orden a Don Luis da Silva para que preparar el filipote de 200 toneladas [...] podra t[ed]emos avisare al Conde de Caracena que tenga preparado por si acaso el filipote *El Espirito Sancto* de mas de 150 toneladas que esta en la Coruña.'
345. Ibid., 'Y porque esto conviene se haga lo mas secreto que fuese posible [...] porque los enemigos no se opongan a la entrada de Dunquerque; se podra echar la voz que no ha de pasar a Flandes hasta la primavera, y que Vuestra Magestad ha ordenado que se junten a la Coruña todos los irlandeses para pasar alli el invierno.'
346. Andres de Prada to Lerma, Valladolid, 8 Dec. 1604 (Archivo Histórico de Loyola, FH/Lerma t. I/c. 27).
347. Casway, 'Henry O'Neill', p. 484.
348. Mountjoy to the privy council, Dublin, 1 May 1601 (*Cal. S. P. Ire., 1600–1*, p. 305).
349. Brendan Jennings, 'Irish swordsmen in Flanders, 1586–1610', *Studies*, 36 (1947), pp. 402–10; 37 (1948), pp. 189–202.
350. 'Report of D.M.', son of R.M.', 22 Jul. 1607 (*Cal. S. P. Ire., 1606–8*, p. 227).
351. 'Opinion of Fr Archer' (AGS, E., Inglaterra, l. 843, f. 120); García Hernán, 'Irish clerics in Madrid', p. 282.
352. Sir Charles Cornwallis to the privy council, Madrid, 10 May 1609 (*Winwood Papers*, vol. 3, pp. 36–7).
353. Puñonrostro to Caracena, Valladolid, 30 Jul. 1604 (AHN, Nobleza, Frias, C67, p. 164): 'El padre fray Florenço [...] esta aquy cuando esta escrivo [...] le suplica vuelva por el de los que van quejosos que cierto pueda dezir con verdad que tienen poca razon que como Su Magestad me le dio por compañero para lo que toca a los irlandeses es de los mejores religiosos que e tratado.'
354. '[...] de los mas insignes y famosos y de grande autoridad por las cosas que en el se vieron'; Pedro de Salazar OFM, *Crónica de la provincia de Castilla* (Madrid, 1616), pp. 95–7. I am indebted to Padre Antolín Abad Pérez OFM of San Juan de los Reyes, Toledo, for this reference. For a history of San Juan de los Reyes, see Gustavo Adolfo Bécquer, *Historia de los templos de España: Toledo* (repr. Madrid: Pareja, 2005), pp. 11–51.
355. Ibid., p. 98.
356. Donnchadh Ó Maonaigh, *Brevis synopsis provinciae Hiberniae FF. minorum,* (Brussels, MS 3,947; in *An. Hib.*, 5 (1934), pp. 119, 171).
357. Ibid.
358. Flaithrí Ó Maolchonaire to Philip III, 1 Aug. 1606 (AGS, E., l. 2797): 'quemando sus conventos como han quemado cinco dellos el año de 1601.'
359. Special report on the kingdom of Ireland, Valladolid, 7 Nov. 1605 (AHL, FH/Lerma t. I/c. 27).

360. Ibid., 'El Reino de Irlanda es una isla que confina con Inglaterra á distancia de mas treinta leguas hácia el poniente. De Escocia dista diez ó doce; y desde España se emplean tres dias de navegacion para ir a ella. Es poco menos que Inglaterra, pues tiene de largo ciento cincuenta leguas y cincuenta de ancho ó 300 y 150 millas inglesas. Esta dividida en cuatro provincias, que llaman Conacia, Ultonia, Momonia, y Laxenia.'

361. Ibid., 'los hijos de Milesio'. His inclusion of the Milesian legend in this report is almost exceptional. In subsequent submissions he preferred to concentrate upon Irish services to the Habsburgs and the losses sustained in doing so.

362. Ibid., 'A persuasion de D. Felipe II sostuvieron siete años contra Inglaterra los Geraldinos [...] Once años han sostenido la guerra los Señores O Nell y O Donell.'

363. 'Para vencerlos se ha visto obligava la reina a enviar contra ellos el ejército de soldados veteranos que en Bretaña peleaba contra los Españoles [...] ha gastado el dinero que empleaba en enviar armadas de piratas contra las flotas españolas que van de Indias, y en ayuda y socorro de los Olandeses.'

364. 'Hasta siete generales ingleses de la flor de la nobleza murieron en aquella guerra por causa se empobrecio tanto aquel reino.'

365. Ibid., 'los irlandeses inglesados [...] por la poca aficion que tienen a aquel Reino'.

366. Special report on the kingdom of Ireland, Valladolid, 7 Nov. 1605 (AHL, FH/Lerma t. I/c. 27): 'Porque siendo sus Rectores ciertos Padres [...] descendientes de Yngleses, mostraron aunque poca aficion a las provincias de Conacia y Ultonia [...] Aunque la intencion de Su Magd era que este Colegio fuese en beneficio de todo aquel reino.'

367. Ibid., 'Con mil excusas como el ser ilegitimos e indociles procuraban excluir a los demas de aquel Reino.'

368. García Hernán, 'Irish clerics in Madrid, 1598–1665', p. 279.

369. Special report on the kingdom of Ireland, Valladolid, 7 Nov. 1605: '[...] por la grandeza y generosidad de Su Magestad florezca en ella para defensa de nuestra Santa Madre Iglesia para la conversion de los Ingleses a la Fé y para conservacion de la Religion en Irlanda.'

370. Ibid., 'que ordenar que en el colegio de Salamanca se guardare inviolablemente la igualidad entre las provincias de Yrlanda. Luego por esta segunda servio la primera, puesto que es imposible, como se ha probado, observar esto segundo si inbierte lo primero. De lo dicho se colige quele debe amicalmente tratar de como han de quedar aqui los yrlandeses'.

371. Ó Maolchonaire to Philip III, 2 Jun. 1606 (AGS, E., NP, l. 1797): 'un compañero de nuestro padre San Francisco fundo el monesterio de Ochill'. See also Francis Harold's manuscript: 'Quis primis conventus Franciscanus in Hibernia' (UCD–OFM, D.02).

372. Ó Maolchonaire to Philip III, 2 Jun. 1606: 'en el Reyno de Irlanda siempre florecio la religion seraphica tanto en aquella Provincia que se tenia por una de las mejores en toda Europa [...] sus conventos que eran hasta ciento y quarenta monesterios no contan los de las monjas'.

373. Ibid., 'por su mucha religion y grandes letras (pues della son hijo el Doctor Subtil Scoto maestro de todos los escotistas y Ocam maestro de los nominales) por lo qual el vulgo de aquel Reyno les tenia grandissima aficcion y devocion, y la gente principal los estimava en tanto que casi todos se enterravan en sus casas y sus confessores eran de ordinario dellos'. Ó Maolchonaire's reference to Occam is intriguing when one considers that his works were out of favour at the University of Salamanca during Ó Maolchonaire's studies there.

374. Ibid., 'aunque Henrrique octavo Rey de Inglaterra y la Reyna Isabel su hija desterraron y acabarron totalmente las demas religiones en aquellas partes, con todo por la grande afficion del pueblo y merecimientos de nuestro padre San Francisco fue Dios servido que nunca hasta ahora se quitasse del todo la religion Seraphica si tuviessen Provincial y algunos conventos en pie aunque perdieron la mayor parte padeciendo grandes subjetos de los moradores martirio'.

375. Ó Maolchonaire to Philip III, 2 Jun. 1606 (AGS, E., NP, l. 1797).

376. Ibid., 'en estas posteras guerras en las quales, de todas las religiones, solos los religiosos franciscanos sirvieron a V Magd desde el principio hasta el fin, predicando y confessando al exercito de los Catholicos. Los hereges con tanta furia les persiguieron que quemaron y assolaron la mayor parte de los conventos que quedaron en pie, como fue el insigne convento de Dungall, por aver recivido en el las municiones y recaudos que Vuestra Magestad embio a los Catholicos.'

377. Ibid., '[...] el año de 601 vaxo un fuego milagrosamente del ciel y quemo el convento con 200 de los hereges que estavan dentro'.

378. Ibid., 'un numero de frayles mozos que pretenden embiar (si V. Magd. les haze esta misericordia) a la Universidad de Lovayna en Flandes'.

379. Ibid., 'dellos que fueron a Flandes y a Francia donde por falta de commodidad no pueden estudiar.'

380. Ibid., 'han embiado frayles moços a estudiar a España, pero por la differencia del clima [...] la mayor parte murieron'. See also Thomas Flynn, *The Irish Dominicans* (Dublin: Four Courts Press, 1993), pp. 106–7.

381. Craig Harline and Eddy Put, *A bishop's tale: Mathias Hovius among his flock in seventeenth-century Flanders*, p. 174.
382. Cardinal Pompeo Arrigone to Lerma, Rome, 15 Oct. 1605 (Fundación Ducal de Medinaceli, Archivo Histórico, legajo 51, ramo 5, carpeta 6).
383. Ó Maolchonaire to Philip III, 1 Aug. 1606 (AGS, E., NP, l. 2797): 'por lo qual queda aquella Provincia siempre obligada a rogar a Dios por V. Magd'.
384. Ibid., 'es impossible porque en el ay mas de quarenta personas seglares y no tiene mas de 25 aposentos, de lo qual es testigo el superior del mismo seminario (que ahora se halla en esta corte)'.
385. Ibid., 'aunque tuviera mas capacidad no conviene que religiosos esten mezclados con seglares ni que tengan seglar por superior'.
386. Ibid.
387. Ibid.
388. Council of state to Philip III, 12 Aug. 1606 (AGS, E., NP, l. 1797).
389. Philip III to Archduke Albert and to Spínola, Madrid, 21 Sept. 1606 (UCD–OFM, C.11).
390. *Louvain Papers*, ed. Brendan Jennings, p. 4.
391. Bruno Bouté, 'Academics in action. Scholarly interests and policies in the early Counter Reformation: the reform of the University of Louvain 1607–1617', *History of Universities*, 17 (2003), pp. 34–89.
392. Benjamin Hazard, 'The foundation letter of St Anthony's College, Louvain', in Edel Bhreathnach and Bernadette Cunningham (eds), *Writing Irish history: the Four Masters and their world* (Dublin: Wordwell, 2007), pp. 114–15.
393. Ibid. *Cf.* Michael E. Williams, 'Campion and the English continental seminaries', in Thomas McCoog (ed.), *The reckoned expense: Campion and the early English Jesuits* (Woodbridge: Boydell, 1996), pp. 285–99.
394. See F. X. Martin OSA, 'Confusion abounding', pp. 38–84.
395. Puñonrostro to Philip III, 28 Nov. 1606 (AGS, E. NP, l. 1797).
396. *Cal. S.P. Ire., 1606–08*, pp. 297–300. See John McCavitt, *The Flight of the earls* (Dublin: Gill & Macmillan), pp. 87–90.
397. Puñonrostro to Philip III, 28 Nov. 1606.
398. Kerney Walsh, *Destruction by peace*, pp. 173–5, 384.
399. Ó Maoltuile to Caracena, 8 Jun. 1603 (AHN, Nobleza, Frias, caja 66, d2, ff 110–11).
400. Davies to Salisbury, Dublin, 1606 (*Cal. S.P. Ire. 1606–8*, pp. 17–18).
401. *Brevis synopsis provinciae Hiberniae FF. minorum*, §38.
402. Examination of Fr Thomas Fitzgerald, Dublin, 3 Oct. 1607 (*Cal. S. P. Ire. 1606–08*, pp. 297–300).
403. 'Report of D.M., son of R.M.', 22 Jul. 1607 (*Cal. S. P. Ire., 1606–8*, p. 227).
404. 27 Aug. 1607 (*Cal. S. P. Ire. 1606–08*).
405. 'Information of James Bathe', Dublin, 7 Oct. 1607 (*Cal. S. P. Ire. 1606–08*, pp. 301–2).
406. Ibid.
407. Benjamin Hazard, '"Writings from Rome and Dublons from Spain": The O'Neills and St Anthony's College, Louvain, 1606–50', *Dúiche Néill: Journal of the O'Neill Country Historical Society*, 16 (2007), pp. 84–95.
408. *Cal. S. P. Ire., 1606–08*, pp. 633–5.
409. Philip III to Spínola, Escorial, 11 Aug. 1607 (AGS, Estado, l. 1843, unfoliated).
410. Marqués de Aytona to Pope Paul V, Rome, 10 Nov. 1607 (Fundación Ducal de Medinaceli, Archivo Histórico, legajo 55, ramo 8): 'El conde de Tiron con su muger y tres higos, y el conde de Odoñel con otros señores y cavalleros se han ydo a España. Atribuiran esto los ingleses a fomentos de España.'
411. *Cal. S. P. Ire., 1606–08*, pp. 496–7.
412. J. J. Silke, 'Outward bound from Portnamurray', in García Hernán et al. (eds), *Irlanda y la monarquía hispánica*, pp. 423–45. For a description of Ó Néill's departure and his reasons for leaving, see McCavitt, *The Flight of the earls*, pp. 92–112.
413. *Cal. S. P. Ire. 1606–08*, pp. 254–5.
414. Chichester to Salisbury, 27 May 1607 (*Cal. S.P. Ire. 1606–8*, pp. 108–9).
415. Bentivoglio to Cardinal Como, 12 Jan. 1608 (*Archiv. Hib.*, 4 (1915), p. 253).
416. Meehan, *Tyrone and Tyrconnell*, p. 111.
417. Sir Thomas Edmondes to Salisbury, 28 Oct. 1607 (*Cal. S.P. Ire. 1606–8*, p. 629).
418. Nollaig Ó Muraíle (eag.), *Turas na dTaoiseach nUltach tar Sáile: from Ráth Maoláin to Rome. Tadhg Ó Cianáin's contemporary narrative of the journey into exile of the Ulster chieftains and their followers, 1607–8* (Rome: Pontifical Irish College, 2007) [hereafter Ó Cianáin], p. 86.
419. *Cal. S.P. Ire., 1606–08*, pp. 122–5.
420. Eoghan Ó hAnnracháin, 'Summit at Binche, 5 November 1607', *The Irish Sword*, 25 (2007), pp. 363–76.

421. Spínola to Philip III, 8 Nov. 1607 (AGS, E., Flanders, l. 2289).
422. 10 Nov. 1607 (*Cal. S.P. Ire. 1606–8*, pp. 332–4).
423. Lombard to Ó Maolchonaire, Rome, 10 Nov. 1607 (Meehan, *Tyrone and Tyrconnell*, p. 119).
424. Ó Cianáin, p. 109.
425. Edmondes to Salisbury, Brussels, Nov. 1607 (*Cal. S. P. Ire. 1606–08*, pp. 638–9).
426. Guadaleste to Philip III, 4 Dec. 1607 (AGS, E., Flandes, l. 2289).
427. Bentivoglio to the papal secretary of state, Brussels, Nov. 1607 (ASV Borghèse II, v. 100, f. 352); Philip III to Albert, Madrid, 15 Apr. 1608 (AGS, E., Flandes, l. 622).
428. Sir Charles Cornwallis to the privy council (*Cal. S.P. Ire. 1608–10*, p. 83).
429. Bentivoglio to Barberini, 15 Dec. 1607 (*Archiv. Hib.*, 4 (1915), pp. 243–6).
430. Bentivoglio to Barberini, 16 Feb. 1608.
431. Bentivoglio to Barberini, Brussels (ASV, Borghèse II, vol. 204–6, p. 2): 'In Hibernia sono due sorte di habitanti, l'una degli antichi Hibernesi, l'altra degli Inglesi, che dopo l'acquisto dell'isola si sparsero in essa con le colonie. Quelli hanno portato sempre odio grandissimo à questi, et con le sollevationi l'hanno mostrato; dell'ultima delle quali fù capo il Conte Tirroni capo della famiglia O Nella, sicome gli O Nelli son capi di tutta l'antica schiatta d'Hibernia.'
432. Bentivoglio to Barberini, 16 Feb. 1608.
433. Ó Cianáin, p. 133.
434. *Louvain Papers*, ed. Brendan Jennings, p. 25.
435. Edel Bhreathnach and Bernadette Cunningham (eds), *Writing Irish history: the Four Masters and their world*, pp. 92–3, 115).
436. Cornwallis to the privy council, Madrid, 19 Apr. 1608 (*Winwood Papers*, vol. 2, pp. 390–2).
437. Brendan Jennings, Introduction to *Wadding papers* (Dublin: Irish Manuscripts Commission, 1953), p. xi.
438. *Archiv. Hib.*, 3 (1914), pp. 268–9.
439. 'Sir Charles Cornwallis to the Lords of the Councel', 19 Apr. 1608 (*Winwood Papers*, vol. 2, pp. 390–2).
440. Ibid.
441. Ó Cianáin, p. 665.
442. Don Juan Vivas to Gastón de Moncada, Genoa, 15 Aug. 1608 (Fundación Ducal de Medinaceli, Archivo Histórico, legajo 56, ramo 1–2).
443. 'Audiencias con el Papa [:] los obispos de Irlanda', Rome, 13 & 20 Dec. 1608 (Fundación Ducal de Medinaceli, Archivo Histórico, legajo 55, ramo 8.)
444. 'Roma in Monte Quirinali Die Lune 30 Martii 1609 fuit Consistorium Secretum', (ASV, Protocollo, 129, p. 62v: Acta Consistorialia coram Paulo P.P. V); 'Roma li xv di ottubre 1605' (Fundación Ducal de Medinaceli, Archivo Histórico, legajo 51, ramo 5).
445. 'Roma in Monte Quirinali Die Lune 30 Martii 1609 fuit Consistorium Secretum', (ASV, Protocollo, 129, p. 62v: Acta Consistorialia coram Paulo P.P. V).
446. 23 April 1609, Rome (ASV, Protocollo, Episcoporum et Alia XIII/33/157/125/126).
447. Ó Néill and Ó Domhnaill to Philip III, Donegal, 14 Jun. 1601 (AGS, E., Es, l. 236, n/f.); 'Irlanda Iglesias', Valladolid, 19 Jun. 1601 (AGS, E. Roma, l. 1856).
448. Silke (ed.), 'The last will of Red Hugh O'Donnell', pp. 51–60.
449. Philip III to the Duke of Sessa, 19 Jun. 1601 (AGS, E. Roma, l. 1856); 'Brief sanctioning of the right of the earl of Tyrone to nominate benefices, 1608', in 'Memoir of the most reverend Peter Lombard', in Matthew J. Byrne (ed.), *The Irish war of defence, 1598–1600: extracts from the De Hibernia insula commentarius* (Cork: Cork University Press, 1930), pp. xxxiv–xxxix.
450. ASV, Protocollo, Episcoporum et Alia XIII/33/157/125/126.
451. Ó Cianáin, 25 & 26 May 1608. See Pietro Martire Fellini, *Trattato nuovo delle cose meravigliose dell'alma Citta di Roma* (repr. Roma: Bartolomeo Zannetti, 1990), pp. 52–4.
452. Carolyn Valone, 'The Pentecost: image and experience in late sixteenth-century Rome', *Sixteenth-Century Journal*, 24 (1993).
453. Ó Cianáin, 25 & 26 May 1608.
454. Edmund Pillsbury, 'Jacopo Zucchi in Santo Spirito in Sassia', *The Burlington Magazine*, 116 (1974), pp. 434–44.
455. Oliver Burke, *The history of the catholic archbishops of Tuam* (Dublin: Hodges Figgis, 1882), p. ii; Knox, *Notes on the early history of the dioceses of Tuam, Killala and Achonry*, p. 1.
456. Davies to Salisbury, Dublin, 12 Nov. 1606 (*Cal. S.P. Ire. 1606–8*, pp. 17–18).
457. See, for instance, Ó Maolchonaire to Alonso Nuñez de Valdiva, secretary of finance, Madrid, 5 Jul. 1610 (AGS, CJH, l. 499–20, ff 44–45). The symbolism of the Red hand would not have been lost on Ó Maolchonaire, whose own family were hereditary genealogists and chroniclers. According to tradition, two Irish leaders decided to resolve a land dispute with a boat race, and the winner and holder of

the land would be the one who put his right hand on shore first. When one built up a lead the other knew he had to act fast so he drew his sword, cut off his right hand and threw it to the shore, thereby establishing the royal line of Uí Néill descendants who ruled over large parts of Ireland for centuries.

458. John Lynch, *Pii Antistitis Icon*, pp. 32–4; James Hardiman, *History of the town and county of Galway* (Dublin: Folds, 1820), pp. 8–9.
459. Philip III to the Duque de Sessa, Valladolid, 19 Jun. 1601 (AGS, E., Roma, l. 1856).
460. *Cf.* Paul Allen, *Philip III and the Pax Hispanica, 1598–1621* (New Haven: Yale University Press, 2000); Bernardo García García, *La Pax Hispanica. Política exterior del duque de Lerma: 1598–1621* (Leuven: Leuven University Press, 1996).
461. Mooney, 'The first impact of the Reformation', in Corish (ed.), *A history of Irish Catholicism*, vol. 3, part 1, pp. 27–8.
462. Thomas O'Connor, 'Florence Conry's campaign for a Catholic Restoration in Ireland', *Seanchas Ard Mhacha*, 19 (2002), pp. 91–105: 104.
463. Óscar Recio Morales, *España y la pérdida del Ulster: Irlanda en la estrategia política de la Monarquía hispánica, 1602–1649* (Madrid: Laberinto, 2002).
464. F. M. Jones, 'The Counter Reformation', in Patrick Corish (ed.), *A history of Irish Catholicism* (Dublin, 1967), 3/2, pp. 52–3.

3

The Mission to Madrid, 1609–18

After accompanying the Ulster earls to Rome, Flaithrí Ó Maolchonaire spent a year in the city where he enjoyed the confidence of Aodh Ó Néill. In accordance with their *regulae*, friars of the Franciscan province of Santiago, such as Ó Maolchonaire, resided at the friary of the Ara Coeli on the Campidoglio hill in Rome in the early 1600s.[1] As a result of Spanish efforts to stabilise their relations with the English and Dutch, there was far less sympathy in Madrid for another Irish military initiative. Denied permission to travel to Spain, Ó Néill sent the new archbishop of Tuam to the court of Philip III as his agent. Ó Maolchonaire spent the next nine years in Madrid as Ó Néill's representative, in combination with the Irish constituency exiled in Spain, Rome and the Low Countries. As Ó Maolchonaire kept abreast of events in Ireland, he also had to devise a political philosophy suitable for the Gaelic pastoral mission, in which he was already deeply involved. This quest found expression first in his protest against the Dublin parliament of 1613–15 and, a year later, in the publication of *Sgáthán an Chrábhaidh* at Leuven. Both these compositions, dealt with below, appeared while the Spanish were negotiating a marriage settlement with James I. Flaithrí Ó Maolchonaire's declared opposition to the idea of a Spanish Match rankled with those Irish who would have preferred to reach some accommodation with James I. Ó Maolchonaire worked for Ó Néill until the latter's death. In 1618, finding his political aims incompatible with those of the Spanish, Ó Maolchonaire departed for the Southern Netherlands.

Ó MAOLCHONAIRE'S RETURN TO SPAIN

Constrained by circumstances at home, where he found himself under increasing pressure from Lord Deputy Chichester, Aodh Ó Néill lacked the funds and weaponry to match his political grievances. He eventually left Ireland hoping to reach the court of Philip III before a swift return at the head of an army.[2] After their arrival in the Southern Netherlands, Ó Néill and Rudhraighe Ó Domhnaill wrote to Philip III repeatedly but received no reply. Nevertheless, they continued to hope that the Spanish king would assist their return to Ireland. Encouraged by words of sympathy from Peter Lombard in Rome, Ó Néill and his retinue made their way there, intending to travel on to meet Philip III in person.[3]

When obliged to wait in Rome after 1608, Ó Néill arranged to send Flaithrí Ó Maolchonaire to Madrid as his representative. Ó Maolchonaire's task on the earl's behalf became all the more urgent when they learned of James I's plans to 'declare confiscated up to six counties of the lands belonging to the earls of

Tyrone and Tyrconnell'.[4] Ó Maolchonaire's response is, perhaps, the earliest recorded reaction of an Irish Catholic to news of the impending plantation of Ulster. Two days before his consecration as archbishop of Tuam, he wrote to the Spanish council of state stating that James was 'offering the said lands perpetually to all the English and Scots and their heirs who wish to inhabit them, provided that they pay a certain amount to the king every year'.[5] According to a pamphlet printed in England a few months earlier, Ó Maolchonaire said, the lands were to be granted on condition:

> [...] they must swear that the king is head of the Church [...] they cannot rent the said lands to any Irishman of the ancient lineage of Ireland. In each county there are to be schools to instruct the young in Calvin's religion. And in every parish, instead of priests, there are to be heretic ministers who consume the income of the church.[6]

Ó Néill had received no direct response to the letters he had written Philip III since December 1607. Addressing this breakdown in communication, Ó Maolchonaire referred to the length of time they had waited and of 'how much reason the earl had to compel his Catholic majesty for the last year to return him to his estates'.[7] Confessing that he had 'always held him back', Ó Maolchonaire revealed that to some extent Ó Néill blamed him for the lack of decision.[8] In reply, Philip III wrote to Francisco Ruiz, Conde de Castro (†1637), his newly appointed ambassador to Rome, instructing him to ask the earl for his conditions to parley with James I. Aodh Ó Néill entrusted his reply to Ó Maolchonaire, who:

> [...] well understands my claims and has been occupied for a long time in the affairs of that kingdom and mine relating to the service of your Majesty. Therefore, I most humbly beg to your Majesty, be pleased to demand that he grant access to the above mentioned archbishop while he seeks the resolution of these affairs.[9]

During the next nine years, Flaithrí Ó Maolchonaire served as *chargé d'affaires* in Madrid for the Uí Néill and Uí Dhomhnaill transacting their business there. Ó Maolchonaire's main problem was clear. Philip III held that the earls' fight was for Catholicism and, as this was the case, responsibility for their plight now rested with the papacy. Paul V, however, would not oblige. Instead he firmly maintained that Spain had fomented the war. According to Rome, therefore, as the papal coffers lacked the necessary funds, Philip was obliged to maintain the earls.[10] Ó Maolchonaire tried to ensure that Ó Néill continued to be provided for in Rome and dealt with his interests in Ireland.

The Spanish council of state, however, turned a deaf ear to Ó Néill and would not allow him to approach the king *ore ad os*. The earl depended upon the new archbishop of Tuam. Before his departure from Rome to Madrid, Pope Paul V provided Ó Maolchonaire with a set of papal letters of credence.[11] These five *recommendatorie* were addressed, respectively, to the cardinal of Toledo, Bernardo Sandoval y Rojas (†1618); his nephew Francisco, the duke of Lerma (†1623); Juan Fernández de Velasco (†1613), the constable of Castile; and Decio Carafa (†1626), papal nuncio to Spain. Written as individual *littere missive*, there were only slight variations between these documents. They related how 'the venerable friar Archbishop of Tuam' was about to make his way to Spain alone, to conduct business on behalf of 'the beloved noble earl of Tyrone'. Entrusting '*Thuamens* the archbishop' to the care of the cardinal and the protection of the nobles, Paul V advised Decio Carafa to carry out his orders carefully by aiding the debate, first with 'our son Philip the Catholic king, then the regal counsellors'. Lerma was asked 'to courteously arrange to undertake the business of the earl'. With blessings bestowed upon his nobility, Don Fernández de Velasco was notified that the letters would be consigned to him by Ó Maolchonaire.[12]

Meanwhile, in Spanish Flanders, Colonel Éinrí Ó Néill, the earl of Tyrone's eldest son, also made preparations for Ó Maolchonaire's mission to Madrid. Three of his captains from the Irish *tercio* were granted leave to accompany him: his first cousin Eoghan Ruadh (†1649) of whom more is said below; Jenquin Fitzsimon, a seasoned campaigner who had fought under Aodh Ó Néill in the Nine Years War; and John Bathe.[13] Ó Maolchonaire arrived at court from Rome in the third week of July, staying with the papal nuncio before being joined by Éinrí and his retinue in September.[14]

Diplomatic missions like this one were 'considerably lacking in the pomp and ceremony of the usual sixteenth- and seventeenth-century ambassadorial entry and reception'.[15] Despite taking up his official duties on arrival in Madrid, Ó Maolchonaire had to wait until the following January before delivering the correspondence entrusted him by Ó Néill, including a renewed proposal for military intervention.[16] Philip III forwarded them to his ambassador in Rome, 'in order that you learn of their contents and respond to him on my part'.[17] The Conde de Castro reiterated the content of earlier correspondence sent to Madrid since December 1607. It explains that, during and after the Nine Years War, 'the Catholics of Ó Néill's league' had remained steadfast in their faith and the service of the Spanish monarchy. Harassed by James I and his advisers, who had reneged on the agreements made after the war, Ó Néill and his allies were forced to flee, fearing that their plans to rise up had been revealed. Ó Maolchonaire then turned to the immediate priority: seeing the earls 'almost abandoned by your Majesty', James I had 'dared to declare, without explanation', all of their lands confiscated.[18]

In May 1610, the king of Spain ordered his ambassador to Rome to demand the earl's conditions of settlement with London.[19] Aggrieved at Philip III's decision to call for his terms for peace with James I, Ó Néill referred to the five *recommendatorie* that Paul V had provided for Flaithrí Ó Maolchonaire before his voyage.[20] These, he had been led to believe, were an expression of papal support for Philip 'to procure the king of England to return his estates and admit him to his favour'.[21] Politically isolated and faced with the imminent seizure of all his property, Ó Néill sought to make use of another of his followers in Madrid:

> Item: that Your Majesty orders to give the Irishman John Bathe the allowance of thirty escudos which the Conde de Puñonrostro assigned to him and that he could serve near the person of Your Majesty's Ambassador in England, in order that he is present there to seek the above mentioned reconciliation.[22]

Ó Néill closed by calling for a reply to be 'handed to the Archbishop of Tuam', in order 'to avoid any further delay in this business' and to ensure that the earl 'receive a just reward'.[23]

CLEARING THE COURT IN MADRID

Flaithrí Ó Maolchonaire's submission of the earl's demands at court coincided with the death of his old ally, the Conde de Puñonrostro.[24] This represented a watershed in Irish affairs at court. Sir Charles Cornwallis (†1629) had wryly observed that Puñonrostro was 'the Raphael that offerreth up the prayers of that people; complaining the desperacy of their case, and the loss of all their hopes'.[25] On 25 February 1610, the council of state discussed an appeal written by Puñonrostro for Flaithrí Ó Maolchonaire after his return to Madrid:

> [...] six months ago Friar Flaithrí Ó Maolchonaire, Archbishop of Tuam, came to this court by order of His Holiness and of the earl of Tyrone to deal with the business of the said earl and the Catholics of Ireland.[26]

Significantly, this document went on to state that Ó Maolchonaire had, to date, 'served your Majesty for twelve years in the wars there offering assistance to the Catholics, especially the earls Ó Néill and Ó Domhnaill whom he has always encouraged to stay resolute in the service of God and of Your Majesty as they have done and as he has done in Spain'.[27] Having considered his record, the six state councillors in attendance accepted Puñonrostro's recommendation and agreed to grant Ó Maolchonaire an ecclesiastical pension of 400 ducados:

> He is someone who can be of very much service in the affairs of Ireland to keep the Catholics of that kingdom in Your devotion, to obtain information from there of the things that they will offer and, because they all respect him here, to move them to any good decision.[28]

It soon became clear why the council of state needed Flaithrí Ó Maolchonaire's expertise as Irish mediator at court. Throughout that year, he had to contend with a public order crisis, provoked by the large numbers of Irish political and economic migrants who had remained in Madrid where their 'disorders and excesses' caused serious offence to the Spanish. The cardinal of Toledo, Bernardo Sandoval y Rojas, was among those on the council of state who, 'for the common good', advocated the expulsion of the Irish and other groups guilty of 'the scandals and offences that continue against Our Lord'.[29]

Puñonrostro's successor, Don Diego Brochero y Añaya (†1625), had links with the Irish. In 1609, Pope Paul V had endorsed him as prior of Hibernia in the order of Malta.[30] A month after the council of state expressed their alarm at Irish misconduct, the duke of Lerma assigned Don Diego Brochero to 'el despacho delos irlandeses' with the sole purpose of clearing them from the court. Brochero believed that it would be best to send the Irish off to the Spanish fleet. He also acknowledged that Spain's shortage of soldiers in the Netherlands needed to be addressed.[31]

According to agents of James I, the Madrid disorders were caused by disagreements between the Gaelic and Old English. In particular, Ó Maolchonaire's promotion to the vacant see of Tuam was identified as a bone of contention.[32] Raymond de Burgo (†1619) had particular difficulties with Ó Maolchonaire, as outlined in the previous chapter. On his arrival with Aodh Ruadh Ó Domhnaill in 1602, the Spanish council of war had judged him 'bona persona de mucha confianca, qualidad y servicio'.[33] However, de Burgo, who 'had been declared illegitimate but styled himself baron of Letram and earl of Clanrickarde', later wrote to Cornwallis twice complaining that, having been overlooked at the Spanish court, he found himself in financial difficulty.[34] Referring to the privileges associated with Spain's military orders, the English ambassador informed the Privy Council a year later:

> [...] having lately made suite to be honoured with the habit of St James, [Raymond de Burgo] was answered that with every good will they would bestowe it on him, were it not that it would be an impediment to their use of his service, if upon any occasions hereafter they should employ him into Ireland.[35]

Ó Maolchonaire's doubts about Raymond de Burgo were probably related to the latter's connections with Cornwallis and with Edward Eustace, who was stationed in Spanish Flanders and associated with James I's ambassador in Brussels.[36] In 1610, de Burgo wrote to the council of state to complain that, due to the antagonism between them, 'el Relator Fray Florencio' had denied him permission to present himself at court for the reward he deserved.[37] As a result, almost all of his 500 vassals and soldiers, veterans of the Nine Years War, deserted him. He asked that a share of payments for Connacht petitions be given to his brothers William and Thomas, in order to send their followers to the Low Countries.[38] Three years earlier, fearing that his company of horse, his infantry and cavalry officers would be broken up, he expressed the view that 'His Majesty should reward everyone of the Irish *naçíon* who conforms to his merits.'[39]

These broils among the Irish irritated the Spanish.[40] Juan Hurtado de Mendoza de la Vega y Luna, duke of Infantado (†1624), informed the council of state that Ó Maolchonaire, 'who resides in this court', had entrusted two sets of papers to him, in the context of solving the problem with the Irish at court.[41] The first document dealt with Irish salaries in Galicia and the allocation of licences to go to Madrid. The council determined that controls should be placed on payments for the Irish based in La Coruña and that they should not be granted permission to go to court. The constable of Castile proposed that all such claims should be determined by individual petition in order to avoid sending women, children, the old and infirm to Spanish Flanders.[42] The second document related to the provision of 500 ducados, which could 'resolve the business of these people and rid this court of them'. The council decided that those Irish in Madrid should be directed to Brussels as soon as possible and recommended that a memorial be drawn up to distribute the 500 ducados among those who stayed. The duke of Infantado added a proviso that, in the forthcoming report, the Irish should also provide the reasons for the allowances they received so as to keep them in check and that reforms at court justified such action.[43]

Matha Óg Ó Maoltuile and his family were among those who had been paid in La Coruña. However, having initially received a combined allowance at court of seventy ducados per month, Ó Maoltuile had been owed his salary for more than sixteen months and his wife had received nothing since May 1609.[44] The former allowance ended at the same time as the breakdown in communications between Philip III and the Ulster earls.[45] Payments made by the Conde de Caracena (†1626) had eased their problems slightly but the archbishop of Tuam had to write to the council of finance on their behalf. He entreated the secretary of finance to procure an order for the treasurer to pay the dues outstanding as Ó Maoltuile, his wife and children were in such great need that Matha's creditors were suing him for his debts.[46]

Since returning to court the previous autumn, and despite the council of state's positive response to the Puñonrostro memorial, Ó Maolchonaire found himself in a difficult financial situation. Ó Maoltuile, who had represented Tyrone's case in Madrid up to the arrival of the archbishop, wrote on Ó Maolchonaire's part restating the points made six months earlier and rounded up the length of service mentioned by Puñonrostro to more than twelve years.[47] Ó Maoltuile continued:

> He finds himself in so much need at court that he cannot work with the decorum that his vocation requires and so he has resolved to leave for his country in disguise where nothing more awaits him than death and if he takes the decision without completing the business of the said earl of Tyrone and of other Catholics of Ireland they would lose all hope of Your Majesty's favour.[48]

Ó Maoltuile humbly begged Philip III, 'in consideration of all the above to be pleased to assign the said archbishop with an *entretenimiento* in this court conforming to his quality, dignity and services while he attends to the said affairs'.[49] At the foot of the next page the following note appears in a secretary's hand:

> [...] this archbishop is a man of example and of good parts. His presence is necessary in this court for dealing with matters which concern his *nación* and he provides important information. In order that he continues this with the decency conforming to his dignity, he could be allocated fifty to sixty ducados per month here so that he receives them punctually.[50]

The serious disruption among the Irish at court, however, remained unresolved. Instead of travelling to London to assist in reaching a settlement with James I, as Aodh Ó Néill had intended, John Bathe became involved in Ó Maolchonaire's efforts to resolve the Irish problem in Madrid. The archbishop told Philip III that Bathe wished 'to make a list of those people, because there are some Irish here in the neighbourhood of the town secretly who dare not show themselves in public for fear of Silva de Torres'.[51] This is a reference to the court gaoler, Silva de Torres, a friend of Lerma's favourite henchman, Villalonga.[52] Therefore, Ó Maolchonaire appealed:

> [...] be pleased to send a warrant to Silva de Torres in order to allow eight days for these Irish to gather together at the inn of the said captain so that he can make a list of them since it is done to remove them from the court as intended.[53]

Individual Irish memorials continued to be lodged and considered, in line with council of state procedure.[54]   In August 1609, for instance, Andres de Prada (†1611) noted that 'fray Florencio Conrrio y el baron de Letrim' had written in support of Morgan O'Farrell vouching for his military service in the Nine Years War and the losses he sustained from the confiscation of 'his patrimony'.[55] The fact that Ó Maolchonaire is not referred to as archbishop here strongly suggests that he wrote the memorial before leaving court to establish St Anthony's College, Leuven. Another of Ó Maolchonaire's letters of recommendation, referring to James Fitzgerald, was intercepted in 1609.[56] This spoke of the latter's fourteen-month imprisonment in London for working on behalf of the earls of Tyrconnell and may have been linked with his petition for a post in the Southern Netherlands.[57]

Again in October 1610, Ó Maolchonaire interceded for the Irish community at court, which found itself in an increasingly uncomfortable situation. He retrieved the king's original instructions to Archduke Albert from the council of state and wrote to remind Philip III how circumstances had arisen:

> [...] at first, on being informed of what the Irish have lost in your royal service and of how they served the Catholic cause in the recent war of Ireland, moved by compassion, and also by justice to reward them in some manner, he [the king] ordered that they be given a great amount of payments and awards.[58]

Consequently, he continued, 'as the fame of your Majesty's bounty towards the Irish spread, many more have flocked here.'[59]

The difficulties that Irish exiles experienced in obtaining payment from the archdukes' coffers in the Southern Netherlands came as no surprise to Flaithrí Ó Maolchonaire. According to a letter sent to Madrid by the Irish Friars Minor, despite providing for the education of twenty-six students since its inception, fifteen months had passed without any of the 1,000 ducados promised to the college as annual alms in 1606.[60] Most of the payment granted to the college for the first six months had been used to set the house in order and to buy books. Finding themselves in 'extreme necessity' as a result, they humbly beseeched that Philip III, 'for the love of God, be served to send a precise order to pay them in full from then on and the said fifteen months arrears'.[61] The council of state acknowledged that it was most just to reimburse a work of such merit and confirmed that the king was to order prompt payment of 1,000 ducados in Spanish Flanders.[62]

UPHOLDING THE *TERCIO* AND THE INTERESTS OF IRISH MILITARY PERSONNEL

In 1605, the numbers of migrants from Ireland had led James Archer SJ to warn the Spanish council of state of an impending crisis. At the same time he alleged that Flaithrí Ó Maolchonaire, their 'Godfather', had encouraged their arrival.[63] Ó Maolchonaire and Puñonrostro had formulated plans to deal with matters the following year but an impasse at Brussels prevented a swift resolution.[64] In an effort to account for the continued arrival of large numbers in Spanish territories,

Ó Maolchonaire vouched that the Ulster earls had raised the *tercio* which accord-ing to the muster-roll taken on 1 June had 1,440 troops.[65] Incorporated into the army of Spanish Flanders since the late 1580s, Irish foot soldiers had become part of an up-to-date force of well-drilled, professional infantrymen. Trained by Spanish officers and led by Irishmen who had served in the Netherlands, they accepted 'the hazard of the open field and the plying of the musket and pike in formal warfare'.[66]

Tercios, on average, consisted of 1,000–1,200 soldiers.[67] It is important to note that this type of military formation was markedly different from the regiments in the army based in Spanish Flanders. At the start of the seventeenth century, only German troops in Spanish service were organised in regiments.[68] Each *tercio*, on the other hand, was its own separate and complete unit under one commander. It was further divided into companies led by captains. This helped instil tactical efficiency and made the army of Spanish Flanders more manoeuvrable on the ground.[69] Spanish veterans accounted for no more than 20 per cent of total infantry numbers. Having originally had a distinct structure of their own, the remaining *naciones* were organised according to the model of the Spanish infantry by the beginning of Philip III's reign.[70]

However, as Geoffrey Parker has revealed, the erratic flow of money from Madrid to Brussels often led to mutiny and desertion among troops in Spanish service.[71] In relation to the Irish case, the Ulster earls reported to Philip III that, due to poor accommodation and ill treatment, almost 300 soldiers from the Irish *tercio* had either died or left the Spanish Netherlands in the two years up to 1608. Many of them had made their way to Madrid in search of their pay.[72] As a result of diplomatic pressure exerted by the English ambassador in Brussels, the *tercio* was then said to be in danger of total collapse. Pleading for better conditions for their soldiers, the earls reiterated Flaithrí Ó Maolchonaire's plea for the Irish in Madrid to be sent to their respective units, thereby allaying Spanish fears of Irish misconduct at court. The council of state recognised the need for experienced soldiers in the Low Countries and advised that the archdukes should be informed.[73]

Amid calls to clear the court of Irish, Ó Maolchonaire repeated his proposal of 1606 to transfer them back to Spanish Flanders. This, he explained, would alleviate matters in Madrid and uphold the Irish *tercio*:

> Being at court by order of His Majesty at the time, I saw how important it was to the service of His Majesty and to his ministers' peace of mind that some remedy be sought so that no more Irish should come to court.[74]

This, in turn, led Ó Maolchonaire to suggest 'to Señor Conde de Puñonrostro (may he be in heaven) that the only means would be to grant them more privi-leges in this court, except that they all be referred to the Archduke'. Then, 'when the same allowances and privileges already awarded by Your Majesty to the Irish should fall vacant, they be allocated in advance to other well-deserving Irish'.[75] In order to accomplish his plan, Flaithrí Ó Maolchonaire proposed that, in his capacity as colonel of the *tercio*, Éinrí Ó Néill should present a report to the arch-duke on the merits and qualities of every one:

In this way the privileges should not be increasing every day, and that the court here should be cleared out, as they wouldn't come to it on seeing that the privileges would be stopped.[76]

Instead, Ó Maolchonaire declared, 'all would flock to serve in the *tercio* in the hopes that they would have of filling some vacancy, and the *tercio* would be well maintained.'[77] In 1606, Puñonrostro and he had 'proposed all this at the council of state and those gentlemen readily accepted it'.[78] In response, Philip III had written to Archduke Albert 'in order to distribute the 500 ducados falling vacant, to certain Irish flocking to this court'. 'This,' Ó Maolchonaire stated at the height of the ensuing crisis, 'has not been carried out to date.'[79] Irish hopes of seeing the proposal properly implemented suffered a further setback with the premature death of Éinrí Ó Néill at Aranda de Duero.

The archbishop of Tuam wrote to the king a fortnight later.[80] In order to ward off English attempts to break up the *tercio*, Ó Maolchonaire related how, at the moment of Éinrí's death, 'he begged Your Majesty, in consideration of his services, for his royal advantage and the consolation of his afflicted father, that the *tercio* was not to be given to anyone who is not to his father's liking.[81] Drawing attention to the serious threats then posed to the *tercio*, the Franciscan described how 'the king of England's ministers have prepared many plots to break it up.'[82]

In the earls' interests, Flaithrí Ó Maolchonaire took up the point again the following year. Due to the fact that Aodh Ó Néill's other son was eleven years of age, Ó Maolchonaire appealed for the earl of Tyrone's nephew Eoghan Ruadh to be appointed major by Philip III, effectively granting him full control of the regiment until the child reached majority. Eoghan Ruadh already held the rank of captain, having served for several years in Spanish Flanders.[83] Archduke Albert, however, appointed Aodh Ó Néill's eldest son Seán to the colonelcy.[84] Notified of the decision from Brussels, Flaithrí Ó Maolchonaire revealed the gravity of his concerns to Philip's secretary of state.[85] Philip III accepted Ó Maolchonaire's view and acceded to Eoghan Ruadh's promotion. The archbishop's role in this compromise rankled with the Old English by hampering their hopes of reaching some accommodation with James I.[86]

On 30 October 1610, Flaithrí Ó Maolchonaire tried to renew his proposal to bolster the *tercio* once more, enclosing the king's original *cédula* to Brussels. This dealt with 'the vacancies so that he may be able to inform and enlighten those gentlemen [the council of state] of all this business, which was the cause that moved His Majesty to make this decision'.[87] Since first presenting these proposals matters had deteriorated further, making the need for a solution even more urgent. Ó Maolchonaire maintained that the best course of action would be an extension of the 1606 plan to stop granting new allowances at court in Spain, redirect payments to the Southern Netherlands to protect the *tercio* by filling vacancies and *plaças muertes*, and to rid the court of unwanted Irish in Madrid:

> I can see no better way then or now in regard to the above mentioned bills, than to command that the said order be executed in the case of the allowances and privileges which fell vacant from that time regarding the *tercio* only, and that the same be done in the case of those about to fall vacant.[88]

The continued survival of the *tercio* depended upon the acceptance of Ó Maolchonaire's calls for Aodh Ó Néill's nephew to be placed in charge. The decision to make Seán Ó Néill colonel reflects the utmost regard shown towards noble lineage during the *ancien régime*, but beyond the obvious shortcomings of giving someone so inexperienced overall command of well over a thousand troops, the archbishop of Tuam identified the need to deal with the administration of payments from the Spanish authorities. Ó Maolchonaire returned to this theme at the end of his letter:

> They have also written to me about the allowances that His Majesty gives for vacancies in the Irish *Tercio* which have not taken effect because His Highness has said that he did not understand this matter and that, until he heard from Your Majesty, he did not know what to do.[89]

According to the papal nuncio in Brussels, Guido Bentivoglio, Albert feared for the fragile peace which had been signed with the Dutch in 1609 and was reluctant to keep a standing army.[90] This consisted of cavalry, lancers, riflemen, an armoured division, a regiment of 300 Germans and 200 Catholic troops from England and Scotland.[91] The Ó Néill *tercio*, approximately 1,000 strong, remained in the Southern Netherlands with three infantry units under Spanish command, two from Italy, one from Burgundy and three from the French-speaking Low Countries.[92]

Flaithrí Ó Maolchonaire, however, aligned the immediate needs of his exiled constituency with events in Madrid. Maintaining the Irish *tercio*, he believed, would help clear the court. Since Philip III had already agreed to the proposal, Ó Maolchonaire wrote:

> I therefore enclose the original letter that His Majesty wrote to Sr Archiduque, where Your Majesty will notice the order which he has issued and that it is right that it continues and succeeds since every day more allowances become available, which they will be able to fill with those that His Majesty has suggested and is to suggest.[93]

Five days later, Ó Maolchonaire wrote to the secretary of state again, suggesting that 'the Archduke be mandated, whenever he should provide these allowances, to give credit to the report which would be given to him by Eoghan Ruadh Ó Néill'. To assist in administration of payments to Irish soldiers, Ó Maolchonaire recommended Aodh Mac Aingil, chaplain major of the *tercio* and guardian of St Anthony's college.[94] The implementation of this proposal would, Ó Maolchonaire assumed, mean that:

> [...] no Irishman will be seen here, nor will it be necessary to make any report about them. If in the first months, not knowing this order, some should come, they will be dispatched by telling them to flock to His Highness.[95]

Philip O'Sullivan Beare's praise for Don Diego de Brochero suggests that he handled the complexities of the situation sympathetically.[96] In this context, the July 1610 report on the Irish at court by Brochero is of interest. Compiled before the death of Éinrí Ó Néill, its seventy-one names fall into three categories. Flaithrí Ó Maolchonaire and Éinrí Ó Néill's cohort take precedence. Next are the names of followers of the Ulster earls who made their way to Madrid after the Flight; and those who had arrived in Spain earlier in the previous decade. Members of the clergy account for 10 per cent of those recorded.[97] Aside from Ó Maolchonaire,[98] these were Thomas Stronge, his confessor and Franciscan con-frère from Waterford; Francis Veahy, abbot of Cong and a close ally of Ó Maolchonaire; Fr Raymond Nealy; Aodh Ó Néill's chaplain, Patrick Duff, who had first intended to stay in Spanish Flanders;[99] Friar Eugene Field, afterwards commissary of the Franciscans in Ireland;[100] and 'Roderigo Escoces de Irlanda', *aliter* Rory Albanagh, described elsewhere as 'of the county of Tyrone, priest and steward' to Éinrí Ó Néill.[101]

Apart from the clergy with whom they mixed in Madrid, the most conspicuous Irish presence in the Spanish capital was the military community.[102] In line with Aodh Ó Néill's interests, Flaithrí Ó Maolchonaire acted on behalf of the earl's allies in exile. Among them was Gerald Fitzmaurice, the Fitzgeralds' kinsman and grandson of Thomas, baron of Lixnaw. He had made his way to Madrid after arriving in Spanish Flanders with Rudhraighe Ó Domhnaill's followers.[103] On 20 July 1609 he sought a salary increase from secretary of state Andres de Prada to join up with the *tercio* of his *naçion*.[104] An undated council of state report filed with Irish memorials for August 1609 states that 'he presents *certificaciones* from the archbishop of Tuam, the earl of Tyrone, from Don Maurice and Don John Fitzgerald':

> [He is] a most noble gentleman and a titled person in Ireland whose father and uncle were the most renowned and capable commanders against the Lutherans until they died in action along with many of their relatives and vassals, the English capturing their estates and belongings.[105]

Gerald Fitzmaurice had then served the earls of Tyrconnell and Tyrone 'for six years in business of great importance which he always completed very well'. For that,

> [...] and for his good parts he is worthy of all the favour he deserves which Your Majesty should be pleased to grant to him. He requests a raise in the salary of 20 ducados he has in Flanders from the vacancies which have arisen in the *tercio* of his *naçion* and the costs to cover the journey.[106]

The case of Tadhg O'Driscoll illustrates further how Irish allies at court would support each others' claims. As the eldest son of Dermot O'Driscoll and nephew of the lord of Castlehaven, his request to have his allowances transferred to serve in Sicily was endorsed by Ó Maolchonaire, Caracena, the earl of Desmond, John Fitzgerald, the O'Sullivan Beare and Eugene MacCarthy, rector of the Santiago Irish college.[107]

In an attempt to explain the prolonged delays, the council of state admitted that the large number of Irish soldiers with good records who sought recompense for their efforts and injuries made it difficult to fully enforce the expulsion policy.[108] A month after financial arrangements were made for the earl of Tyrone's sons

Seán and Brian, the projected policy for the Irish was declared consistent with the reports of allowances and privileges calculated in 1608. Of the 3,311 ducados paid per month to Éinrí Ó Néill's *tercio*, 884 had been assigned by the archdukes.

According to Ó Maolchonaire, many posts had been vacated since then and the remaining number would be reduced by a further third in the general reform of the army, leading to a much lower total than that paid in 1608. To 'proceed with certainty in the provision of these salaries', the council of state accepted Ó Maolchonaire's suggestion that Archduke Albert should refer to reports given by Eoghan Ruadh and Aodh Mac Aingil. A note added to the foot of the document states that Juan de Mancicidor, secretary of state and war to the archducal couple (†1618), was to send Philip III an account of the debts due in Spanish Flanders, complete 'with marginal glosses for each one'.[109] Of the others named on the list, Flaithrí Ó Maolchonaire later vouched for Anthony de Burgo. Accompanying accreditation was provided by the earls of Desmond and Bearhaven, who describe him as 'Señor del Condado de Mayoo'.[110] Ó Maolchonaire's *certificación* of Anthony de Burgo appears to have been written at the start of his military career:[111]

> I know Don Antonio de Burgo to be a noble son of the de Burgo family, a cousin of the Mac William Burc, and that he and his relatives have served in the last war of Ireland and lost many people and estates in the service of Your Majesty.[112]

The young de Burgo wished to serve in the Spanish fleet. On his behalf, Ó Maolchonaire continued:

> For the services of his parents and relatives, I believe that the said Antonio is worthy of Your Catholic Majesty's favour which He should be pleased to grant him. At His [Philip III's] request, I gave him this testimonial, signed and sealed with my seal.[113]

Don Diego Brochero presented an updated list of Irish recipients of payments in Madrid the following month.[114] Fifteen of the twenty-seven names occur in the first report with Ó Maolchonaire to the fore once more. It seems that the young de Burgo had left the court as he is missing from the new list, as is Matha Óg Ó Maoltuile. Having requested that he be transferred back to the north of Spain the previous September, he had died during the winter. Instead, his widow Elena is named along with a small retinue.[115]

Francis Veahy remained in Madrid along with Eoghan Ruadh, Jenquin Fitzsimon and Patrick Maguire, all of whom had accompanied Éinrí Ó Néill on his mission from Spanish Flanders.[116] John Bathe, who Aodh Ó Néill had asked to be sent to London on his behalf, is not on the list for 1611. Instead he awaited a commission for raising an infantry company in Madrid, pending the arrival of two thirds of them in the Low Countries. According to Brochero, the archbishop of Tuam gave Bathe one of the four testimonials that accompanied his memorial to Philip III.[117] This states that at least 100 Irish soldiers at court wished to serve in the *tercio*, a claim substantiated by Denis O'Brien in a separate application which spoke of 'many vassals of his own scattered throughout Spain'.[118] Denis

MacCarthy, his wife and mother-in-law, were also in Madrid following his request for the same pay in Spanish Flanders as he had received in La Coruña.[119]

Thus, it seems, the thirty-six petitioners originally catered for in Philip III's *cédula* had made their way to Spanish Flanders, taking with them their groups of followers and the four religious who were absent from the new register. Isolated incidents of Irish criminality continued into the same year.[120] Nevertheless, the eventual outcome of the year's events represented a minor triumph for Flaithrí Ó Maolchonaire. For now, the Irish *tercio* was safe. Notwithstanding the loss of significant numbers because of the poor standard of their quarters and erratic pay, according to the muster-roll of 1 June 1610 referred to by Ó Maolchonaire,[121] Éinrí Ó Néill still commanded a force of 1,440 which, in turn, helped lead to other Irish formations. The commanding officer, or *maestre de campo*, of a *tercio* was effectively its administrator and, as such, accountable for its maintenance.[122] Without adequate internal administration of *sueldo*, therefore, the Uí Néill companies may well have been disbanded as part of the regular reform of Spanish forces in the Southern Netherlands and through the efforts of Thomas Edmondes (†1639). Instead, his successor in Brussels grudgingly acknowledged 'this Irish regiment which is the very best in the king of Spain's service'.[123] Despite meeting with further adversity in later years, the Uí Néill *tercio* survived until 1681. This was exceptional. Of the military units raised from the British Isles during the sixteenth and seventeenth centuries, less than 33 per cent survived more than a decade.[124]

'A STIRRING MAN': CONTEMPORARY CRITICISM OF Ó MAOLCHONAIRE

Assured of the survival of the Irish *tercio* in Spanish Flanders and having seen his proposal to clear the Irish from court implemented, Flaithrí Ó Maolchonaire continued his work for Ó Néill and his interests in Madrid.[125] His political activity in the Spanish capital, however, drew sharp criticism from Rome, which was concerned at his neglect of his pastoral duties less than a year after his accession to the see of Tuam. Cardinal Pompeo Arrigone, protector of the Irish, declared that Ó Maolchonaire was exceeding the limits of his office and making unreasonable demands on the papacy.[126] Instead of administering to his archdiocese or even his region, he was dealing with matters pertaining to the kingdom of Ireland.[127] Defending himself against Arrigone's accusations, Flaithrí Ó Maolchonaire wrote to Rome on St Patrick's Day, 1610, pleading papal permission to serve Ó Néill.[128] He pointed to his nomination of a vicar general to the archdiocese.[129] As soon as Philip III favourably resolved the earl's business and other Irish matters, Ó Maolchonaire promised to return to Ireland.[130] He then mentioned the links between the Society of Jesus and the Catholic archbishop of Cashel, David Kearney (†1624) who, he said, intended to travel to Rome hoping to support Old English candidates to the episcopacy in Ireland. Ó Maolchonaire raised this issue at court in Madrid, apparently in defence of Ó Néill-approved Gaelic candidates.[131] Informed of these plans, Philip III wrote to his ambassador in Rome, whereupon Kearney's journey was delayed.[132]

A letter written by Flaithrí Ó Maolchonaire later that year again took up the vexed question of appointments to Irish sees. Ó Maolchonaire complained about the lack of suitable candidates to send to his suffragan bishoprics.[133] In his view, placing members of the Irish Jesuit province in charge of the Irish college at Salamanca had had a detrimental effect upon students from Connacht and Ulster.[134] Apparently blind to other possible reasons for the lack of suitable candidates for these sees, Ó Maolchonaire claimed that both provinces had found themselves in 'extreme necessity' since James I issued orders to place Protestant preachers in all their parishes.[135] This was, perhaps, a plea for special treatment. After giving an account of these developments to Aodh Ó Néill, 'the unworthy archbishop of the province of Connacht' simply communicated the earl's grievances about Ulster at court in Madrid. He had, he averred, proposed nothing to Philip III.[136] Contrary to Ó Maolchonaire's wishes, however, Thomas White SJ was appointed rector of the Irish college at Santiago two years later. He replaced Eugene McCarthy of Fermoy, whose administration is said to have displeased Philip III as students there often returned to Ireland without being ordained.[137]

The following year brought some good news to Ó Maolchonaire regarding the promotion of his own men to Irish sees. When Mateo de Oviedo, archbishop of Dublin, died in January 1610 at Valladolid,[138] Dr Eóghan Mag Mathghamhna, bishop of Clogher was selected as his successor. This satisfied the earl of Tyrone but deeply frustrated Old English Catholics.[139] The son of Éimhear Mag Mathghamhna of Monaghan, Eóghan knew Flaithrí since their Salamanca days together. Eight years earlier, Ó Maolchonaire arranged payments for Mag Mathghamhna's own use at the university and 'to help the Catholics of his country'.[140] Following his consecration, Mag Mathghamhna made his way from Leuven to his diocese.[141] English agents continued to report trouble among Gaelic and Old English émigrés from Ireland, due in part, it was said, to ill-feeling at Ó Maolchonaire's appointment as archbishop.[142] Mag Mathghamhna's appointment can only have exacerbated this animosity. Similar tensions were apparent in the Franciscan college in Leuven where Aodh Mac Aingil appears to have caused friction between the friars. Donnchadh Ó Maonaigh explained how matters had developed:

> While I was in France reading for the good of my province as someone that the brothers would have known, I left behind in this house of Leuven Aodh Mac Aingil, elected by the brothers as guardian. Father Flaithrí had sent his affirmation to him from Rome.[143]

The affirmation from Ó Maolchonaire referred to here may be the letters patent he wrote while still minister-provincial, placing Mac Aingil in charge of the college.[144] Ó Maonaigh subsequently wrote to the guardian of Multyfarnham friary:

> [...] the best young men in the colleges are coming from the hands of the Jesuits and Capuchins, and Mac Aingil is rejecting them insultingly even after the friars had given a promise to accept them. He does not accept my advice on this matter or the advice of the whole house. I myself was going along this road and news reached me from Flaithrí not to go there [Leuven] yet.[145]

These tensions did not hamper Catholic pastoral activity in Ireland, a point borne out by the apprehension expressed by the lord deputy in Dublin, who referred to 'the access of bishops, priests, Jesuits and friars into this land from other parts since Christmas last, [which occurred] in far greater numbers than at anytime heretofore'.[146] In this regard, Sir Arthur Chichester (†1625) referred specifically to Flaithrí Ó Maolchonaire as 'a stirring man'. 'Made archbishop of Tuam,' Chichester said, Ó Maolchonaire was 'well-known to be in favour in the courts of Spain and Rome, beyond all others of his profession of this nation.'[147] Ó Maolchonaire's role in Leuven enabled him to exercise considerable control in Ireland, where the newly trained friars were deployed. This also won him the plaudit of the Brussels nuncio who reported that there were 100 friars in Ireland, where the order was always held 'in great esteem'.[148]

Ó Maolchonaire's continued absence from his see, however, raised eyebrows in Rome and caused concern to Peter Lombard, Catholic primate of Ireland and archbishop of Armagh.[149] For his part, Ó Maolchonaire continued to plead that his special responsibilities on behalf of the Uí Néill made his presence in Madrid imperative. The papal briefs written to Philip III in 1609 and carried to Madrid by Ó Maolchonaire confirmed this, he argued.[150]

At this time, Lombard became more vocal in his criticism of Ó Maolchonaire and of Ó Néill. This was in the context of his own changing political position. To help convince James I of 'the desirability of unity and coming to a better understanding with his Irish subjects', Lombard had composed a Latin treatise 'to show how the cause of that country could be best served by retaining the Irish in the old faith to which they have clung despite the efforts to deprive them of it'.[151] In 1612 he wrote to the pope, expressing his displeasure with the Ó Maolchonaire and Mag Mathghamhna appointments stating that they had only been promoted on the earl of Tyrone's insistence and against the primate's wishes.[152] Flaithrí Ó Maolchonaire, he alleged, was unjustified in his resistance towards the king of England and his ministers. Rather than returning to his archdiocese, Ó Maolchonaire, Lombard argued, was more eager to renew the war than the military commanders themselves.[153] In a letter to Maffeo Barberini, one Thomas White reiterated the Catholic primate's concerns about the promotion of 'il Padre Fra Florento' and his agency for Ó Néill.[154]

Some of Lombard's entourage were also hostile to Ó Maolchonaire. Having lodged 'with his unkle in the same palace with the earle of Tyrone', Robert Lombard of Waterford informed Sir Dudley Carleton (†1632) of Ó Néill's 'purpose to leave Rome and go into Flanders […] to transport those Irish companies which are there in the king of Spaine's service into Ireland, and there raise rebellion'.[155] Perturbed to hear that the *tercio* remained intact after the reform of forces in Spanish Flanders, Carleton was told that the Conde de Castro had presented Ó Néill with letters from Philip III 'for their transmigration to Brussels', offering money while awaiting funds from Madrid and papal approval for the expedition. Describing Flaithrí Ó Maolchonaire as 'able and active as wicked and malicious', the young Lombard declared that 'upon this man's practising […] he conceives more of this enterprise to be founded.'[156] On being asked 'what were his inducements to make this discovery', the archbishop of Armagh's nephew expressed the view that 'religion was the pretence of their designs, but ambition the true motive' and stated that he wished 'to obtaine hereby the grace and favour' of James I:

The condition of all the other provinces to be subject to those Ulster lords would be most miserable [and] your Majestie's Clemency ... would be turned into so great displeasure that they would promise themselves nothing but the oppression of their persons and the utter extirpation of their religion.[157]

Seizing upon the lack of trust between Irish exiles, Carleton was particularly struck by Robert Lombard's insistence upon the 'integrity and loyalty' of his uncle, 'besides his love and devotion to your majestie's person and service – as if the effect of his coming unto me had been to negotiate in his favour'.[158]

In an effort to quell dissent among the secular and regular clergy in Ireland, Peter Lombard had sent David Rothe (†1650) there as vice-primate of Armagh about 1609.[159] Ó Maolchonaire, although he stoutly supported the interests of the regular clergy, was also sensitive to episcopal authority. In 1613, to counteract criticism of the Franciscans, he instructed them to dress and act as recollects.[160] Though Ó Maolchonaire does not identify exact cases of indiscipline, according to Cathaldus Giblin, the provincial chapters of 1612 and 1615 indicate that among other things some Irish friars were not wearing the religious habit as prescribed by the *regulae* of their order.[161] In response, perhaps, Ó Maolchonaire composed a tract on episcopal jurisdiction over mendicant friars, particularly in cases of misconduct, drawing upon specific canons of the Council of Trent, together with the teachings *multorum aliorum Pontificum*.[162]

Controversies about mendicancy were nothing new but, as Rothe's opposition shows, it remained something of a jurisdictional hornet's nest.[163] The friars had been granted apostolic privileges by Sixtus IV (†1484) to preach and exercise the pastoral ministry in 1471. According to Cardinal Giovanni Maria Del Monte (†1577), president of the Council of Trent and later Pope Julius III (†1555), these privileges 'did not injure the divine right of the bishops'. Nevertheless, this question remained one of the most contentious of the entire proceedings until, during session twenty-five, the legates agreed to uphold the mendicants' privilege.[164]

In his document, Flaithrí Ó Maolchonaire applied specific decrees on how episcopal authority could be brought to bear in cases of ill-discipline among the regular clergy.[165] Opening his argument, Ó Maolchonaire applied *Ius novum Tridentini* from session 6, chapter 3 to Irish friars.[166] This stated that 'the excesses of secular clerics and regulars, who live out of their monasteries, shall be corrected by the Ordinary of the place.' No regular 'living out of his monastery, shall, under pretext of a privilege of his order, be accounted, if he transgress, exempt from being visited, punished, and corrected'.[167] In the case of Ireland, however, the suppression of the monasteries and the confiscation of ecclesiastical property had led to itinerant practices among the Catholic clergy.[168] Next, Ó Maolchonaire drew attention to session 7, chapter 14 of the decree on sacraments for 'civil causes of exempted persons which may be taken cognisance of by bishops'.[169] This upheld the decree of Pope Innocent IV (†1254) at Lyons,[170] adding that 'relative to wages, and to persons in distress, clerics, whether seculars, or regulars who live out of their monasteries, howsoever exempted [...] may be brought before the Ordinaries of the places, and be constrained and compelled by course of law to pay what they owe'.[171]

Ó Maolchonaire then turned to session 25, chapter 14.[172] It concerned 'by whom punishment is to be inflicted on a regular who sins publicly':

> A regular who, not being subject to the bishop, and residing within the enclosure of a monastery, has out of that enclosure transgressed so notoriously as to be a scandal to the people, shall, at the instance of the bishop, be severely punished by his own superior, within such time as the bishop shall appoint.[173]

The decree continues that the superior was expected to 'certify to the bishop' that the punishment had been exacted, 'otherwise he shall be himself deprived of his office by his own superior, and the delinquent may be punished by the bishop.'[174] In view of contemporary Irish religious politics, Ó Maolchonaire summed up by emphasising the importance of adhering to the decrees. As long as the quarrelling went on between Irish regular and secular clergy, Ó Maolchonaire said, it gave the upper hand to the heretics, who were 'boasting and leaping over' the Catholics with their jurisdiction. It was this that made it difficult, he continued, for Catholic bishops, such as himself, to make public use of their own authority 'in the kingdom of Ireland'. For the mendicants to relinquish their apostolic privileges to preach and exercise the pastoral ministry would only allow the established state church to stretch forth their authority in Ireland. Without a resolution to the problem, ill-discipline was being punished with imprisonment instead of being settled from within.[175]

The most senior Catholic cleric in Ireland at that time was the vice-primate of Armagh, David Rothe, a severe critic of the mendicants on the grounds that their way of life led to 'a vagabond clergy'. Nevertheless, the Franciscan mission to Ulster in 1610 showed that the diocesan system was in a state of collapse. In Clogher and Down, friars had to live in *domus refugi* complete with a chapel and often set in forests.[176] Mass was celebrated in the homes of their patrons and preaching appears to have become confined to the friars. It was in this context that they developed the concept of a Gaelic Maccabean battle and their sermons referred to contemporary events in apocalyptic terms.[177] In 1612, at the Franciscan general definitory, the Irish province of the order had been granted the privilege of presenting the names of Irish friars for nomination as canonical visitors of their own province. According to Benignus Millett, this special right was granted:

> [...] because of persecution, as the times were too disturbed for a foreign friar to enter the country and perform the canonical visitation of the friaries and their communities without being detected by the civil authorities and imprisoned.[178]

When one takes all these factors into consideration, it seems fair to say that, despite objections from the Irish secular clergy, there was a strong case in favour of the regulars. As far as Ó Maolchonaire was concerned, it seems, drastic conditions in the country urgently needed to be addressed. In the event that episcopal jurisdiction had to be exercised over mendicant friars, particularly in cases of misconduct, he held that sufficient measures were already in place for action to be taken. Nevertheless, this document also drew attention to the Catholic archbishop of Tuam's absence from his own archiepiscopal see. The criticism levelled at Ó Maolchonaire by Lombard and his allies in this regard was set to intensify during the next decade.

ALIGNING IRISH PRIORITIES WITH THOSE OF SPAIN

In spite of the criticism which greeted his elevation to the archbishopric of Tuam, Flaithrí Ó Maolchonaire continued his mission as resident at court in Madrid from 1609 to 1618.[179] His voice represented one political group among many competing for attention and causing friction at this time. Envoys from Portugal, the Italian and German states, Flanders and Brabant, England and Scotland all congregated in Madrid.[180] Residents at court were not just the personal representative of the political figure who sent them, but active agents 'for gathering information and weaving intrigue'.[181] With fewer important matters to press, lengthy service at court made agents 'less negotiators, more purely observers'.[182] Ó Maolchonaire's mission was in part to ensure that the Spanish continued their financial support of the earls' entourage. It was inevitable that Philip III and his ministers should expect continued service for the subsidy awarded to members of the Irish military and religious communities in Habsburg territories. As highlighted by Óscar Recio Morales, the Irish at court tried to ensure that their priorities were presented as those of Spain to safeguard their political interests.[183]

Since the turn of the twentieth century, historians have drawn attention to the strong links which persisted between Ireland's southern and western ports and Spain and France in the 1600s.[184] Spanish gold and silver was described in contemporary sources as 'the coin that most aboundeth and is chiefly reckoned on in that nation, especially in Connaught and Munster'.[185] Wine continued to be the main Spanish import to Ireland: and of the inhabitants of Galway it was said: 'They do greatly trade with other countries, especially Spain, from whence they used to fetch great stores of wine and other wares every year.'[186]

The cargoes of salmon, herrings and pilchards and other Irish fish shipped to several ports of Spain and Venice throughout the 1600s 'would startle common people' according to contemporary reports.[187] Large quantities of ambergrease for the fishing industry were brought by merchants from Galway to Spain where it was 'held to be as good and perfect as any'.[188] Woollen goods were manufactured for export to Spain for a higher return than England. When in later years restrictions were placed upon its sale, Irish wool was smuggled to Spain under the pretence of shipping it to England.[189]

By 1614, a significant increase in Irish trading contacts with ports in England, Wales and Scotland became apparent. For example, a substantial proportion of the wine which continued to be the main Spanish import to Ireland was transported in English ships.[190] The victualling in Irish ports of ships from England became regarded as 'one very valuable species of trade'.[191] In the same year, Oliver St John (†1630) noted that 'great good will come to this kingdom by transporting cattle and corn hence into England, for this kingdom will be able to spare great quantity of both.' Tillage yields remained at an exceptional level throughout the decade and large numbers of hides also continued to be exported to Spain.[192] In return, salt, hops, iron ore and clay for glass-making were imported into Ireland.[193]

In the absence of official diplomatic contact with Ireland, it was Ó Maolchonaire who kept Antonio de Aroztegui, secretary of state, informed of developments. He appears to have operated outside official state circles, using a combination of messengers and merchant post to communicate with Ireland. In 1611, Ó Maolchonaire wrote that he received news from Irish ships which sailed from Dublin and Waterford to Bilbao.[194] Seven years later, he provided a testimonial to Stephen England, an Irish resident of the Basque port and one of a network of Irish couriers who carried letters and helped new arrivals in the north of Spain.[195] His duties there may have included delivery of secret correspondence described by Ó Maolchonaire.[196] An Irishman based in Galicia, Gaspar Grant, also relayed messages from Ireland to Spain.[197] It is quite clear, however, that Ó Maolchonaire's most trusted source of intelligence on Ireland was St Anthony's, Leuven. According to a physician who treated Aodh Ó Néill, 'the frères in Flanders receive letters every three months from Ireland. There is but few things done in the court of Ireland, be it ever so secret, but it will be heard or else sought out by them.'[198]

Flaithrí Ó Maolchonaire's correspondence at this time reveals that he accumulated information before delivery, condensing the different subject categories per report.[199] This enabled him to provide the court with reports of religious persecution against Catholics, the colonisation of Virginia, and the activities of English pirates off the Irish south coast which severely hindered trade contact. Each of these points appealed to Spain's ambassador to the court of James I from 1613, Don Diego Sarmiento de Acuña, Conde de Gondomar (†1626), especially 'buccaneering'.[200] This was not the first or last time that the paths of Ó Maolchonaire and Gondomar crossed. Both had been at Valladolid earlier in their careers where the latter served as *Corregidor*, royal representative, from 1602 to 1605.[201] They subsequently corresponded with one another and, until the start of negotiations for a Spanish Match, Ó Maolchonaire related his political interests to those of Philip III's ambassador to London.[202] Up to that point, in letters to Joseph Creswell and to Ó Maolchonaire, Gondomar expressed soft words of admiration for Irish Catholics and his hopes that James I would offer them a statute of toleration.[203]

For the time being, Irish hopes of Spanish military intervention were not compatible with 'the desired stalemate' for his king: preventing James I from entering a renewed war against Spain.[204] With few exceptions, Aodh Ó Néill's calls for an armed response to the confiscation of his lands fell on deaf ears in Madrid. Thus, for the short term at least, Flaithrí Ó Maolchonaire left aside his 'militancy' and adopted a more circumspect approach to dealing with Philip III. During this period of peace, he sought to improve Irish economic interests within Spain's sphere of influence. In doing so he competed against the claims of English merchants who were eager to advance their cause at court.[205] As we shall see, Ó

Maolchonaire's treatise on the Spanish Match pays particular attention to the potentially adverse effects of an Anglo-Spanish marriage on the Indies trade.[206]

According to contemporary reports, the 'hordes of pirates [which] infested the southern coast' had a very harmful effect upon Irish trade.[207] In 1611 Ó Maolchonaire received news that 'all of the English corsairs' responsible for naval raids against Spanish interests were sheltering off the coast of west Cork. They revictualled and repaired their vessels there before setting out on new raids against Spanish and Flemish ships at sea. Unprotected by either a fort or garrison, Ó Maolchonaire asserted they were susceptible to a Spanish naval attack.[208]

The council of state in Madrid was concerned about the issues Ó Maolchonaire raised concerning English piracy. On 9 October 1611, a report about the pirate ships leaving from Ireland under English protection was sent to Philip III's ambassador to be presented to James I, whereupon a group of three advisers were assigned to find a remedy for the problems caused by buccaneering.[209] Despite a statute of James I which entitled the Irish to trade freely overseas,[210] the English consul in Andalucía was accused of unfairness towards Irish merchants. To overcome this, Flaithrí Ó Maolchonaire applied to the council of state to provide merchants from Ireland with their own representative in southern Spain.[211] In return for sustaining Irish and Spanish trading contacts, Philip III's state coffers would benefit as a result of the customs duties of increased commerce. 'Each year,' Ó Maolchonaire reported, 'many Irish ships and much Irish merchandise comes to the Sanlúcar de Barrameda port of Santa María y Cadiz':

> [...] usually visited by an Englishman named Thomas James Morador with whom the said Irish do not get on well and he causes them much inconvenience and harm for being from an enemy *naçion* and of a different language.[212]

To remedy the situation 'en nombre de toda la naçion irlandessa', Ó Maolchonaire proposed that Nicholas Wise, an Irish innkeeper who lived in Sanlúcar with his Spanish wife, be made 'consul of all the Irish on that coast'.[213] In October 1608, a soldier of the same name in Thomas Stanihurst's Irish *tercio* company received 50 ducados. He may also have been the same Nicholas, brother of Andrew Wise, a knight of the order of Malta, who supported Domhnall O'Sullivan Beare's application to enter the military order of Santiago.[214]

Responding to Ó Maolchonaire's memorial, the council of state declared that, even though Wise was 'a most commendable Catholic', it would be inconvenient to make him consul, justifying the decision by saying that the 'very Catholic and loyal' Morador was 'intelligent and trustworthy', and well deserving of his office, which included *entretenimiento* from the king of Spain. The Marqués de Villafranca (†1627) and Don Agustín Messía acknowledged that, due to 'the complaints and enmity between the Irish and English' it would be equitable to appoint an Irish representative.[215]

Nevertheless, the consejo decided that Nicholas Wise could not be accepted as consul of the Sanlúcar Irish without giving him 'more authority and jurisdiction'. Besides, the comendador mayor de León said, consuls were in the habit of acting 'for all the peoples of their king even though they are different'. James Morador was 'consul of Great Britain in which Ireland and Scotland are included for being all of the Crown of England'.[216] Allegations of Morador's partiality seem to have continued, however, leading to the appointment of Ó Maolchonaire's ally James Fitzgerald as 'consul de la *nación* yrlandesa en la costa de Anduluçia' by 1620, a time when Irish appeals to court on economic grounds re-emerged.[217]

The safekeeping of Spain's recently discovered possessions in the New World, and the commercial benefits which resulted from them, caused considerable unease among the counsellors of Philip III.[218] Flaithrí Ó Maolchonaire took advantage of this sense of anxiety when, in 1610, he presented them with a detailed account of what an Irishman, Francis Magnel, had learned in Virginia over the eight months he was there.[219] A crew member under the command of Captain Christopher Newport, Magnel has been identified by D. B. Quinn as one of the original settlers of the new colony.[220] The report that Ó Maolchonaire provided to the council of state revealed the different routes to Virginia taken by the English and provides a full description of their settlement and fortifications there; and the colony's rich, unexploited natural resources. Moreover, the archbishop advised, the native population were liable to believe 'in the God of the English'.[221]

Magnel's information enabled Ó Maolchonaire to report 'the designs and intentions of the English against His Catholic Majesty'; that is, the serious threat posed by the new English colony to Spain's overseas territories and commerce. Magnel had learned of three routes to the South Atlantic which he had 'seen or heard said and dealt with among the most important of the English' when he was in Virginia:

> The English intend nothing else so much as to make themselves lords of the southern sea in order to have their part of the riches of the Indies and to cut off the trade of the king of Spain and to seek new worlds for themselves.[222]

In order to achieve their aims, Ó Maolchonaire explained, the new settlers intended to construct a succession of forts along the routes and, to this end, James I had 'sent the best carpenters of his kingdom'. Further, Virginia abounded in the natural resources necessary for shipbuilding. At the new colony's iron mines they had already erected machinery. With 'a great abundance of the best timber', and plentiful quantities of pitch, resin tar and hemp to make cables and ropes, the English intended to extend their influence south towards Spanish territory.[223] Drawing attention to this threat, Ó Maolchonaire signalled the value of Magnel's information to the Spanish:

> [...] so great is their caution that the secrets of this country [Virginia] shall not be disclosed that they have given orders forbidding anyone from taking letters with him out of the country, and especially from sending any to private individuals without first being seen and read by the governor.[224]

As Spain struggled to avoid bankruptcy in the early seventeenth century, trade from the Indies was even more highly valued and this only deepened Spain's concerns about the vulnerability of its outposts across the Atlantic.[225] A fortnight after Flaithrí Ó Maolchonaire's report, the council of state notified Philip III of the archbishop's news which he had accompanied with a request to employ

Magnel in the king's service, 'because it will not be good to lose him'.[226] The protector of the Irish at court, Don Diego Brochero, himself a naval commander, was ordered 'that, having informed himself of this Irishman's qualities, he should advise the best course of action', stating that Magnel's reputation as a gunner suggested he was deserving of a post in the navy.[227] The admissibility of Magnel's evidence was called into question the following year, however, when the Spanish learned that the southern sea was 400 leagues from Virginia, across harsh terrain unfamiliar to the native people themselves.[228]

Flaithrí Ó Maolchonaire's control of information from Irish sources during this decade ensured that the interests of Ó Néill and his allies continued to be represented at court in Madrid. Nonetheless, Ó Maolchonaire's partisan reports to Philip III and his advisers were of limited use in so far as they helped the Spanish quantify the threat posed by England. In the interests of preserving Spain's peace deal with England, the Spanish authorities appear to have been willing to turn a blind eye to a mainstay of Ó Maolchonaire's case for intervention in Ireland – religious persecution. His frustrated hopes of closer economic ties with the Iberian Peninsula also proved incompatible with improving Anglo-Spanish relations. The most he and his allies could now look forward to was the possibility of renewed military action in the event that peace with England collapsed.

SECURING IRISH EARNINGS FROM SPANISH COFFERS

During this period, Ó Maolchonaire continued to try to infuence control of Spanish funds for the Irish. In the changing circumstances of the time, this was not a straightforward process. Following the death of the earl of Tyrone's eldest son in August 1610, Ó Maolchonaire and Ó Néill tried to recover what was owed to him by the Spanish crown. Ó Maolchonaire wrote to Lerma asking him to make arrangements with the president of finance for payment of the 2,288 escudos due for Éinrí's military service and 1,200 ducados owed to the legatees named in his will. Objections had been raised on the grounds that, as Éinrí had served in the Southern Netherlands, the will should be executed in Brussels rather than Spain.[229] In Brussels there was a reluctance to meet these demands.[230]

In the event, Lerma responded favourably to Ó Maolchonaire's request, but dealt solely with the question of the dead colonel's debts.[231] Spanish financial constraints explain the failure to settle matters properly at this time.[232] It is worth noting that Lerma kept Éinrí Ó Néill's papers along with the receipts for payments on behalf of the Ulster earls in 1602. These consisted of 500 ducados for Aodh Ó Néill, 3,500 reales for Aodh Ruadh Ó Domhnaill's funeral and Masses for the repose of his soul, 200 ducados to two of his creditors, and 750 ducados to nineteen of his followers, including Flaithrí Ó Maolchonaire.[233] He paid the monies for Ó Domhnaill's obsequies a full week before the young earl's death.[234]

Éinrí's debts remained unsettled and in the absence of any increase to his own monthly pension, Aodh Ó Néill appealed to the king through the Conde de Castro, Spain's ambassador in Rome, for a resolution.[235] Four months before the earl's death, Philip III assured de Castro that 'the necessary steps will be taken to procure prompt payment of the amount owed.'[236] The trail of evidence seems to run cold here, though, suggesting that matters went no further.

Ó Maolchonaire found it difficult enough to secure an ecclesiastical allowance for himself at court. Payment of this allowance depended on three *cédulas* from the Consejos de Cámara and Hacienda followed by instructions issued from secretary of state Antonio de Arostegui to the treasurer general Don Juan Ybañéz de Segobia. The latter recorded that, 'not having enjoyed the benefits of his dignity' and 'after enduring discomfort at court', Ó Maolchonaire was to receive 1,000 ducados per year 'in consideration of his many good parts'.[237]

Acknowledging his services to Philip III, the archbishop was to be reimbursed 800 ducados for each year he had spent at court since his return from Rome in 1609. Four payments were to be made annually to Ó Maolchonaire from *las arcas de tres llaves*, the most reliable source of finance at the Spanish court, and were obtained from funds provided for the *tercios*.[238] Unlike numerous unanswered petitions at court, this record, coming as it does from the treasurer general's own accounts, provides us with clear evidence that Ó Maolchonaire received what he had been promised. Taking care to ensure his hard-earned income was maintained prior to his departure for Spanish Flanders several years later, Ó Maolchonaire approached Lerma, who notified the president of finance of Philip III's resolve to continue the stipend.[239] This was confirmed three weeks later with a *cédula* from the king, declaring that the archbishop of Tuam also receive 500 ducados to offset the costs of his journey. The eleven consejeros each endorsed the order with their rubrics, autographed initials, and stated that the money be paid by Don Juan Ybañéz de Segobia.[240] Philip III followed this up with a letter to Archduke Albert, recommending that Ó Maolchonaire receive the same allowance in the Southern Netherlands that he had been paid in Spain.[241] As the next section shows, Flaithrí Ó Maolchonaire's reaction to the Dublin parliament of 1613–15 signalled a return to a consideration of military solutions to their difficulties.

PARLIAMENT IN DUBLIN, 1613–15

Since 1611, Flaithrí Ó Maolchonaire knew of government plans in Dublin to contain the Catholic clergy and enforce an oath of supremacy, following the rejection of these proposed measures by the earl of Clanricard.[242] That year, the archbishop of Tuam notified Madrid of the arrest and imprisonment of Conor O'Devany (†1612), 'a saintly old bishop', along with Patrick O'Loughran (†1612), a former confessor of Aodh Ó Néill, and other priests 'who were there serving God in secret'.[243] Ó Maolchonaire explained this in the context of an edict ordering 'that all priests and religious leave within a period of six months ending next December under pain of death' which Clanricard, 'Irish governor of the province of Connacht', had rejected as an invention of James I's counsel.

At a meeting of the Council of Ireland in Dublin, Chichester called upon Clanricard to sign the decree so that it could be published, but he had refused.[244] Believing it to be an invention of the lord deputy, the earl had then set sail for

England to give an account of events to James I. The Spanish council of state's annotations on the reverse side of Ó Maolchonaire's letter recommend that Don Alonso Velasco be directed to bring up all these matters in London.[245]

In receipt of correspondence from Ireland every twelve weeks, Flaithrí Ó Maolchonaire kept the Spanish secretary of state, Antonio de Aroztegui, informed of these developments.[246] From London, Philip III's ambassador substantiated claims of persecution against English and Irish Catholics, which had increased since the publication of 'el libro y la doctrina del Padre Suarez' in 1613.[247] Within a year the book was burned in London and Paris. Sir John Digby, James I's ambassador to Madrid, called for the work of Suárez to be condemned in Spain. Philip III responded by calling for an enquiry which judged that the Suárez thesis concurred with the teachings of the Church Fathers. This was conveyed to James I, accompanied with calls to show tolerance towards his Catholic subjects.[248] As stated below, in common with other political thinkers of his time, Ó Maolchonaire found in the works of Suárez 'an arsenal of polemics [...] ready to seek and receive truth'.[249]

Otherwise unable to secure government interests in Ireland, Chichester and Davies had made arrangements for the calling of an Irish parliament as soon as the Ulster plantation was underway.[250] In response to Chichester's invitation to 'the nobility at large to suggest legislation which might be considered', six Catholic lords wrote in protest to James.[251] Plans for the parliament of 1613, the first in Ireland for over a quarter of a century, were greeted with consternation by the Catholic hierarchy. In a letter written to the Irish college at Salamanca, the archbishop of Cashel, David Kearney, expressed the view that 'the heretics intend to vomit out all their poison and infect with it the purity of our holy religion, and it is expected that things will take place in it such as have not been seen since the schism of Henry VIII began.'[252] In the meantime, reports to Rome from the nuncio at Brussels stated that Irish Catholic nobles wished to avoid being forced to accept laws against their religion, which were said to include an oath of allegiance to James I.[253]

Davies was determined to have a Protestant majority in the lower house.[254] The lack of 'a standard survey of property in Ulster' enabled him to alter the parliamentary franchise, thereby helping to ensure the desired outcome in the Commons.[255] He described the newly created pocket boroughs as 'perpetual seminaries of Protestant burgesses' as those who packed them would assuredly take the oath of allegiance.[256] However, many of the constituencies incorporated returned members 'incapable by law, not resident in these boroughs, and utter strangers to the places which elected them'.[257]

Controversy was ensured when both houses gathered in the great hall at Dublin Castle and the parliament opened on 18 May 1613.[258] A delegation of Catholic lords protested to James I against the illegally incorporated boroughs and other measures designed to emasculate the Anglo-Irish.[259] At the second session, the start of which had been delayed for over a year, an act for the attainder of 'Tirone, Tirconnel, Sir Cahir O Dougherty (†1608) and some others concerned in rebellion or conspiracy' was presented to the Commons by Everard. This declared, by parliamentary statute and without recourse to trial, that those named were guilty of sedition. Passed unanimously, the bill 'received the royal assent at the prorogation of 29 November 1614'.[260]

After a reasonably successful campaign of obstruction, especially at the first session, Ó Maolchonaire was incensed to learn that Catholic members of parliament had voted Ó Néill's attainder. He was particularly displeased at the advice they continued to receive from members of the clergy. Writing from the convent of St Francis in Valladolid the following March, he regarded the conduct of the Catholic party as unconstitutional. Due process had not been adhered to, he argued, and injustice could not be allowed in the hope that good would arise from it. His Leuven confrères sought to use Ireland's cultural legacy to galvanise their pastoral mission and, in his letter of protest, Ó Maolchonaire speaks of restoring Ireland's laws and customs to their 'ancient greatness and splendour'.[261] In a comment reminiscent of his protest against the Irish college at Salamanca in May 1602, he contended that those who had refused help to Ó Néill against heresy were complicit in accepting the attainder and God would strike against Ireland in retaliation. Describing the resulting deed as a breach of divine law, he declared that civil obedience should only be shown towards a just Catholic ruler who has received power from God. Acting out of shortsighted self-interest, Ó Maolchonaire predicted, had merely delayed their own retribution at government hands.[262] Interestingly, the key issue of land versus faith re-arose in the 1640s when a number of Catholic confederates showed their aversion towards Rinuccini's mission for an Irish restoration.[263]

Since the arrival of the newly established state Church and its reforms in the reign of Elizabeth Tudor, Flaithrí Ó Maolchonaire's family had witnessed the abrupt transition brought by new landholding practices in Gaelic society.[264] Six years prior to Ó Maolchonaire's departure from Ireland, 'the Grange of the O'Mulconry' was recorded as belonging 'to the queen'.[265] These ongoing developments certainly help to explain the vehement tone of his Valladolid remonstrance.

The Uí Mhaoilchonaire continued to hold large amounts of land in the early seventeenth century but, as there was no formal plantation in Roscommon, Gaelic landowners such as Flaithrí Ó Maolchonaire's brother Maoilechlainn had to take on protracted legal action to retain possession.[266] This caused indebtedness and the mortgage of property. Thus, the illusion of landowning was kept alive in many native families, while its actual control was in the hands of newcomers or anglicised natives.[267] Unfamiliar with the new forms of landholding introduced, native landowners such as the Uí Mhaoilchonaire maintained the Gaelic practice of partible inheritance among sept members. Sub-division led to the fragmentation of holdings as common law recognised only a sole owner, rather than reversible entitlement between kinsmen.[268] Those with access to office and money benefited from the 'consequent conveyance and consolidation of such small holdings'.[269]

The borough of Roscommon was incorporated in February 1613 and, as was the case with most Protestant representatives in the Commons, those returned were members of the military and planter class, namely Sir John King and Sir Oliver St John.[270] The plantation of the neighbouring counties of Leitrim and

Longford encouraged the arrival of settlers in Roscommon, one of the few areas of English settlement in Connacht after 1614.[271] Sir John King, a leading English administrator and large-scale speculator, was granted five quarters of former Uí Mhaoilchonaire freehold on lease as crown land.[272] This decision was upheld in 1619.[273] A series of exchequer inquisitions held to ascertain ownership in the surrounding district included eight claims to smaller freeholdings by Flaithrí Ó Maolchonaire's brother Maoilechlainn and his relatives.[274]

Sir Oliver St John was a privy councillor and James I's master of the ordnance in Ireland. Having commanded 25 horse and 150 foot in Roscommon, he was recommended by Cecil for the office of vice-president of Connacht in 1602.[275] While in Roscommon he acquired manuscripts such as the Annals of Boyle, compiled in the monastery founded by Clarus Ó Maolchonaire on Holy Trinity Island in Loch Cé. St John subsequently donated this manuscript to the Cotton library.[276] An active participant in the parliament, particularly in the dispute about the speakership, St John was one of three *avant-couriers* sent ahead of the Catholic lords by Chichester 'to counteract their practices' in June 1613.[277]

MILITARY PETITION RENEWED

As discussed earlier in this chapter, faced with Habsburg reserve towards the earl of Tyrone's calls for a new military expedition to Ireland, Ó Maolchonaire was impelled to turn his attention to the needs of the exiled Irish constituency in Spain. In March 1615, however, at the moment when the archbishop penned his remonstrance against the Bill of Attainder, Aodh Ó Néill renewed the case for his return to Ireland at the head of an army.[278] To this end, he entrusted Ó Maolchonaire with correspondence for Lerma and the council of state.[279] Ó Néill then sent the recusant leader William Miagh to assist the archbishop in Madrid.[280]

In 1603, as recorder of the corporation of Cork, Miagh had resisted calls to declare James VI of Scotland successor to Elizabeth as king of Ireland. 'With the demise of the crown,' the corporation proclaimed themselves 'sovereign within their own liberties.'[281] Mass was celebrated in public, religious objects were openly venerated and the churches were re-consecrated in Miagh's presence. 'The gentlemen jurists of Cork' refused to find him guilty of treason, 'in spite of most violent and unlawful courses taken to influence them and procure a conviction.'[282] Instead Catholic nobles from Munster sent Miagh to Spain, offering Philip III the kingdom of Ireland.[283] From there he made his way to Naples where he was retained on forty ducados per month.[284]

William Miagh arrived at court in June 1615.[285] Philip III's intelligence chief, André Velasquez de Velasco, held discussions with the archbishop, with John Bathe, Miagh and O'Sullivan Beare on the situation in Ireland.[286] Instructions were then sent to Rome telling the earl that his pleas would be considered, whereupon Ó Maolchonaire wrote to Velasquez de Velasco asking for the Irish *tercio* to be given leave to sail from Flanders.[287] This he accompanied with calls to assist the Ulster earls' Scottish kinsman James MacDonnell, the lord of Kintyre, who had raised forces after escaping captivity in Edinburgh.[288] Underlining his combined approach to the religious mission and military action,

Ó Maolchonaire advocated sending friars from Leuven to Scotland while also seeking Spanish aid for an invasion of the country.[289] On receipt of renewed protests from London, Velasquez de Velasco responded to Ó Néill's proposed return to Ireland at the head of an army by advising Ó Maolchonaire against announcing the earl's intentions to Lerma.[290]

There appears to be little original evidence to support the claim made by some that Ó Maolchonaire curtailed his work in Madrid to make the voyage to Rome, resolved his differences with Peter Lombard and joined him to console the dying earl.[291] This was, after all, 'an age of slow communication in which the most routine absence was inevitably long' and one could not travel on credit.[292] On average, the journey from Madrid to Rome took twenty days.[293] Aodh Ó Néill died after continuous fevers on 20 July 1616. Cardinal Gaspar de Borja y Velasco notified Gondomar that he had paid for Ó Néill's funeral, 'a most solemn burial', which was held the following day.[294] Less than a month later, 'upon the news of his death', Ó Maolchonaire travelled from Alcalá de Henares to the Escorial palace on the outskirts of Madrid where he discussed the state of Irish affairs with Philip III. Plans to land another military expedition in Ireland during the third Habsburg's reign had died with Ó Néill.[295]

SGÁTHÁN AN CHRÁBHAIDH: MIRROR OF DEVOTION

Waiting on political events, Ó Maolchonaire availed of the opportunity to immerse himself in scholarship once again.[296] He and Luke Wadding were well acquainted with one another in Madrid where Ó Maolchonaire studied St Augustine in great detail, especially his doctrine of grace.[297] The influence of St Augustine is clear in Ó Maolchonaire's Sgáthán an Chrábhaidh, which refers to the bishop of Hippo as 'the marvellous eagle of the Scriptures who surpassed the other Doctors of the Church'.[298] A translation into Irish of the allegorical Catalan tale Spill de la Vida Religiosa, it was published at Leuven in 1616. According to the philologist R. I. Best, Sgáthán an Chrábhaidh can be 'justly regarded as a masterpiece of Irish prose'.[299] Ó Maolchonaire may have become familiar with the original text during his studies at Salamanca where the eleventh Castilian edition had been published in 1580. He also used a copy of the original Catalan for his Irish translation.[300] The Castilian source, however, was essential to Ó Maolchonaire's work. It used allegories from Franciscan devotional texts concerned with the via mystica: the love of God; the shepherd well equipped to watch his flock, who may, in turn, symbolise the episcopacy; the difficult path through a harsh desert; the virtuous female adviser who accompanies the protagonist Desiderius on his way; the watchdog of goodwill and the servant of chastity.[301]

The Franciscan theme continues with Ó Maolchonaire's title page woodcut showing Christ on the road to Calvary followed by members of the three Franciscan orders each carrying their own cross.[302] This example of Franciscan iconography was replicated by Fra Giovanni Sgaury in his Wadding cloister frescoes at St Isidore's College, Rome. In keeping with his family's manuscript tradition, at the very start of the work, Ó Maolchonaire opens with an invocation to Emanuel.[303] While recognising the original work's popular appeal, Ó

Maolchonaire added substantial sections to the Spanish text. These, his own interpolations, may have been drawn from polemical literature of the period.[304]

Of these passages, 1,500 lines added in the middle of *Sgáthán an Chrábhaidh* relate directly to contemporary Irish politics, encouraging Catholics to persevere in the face of religious persecution.[305] Ó Maolchonaire begins by highlighting the falseness of heresy before applying Bellarmine's distinction between temporal and spiritual authority to early seventeenth-century Ireland.[306] It is the duty of men, he averred, to know that temporal authority only applies to the temporal sphere and is, in turn, obtained from God. Spiritual authority therefore remains paramount.[307] Rather than being invested with power from Rome, bishops of the newly established state Church based their authority on the false teachings of Luther and Calvin, which have the colour of truth to deceive ordinary people.[308] At this point, since James I lacked true spiritual power, and his temporal power depended on the will of the Irish people, Ó Maolchonaire advised Catholics against taking the oath of allegiance regarding the authority exercised by a prince over the Church.[309] Neither jurisdiction nor moral authority extended to such rule since an unjust law could not in itself have any moral authority.[310] While it may be true to say that the *monarquía* discouraged the promulgation of those parts of the Council of Trent that dealt with the primary loyalty of bishops to Rome, Ó Maolchonaire only asserted the independence of bishops in matters spiritual and their indirect temporal authority.

In the same vein as his Valladolid remonstrance, Flaithrí Ó Maolchonaire applied the thinking of Suárez on the *res publica* to the Irish experience, advocating that people invest power in their rulers just as Christ gave power to Peter and the apostles and God gives authority to the bishops.[311] Ó Maolchonaire's book appears to be the first formal application of Bellarmine and Suárez to the political situation in Ireland. The latter's work of 1613, *De Defensio Fidei Catholicae Adversus Anglicanae Sectae Errores*, refuted James I's ideas on the divine right of kings. Flaithrí Ó Maolchonaire therefore chose to publish at a time when the work of Suárez was causing maximum controversy in Europe.[312] In common with other Irish Franciscans, he resolved any apparent contradiction with his loyalty to the Spanish *monarquía* by accepting the view that subjects should recognise existing monarchical rule only when clearly sanctioned by the pope. This reflected contemporary political thought which advocated, controversially for its time, that established order could justifiably be opposed so as to rescue a ruler from malevolent counsel. This was, however, very carefully argued. Even Catholic diehards avoided using it to undermine authority, even when that authority was exercised by a perceived heretic.[313]

In Ó Maolchonaire's version of the allegorical tale, Desiderius is threatened with prison and the loss of all his belongings unless he attends the newly established Church. His guide Simplicity warns him, however, that while defying heresy means imprisonment, defying the will of God leads to eternal fire. Ó Maolchonaire asserted that accepting the rule of a king need not include following his religion. Caesar is only entitled to his own right, he continued, and while it is right to fear a king on earth, God is far greater.[314] Towards the end of this interpolation, Ó Maolchonaire points out the need to provide for the ordinary people to keep them strong in faith, leaving questions of doctrine to the prelates.[315] Ó Maolchonaire justifies political resistance on a theological and philosophical basis by asserting that Catholicism represents the 'very essence' of salvation for the faithful.[316] Irish sufferings and the lack of help from Philip III were, Ó Maolchonaire believed, due to God's wrath, *d'fheirg an Ardriogh* – anger of the high-king – towards the sins of Ireland, Spain, and himself.[317] This is redolent of the views expressed at court in the self-deprecation of the *arbitristas* who attributed Spain's ensuing decline to its failure in the trials of faith.[318]

Flaithrí Ó Maolchonaire's comments on recusancy fines, enforced for non-attendance at Protestant Church services, on the oath of allegiance and the authority of bishops were of direct relevance to his own family's current experience and to the experience of many of their contemporaries. The diocese of Elphin, where Ó Maolchonaire's family held their lands, represented 'an exception to the general poverty and inadequacy of the Church of Ireland in this region'.[319] Following the Ulster precedent, therefore, provision was made for the new state Church in the allocation of lands.[320] William Daniel (†1628), archbishop of Tuam for the established state church, was granted two quarters of former Ó Maolchonaire lands 'in right of his see'.[321] Large landowners, such as Ó Maolchonaire's brother Maoilechlainn, served as jurists. Since 1612 there had been 'a renewed outburst of persecution of recusants' and juries throughout Ireland were subject to punitive fines for refusing to present them.[322] Coming to terms with the accompanying changes in landholding practices, Maoilechlainn befriended Sir Richard Lane (†1668), sheriff of County Roscommon, whose mother and wife were both Irish.[323] Maoilechlainn conducted scribal work on behalf of Sir Richard, who acted as his trustee.[324] When Maoilechlainn drafted his last will and testament in Latin and English he distributed his property between kinsmen and assigned the document to Lane along with deeds of settlement.[325]

FLAITHRÍ Ó MAOLCHONAIRE'S CASE AGAINST THE SPANISH MATCH

Don Diego Sarmiento de Acuña, Conde de Gondomar, served as Spanish ambassador in London from 1612.[326] During his first term of office, Gondomar introduced James to the idea of a marriage alliance between the crowns of Spain and England, offering a dowry of £600,000 to the cash-strapped Stuart.[327] In the years before his death, Aodh Ó Néill requested that the return of his lands and those of the Uí Dhomhnaill be included in the terms of negotiations.[328] Whereas there are clear indications of Peter Lombard's support for the Spanish Match,[329] Ó Maolchonaire was unequivocally opposed to it from the time of Gondomar's first embassy to London. He set out his objections in a hitherto unpublished document.[330]

He argued, firstly, that it was 'not good for His Catholic Majesty to rely on the friendship of the English', which Ó Maolchonaire described as a 'route to sorrow'. Instead, he suggested that accord should be reached with 'a Christian Prince, such as the king of France'.[331] Louis XIII (†1643) had yet to reach the age of majority and his mother María de Medici (†1642) governed France in his stead.[332]

Ó Maolchonaire urged: 'Now is the time, while the king of France needs the

friendship of Spain' and *entente* should be arranged 'before he comes of age, when
it could well be that he be of the same humour as his father', Henry IV (†1610).[333]
Such an arrangement would have negated the offensive alliance between France
and the duke of Savoy, thereby recovering the military corridor through the Alpine
valleys for Habsburg forces. During the reign of Philip II, the duke's desire for
French terrain led him to grant the king freedom of access, linking Spain's
Milanese and Franche-Comté dominions. The territorial integrity of Savoy is
said to have mattered more to the king of Spain for the passage to the Southern
Netherlands than it did to the duke. After 1602, however, Savoy switched allegiance to Henry IV when offered the prospect of annexing Spanish lands in
Lombardy.[334] The following decade, Flaithrí Ó Maolchonaire revealed, to maintain the impasse, Spain's enemies had secretly paid the duke 200,000 ducados for
the upkeep of his cavalry.[335]

As things stood, 'it is certain that all the princes of Christendom are so fearful
seeing how much power Spain has and so envious of seeing all the wealth of this
world which comes every year from the Indies.'[336] Closer union with England, Ó
Maolchonaire remarked, would merely assure James I that the vassals of Philip
III 'will not dare to do anything against him'.[337] Therefore, rather than making
matters more secure for Spain, a marriage agreement would only give James I
more freedom of action. The harmful consequences of the Spanish Match would
be two-fold:

> [...] to promote his heresy more and more in Spain, under the cloak of
> friendship and exchange, and to keep on gaining more ground on the way
> to the Indies, until he sees his opportunity to take them.[338]

'So many opportunities present themselves,' Ó Maolchonaire went on, 'that it
wouldn't be a miracle' to see the Indies fall into English hands. This, he
explained, was because the inhabitants there 'are so tired and desirous of seeing
another type of government'. Indeed, 'the boisterous Spanish who are born and
have estates there are subject to rise up with a great show of strength against his
Majesty, for once too preoccupied to turn somewhere so distant and far from his
forces.'[339]

In a second set of arguments, Ó Maolchonaire held that it might be thought that
'His Majesty does much good for the Catholics of the *septentrion* [of northern
Europe], obliging the English king to give freedom of conscience to his vassals ...
his is the word of a heretic which he will not honour tomorrow.'[340] Guaranteed of
peace with Spain 'by reason of the marriage', James could act with impunity:

> He will look for a thousand ways under other civil pretexts to put an end
> to the Catholics and relieve them of their property and estates, without
> there being anyone who may pity them, as it could be said then that they
> wouldn't be suffering for the faith but because of rebellion.[341]

Today, Ó Maolchonaire declared, the ministers of the king of England told a
thousand other lies to falsely accuse the bishops and priests. James I's advisers
did this 'not because the clergy were Catholic but because of the crime of *lèse
majesté* which they may commit'.[342] Recalling the interdict against Ó

Maolchonaire, this comment readily applied to him.[343] While not doubting Philip III's desire 'from the heart' to protect Catholics with his word and see them granted freedom of conscience, Ó Maolchonaire considered that this would not be 'to the service of His Catholic Majesty'. To Ó Maolchonaire's mind, James I and his vassals would only exploit closer union with Spain in pursuit of their aims to capture the Indies.[344]

In his third set of arguments, Ó Maolchonaire held that despite any pretence to the contrary, allowing the foes of Spain to see that 'they are such friends of peace' in the country, would dishonour the monarchy. Such a reverse, Ó Maolchonaire believed, was unworthy of the Spanish monarchy, which would be weakened, 'as she feels such horror and fear that in times past all the world felt towards Spain'.[345]

At present, Flaithrí Ó Maolchonaire claimed, 'the enemies are arrogant and intimidating, saying they will break the peace.'[346] Consequently, he said, 'by remaining reconciled, Spain remained in perpetual danger.' Yet, it was obvious that 'her enemies are at war with her' as, whenever England 'presented herself against the wellbeing of His Catholic Majesty, none of the enemy ever let the opportunity pass'.[347] Indeed, while the truce in the Netherlands teetered on the brink, Philip III's ambassador to London protested against English and Dutch raids in the Caribbean.[348] According to Ó Maolchonaire, combined with their colonies in Virginia and Bermuda, a navy assembled by the English and Dutch would represent a serious threat to Spain's Atlantic fleet. This, in turn, encouraged other rulers in their hostility towards Spain which 'suffers everything for preserving the peace'.[349] Every day, 'the English and Dutch enjoyed the benefits of peace by fortifying Virginia and the Bermudas'.[350] The king would 'of course accumulate many millions by the peace to shower his enemies with his most tolerable patience and silence', but Ó Maolchonaire feared 'he may not save.'[351] That which Philip III 'would spend now in ejecting them, could well cost him six times as much if he delays for long'.[352]

Having 'rooted out and annihilated Spain's Catholic friends in Ireland, the only place of fear' for the king of England, his three kingdoms would be 'secure and planted with heretics'.[353] James I's confiscation of the estates belonging to the earls of Tyrone and Tyrconnell, almost one fifth of the kingdom, offered sufficient warning.[354] It could be 'conjectured with what aggression he will approach Spain then, and what leagues he will make with enemy princes':[355]

'For the conservation of the monarchy of Spain,' Flaithrí Ó Maolchonaire argued, 'all of the above showed the importance of applying a remedy to the said problems':[356]

> [...] liberate Ireland by decree of Spain, something that does not have any more difficulty than it begins well and in secret for the many exiled gentlemen of that land [...] for the *tercio* in Flanders in which there are knights of every family of the kingdom, and to provide for the knights in it who are oppressed and tyrannised by English heretics.[357]

'Great glory to the service of God and His Church' would follow. By fulfilling his commitment to the Irish 'for that which they lost for having served him', Philip III could avoid 'all the dangers and misfortune with which the enemies threaten Spain'.[358] Just as Lombardy and Spanish Flanders 'serve as a brake against the French king', Ó Maolchonaire averred, Ireland had the potential to keep James I in check so that he could not 'do against Spain all that he may desire'.[359] Moreover, having Ireland in Spanish hands would 'render the Indies very secure against the north'.[360]

Ó Maolchonaire acknowledged Philip III's support for the claims of Duke Wolfgang Wilhelm of Neuburg (†1653) in the Palatinate and the value of keeping him hostage to avert further Dutch hostilities. 'Thus is it necessary,' Ó Maolchonaire advocated, 'to keep another hostage, one against the English king.' Otherwise James I would be taken up with events in the Low Countries and 'activities that may take his fancy'. By holding Ireland, Philip III could 'tie the hands of James so that he wouldn't dare to do anything against Spain, not even in secret'.[361] Were James I to die soon, seeing help so near, English and Scottish Catholics would never acknowledge his son-in-law, the Protestant elector Frederick V (†1632), as his successor. That, Flaithrí Ó Maolchonaire averred, 'would be of no little service to Spain' as, being the nephew of Maurice of Nassau (†1625),

> [...] were he to become king of England, it is clear that he would help the Dutch with all his forces [...] he would attempt to emerge as emperor with help from the Dutch and from the other heretics of Germany and France, and would do all he could do against Spain.[362]

So encouraged at seeing Ireland on the side of Spain, the Catholics of England and Scotland would turn on 'the heretic king, who caused them so much harm, that he wouldn't have a day's peace'. With the rebellions launched against him, the government of England would promptly fall.[363]

Historians have discussed how Ambrosio Spínola's successful yet highly expensive recapture of Oostende showed that 'Spain and her Netherlands were still powers to be reckoned with' in 1604.[364] Irish troops had fought there with distinction.[365] At the close of his case against negotiations for a marriage agreement with James I, Ó Maolchonaire referred to the Oostende siege. Since the towns of Ireland, Scotland and England lacked fortification, Ó Maoilchonaire said they could fall to Phillip III without the expenses he incurred in Flanders where defences like those at Oostende were found far and wide.[366]

The intervention of the state in Church affairs had as its counterpart the active participation of the Church in the state.[367] Placed in the context of European discourse on the Match, Flaithrí Ó Maolchonaire's contribution to the debate is best understood when compared with the views of those opposed to Lerma's ineffective foreign policies. Among the most prominent were Don Alfonso de la Cueva, marqués de Bedmar, and his allies Conde de Fuentes, the Duque de Osuna and the Marqués de Villafranca.[368] They held that James I was merely using the talks as a foil while conspiring to stir up renewed conflict.[369] Knowing also that Pope Paul V was 'the unwavering opponent of the Spanish Match',[370] Ó Maolchonaire was unafraid to express his resistance to the proposed marriage.

DONAL O'SULLIVAN BEARE AND JOHN BATHE

Following the demise of Aodh Ó Néill, attention turned to the earl of Bearhaven, Domhnall Ó Súilleabháin Béarra (†1618), who assumed a central role in the campaign to convince the Spanish to intervene militarily in Ireland.[371] That he and Ó Maolchonaire had known one another since 1602 is apparent from Ó Maolchonaire's testimony recommending Bearhaven for the military order of Santiago in Madrid.[372] Acceptance into one of Spain's four military orders conferred considerable social prestige 'for it meant the wearer was of pure noble blood'.[373] Domhnall Ó Súilleabháin Béarra was among the privileged few from the upper echelons of the Irish community on whom the habit was bestowed.[374] In his case, it also confirmed his entitlement to a share of the income from the military orders' considerable estates.[375]

A sign of the vitriolic rivalries among Irish exiles was about to manifest itself, however. The Old English representative in Madrid, John Bathe of Drumcondra, a brother of the *Janua Linguarum* author William Bathe SJ, was apparently jealous at the preferment shown towards Ó Súilleabháin Béarra.[376] Captain Bathe had accompanied Éinrí Ó Néill to the capital in 1609.[377] Aware that Flaithrí Ó Maolchonaire wished to go to Spanish Flanders nine years later, Bathe sought to fill his vacancy at court, complete with equivalent income and accommodation.[378] In a letter to the king, Ó Maolchonaire alleged that John Bathe was a double agent and advised against trusting him:

> All those of my nation are under strong obligation to serve your majesty because of the royal protection and favours extended to them, and particularly to myself whom Your Majesty has always trusted with the important affairs of that nation.[379]

For that reason, the archbishop explained, before setting out on his journey to Spanish Flanders, he felt it his duty to provide Philip with 'adequate information about a certain person of my nation who may in time do serious disservice to Your Majesty if the council of state are not forewarned and put on their guard'.[380] He continued:

> In this court there resides an Irishman, John Bathe, to whom Your Majesty gives forty ducados a month, not for service to Your Majesty, nor of those of his ancestors, all of whom served the crown of England ... but because of his good parts and particularly because of what he calls his art of memory.[381]

Ó Maolchonaire learned from 'a secret and reliable source' that Bathe had 'promised the then viceroy of Ireland, Arthur Chichester, to inform him of affairs of state which he might hear and find out in this court'. As a sign of his loyalty, and 'to be of service to the king of England', Bathe sent back information concerning the Spanish fleet when he landed in Lisbon.[382] Initially, Ó Maolchonaire thought that 'he would not give information of importance' and that despite his promise 'it was only to comply with the demands of the English so that his family, who are well regarded by them, should not come under suspicion on his account.' However, much to the surprise of the Irish in Madrid, when Bathe travelled to Ireland in 1617:

[…] not only did he come to no harm at all, but on the contrary, during his visit which lasted many months, the viceroy and all the councillors treated him with honour and any time he wished he had meals at the table of the viceroy, of the chancellor and of the other councillors.[383]

In the case of other Irishmen arriving from Spain, the English usually harassed them.[384] Moreover, according to 'a person of repute', John Bathe left Ireland with permission from the viceroy. Describing Bathe as 'a very clever and astute man of great intelligence', Ó Maolchonaire believed it 'dangerous that he should be at the court'. To resolve matters, he suggested that Philip III could order Bathe 'to join the company of Irish soldiers serving in the Spanish fleet'. To keep such action secret:

[The king] could issue a general order that no Irish should receive payments of salary or allowances at the court and that all those that are here should go to serve in the fleet. If Bathe should not wish to go, as I expect, Your Majesty could then with justice stop his salary.[385]

The archbishop closed solemnly, declaring: 'I do not wish him any harm […] God knows that it goes to my heart to have to uncover the faults of another, although it be to avoid a greater evil.'[386] The council of state raised the subject the following month.[387] While recommending that Bathe should no longer be trusted or admitted to the court, no action was taken, however. Later that summer, following an argument and duel with Philip O'Sullivan Beare (†1634), John Bathe stabbed and killed the earl of Bearhaven, who came upon the scene. Domhnall Ó Súilleabháin Béarra, 'in whom the Irish had then their greatest hope', was fifty-seven years of age at the time of his death. Philip O'Sullivan Beare's record of the event indicates that the murder was premeditated.[388] The council of state subsequently retrieved Flaithrí Ó Maolchonaire's letter, appending the following note to it:

[…] this matter takes on a different complexion. If the Church protects [Bathe] he could be banished from all the dominions of His Majesty. Those who are dealing with his case should be notified accordingly.[389]

Domhnall Ó Súilleabháin Béarra appears to have been planning to lead an uprising in Ireland. Tadhg O'Houlihan, a priest from Kerry, wrote from Bearhaven assuring Ó Súilleabháin Béarra:

[…] both spiritual and temporal, both cities and country men, are so willing and ready to concur with the matter and arise with good courage and free will. But they are slow in beginning any stirring before they see some assistance, being already many times deceived.[390]

O'Houlihan had spread the word in Connacht also, 'which is ready to your contentment; but none of them will stir until they see yourself in person or your letters, but above all they expect yourself with good succour.'[391]

Traces of Bathe's counter-intelligence occur in duplicate copies of original Spanish documents such as Philip O'Sullivan Beare's 'Briefe relation of Irland and diversity of Irish in the same', a translation of which found its way into

James Ussher's library.[392] Another example is Ó Maolchonaire's provisions for a replacement as Irish representative in Madrid. This reveals that Maurice Cornelio of Kerry had been stripped of his office and banished from court 'for disservice to your Majesty and other crimes'.[393] Maurice Cornelio had served in Ó Maolchonaire's stead as assistant to the protector of the Irish in Madrid. When the earl of Bearhaven's son Diarmaid (†c.1664), a page at court, sought to join the military order of Santiago, for instance, Cornelio testified in his favour along with Ó Maolchonaire's confessor Thomas Stronge OFM, Francis Veahy, the abbot of Cong, and Captain John Bathe.[394] Considering the widespread corruption in Lerma's administration,[395] Cornelio may subsequently have been removed for fraudulent use of funds.

Entreating the king to restore the privilege of 'an Irishman at court named Agent for Ireland', Ó Maolchonaire suggested that Don Diego Brochero, Puñonrostro's successor on the council of war, should nominate suitable candidates. Most revealingly, it is said that the English regarded the position as a sign of 'agreement between your Majesty and the Catholics of Ireland' which they feared more than the *tercio* in the Spanish Netherlands.[396]

EXILE IN SPANISH FLANDERS

Commending him to their protection, Philip III told the archdukes to treat Flaithrí Ó Maolchonaire with all honour and explained that he was leaving 'for the good of his health and other reasons'.[397] During the twelve years' truce, the sea route to the Southern Netherlands was comparatively safe to travel.[398] The voyage from San Sebastian to Dunkirk, for instance, took an average of eight days across the Bay of Biscay and up the Channel. Those with official accreditation, such as Flaithrí Ó Maolchonaire, then made their way to the court of the archdukes at Brussels where they presented their papers.[399]

Ó Maolchonaire's departure for the Low Countries made sense for a number of reasons. Talk of the Spanish Match dragged on and, for the time being at least, Madrid would not hear of proposals for war against the English. Thus, it seems, he was among those to become *persona non grata* at court. Other prominent Irish exiles also appear to have beaten a retreat from Castile, such as Philip O'Sullivan Beare and Raymond de Burgo in Lisbon, and John Fitzgerald, brother of the Sugán earl of Desmond, who had made his way to Galicia.[400] This corresponded to the wider developments identified by Elliott. In Madrid, Lerma was associated with defeatism and disgrace by 'fervent partisans' of the militant Spanish tradition symbolised by their patron Santiago. Denied their way in Spain by a regime they reviled, figures such as the Conde de Fuentes, Marqués de Bedmar, Marqués de Villafranca and the Duque de Osuna chose to conduct their own bellicose policy away from court.[401] How this related to Ó Maolchonaire in Spanish Flanders is dealt with further in the next chapter.

From the death of Philip II to that of Albert, the archdukes are said to have enjoyed a sovereignty more nominal than real over the ten states of the Southern Netherlands. The anomaly of their international status suggests that the archduke was, for the king of Spain, neither a foreign monarch nor a simple governor. His duties, however, show that he can be regarded as both, 'with an intermediate role discernible as well, that of the dependent sovereign of a client state'.[402] With the increasingly unsustainable Dutch truce near to collapse,[403] Ó Maolchonaire moved closer to the Irish *tercio* he had helped to establish and maintain in Spanish Flanders. Beyond the Jesuits' main sphere of influence in Castile, being at Leuven also provided him with access to the university's likeminded theology faculty.[404] Ó Maolchonaire also had more room for manouevre in the Spanish Netherlands now because John Roche, a strong ally of Lombard and Rothe with connections to the Irish college at Douai, had been transferred to Paris with Guido Bentivoglio.[405]

In conclusion, following his appointment as archbishop of Tuam, Flaithrí Ó Maolchonaire endeavoured to position Irish affairs from a Habsburg perspective on behalf of Aodh Ó Néill in Madrid where the limitations of early-modern communications meant that individual action and judgment was his. The response to events evinced by his writings confirms Ó Maolchonaire's great strength of intellect, although his challenge to the Spanish Match shows how entrenched he was in his views. Ó Maolchonaire helped Irish exiles and their Habsburg hosts to overcome the problems they faced in the second decade of the seventeenth century, assisting in clearing the court of Irish exiles, thereby protecting St Anthony's College and the Uí Néill *tercio*. Realising that the reticence of Lerma and Philip III ruled out renewed military action, Ó Maolchonaire tried to place Irish affairs in line with Spain's global interests before leaving for the Southern Netherlands. The next chapter discusses how he continued to represent the interests of exiled Irish nobles, redeploying his efforts in the Spanish Netherlands with an increase in his ecclesiastical activity. From St Anthony's, he helped launch the Irish Franciscans' pastoral mission to Scotland and primed a new generation of Irish military leaders before returning to Madrid.

NOTES

1. *Cronica de la provincia franciscana de Santiago. 1214–1614. Por un franciscano anónimo del siglo XVII. Introducción, rectificaciones y notas por Manuel de Castro, OFM* (Madrid, 1971), p. 323. Aodh Mac Aingil and Luke Wadding also stayed at the Ara Coeli friary on their arrival in the city.
2. Richard Bagwell, *Ireland under the Stuarts* (3 vols, London: Longman, 1909–16), vol. 1: 1603–42, pp. 41–2; Allen, *Philip III and the Pax Hispanica, 1598–1621*, p. 273.
3. For Lombard's letters of 10 November 1607 to Ó Domhnaill, Mag Uidhir and Ó Maolchonaire, see Charles Meehan, *Fate and fortunes of the earls of Tyrone and Tyrconnell*, pp. 186–9.
4. Ó Maolchonaire to Andres de Prada, Rome, 1 May 1609 (AGS, E. Roma, l. 992): '[…] llegò a mis manos un librillo ingles impresso en Londres poco meses ha que contiene unos articulos del Rey de Inglaterra en los quales declara confiscados para si las tierras de los condes de Tiron y Tirconel hasta seis condados, sin declarar la causa porque.'
5. Ibid., '[…] offresce las dichas tierras perpetuamente (para si y para sus herederos) a todos los Ingleses y Escoceses que quisieren yr a habitar las con tal que paguen un tanto al Rey cada año y no pueda una persona tener quanta tierra quisiere sino cierta cantidad que alli prescribe para cada uno.'
6. Ibid., '[…] que primero jurer que el Rey es cabeça de la Iglesia. Item que no puedan arrendar las dichas tierras a ningun Irlandez que sea de la antigua stirpe de Irlanda. Que en cada condado aya escuelas para instruir a los mancebos en la Religion de Calvino. Y que en todos las Iglesias parrochiales en lugar de sacerdotes aya ministros herejes que comen la renta de la Iglesia.'
7. Ó Maolchonaire to Andres de Prada, Rome, 1 May 1609: 'que quise escrivir a V Md para que echasse de ver quan[do razon] tenia el conde de dar priessa a Su Magestad Catholica todo este año passado paraque le bolviesse a sus Estados'.
8. Ibid., 'A mi me pone alguna culpa por no le aver dexado dar mas priessa a Su Magestad de la que dio,

que siempre le yva yo a la mano en no dar priessa por parezerme que bastava la que se dava que Su Magd yva disponiendo las cosas del conde bien.'

9. Aodh Ó Néill to Philip III, Rome, 9 Jun. 1609 (AGS, E. Roma, l. 994).
10. Bentivoglio to the papal secretary of state, Brussels, 12 Jan. 1608 (ASV, Borghèse II, vol. 204–206, ff 2–6).
11. 'Paulus Papa Quintus', Rome, 5 Jun. 1609 (ASV, Protocollo XLV, tomo 5, ff 4–5).
12. Ibid., *Dilecto filio nostro Bernardo tti. Sanctae Anastasiae Pbro Cardinali Toletano; Dilecto filio Nobili viro Duci Lermae; Dilecto filio Nobili viro Comestabili Castellae; Venerabili fratri Decio Archiepiscopo Damasceno nostro, et Sedis Apostolicae apud Hispaniarum Regem Nuncio.*
13. Kerney Walsh, *Destruction by peace*, p. 114.
14. 'Sir Charles Cornwallis to the lords of the council', Madrid, 20 Jul. 1609 (*Winwood Papers* (London, 1725, vol. 3, pp. 55–6); Cottington to Edmondes, Madrid, 27 Sept. 1609 (HMC *Downshire*, vol. 2, 1605–10, pp. 136–7).
15. Jensen, *Bernardino de Mendoza and the French Catholic League*, pp. 96–7.
16. Philip III to Francisco, Conde de Castro, Aranjuez, 24 Jan. 1610 (AGS, E. Roma, l. 994). Such a delay was by no means exceptional, however. The nuncio to Ireland, Ludovico Mansoni SJ, for instance, waited six months before he could get a royal audience at court in Valladolid. See S. P. Ó Mathúna, *William Bathe, SJ, 1564–1614*, p. 53.
17. Ibid., 'El Arçobispo Tuamense que como sabreis ha venido aqui de parte del Conde de Tiron me ha dado el memorial y carta del dicho conde de cuya copia se os embia para que sepais lo que contiene y le respondais a el de mi parte.'
18. Memorial to Philip III, Rome (AGS, E. Roma, l. 994).
19. Kerney Walsh, *Destruction by peace*, pp. 254–9.
20. Ó Néill to Philip III, Rome, 29 Jul. 1610 (AGS, E. NP, l. 1754): 'Lo qual podra Vuestra Magestad muy bien hazer, a lo menos socolor de que Su Santidad selo ha pedido, como lo pidio en el Breve que escrivio a Su Nuncio el año passado, mandandole encarecidamente que tratasse con Vmagd los negocios del supplicante muy de veras y procurasse el buen successo dellos y en los Breves que con el Arçobispo Tuamense embio al Cardenal de Toledo, al Duque de Lerma y al Condestable en las mesma conformidad.'
21. Ó Néill to Philip III, Rome, 29 Jul. 1610: 'es procurar con instancia que el Rey de Inglaterra le buelva sus estados y le admita en su gracia.' On letters of credence, see Jonathan Wright, *The ambassadors: from ancient Greece to the nation state* (London: Harper, 2006), p. 117.
22. Ó Néill to Philip III, 29 Jul. 1610, 'Item: que mande Vuestra Magestad dar â Juan Batheo Irlandes el Entretenimiento de Treinta escudos que el conde de Puñonrostro le señalo y que los pueda gozar acerca de la persona del Embaxador de Vmagd en Inglaterra, para que assista alli â solicitar la dicha reconciliacion.'
23. Ibid., 'que se de la Respuesta deste Memorial al Arçobispo Tuamense […] para no dilatar mas este negocio y recibira merced'.
24. Philip III to the Conde de Castro, Madrid, 22 Jan. 1610 (AAEE, FSS, legajo 56, f. 97).
25. 'Sir Charles Cornwallis to the lords of the counsayle', Madrid, 10 May 1609 (*Winwood Papers*, vol. 3, pp. 36–7).
26. Conde de Puñonrostro to the Spanish council of state, Madrid (AGS, E. NP, l. 2745): 'ha 6 meses que vino a esta Corte Fray Florencio Conrrio Arcobispo Tuamense por orden de Su Santidad y del Conde de Tiron a tratar los negocios del dicho Conde y de los Catholicos de Yrlanda'.
27. Ibid., 'que ha 12 años sirve a Vuestra Magestad el dicho Arcobispo en Yrlanda en las guerras que alli se han offrecido asistiendo a los Catholicos particularmente a los Condes Oneill y Odonnell y siempre les persuadio que quedasen firmes en el servicio de Dios y de Vuestra Magestad como lo han hecho que lo mismo ha hecho en España'.
28. Ibid; Spanish council of state to Philip III: '[…] es persona que se puede ser de mucho servicio en las cossas de Yrlanda y para conservar los Catholicos de aquel Reyno en su devoçion y informarles desde alla de las Cossas que se offreçieren y de los animos y secretos de los dichos Catholicos y para moverles a qual quiera buena resoluçion porque todos ellos le respectan […] Al Conssejo pareze que seran muy bien empleados en su persona quatroçientos ducados'.
29. 14 Aug. 1610 (AGS, E. Corona de Castilla, l. 228–1): 'desordenes y excesos'.
30. Andres de Prada to Gastón de Moncada, marqués de Aitona, Madrid, 7 Apr. 1609 (Fundación Ducal de Medinaceli, Archivo Histórico, l. 56, ramo 1).
31. Óscar Recio Morales, 'De *nación* irlandés: percepciones socio-culturales y respuestas políticas sobre Irlanda y la comunidad irlandesa en la España del XVII', in Enrique García Hernán et al. (eds), *Irlanda y la monarquía hispánica*, pp. 337–8.
32. Francis Cottington to Salisbury, Madrid, 26 Jun. 1610 (*Cal. S.P. Spain*, 94/17/II, 109).
33. 'Sobre el despacho de los irlandeses', Valladolid, 25 Sept. 1602' (AGS, GA, l. 589).

34. Cornwallis to Salisbury, Madrid, 2 Jun. 1608 (HMC *Salisbury*, vol. 20, pp. 179–80).
35. 'Sir Charles Cornwallis to the lords of the council', Madrid, 20 Jul. 1609 (*Memorials of affairs of state [...] from the original papers of the right honourable Sir Ralph Winwood, Kt.*, ed. Edmund Sawyer (3 vols, London, 1725), vol. 3, pp. 55–6.
36. HMC *Downshire*, 4, p. 150.
37. Ciarán O'Scea, 'The significance and legacy of Spanish intervention in west Munster during the battle of Kinsale', p. 59.
38. 'Don Raymundo de Burgo Baron de Letrym', Madrid, 4 May 1610 (AGS, E. NP, l. 1751).
39. Raymond de Burgo to Andres de Prada, 15 May 1607 (AGS, E. NP, l. 1748).
40. Recio Morales, 'De *nación* irlandés', pp. 337–8.
41. Madrid, 18 Jul. 1610 (AGS, E., Inglaterra, l. 2513): 'El duque de Infantado dixo que el Arçobispo Tuamense que reside en esta corte le dio los dos papeles primero y segundo encargando le que corriesen con mucho secreto por el riesgo que correria si se supiese que los avia dado.'
42. Ibid., 'Pareçe al Condestable de Castilla muy combeniente que a los que estan en La Coruña no seles de liçençia para venir aca y que se pida relacion particular de todos paraque los que no tienen hijos ni mugeres ni estan viejos ni impedidos se vayan a Flandes.'
43. Ibid., 'En lo que contiene el segundo papel sobre proveer los quinientos ducados como esta resuelto para el despacho desta gente y hecharla desta corte, pareçe al consejo que a los que ay aqui se podrian encaminar a Flandes con la brevedad pusible socorriendo a los que hubieren quedado de una memoria que se hizo para repartir los dichos quinientos ducados y no a los demas.'
44. Flaithrí Ó Maolchonaire to Alonso Nuñez de Valdiva, 5 Jul. 1610 (AGS, CJH, l. 499–20, ff 44–5): 'Matheo Tulio que solicita aqui los negocios del Conde de Tiron y esta dará a Vuestr. merced el y su muger sesenta ducados de entretenimiento al mes en las arcas, ha mas de un año que su muger no recibo blanca y a el sele deven mas de diez y seis meses.'
45. Aodh Ó Néill to Philip III, Rome, 9 Jun. 1609 (AGS, E. Roma, l. 994).
46. Ó Maolchonaire to Alonso Nuñez de Valdiva, 5 Jul. 1610: 'Tienen cargo de hijos y familia y andan muy necessitados de manera que sus acreedores le molestan por via de justicia y porque se que su necesidad es muy grande y anda empeñado supplico a Vuestr. merced procure con el Señor Presidente que de orden al Thesorero para que le pague lo quese resta deviendo para lo qual tiene cedula de Su Magd y yo recibire muy particular merced en que se le hagen Vuestra Magestad.'
47. Matha Óg Ó Maoltuile to the council of state, Madrid, 10 Jul. 1610 (AGS, E. NP, l. 2745).
48. Ibid., 'se halla con tanta necessidad en esta corte que no puede andar con la Deçençia que requiere su Vocaçion y por esto resuelto de yrse disfraçado a su Tierra donde no puede esperar mas que la muerte y si toma esta ressolution dexando por acabar los negocios del dicho Conde de Tiron y de los demas Catholicos de Irlanda desesperaran del favor de Vuestra Magestad.'
49. Matha Óg Ó Maoltuile to the council of state, 10 Jul. 1610: 'Supplica a Vuestra Md muy humilidamente que en consideracion de todo lo referido se sirva de mandar señalar al dicho Arçobispo un entretenimiento en esta Corte conforme a su Calidad Dignidad y Servicios mientras assistiere a los dichos negocios.'
50. Ibid., 'este Arçobispo es Hombre exemplar y de buenas partes y de buena Vida y es necessario en esta corte para las cosas que se ofrecieron de su naçion y da avisos de importancia y assi le pareçe que para que se pueda continuarlo con alguna Deçençia conforme a la Dignidad que tiene sele podrian señalar aqui de cinquenta a sesenta ducados al mes de forma que los cobre con puntualidad.'
51. 'Fr Florencio Conryo Arçobispo Tuamens', Madrid, 9 Oct. 1610 (AGS, E. NP, l. 1754).
52. Patrick Williams, 'Lerma, Old Castile and the travels of Philip III of Spain', *History*, 73 (1988), p. 392.
53. Madrid, 9 Oct. 1610 (AGS, E. NP, l. 1754): 'Por tanto supplico a Vuestra Magestad se sirva de embiar un recaudo a Silva de Torres para que permita por estas ocho dias â los dichos irlandeses acudir a la posada del dicho Capitan para que haga lista dellos pues se haze para sacarlos de la corte que es lo que se pretende.'
54. 'Sobre el despacho de los irlandeses', Madrid, 18 Jul. 1610 (AGS, E. In., l. 2513).
55. 'Don Morgan Farel a Secretario Prada', 8 Aug. 1609 (AGS, E. NP, l. 1754): 'su patrimonio'.
56. 'Florin O Mulchonor and James Geraldine', 12 Oct. 1609 (HMC *Downshire*, vol. 2 (1605–10) p. 154).
57. James Geraldine's request for preferment, 3 Sept. 1608 (AGS, E. NP, l. 1751).
58. Flaithrí Ó Maolchonaire to Antonio Aroztegui, Madrid 30 Oct. 1610 (AGS, E. Flandes, l. 2292): '[…] siendo al principio su Magd enformado de lo que an perdido los yrlandeses en su real serbicio, y de lo que an serbido a la causa cattholica en la ultima guerra de Yrlanda, movido de compassion, y tambien de equidad para recompensarles en alguna manera sus serbicios y perdidas les mando dar gran golpe de entretenimientos y vantajas.'
59. Ibid., '[…] como currio la fama desta liberalidad que su Magd uso con los irlandeses an acudido tantos'.

60. Letter of the seminary of Irish Franciscan friars, August 1608 (AGS, E. NP, l. 1802): 'aura cerca de dos años el padre fray Florencio Conrrio Provincial de la dicha orden en el Reyno de Irlanda […] V. Magd les hizo merced de mil ducados al año […] el dicho Provincial fundo una casa en Lovayna la qual tiene continuamente veinte y seis frayles estudiando'.

61. Ibid., 'Y tambien dizen que de los seis meses de la dicha limosna que han recibido han gastado la mayor parte en assentar su casa y comprar libros […] Por lo qual humilmente supplican a V. Magd. por amor de Dios de embiarles una precisa orden para que les paguen adelante enteramente y los dichos quinze meses atrasados.'

62. Ibid., 'es muy justo ordenarlo como lo piden por ser una obra de tanto merito […] puntualidad con la paga del mil ducados que V. Md. les mando senalar en Flandes'.

63. Recio Morales, *El socorro de Irlanda en 1601*, pp. 139, 260.

64. Flaithri Ó Maolchonaire to Antonio Aroztegui, Madrid 30 Oct. 1610 (AGS, E. Flandes, l. 2292).

65. Ó Maolchonaire to Philip III, Madrid, 9 Sept. 1610 (AGS, E. NP, l. 1751).

66. Hayes-McCoy, 'The Renaissance and the Irish wars', pp. 43–51; Geoffrey Parker, *The military revolution* (Cambridge: Cambridge University Press, 1967); Gráinne Henry, *The Irish military community*, pp. 22–3.

67. Parker, *The army of Flanders and the Spanish road*, p. 274.

68. Julio Albi de la Cuesta, *De Pavia a Rocroi*, pp. 48–57.

69. Domínguez Ortiz, *Golden Age*, p. 36.

70. Julio Albi de la Cuesta, *De Pavia a Rocroi*, Chapter 5.

71. Geoffrey Parker, 'Mutiny and discontent in the Spanish army of Flanders, 1572–1607', *Past & Present*, 58 (1973), pp. 38–52.

72. Kerney Walsh, *Destruction by peace*, pp. 223–4.

73. Ibid.

74. Ó Maolchonaire to Aroztegui, Madrid, 30 Oct. 1610 (AGS, E. F., l. 2292): 'viendo lo mucho que importaba al serbicio de Su Magd y a la quietud de sus ministros buscar algun remedio paraque no viniessen mas yrlandeses a la corte propuse Sr Conde de Puñonrostro (que esta en gloria) que el unico medio seria haçelles mas merçedes en esta corte'.

75. Ibid., 'que fuessen todos remittidos al Sr Archiduque y que de los mesmos entretenimientos y ventajas que estaban ya dadas alos yrlandeses por Su Magd, quando fuessen vacando se fuessen proveiendo en adelante en otros yrlandeses benemeritos'.

76. Ibid., 'la relacion que diesse Don Henrique O Nel a Su Alteza de los meritos y qualidades de cada uno, y que desta manera no irian las merçedes creçiendo cada dia, y se limpiaria la corte aqui, porque no vernian a ella viendo que cessaron las merçedes'.

77. Ó Maolchonaire to Aroztegui, Madrid, 30 Oct. 1610: 'las merçedes accudirian todos a serbir en el tercio por las esperanças que ternian de alcançar alguna vacantia, y que assi se conserbaria bien el tercio.'

78. Ibid., 'Todo esto propusimos en consejo de estado, lo qual approbaron aquellos señores de buena gana.'

79. Ibid., 'y en conformidad dello escrivio Su Magd despues la carta que va con este à Su Alteza para distribuir 500 ducados que vacaron en España en cierto yrlandeses que acudieron a esta corte lo qual no se effectuo hasta agora.'

80. Ó Maolchonaire to Philip III, Madrid, 9 Sept. 1610; Kerney Walsh, *Destruction by peace*, p. 266.

81. Ibid.

82. Ibid.

83. Jerrold Casway, *Owen Roe O'Neill and the struggle for Catholic Ireland* (Philadelphia: University of Pennsylvania Press, 1984), pp. 20–32.

84. Kerney Walsh, *Destruction by peace*, p. 268.

85. Ibid, pp. 236–7, 271.

86. O'Connor, '"Perfidious machiavellian friar": Florence Conry's campaign for a Catholic Restoration in Ireland', p. 99.

87. Ó Maolchonaire to Aroztegui, 30 Oct. 1610 (AGS, E. Flandes, l. 2292).

88. Ó Maolchonaire to Aroztegui, Madrid, 30 Oct. 1610 (AGS, E. F., l. 2292): 'Yo entonces y agora no veo mejor medio para los sobre dichos effectos, que mandar que se executa la dicha orden en los entretenimientos y ventajas que vacaron desde entonces en el tercio solamente y lo mesmo se haga en los que vacaren en adelante.'

89. Ibid., 'Tambien me han escrito acerca de los entretenimientos que Su Magestad dade vacancias en el Tercio Irlandes que no tenian effecto porque Su Alteza decia que no entendia aquellas Vacancias y que hasta que lo supiesse de Su Magestad que no sabia que hazer.'

90. Bentivoglio to the papal secretary of state, 6 Apr. 1613 (ASV, Borghese, I, vol. 269–72, pp. 42–6): 'Dell'essercito che mantiene il Rè Cattco in Fiandra … in grandissime angustie gli Archiduchi'.

91. Ibid., '[...] le compagnie di cavalli; distinte in Lancie; corazze, et archibuggeri [...] gli Alemani intorno a trecento; e gli Inglesi, e Scozzesi ducento.'

92. Ibid., 'Trè sono i Terzi de gli Spagnuoli, due quelli de gli Italiani; uno di Borgugnoni; uno d'Irlandesi e trè di Valloni [...] gli Ifanti Irlandesi mille.'

93. Ó Maolchonaire to Aroztegui, Madrid, 25 Oct. 1610 (AGS, E. Flandes, l. 2292): 'por tanto embio aqui a Vuestra Magestad la original carta de Su Magestad esinta al Sr Archiduque, por donde echarà Vuestra Magestad de ver la orden que tiene y que es raçon que se continue y tenga effecto pues cada dia vacan mucho entretenimientos los quales se podran proveer en los que Su Magd ha señalar.'

94. Ó Maolchonaire to Aroztegui, Madrid, 30 Oct. 1610 (AGS, E. Flandes, l. 2292): 'que se ordene al Sr Archiduque quando proveiere estos entretenimientos dar credito a la relacion que le dieren el Capitan Don Eugenio O Nel sobrino del Conde O Nel y el Padre fray Hugo Cavello Guardian del Collegio Yrlandes de Lovayna y Capellan Mayor del dicho Tercio Yrlandesa de aura virtud y buenas partes Su Alteza tiene harta satisfaction'.

95. Ibid., 'haciendo esso no se vera yrlandes aqui, ni sera menester hacer alguna relacion dellos, y si los primeros messes por no saber esta orden vinieron algunos, ia son despachados con decilles que accudan a Su Alteza'.

96. Philip O'Sullivan Beare, *Hist. cath. Ibern.*, pp. 337–8.

97. Report of the Irish found at court, 6 Jul. 1610 (AGS, E. In., l. 2513).

98. For both, see their testimonies on behalf of 'Dermicio O Sulivan', Madrid, 1613 (Archivo Histórico Nacional (hereafter AHN) Madrid, Ordenes militares; Pruebas de Caballeros de Santiago, expediente 7957).

99. Archduke Albert to Philip III, Vintz, 8 Nov. 1607 (AGS, E. Flandes, l. 625).

100. *Wadding Papers*, ed. Brendan Jennings, pp. 77, 353.

101. 'Information of James Bathe, Drogheda', 7 Sept. 1607, (*Cal. S. P. Ire.*, 1606–8, pp. 301–2).

102. Recio Morales, 'De nación irlandés', pp. 315–40.

103. Archduke Albert to Philip III, Vintz, 8 Nov. 1607 (AGS, E. F., l. 625).

104. 'Don Xeraldo Mauriçio cavallero yrlandez' (AGS, E. NP, l. 1750).

105. 'Don Geraldo Mauricio caballero irlandes' (AGS, E. NP, l. 1746): '[...] cavallero muy noble y titulado en el Reyno de Irlanda, que su padre y tio fueron los mas nombrados y calificados caudillos contra luteranos hasta que con muchos parientes y vasallos suyos. Murieron en la demanda confiscandoles su estado y bienes los ingleses'.

106. Ibid., 'que el suplicante a servido seys años a los condes de Tirconnel y Tiron, en negocios de mucha fidelidad y importancia de que siempre dio muy buena parte qta. Por lo qual y sus buenas partes les parece digno de toda la merced que Su Magd fuere servido hazerle. Pide acrecimiento de los 20 ducados de entretenimiento que tiene en Flandes, de los que subieron vacado en el tercio de su nacion y alguna ayuda de costa para el camino.'

107. 'Don Thadeo Odriscol', 1609–10 (AGS, E. NP, l. 1751).

108. Recio Morales, *El socorro de Irlanda*, p. 263.

109. Report of the council of state, Dec. 1610; 'Relacion de los entretenimientos que goçan [...]', Brussels, Oct. 1608 (AGS, E. F., l. 2292).

110. 'Don Antonio de Burgo cavallero yrlandes' (AGS, Guerra Antigua (Servicios de Militares), l. 5, f. 78). Occurring midway between the sixteenth-century *memorial* and the eighteenth-century *hoja* or service record, these sets of folios, known as *relaciones de servicios*, followed definite diplomatic norms: official certification of the functions performed and length of time served by an individual in the armed forces. Directed to the council of war for consideration, they were usually provided by military command, by officers and, to a lesser extent, by civil servants of central government administration, such as regiment accountants. Members of the services and their families closely guarded such documentation to guarantee continued remuneration and support further claims for promotion. See José María Burrieza Sánchez, *Guía del Investigador a los fondos de la Sección Guerra Antigua, Servicios de Militares* (Valladolid: Archivo General de Simancas, 2000), pp. iii–v.

111. 'Pide Entretenimiento para la Armada. Don Antonio de Burgo cavallero yrlandes' (AGS, Guerra Antigua (Servicios de Militares), l. 5, f. 78).

112. Ibid., 'Don Fray Florencio Conryo por la gracia de Dios y de la Santa Sede Apostolica, Arçobispo Tuamense en Irlanda, hago fe que conosco a Don Antonio de Burgo ser hijo de un cavallero de la familia de los Burgos, primo de Mac Villiam Burc, y que el y sus parientes han servido en la ultima guerra de Irlanda, y perdido mucha gente y haçienda en serviçio de Su Magestad.'

113. Ibid., '...por los quales serviçios de sus padres y parientes, me parece que el dicho Antonio es digno de la merced que Su Magestad Catholica fuere servido haçele, y a Su pedimiento le di esta fe, firmada y sellada con mi sello'.

114. Recio Morales, *El socorro de Irlanda*, p. 145.

115. Kerney Walsh, *Destruction by peace*, pp. 273–4.

116. Brendan Jennings (ed.), *Wild Geese in Spanish Flanders*, pp. 118–20; Archduke Albert to Philip III, Vintz, 8 Nov. 1607 (AGS, E. Flandes, l. 625).

117. 'Don Diego Brochero', 22 May 1610 (AGS, E. NP, l. 1752).

118. Kerney Walsh, *Destruction by peace*, pp. 254–5, 261.

119. 'Don Dionisio Carty yrlandes, hermano de Macarthy Mor', Madrid, 30 Oct. 1610 (AGS, Guerra y Marina, l. 704, f. 260).

120. Recio Morales, *El socorro de Irlanda*, p. 146.

121. Ó Maolchonaire to Philip III, Madrid, 9 Sept. 1610 (AGS, E. NP, l. 1751).

122. Julio Albi de la Cuesta, *De Pavía a Rocroi*, Chapter 2.

123. William Trumbull to the secretary of state, Brussels, February 13, 1612 (HMC *Downshire*, vol. 3, 1611–12, pp. 237–8).

124. For the later period, see David Murphy, *The Irish brigades, 1685–2006* (Dublin: Four Courts Press, 2007).

125. Report of the council of state, Madrid, 8 Mar. 1611 (AGS, E. Es., l. 2746); Sir Dudley Carleton to James I, Venice, 18 Mar. 1613 (HMC *Buccleuch*, vol. 1 (1899), pp. 152–5); Edward Eustace to William Trumbull, Paris, 6 Oct. 1613 (HMC *Downshire*, vol. 4, 1/13–8/14).

126. Arrigone to Cardinal Barberini, Rome, 22 Jan. 1610 (Biblioteca Apostolico Vaticano (BAV), Barberini Latini (Barb. Lat.), 8676, 236).

127. Ibid., '[…] mi ricordo chi l'Archiviscovo Tuamensi dimando cosa ch'io restai stupido et voliva non solamenti per la sua diocisi, et provincia ma no noliva far il Papa per tutto quel regno et lo sempri li diecli la negativa.'

128. Ó Maolchonaire to Cardinal Borghèse, Madrid, 17 Mar. 1610 (BAV, Barb. Lat. 8581, 43–4): 'Subito chi'arrivai in questa corti' visto chi' per forza havevo da sta qui qual chi' tiempo, per asistieri' ai Negotii del Conti' di Tiron, ai quali venni per ordini' di Sua Santità.'

129. Ibid., '[…] e del detto Conti', spedii una patenti mia, ordinando un vicario generali' nel mio arcivescovato'.

130. Ibid., '[…] et finiti questi negotii spero veniri' Io costi in persona comi' proposi […] già Sua Maestà ha risolto il negotio principale del Conte di Tiron'.

131. Ibid., 'L'Archivescovo Casselensi' nuovamenti' venuto d'Irlanda […] tieni fama di esseri partiali' in favorire alli Gesuiti.'

132. Philip III's instructions to the Conde de Castro, Madrid, 15 April 1610 (AAEE, FSS, legajo 55, f. 218.)

133. 'Florencio Conryo Arçobpo Tuamen, Madriti', 23 November 1610 (RLM, S52/9/6, f. 4): '… no tengo en toda mi provincia personas suficientes para ser vicarios generales en los obispados sofraganeos'.

134. '… poca aficion que tienen aquellos padres de misma naçion a las desventuradas provincias de Conacia y Ultonia'.

135. Ibid., '… especialmente si consideren la estrema necesidad de aquellas provincias en las quales mando el Rey de Inglaterra que se pusiesen predicantes de su secta en todas las parochias'.

136. Ibid., 'Yo escribi a Roma dando quenta al Conde O Neil de lo que passa, y aunque por ser Arçobispo indigne de la provincia de Conacia pudiera con razon volver sobre sus agrabios, aguardo al parecer del dicho Señor Conde antes que propongo nada a Su Magestad.'

137. Thomas Morrissey's entry on Thomas White, in Charles O'Neill and Joaquín María Dominguez (eds), *Diccionario histórico de la de Jesús* (Rome, 2001), vol. 4, p. 4031.

138. Recio Morales, *El socorro de Irlanda*, pp. 186–7.

139. J. J. Silke, 'Later relations between Primate Peter Lombard and Hugh O'Neill', *Ir. Theol. Quart.*, 22 (1955), pp. 15–30.

140. 'Eugenio Mahon Sacerdote', 1 Aug.1603 (AGS, CJH, l. 429–11 Armada & Ejercito).

141. Silke, 'Primate Peter Lombard and Hugh O'Neill', p. 29.

142. William Trumbull, ambassador in Brussels, to Salisbury, 18 Jul. 1610 (*Cal. S. P. Flanders*, 77/9/II, 398v).

143. Donnchadh Ó Maonaigh to Maurice Walsh, Antwerp, 12 May 1610 (Paul Walsh (ed.), *Gleanings from Irish manuscripts* (Dublin: Three Candles, 1933), pp. 53–60).

144. *Louvain Papers*, ed. Brendan Jennings, p. 11.

145. Ó Maonaigh to the guardian of Multyfarnham friary, Antwerp, 12 May 1610 (Walsh (ed.), (*Gleanings from Irish manuscripts*, pp. 53–60).

146. Chichester to Salisbury, 13 Jun. 1610 (*Cal. S.P. Ire. 1608–10*, p. 461).

147. Ibid.

148. *Archiv. Hib.*, 3 (1914), pp. 300–2.

149. Ó Néill to Philip III, 29 Jul. 1610 (AGS, E. NP, l. 1754). Su Santidad selo ha pedido, como lo pidio en el Breve que escrivio a Su Nuncio el año passado […] y en los Breves que con el Arçobispo

Tuamense embio al Cardenal de Toledo, al Duque de Lerma y al Condestable en las mesma conformidad'; Ó Maolchonaire to Borghèse, 17 Mar. 1610 (BAV, Barb. Lat. 8581, 43–44): '[…] per asistieri' ai Negotii del Conti' di Tiron, ai quali venni per ordini' di Sua Santità'.

150. 'Paulus Papa Quintus', Rome, 5 Jun. 1609 (ASV, Protocollo xlv, tomo 5, ff 4–5).

151. *Petro Lombardo Archiepiscopo Ardmacano Primae Hibernia ad Jacobum Primum Magnae Britanniae Franciae et Hiberniae, Destinatum ac Dictatum pro Religione et Patria* (Archivum Romanum Societate Iesu (hereafter ARSI), 'De Rebis Hibernicis, 1576–1698', 6); for details see *Archiv. Hib.*, 4 (1915), p. 264.

152. *Archiv. Hib.*, 3 (1914), pp. 296–8.

153. Ibid, p. 297: 'officialibus studiosior esse belli suscitandi'.

154. 'Thomas Vito, Rome, 24 di marto 1612', (BAV, Barb. Lat., vol. 8928; ff 29r–30v).

155. Sir Dudley Carleton to James I, 8 Mar. 1613, Venice (*Winwood Papers*, vol. 2, pp. 501–4).

156. Ibid.

157. Ibid.

158. Ibid.

159. *Spic. Ossor.*, vol. 1, p. 235.

160. Declaration by Flaithrí Ó Maolchonaire, Catholic archbishop of Tuam, Madrid, 13 Feb. 1613 (UCD–OFM, D.01, p. 791). Andrés de Soto, commissary general of the Friars Minor and confessor to the Archduchess Isabel, endorsed this declaration in Brussels on 16 Aug. 1617.

161. Cathaldus Giblin, 'Aspects of Franciscan life in Ireland in the seventeenth century', *The Franciscan College Annual* (1948), pp. 67–72.

162. 'Frater Florentius Conrius, Archiep. Tuamen.', *circa* 1613 (BAV, Barb. Lat., vol. 1575, pp. 1r–6v/ ff 238r–243v). The papacies are those of Clement IV, Nicolas IV, Boniface VIII, Benedict II, St Martin, Boniface IX, Pius IV, Innocent IV, Benedict XI and Pius VI.

163. This had arisen after the death of St Francis of Assisi (1182–1226) and was first addressed in detail by St Bonaventure (1221–1274) in his *Apologia Pauperum* of 1269. Nicholas Havely, *Dante and the Franciscans: poverty and the papacy in the 'Commedia'* (Cambridge, 2004), Chapter 4: 'Paradiso: poverty and authority'. See also José de Vinck (ed. and trans.), *St Bonaventure: Apologia Pauperum* (Paris, 1966). Ten years later, on the Feast of the Assumption, Pope Nicholas III (*c.* 1216–1280) accepted this defence and gave his approval to the *regulae* of the Franciscans in a document entitled *Exiit qui seminat*. In 1311 at the Council of Vienne, Clement V (1264–1314) issued a definitive decree, *Exivi de paradiso*. See 'Declaration of the Lord Pope Clement V concerning the rule of the Friars Minor. Clement, Bishop, servant of God's servants, in perpetual memory of the matter', Vienne, 5 May, 1312 (*Declarations of Popes Nicholas III, Clement V, and Innocent on the rule of the friars minor (pro manuscripto)* (Dublin, 1947), pp. 19–29. For the decree in Latin, see Wadding, *Annales Minorum* (vol. 6.), pp. 202–11.

164. Hubert Jedin, *The Council of Trent, 1545–63* (2 vols, Edinburgh: Thomas Nelson & Sons, 1961) vol. 2, pp. 101–22; Henri Daniel-Rops, *The Catholic Reformation* (London: J.M. Dent, 1963), pp. 83–116.

165. 'Frater Florentius Conrius, Archiep. Tuamen' (BAV, Barb. Lat., vol. 1575): 'Cum huius questionis resolutio Canonum dispositionem tantum modo concernat et ad Theologiam scholasticam minime pertineat ea omnia, ex sacris Canonibus, et ex principiis, que a Canonistis probantur, et ad ducuntur ad alias quaestiones resolue.'

166. Ibid., 'Religiosi mendicantes ubique precipue in Hibernia extra monasteria degentes etibi delinquentes, subsint punitioni visitationi, et correctioni episcopo et alio ordinario.'

167. See James Waterworth (ed. and trans.), *The canons and decrees of the sacred and œcumenical Council of Trent* (London: Dolman, 1848), p. 52.

168. Giblin, 'Franciscan life in Ireland in the seventeenth century', pp. 67–72.

169. Waterworth (ed. and trans.), *The canons and decrees*, pp. 64–5.

170. 'Frater Florentius Conrius, Archiep. Tuamen.' (BAV, Barb. Lat., vol. 1575 pp. 1r–6v/ ff 238r–243v): '[…] decreto et sub prefata constitutione Innoc. 4 posita in c. Volentes de privi'.

171. Waterworth (ed. and trans.), *The canons and decrees*, pp. 64–5.

172. 'Frater Florentius Conrius, Archiep. Tuamen.' (BAV, Barb. Lat., vol. 1575): 'Pro explicatione huius controversiae animadvertendum est […] in remissione religiosi intra claustra degentis et deprehensi in flagranti delicto foris ad suum superiorem.'

173. Waterworth (ed. and trans.), *The canons and decrees*, p. 246.

174. Ibid.

175. 'Frater Florentius Conrius, Archiep. Tuamen' (BAV, Barb. Lat., vol. 1575): '[…] in Regno Hiberniae ubi haec controversia incepta est, tibi ministrabitur ansa haereticis gloriandi, et insultandi contra Catholicos super sua Iurisdicion sic semper litigantes cum hereticos et Catholicos secularium scandalo et si adhuc illis ordinariis in Hibernia concederemus hanc Iurisdictionem non poterunt

eam exerere, cum in illis partibus non possint ob hereticos et persecutiones uti publice sua iurisdictione, neg. carceres habere ni quibus hoc monumentum sibi suisque [oi.] delinquentes puniant […] puniendi religiosos delinquentes cum non possunt […] vel ex communicationis eos ueleorum benefactores.'

176. Brian Mac Cuarta, *Catholic revival in the north of Ireland, 1603–41* (Dublin: Four Courts Press, 2007), pp. 18–19, 71–2, 130.
177. Ibid., pp. 84–90. The theme of Gaelic Maccabean thought is returned to in the next chapter.
178. Benignus Millett, *The Irish Franciscans, 1651–1665* (Rome: Analecta Gregoriana, 1964), pp. 4–5.
179. Report of the council of state, Madrid, 8 March 1611 (AGS, E. Es., l. 2746); Sir Dudley Carleton to James I, Venice, 18 March 1613 (HMC *Buccleuch*, vol. 1 (1899), pp. 152–5); Edward Eustace to William Trumbull, Paris, 6 October 1613 (HMC *Downshire*, vol. 4, 1/13–8/14).
180. Miguel Ángel Echevarría Bacigalupe, *La diplomacia secreta en Flandes, 1598–1643* (Leioa–Vizcaya, 1984), pp. 36–7; José García Oro, *Don Diego Sarmiento de Acuña, Conde de Gondomar y embajador de España (1567–1626): estudio biográfico* (Santiago: Xunta de Galicia, 1997), pp. 240–3.
181. Ortiz, *The Golden Age of Spain*, p. 43.
182. Charles Carter, 'The ambassadors of early-modern Europe', in idem (ed.), *From the Renaissance to the Counterreformation* (London: Jonathan Cape, 1966), pp. 280–1.
183. Recio Morales, *El socorro de Irlanda*, p. 104.
184. See Murray, *A history of the commercial and financial relations*; George O'Brien, *The economic history of Ireland* (Dublin: Maunsel, 1919); Hugh Kearney, 'The Irish wine trade, 1614–1615', *IHS*, 9/36 (1955), pp. 400–42; Schüller, *Die Beziehungen zwischen Spanien und Irland im XVI und XVII Jahrhundert*.
185. *Cal. S. P. Ire. 1600–01*, p. 126; cited by O'Brien, *The economic history of Ireland*, pp. 95–8.
186. Boate, *A natural history of Ireland*; quoted by Murray, *A history of the commercial and financial relations*, p. 18.
187. O'Brien, *The economic history of Ireland*, p. 195.
188. Ibid, p. 82.
189. *Cal. S. P. Ire., 1660–62*, pp. 151–2; cited by O'Brien, *The economic history of Ireland*, p. 180–3.
190. Kearney, 'The Irish wine trade, 1614–1615', pp. 400–42.
191. O'Brien, *The economic history of Ireland*, pp. 163–4.
192. *Cal. S. P. Ire., 1611–14*, p. 502; *Cal. S. P. Carew, 1603–24*, p. 138; Barnaby Rich, 'Remembrances of the state of Ireland, 1612,' ed. C. Litton Falkiner, in *Proc. RIA*, vol. 26 (1907), section c., p. 126; O'Brien, *The economic history of Ireland*, pp. 41–2.
193. O'Brien, *The economic history of Ireland*, p. 83; Karin Schüller, *Die beziehungen zwischen Spanien und Irland*, pp. 212–13.
194. Flaithrí Ó Maolchonaire to the Spanish secretary of state, Madrid, 29 Sept. 1611 (AGS, E. In. l. 2588, f. 67).
195. Ciarán O'Scea, 'The role of Castilian royal bureaucracy', p. 230.
196. 'El arçobispo fray Florencio Conrrio', 29 Sept. 1611 (AGS, E. In. l. 2588, f. 67).
197. Recio Morales, *El socorro de Irlanda*, p. 265.
198. Thomas Doyne to John Bourke, Venice, 17 September 1615 (*Cal. S.P. Ire., 1615–25*, pp. 89–91).
199. See, for instance, Ó Maolchonaire to Aroztegui, 29 Sept. 1611 (AGS, E. In. l. 2588, f. 67).
200. For his many letters to Philip III and the council of state on the dangers of piracy, see Real Biblioteca, Madrid, volumes II-2108; II-2115; II-2168; II-2191; II-2221.
201. García Oro, *Don Diego Sarmiento de Acuña*, pp. 123–8.
202. Ibid., pp. 242–4.
203. Gondomar to Ó Maolchonaire, London, 17 May 1615 (AGS, Estado, legajo 370, ff 252r–253v). A copy of this letter was sent to Antonio Orquines SJ.
204. Garrett Mattingly, *Renaissance diplomacy* (New York: Jonathan Cape, 1988), p. 266.
205. Cf. Echevarría Bacigalupe; *La diplomacia secreta en Flandes*, pp. 37–8, 91–7.
206. 'Parece contrario al casamiento de fray Florencio Conrrio, arçobpo de Tuemia en Irlanda' (AGS, E. In., Libro 369 (l. 7,026), pp. 72–4).
207. 'Stafford to the lords of the council', Dublin, 23 Nov. 1627 (*Cal. S. P. Ire., 1625–32*, p. 645).
208. Flaithrí Ó Maolchonaire to the Spanish secretary of state, Madrid, 29 Sept. 1611 (AGS, E. In. l. 2588, f. 67); Kerney Walsh, *Destruction by peace*, pp. 278–9.
209. Recio Morales, *El socorro de Irlanda*, p. 244.
210. 3 Jac. c. 6 (Engl.); quoted by Murray, *A history of the commercial and financial relations between England and Ireland*, p. 7.
211. 'Sobre lo que ha pedido la nacion irlandesa acerca detener consul de su nacion en el Andaluzia', Madrid (AGS, E. Indiferente de España y norte, l. 4191).

212. Ibid., 'y los que ban a San Lucar suelen visitados por un ingles llamado Thomas Jaimes Morador alli con quien no se entienden los dichos irlandeses y les haze muchas molestias y agravios por ser de naçion enemiga y diferente en la lengua'.

213. Ibid., 'suplico a VMD en nombre de toda la naçion irlandessa fuesse servido de mandar al Duque de Medina, que reciviesse por consul de todos los irlandeses que aportasen a aquella costa a un Nicolas Vis de su naçion vecino de San Lucar y casado con española persona de muy buenas partes.'

214. For one 'Nicolas Wisse', see 'Relacion de los entretenimientos que goçan', Brussels, Oct. 1608 (AGS, E. Flandes, l. 2292); see also the prueba for 'Daniel O Sulivan Bearra', Madrid, 1617 (AHN, Ordenes militares; Pruebas de Caballeros de Santiago, expediente 5808).

215. Report of the council of state to Philip III, 2 Aug. 1614, Madrid (AGS, E. Indiferente de España y norte, l. 4191).

216. Ibid., 'en persona muy benemerita que es el dicho Thomas Jaimes ingles con entretenimiento de VMD y muy catolico y fiel y es consul de la Gran Bretaña en quese incluye Irlanda y Escocia por ser toda de la Corona de Inglaterra.'

217. 'Diego Geraldin Consul', Seville, 17 Nov. 1620 (AGS, E. Es., l. 2646); Thirty-five-point list of Ireland's resources, 1623 (AGS, E. In., l. 2516, carpeta 985).

218. K. R. Andrews, 'Caribbean rivalry and the Anglo-Spanish treaty of 1604', History, 59 (1974), pp. 1–17.

219. 'Relacion de Virginia al Consejo de Estado', Madrid, 1 Jul. 1610 (AGS, Estado 2587, f. 98).

220. Brian McGinn, 'Virginia's lost Irish colonists', Irish Roots (1993), pp. 21–4.

221. 'Relacion de Virginia al Consejo de Estado', 'Del Emperador y naturales de la Tierra […] El emperador y sus hijos prometieron a los Ingleses que dexarian su Religion y creerian en el Dios de los Ingleses y por la familiaridad grande que muestran pareze que son faciles para convertirse.'

222. Ibid., 'Los Ingleses no pretenden ninguna otra cosa tanto como hazerse señores del mar del sur para tener su parte de las Riquezas de Indias y para estorvar el Trafago del Rey de España y para buscar otros nuevos mundos para si.'

223. Ibid., 'Para el sobre dicho efecto embio el Rey de Inglaterra alla muchos de los mejores Carpinteros de su Reyno […] Para fabricar navios y barcos en aquellos rios y mares para lo qual tienen alli grandissima comodidad, por que tienen mucha abundancia del mejor maderamiento que se puede hallar para haber navios, y la tierra de suyo es abundamente de Pez, Rezina y Trementina, y hazce naturalmente en ella mucha Cañamo de que piensan hazer cables y cuerdas para los navios […] podran hazer mas daño al Rey de España.'

224. Ibid.

225. K. R. Andrews, Trade, plunder and settlement (Cambridge: Cambridge University Press, 1991); Elliott, 'Foreign policy and domestic crisis: Spain, 1598–1659', in idem (ed.), Spain and its world, 1500–1700 (New Haven, CT: Yale University Press, 1989), pp. 114–36.

226. 'Sobre lo que pide el Arçobispo Tuamense por un irlandes que ha estado en La Virginia', Madrid, 17 Jul. 1610 (AGS, E. NP, l. 2745).

227. Ibid., 'El consejo ordeno a Don Diego Brochero que haviendo se Informado de las partes deste Irlandes avisase lo que seria bien hazer con el, y dize que ha tenido del muy buena relaçion que demas de ser Gran Artillero tiene mucha platica de piloto que sera muy aproposito para servir en la Armada.'

228. Alexander Brown, The Genesis of the United States (New York: Russell & Russell, 1890), vol.1, p. 457.

229. Flaithrí Ó Maolchonaire to Lerma, Madrid, 10 Jan. 1612 (AGS, Consejo y Juntas de Hacienda (CJH), legajo 428-17).

230. Bentivoglio to the papal secretary of state, 6 Apr. 1613 (ASV, Borghese, I, vol. 269–72, pp. 42–6): 'Dell'essercito che mantiene il Rè Cattco in Fiandra […] in grandissime angustie gli Archiduchi'.

231. 'El Duque a 9 de enero 1613. El Coronel Don Enrrique Onel', Palacio (AGS, CJH, legajo 522-22-9).

232. O'Scea, 'The role of Castilian royal bureaucracy', in O'Connor and Lyons (eds), Irish communities in early-modern Europe, pp. 200–39.

233. 'Al Presidente de Hazienda', 3 Sept. 1602 (AGS, Consejo y Juntas de Hacienda (CJH), legajo 428-17).

234. 'Señor Duque, 3 de septiembre 1602', Valladolid (AGS, Consejo y Juntas de Hacienda (CJH), legajo 428-17).

235. Conde de Castro to Philip III, 15 Sept. 1615, Rome; cited by Kerney Walsh, Destruction by peace, p. 366.

236. Philip III to the Conde de Castro, 4 Apr. 1616, Madrid; cited by Kerney Walsh, Destruction by peace, p. 375.

237. 'Las dichas consignaciones', Aug. 1613, Madrid (AGS, Contaduría Mayor de Cuentas, 3a epoca, l. 3,159, sección 23, ff 23v–24v).

238. Ibid.
239. 'A suplicacion de Don Fray Florencio Conrio Arçobispo Tuamense en Irlanda', 7 Oct. 1617, Lerma (AGS, CJH 549-27-8, Particulares).
240. Philip III to the Council of Finance, 26 Oct. 1617, Ventosilla (AGS, CJH 556-15-2, Particulares).
241. Same to Albert, 4 Nov. 1617, Pardo (AGR, Secrétairerie d'État et de Guerre, registre 181).
242. Flaithrí Ó Maolchonaire to the Spanish secretary of state, Madrid, 29 Sept. 1611 (AGS, E. In. l. 2588, f. 67).
243. Spanish council of state to Philip III: 'Que han presso a algunas sacerdotes y a un Arzobispo y persiguen mucho los Catholicos' (AGS, E. In. l. 2588, f. 67).
244. Ibid., 'Que en Irlanda quisieron publicar un edito paraque dentro de seis meses saliesen de alli todos los religiosos que ay en aquel Reyno y para que todos jurasen por caveza de la Iglessia al Rey. Que El Conde de Clanricard que es Irlandes no bino en esto y paso a Inglaterra a dar quenta que se hazia aquello por orden del Rey.'
245. Ibid.
246. See, for instance, the Irish Franciscans' manuscript description of the parliament's proceedings in 1613, dated 4 October (Archivium Collegii S. Isidori de Urbe (ACSI), Rome, Sectio W.1.5/P208/5).
247. 'El Consejo de Estado' (AGS, E. In., l. 844, ff 183–7).
248. Cesáreo Aguilera, 'La teoría del estado en la España de los Austrias', Revista de Estudios Políticos, 36 (1983), pp. 131–58.
249. Domínguez Ortiz, Golden Age, pp. 238–9.
250. R. F. Foster, Modern Ireland 1600–1972 (Harmondsworth: Penguin, 1989), pp. 45, 50.
251. Edmund Curtis and R. B. McDowell (eds), Irish historical documents: 1172–1922 (London: Methuen, 1943), pp. 133–5. The six were: Gormanston, Slane, Kileen, Trimbleston, Dunsany and Louth.
252. Patrick Moran (ed.), Spic. Ossor. vol. 1, p. 122; Richard Bagwell, Ireland under the Stuarts, vol. 1, p. 110.
253. 'Auisi d'Inghilterra, 19 vii 612' (ASV, Inghilterra 19, ff 50–66): 'Sua Maestà […] ordine a tutti si ministra il giuramento […] All'istesso tempo che venne questa scatola Sua Maestà hebbe auiso che in Irlanda la parte di Catolici nel parlamento non si voleua rendere ne accettare le leggi di Sua Maestà contra la religione loro.'
254. T. W. Moody, 'The Irish parliament under Elizabeth and James I: a general survey', RIA Proc., 45 (1939), pp. 49–81.
255. Mark Netzloff, 'Forgetting the Ulster plantation: John Speed's The theatre of the empire of Great Britain (1611) and the colonial archive', Journal of Medieval and Early-Modern Studies, 31 (2001), pp. 313–48.
256. Cal. Carew MSS, 1603–24, p. 280; Moody, 'The Irish parliament under Elizabeth and James I', p. 54.
257. Thomas Leland, The history of Ireland (Dublin: Brett Smith, 1814), p. 447.
258. C. Litton Falkiner, 'His Majesty's Castle of Dublin', in idem (ed.), Illustrations of Irish history and topography, mainly of the seventeenth century (London: Longmans, Green, & Co. 1904), p. 28.
259. Leland, The history of Ireland, p. 451.
260. 11 Jac. 1, Irish Stat. 11, 12, 13; cited by Leland, The history of Ireland, p. 456.
261. Philip O'Sullivan Beare, Hist. Cath. Ibern., tom iv, lib. ii, cap. ix; Charles Meehan, Fate and fortunes of the earls of Tyrone and Tyrconnell, p. 395.
262. Ibid.
263. Thomas O'Connor, 'Review of Tadhg Ó hAnnracháin, Catholic Reformation in Ireland: the Mission of Rinuccini, 1645–1649', Ríocht na Midhe, 14 (2003), pp. 264–8.
264. Cf. Bernadette Cunningham, 'Native culture and political change', pp. 148–70.
265. Exchequer Inquisition, 24 Jan. 1584 (NAI, Repertories to Inquisitions (Exchequer), County Roscommon, Elizabeth, 4).
266. See, for instance, 'Melaghlin Modder claim as rightful inheritance […] Ardanafrine and Corlisconnel, 2 quarters', 18 Sept. 1610 (NAI, Repertories to Inquisitions (Exchequer), County Roscommon, James I, 7).
267. Brendan O'Bric, 'Galway townsmen as landowners in Connacht' (NUIG, MA thesis, 1974).
268. Patrick Duffy, 'The territorial organisation of Gaelic landownership and its transformation in County Monaghan, 1591–1640', Ir. Geography, 14 (1981), pp. 1–26. See also, Mary O'Dowd, 'Land inheritance in early-modern Sligo', in Irish Economic and Social History, 10 (1983), pp. 5–18.
269. Brian Mac Cuarta, 'The plantation of Leitrim, 1620–41', IHS, 32 (2001), p. 318.
270. Moody, 'The Irish parliament under Elizabeth and James I', pp. 74, 79.
271. Carew Cal. 1603–24, p. 292, Alan Ford, The Protestant reformation in Ireland, 1590–1641 (Dublin: Four Courts Press, 1985), pp. 123–51. See also Tadhg Cronin, 'The Elizabethan colony in Co. Roscommon', in Harman Murtagh (ed.), Irish Midland Studies (Athlone: Old Athlone Society, 1980).

272. 8 Jun. 1608: '5 qrs of Clonpluckan' (*Cal. pat. rolls Ire., Jas I* (Pat. 6), p. 126a, 406a).
273. 7 Jan. 1619: '5 qrs of Clonpluckan to Sir John King, muster master and privy councillor', (*Cal. pat. rolls Ire., Jas I*, p. 460).
274. 21 Jan. 1616, Tulsk, County Roscommon (N.A. Exchequer Inquisitions, James I; 2–4, 7, 12–13, 20): 'Shennaghin O Mulconry of Ballicomin [...] Maurice O Molconrie, Clonehihe [...] Mallin O Mulconry [...] Padin Roe O Mulconry [...] Gillacollum Duffe O Mulconrie'; 3 Feb. 1616 (N.A., Exchequer Inquisitions, James I; 18, entries 9–12): 'Torne O Mulconrie [...] John and Phihell O Mulconera'.
275. See *Oxford New DNB* entry.
276. Robin Flower, 'Introduction', in idem (ed.), *Catalogue of Irish manuscripts in the British Museum*, vol. 3 (London, 1953), pp. 3–4.
277. Leland, *The history of Ireland*, p. 451; Moody, 'The Irish parliament under Elizabeth and James I', pp. 65–7.
278. Ó Néill to Philip III, Rome; Kerney Walsh, *Destruction by peace*, p. 343.
279. Ó Néill to Velasquez de Velasco, 23 May 1615, Rome; Kerney Walsh, *Destruction by peace*, pp. 351–3.
280. Velasquez de Velasco, 28 Jun. 1615; Kerney Walsh, *Destruction by peace*, pp. 355–7.
281. Bagwell, *Ireland under the Stuarts*, pp. 8–9.
282. HMC *Egmont*, vol. 1, pt. 1, p. lxx.
283. Kerney Walsh, *Destruction by peace*, pp. 148–9.
284. Sir Dudley Carleton to James I, Venice, 8 Mar. 1613 (*Winwood Papers*, vol. 3, pp. 501–4).
285. Velasquez de Velasco to Lerma, Madrid; Kerney Walsh, *Destruction by peace*, pp. 355–6.
286. Ibid., 4 Jul. 1615. From them he learned that, while the Irish would recognise the earl of Tyrone as their leader 'in the fortunes of war', they would not bow to him as their king. See Kerney Walsh, *Destruction by peace*, pp. 357–9
287. Philip III to the Conde de Castro, Madrid, 8 Jul. 1615, Madrid; Kerney Walsh, *Destruction by peace*, p. 413; Flaithrí Ó Maolchonaire to Andrés Velasquez de Velasco, Madrid, Saturday, Sept. 1615: '[...] se pida a Su Magestad es que el tercio questa en Flandes y el Conde de Tiron bacian a Irlanda' (AGS, Estado, legajo 629, f. 153).
288. Ó Maolchonaire to Velasquez de Velasco: '[...] con muy poca ayuda basta este cavallero para alborotar a toda Escocia' (AGS, Estado, legajo 629, f. 153.)
289. 'Don Diego Magdonel' (AGS, Estado, Inglaterra, l. 845 (1615–22), ff 82, 102–3); Nuncio Morra to Cardinal Borghèse, Brussels, 9 Sept. 1617 (ASV, Borghèse II, 137, ff 64–5).
290. Madrid, 13 Sept. 1615; Kerney Walsh, *Destruction by peace*, pp. 363–4.
291. See, for example, Felim O'Brien, 'Florence Conry, archbishop of Tuam', *Irish Rosary*, 32 (1928), p. 457.
292. Carter, 'The ambassadors of early-modern Europe', pp. 276–7.
293. 'Cartas de españoles destacados como agentes en las principales ciudades italianas', Fundación Ducal de Medinaceli, Archivo Histórico, legajo 56, ramo 2 (1606–9).
294. Cardinal de Borja to the Conde de Gondomar, Rome, 23 Jul. 1616 (RBPM, II–2152). Fearing that such news could threaten peace with James I, 'aber sido tenido por rebelde el conde', this part of the letter was ciphered.
295. Francis Cottingham to Ralph Winwood, Madrid, 19 Aug. 1616; cited by Charles Meehan, *Fate and fortunes of the earls of Tyrone and Tyrconnell*, p. 477.
296. O'Connor, 'Perfidious Machiavellian friar: Florence Conry's campaign for a Catholic restoration in Ireland', p. 99.
297. Luke Wadding, *Scriptores Ordinis Minorum*, p. 109.
298. *Desiderius, otherwise called Sgáthán an Chrábhaidh by Flaithrí Ó Maolchonaire*, ed. Thomas O'Rahilly (Dublin: Dublin Institute for Advanced Studies, repr. 1975), p. xv.
299. R. I. Best, 'Distinguished Connaught men', in Fletcher (ed.), *Connaught*, p. 158.
300. Seán Ó Súilleabháin, 'Údar *Sgáthán an Chrábhaidh*', *Maynooth Review*, 14 (1989), pp. 42–50; idem, '*Sgáthán an Chrábhaidh*: Foinsí an aistriúcháin', *Éigse*, 24 (1990), pp. 26–36.
301. August Bover i Font, 'Notes sobre les traduccions no castellanes de l'Spill de la vida religiosa', *Estudis de la llengua i literatura catalanes*, 3 (1981), pp. 129–38.
302. *Tolle crucem tuam & sequere me* (Take up your cross and follow me), Matt. XVI: 24.
303. Benjamin Hazard, 'Gaelic political scripture in the sixteenth century: Uí Mhaoil Chonaire scribes and the *Book of Mac Murchadha-Caomhánach*', in *Proceedings of the Harvard Celtic Colloquium, 2003* (Harvard University Press, 2009), pp. 149–64.
304. Thomas O'Connor, 'The ideology of state building in early-modern Europe: Ireland and the formation of an Irish Catholic *natio* in the early seventeenth century', in Gudmundur Hálfdanarson and Ann Katherine Isaacs (eds), *Nations and nationality in historical perspective* (Pisa: Edizioni Plus, 2001) p. 250.

305. O'Rahilly, Introduction to *Desiderius [...] Sgáthán an Chrábhaidh*, p. xvi.
306. Ó Buachalla, *Aisling ghéar*, pp. 23–4.
307. *Desiderius*, p. 127.
308. Ibid, pp. 119, 125–6.
309. Ibid, p. 128; Mac Craith, 'The political and religious thought of Florence Conry and Hugh McCaughwell', pp. 183–202.
310. Melquíades Andrés Martín (ed.), *Historia de la teología española* (2 vols, Madrid: Fundación Universitaria Española, 1983–7), vol. 1, pp. 350–3.
311. *Desiderius*, p. 128.
312. *Cf.* Council of state to Philip III, Madrid, August 1614 (AGS, E. In., l. 844, ff 183–7).
313. Nicholas Canny, *Making Ireland British* (Oxford: Oxford University Press, 2002), p. 428; Paul Kléber Monod, *The power of kings: monarchy and religion in Europe, 1589–1715* (New Haven, CT: Yale University Press, 1999), p. 52.
314. *Desiderius*, p. 133.
315. Ibid., pp. 158–9.
316. Thomas O'Connor, 'The ideology of statebuilding', pp. 250–2.
317. Ó Buachalla, *Aisling ghéar*, p. 30.
318. Fernández Armesto, 'The improbable empire', p. 145.
319. Ford, *The Protestant reformation in Ireland*, p. 147.
320. Mac Cuarta, 'The plantation of Leitrim', p. 304.
321. 21 Jan. 1616, Tulsk, County Roscommon (NAI, Repertories to Inquisitions (Exchequer), County Roscommon, James I, 20).
322. HMC *Egmont*, p. lxx.
323. Sir Richard Lane was granted the 1st baronetcy of Tulsk, Roscommon in 1661. His mother was an O'Farrell and his wife, Mabell, a daughter of Gerald Fitzgerald of Rathaman (*Linea Antigua*, Royal Irish Academy, MS E44, National Library of Ireland, Dublin, Genealogical MS 155). I am indebted to Kenneth Nicholls for the aforementioned information on Ó Maolchonaire's brother and Sir Richard Lane.
324. Gaelic deed, Roscommon, 1623 (TNA, Chancery Master Exhibits, unsorted collection, C.106/104, box 2).
325. Last will and testament of Maoilechlainn Modartha Ó Maolchonaire, 7 Aug. 1612 (NAI, Chancery Master Exhibits, unsorted collection, C.106/104, box 2).
326. José Pablo Alzina, *Embajadores de España en Londres: una guia de retratos de la embajada de España* (Madrid: Ministero de Asuntos Exteriores, 2001), pp. 89–105; Mattingly, *Renaissance diplomacy*, pp. 202–21.
327. García Oro, *Don Diego Sarmiento de Acuña*, pp. 307–8. See also Glyn Redworth, *The Prince and the Infanta: the cultural politics of the Spanish match* (New Haven, CT: Yale University Press, 2003). For a reappraisal, see Robert Cross, 'Pretence and perception in the Spanish Match, or history in a fake beard', *Journal of Interdisciplinary History*, 37 (2007), pp. 563–83.
328. Kerney Walsh, *Destruction by peace*, pp. 293, 346.
329. See Samuel Gardiner (ed. and trans.), *El hecho del matrimonio pretendido por el Principe de Gales con la Serenissima* (London: Camden Society, 1869).
330. 'Paracer contrario al casamiento de Fr. Florencio Conrrio, Arzobispo de Tuemia, en Irlanda' (AGS, Estado, libro 369, pp. 72–4).
331. Ibid., 'no esta bien a Su Cathca Magd fiarse en amistad de los Yngleses por mas union que aja entre las dos naçiones Española y Ynglesa … por esperiencia pues se vee que por estabia a penas. Se puede oj dia ganar la voluntad de un Principe Xptiano como el Rey de Françia.'
332. Bonney, *The European dynastic states*, p. xxv.
333. 'Paracer contrario al casamiento' (AGS, Estado, libro 369, pp. 72–4): 'Que haora es el tiempo mientras el Rey de Françia tiene neçessidad de las amistades de España y antes que venga a he edad de Ombre que entonçes podra ser que sea del umor de Su padre.'
334. Geoffrey Parker, *The army of Flanders and the Spanish road, 1567–1659*, pp. 60–71, 91.
335. 'Paracer contrario al casamiento': 'que hiçieron ultimamente en ayuda del Saboyano embiandole ocultamente doçientos mill ducados para pagar la cavalleria.'
336. Ibid., 'Que es çierto que todos los principes de la christianidad estan tan temerosos de ver tanta potencia como la de España y tan ymbidiosos de ber que toda la Riqueza de este mundo que es lo que viene cada año de las Yndias.'
337. Ibid., 'Que con semejante union a segura el Rey de España al Yngles sus estados que estando en union con España no se atreveran sus Vasallos a haçer cossa contraer y el Rey de España tendra sus estados menos seguros.'
338. Ibid., '[…] se sacare della sera tener el Rey de Yngalatierra mas comodidad para […] pegar mas y

mas cada dia su herejia en España secretamente socapa de amistad y trato e yr ganando mas tierra en el Camino de las Yndias asta que bea su coyuntura de a cometer a todas.'

339. 'Paracer contrario al casamiento': 'Que tantas coyunturas se ofreçen que no seria milagro ver semejante ocasion especialmente estando los Yndianos tan cansados y deseosos deber otro genero de govierno y los Españoles que naçen y tienen haçienda alla bulliçiosos y sujetos a levantarse con todo allando a Su Magestad una vez muy ocupado por aca por berse tan distante y lejos de sus fuerças.'

340. Ibid., 'Lo segundo se piensa que Su Magestad haçe mucho bien a los Catholicos del septentrion obligando al yngles a que diese livertad de conciençia a sus Vasallos dejando a parte quando viniese en ello el yngles que es la palabra de hereje que no la cumplia mañana.'

341. Ibid., '[...] obligando al yngles a que diese livertad de conciençia a sus Vasallos dejando a parte quando viniese en ello el yngles que es la palabra de hereje que no la cumplia mañana no pareçe sino lo contrario que no se haçe bien en ello a los Catholicos sino mal por quee estando el yngles seguro de España por Raçon de Casamiento [...] para extinguir los Catholicos y privar los de sus tierras y haçiendas'.

342. Ibid., '[...] otras mill mentiras que los ministros del Rey de Yngalatierra les levantarian cada momento como los levantan oy dia a los obispos y sacerdotes que mentiriçan significando que no lo hacen por ser ellos Catholicos sino por crimen de lesa Magd. que cometiesen.'

343. *Scriptores Ordinis Minorum*, pp. 75–6. According to Wadding, Ó Maolchonaire was 'per Anglos proscriptus'.

344. 'Paracer contrario al casamiento' (AGS, Estado, libro 369, pp. 72–4): 'Quanto y mas que quando les diese de coraçon Livertad de Conçiençia y les guardase bien su palabra no estaria esso bien al servicio de Su Catholica Magd porque en tal cassio sus Vasallos del Yngles le querrian mas que a ningun otro principe y le servirian de beras contrato el mundo y en la conquista de las Yndias que nunca dexara el Yngles de proseguir por mas union que tenga con España.'

345. Ibid., 'Lo tercero como los enimigos ven que en España son tan amigos de la paz que por mas tiros que ellos hagarian desimulando en España por el mesmo casa que España con menos reputaçion obligada a conserver y aun a mendigar las voluntades de los enemigos con dadivas disimilaçiones. Y subjeciones muy endignas de tanta monarquia y queda echada por tiene aquel espanto y temor que en tiempos pasados todo el mundo tenia a España.'

346. Ibid., '[...] quedan los enemigos muy ufanos y arrogantes espantando y a temoriçando con deçir que romperan las paçes'.

347. Ibid., '[...] por la mesma Raçon queda España en perpetuo peligro porque queda en paz con sus enemigos y los enemigos en guerra, con ella como se echa deber en todas las ocassiones que se ofreçe contra el serviçio de Su Catholica Magestad que ninguna de han pasar'.

348. Charles Carter, *The secret diplomacy of the Habsburgs, 1598–1625* (New York: Columbia University Press, 1964), p. 278; Peter Brightwell, 'The Spanish system and the twelve years' truce', *English Historical Review*, 89 (1974), pp. 270–92.

349. 'Paracer contrario al casamiento': 'la conquista de la Virginia y Bermudas cosas que puedan ser de mucho peligro a España'; 'Y quien les quitara que armen una fuerte armada de Yngleses y Olandeses quando vean su ocassion y tomen alguna vez la flota de Yndias [...] y ellos dieron exemplo a otros principes a que hagan otra conquista contra España pues sufre todo por conservar las paçes.'

350. 'Paracer contrario al casamiento': 'Ademas que cada dia sea provechan los enemigos de las paces fortificandose en la Virginia y Bermudas.'

351. Ibid., 'Que si el Rey ahorrara muchos millones con la paz y los amontonaria para dar despues sobre sus enemigos su paçiençia Y silençio mas tolerable pero temese que no ahorra.'

352. Ibid., '[...] lo que gastara Su Magestad ahora con echarlos por ventura le costaria seis veçes tanto si tarda mucho'.

353. Ibid., 'Y tenban los enemigos desarragando y aniguilando Los Catholicos de Yrlanda que son amigos de España y el unico puesto por donde el Yngles teme [...] y teniendo el Rey de Yngalatierra sus tres Reynos una bez seguros y plantados de hereges como pretende.'

354. Ibid., 'es indiçio bastante la confiscaçion que hiçieron ahora de las tierras de los condes de Tiron y Tirconel que contenienen cassi la quinta parte del Reyno'.

355. Ibid., '[...] lo que haçe agora se puede conjeturar que toros hara entonces a España y las ligas que hara con Principes enemigos.'

356. Ibid., 'De lo suso se saca quan ymportante es a la conservaçion de la monarquia de España poner algo remedio a los dichos yncombinientes.'

357. Ibid., 'Y el Remedio es poner a Yrlanda en livertad que se del bando de España cossa que no tiene mas dificultad que empeçarlo bien y con secreto por los muchos señores que ay de aquella tierra desterrados y por el terçio que ay en Flandes en qual ay cavalleros de cada familia del Reyno y por la disposiçion de los cavalleros que en el estan oprimidos y tiraniçados de los herejes yngleses.'

358. 'Paracer contrario al casamiento': 'Y echo esto una bez fuera de la grande Gloria que se sigue dello al serviçio de Dios y de su Yglesia y de cumplir con la obligacion que tiene Su Magd a los dichos Catholicos por que se perdieron por haver le serbido se ebitan todos los peligros y desbenturas que los enemigos y la adbersa fortuna amenaçan a España.'

359. Ibid., '[...] que como Lombardia y Flandes sirven a Su Catholica Magd por freno contra el francés para detenerle a [que] no haga contra España todo lo que desee.'

360. Ibid., 'teniendo Su Catholica Magd a Yrlanda [...] dara las Yndias muy seguras del sepentrion.'

361. 'Paracer contrario al casamiento': 'Y como Su Magd alço al Duque de Neoburgo y le ayuda para tenerle por contrapresso contra los Olandeses assi es necessario tener otro contra preso contra el Ingles que de otra manera estando metido en Sus Islas y tiros que quisiere pero teniendo Su Catholica Magd a Yrlanda le ata las manos de manera que no se atreviera a haçer nada contra España ni aun en secreto.'

362. Ibid., 'Y si el Rey de Yngalatierra muere presto [...] en tal caso teniendo Su Magd Catholica gente de Yrlanda los Catolicos de Yngalatierra viendo el socorro tan cerca nunca admitaran al Palatino que es hereje y estrangero [...] siendo el sobrino del Conde Mauriçio si biniese a ser Rey de Yngalatierra claro esta que ayudaria a los Olandeses con todas sus fuerças. Y que tentaria salir por Emperador con ayuda de los Olandeses y de los demas herejes de Alemania y Francia y proveraria haçer todo quanto pudiese contra España.'

363. Ibid., '[...] teniendo Su Magd a Yrlanda quedaran los Catholicos de Yngalatierra, Escoçia tan animados que no tendra el Rey herege que les hiço tantos agravios un dia dequietud por los lebantamientos que harian contra el demanera que bendria el gobierno de Yngalatierra a caer presto'.

364. Parker, *The army of Flanders and the Spanish road, 1567–1659*, pp. 249–50; Paul Allen, *Philip III and the Pax Hispanica*, Chapters 3 and 7.

365. Gráinne Henry, *The Irish military community*, pp. 66, 89.

366. 'Paracer contrario al casamiento': '[...] no gastando con todo ello lo que gasto con obstende porque ni en Yrlanda ni en Escoçia ni en Yngalatierra ay Plaças fuertes en que el que fue Señor de la Campaña lo sera luego de todo y en cada tres leguas de Flandes ay un Ostende'.

367. Domínguez Ortiz, *The Golden Age of Spain*, pp. 88, 129.

368. Elliott, *Imperial Spain*, pp. 324–5.

369. García Oro, *Don Diego Sarmiento de Acuña*, pp. 307–8.

370. Albert Loomie, 'Spanish secret diplomacy at the court of James I', *Politics, religion and diplomacy in early-modern Europe*, 27 (1994), p. 238.

371. Declan Downey, 'A Salamancan who evaded the Inquisition: Florence Conry, pro-Habsburg archbishop, diplomat and controversial theologian', p. 98.

372. Brian Ó Cuív (ed.), 'An appeal to Philip III of Spain by Ó Súilleabháin Béirre', *Éigse*, 30 (1997), pp. 18–26; Madrid, 1617 (AGS, Guerra Antigua, l. 3144; AHN, Madrid, OO. MM. Pruebas de Caballeros de Santiago, expediente 5808).

373. Ortiz, *The Golden Age*, Chapter 8: 'The privileged estates of nobles and clergy'. The Spanish council of orders was instituted in the fifteenth century. The four orders were those of Alcántara, Calatrava, Montesa and Santiago.

374. Elena Postigo Castellanos, *Honor y privilegio en la corona de Castilla: el Consejo de las Ordenes y los caballeros de hábito en el siglo XVII* (Soria: Junta de Castilla y León, 1988), p. 205; Micheline Kerney Walsh (ed.), *Spanish knights of Irish origin*, vol. 1, pp. 5–6.

375. 'El Duque a 15 de septiembre, 1613' Palacio (AGS, CJH legajo 522-22).

376. Óscar Recio Morales, *España y la pérdida del Ulster*, p. 124.

377. See Brendan Jennings (ed.), *Wild Geese in Spanish Flanders*, pp. 118–20.

378. Recio Morales, *El socorro de Irlanda*, pp. 105, 244.

379. Ó Maolchonaire to Philip III, Madrid, 12 Apr. 1618, cited by Micheline Kerney Walsh, 'O'Sullivan Beare in Spain: some unpublished documents', *Archiv. Hib.*, 45 (1990), pp. 46–63; idem, *An exile of Ireland: Hugh O'Neill, prince of Ulster* (Dublin: Four Courts Press, 1998), pp. 102–7.

380. Ó Maolchonaire to Philip III, Madrid, 12 Apr. 1618.

381. Ibid.

382. Ó Maolchonaire to Philip III, Madrid, 12 Apr. 1618.

383. Ibid.

384. Kerney Walsh, *An exile of Ireland*, pp. 102–7.

385. Ibid.

386. Ibid.

387. Council of state to Philip III, Madrid, 19 May 1618; see Kerney Walsh, *An exile of Ireland*, pp. 102–7.

388. Philip O'Sullivan Beare, *Hist. Cath. Comp.*, ed. M. Kelly (Dublin, 1850), pp. 334–8.

389. Kerney Walsh, 'O'Sullivan Beare in Spain', pp. 46–63; idem, *An exile of Ireland*, pp. 102–7.
390. Ibid.
391. Ibid.
392. 'Breviate of Ireland' (TCD, Collectanea Historica, MS E. 580, E.3.8, ff. 22, 49–52); Downey, 'Irish–European integration: the legacy of Emperor Charles V', p. 101. For a contemporary copy of this translation preserved among Luke Wadding's papers, see UCD–OFM, D.01, vol. 1, pp. 15–26.
393. 'The Archbishop of Tuam and others to the King of Spain', 18 Feb. 1618 (HMC *Downshire*, vol. 6, 841/IX/26).
394. 'Dermicio O Sulivan Bearra', Madrid, 1613 (AHN, Madrid, OO. MM. Pruebas de Caballeros de Santiago, expediente 7957, p. 2).
395. Ciarán O'Scea, 'The role of Castilian royal bureaucracy', p. 204.
396. HMC *Downshire*, vol. 6, 841/IX/26.
397. Philip III to Albert, 4 Nov. 1617, Pardo (AGR-ARA, Sécrétairerie d'État et de Guerre, registre 181).
398. *The life of Captain Alonso de Contreras, knight of the military order of St John, native of Madrid, written by himself (1582–1633)*, ed. C. A. Phillips (London: Jonathan Cape, 1926), p. 164.
399. Ibid.
400. Cottingham to Secretary Winwood, Madrid, 19 Aug. 1616, cited by Charles Meehan, *Fate and fortunes of the earls of Tyrone and Tyrconnell*, p. 477.
401. Elliott, *Imperial Spain*, pp. 324–5.
402. Carter, *Secret diplomacy of the Habsburgs*, p. 80; Elliott, *Imperial Spain*, p. 290; Allen, *Pax Hispánica*, p. 17.
403. Brightwell, 'The Spanish system and the twelve years' truce', pp. 270–92.
404. Brussels, Bibliothèque Royale, MSS 22172–3, J. L. Bax, *Historia Universitatis Lovaniensis* (16 vols, 1804–25); Edmond Reusens (ed.), *Documents à servir à l'histoire de l'ancienne université de Louvain, 1425–1797* (repr. Brussels, 1999), pp. 427, 1527.
405. Rothe was educated at Douai like his kinsman Roche, who served as secretary to papal nuncio Bentivoglio in Brussels until they departed for France in 1615. See John Brady, 'Father Christopher Cusack and the Irish college of Douai, 1594–1624', in Sylvester O'Brien (ed.), *Measgra Mhichíl Uí Chléirigh: miscellany of historical and linguistic studies in honour of Brother Michael Ó Cléirigh, chief of the Four Masters, 1643–1943* (Dublin: Assisi Press, 1944), pp. 98–107; Patrick Corish, 'The beginnings of the Irish College, Rome', in Daire Keogh and Albert McDonnell (eds), *The Irish College, Rome and its world* (Dublin: Four Courts Press, 2008), pp. 3–4.

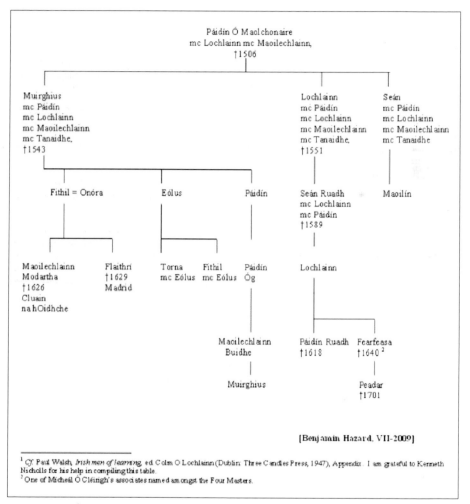

Páidín Ó Maolchonaire
mc Lochlainn mc Maoilechlainn,
†1506

Muirghius
mc Páidín
mc Lochlainn
mc Maoilechlainn
mc Tanaidhe,
†1543

Lochlainn
mc Páidín
mc Lochlainn
mc Maoilechlainn
mc Tanaidhe,
†1551

Seán
mc Páidín
mc Lochlainn
mc Maoilechlainn
mc Tanaidhe

Fithil = Onóra

Eólus

Páidín

Seán Ruadh
mc Lochlainn
mc Páidín
†1589

Maoilín

Maoilechlainn
Modartha
†1626
Cluain
na hOidhche

Flaithrí
†1629
Madrid

Torna
mc Eólus

Fithil
mc Eólus

Páidín
Óg

Lochlainn

Maoilechlainn
Buidhe

Páidín Ruadh
†1618

Fearfeasa
†1640 [2]

Muirghius

Peadar
†1701

[Benjamin Hazard, VII-2009]

---

[1] Cf. Paul Walsh, *Irish men of learning*, ed. Colm Ó Lochlainn (Dublin: Three Candles Press, 1947), Appendix. I am grateful to Kenneth Nicholls for his help in compiling this table.
[2] One of Mícheál Ó Cléirigh's associates named amongst the Four Masters.

Plate I: Flaithrí Ó Maolchonaire's family tree, paternal line cf; Paul Walsh, *Irish men of learning*, ed Colm Ó Lochlainn (Dublin: Three Candles Press, 1947), Appendix). I am grateful to Kenneth Nicholls for his help compiling this table.

Plate II: A lecture at the University of Salamanca, where Ó Maolchonaire studied in the 1590s; detail from a painting by Martín de Cervera, *c.* 1614, (Manuel Fernández Álvarez, Luis Rodríguez San Pedro, Julián Álvarez Villar, *The University of Salamanca: eight centuries of scholarship* (Salamanca: Ediciones Universidad de Salamanca, 1992) p. 71)

Plate III: Simancas Castle, now the Archivo General de Simancas, where Ó Maolchonaire attended to Aodh Ruadh Ó Domhnaill in his final days, signing his will and acting as his interpreter (courtesy of the Ministerio de Cultura, Madrid)

Plate IV: The Monastery of San Juan de los Reyes, Toledo, where Ó Maolchonaire was elected Irish minister-provincial at the Franciscan General Chapter, 1606 (reproduced by kind permission of the guardian and friars, Monasterio de San Juan de los Reyes, Toledo)

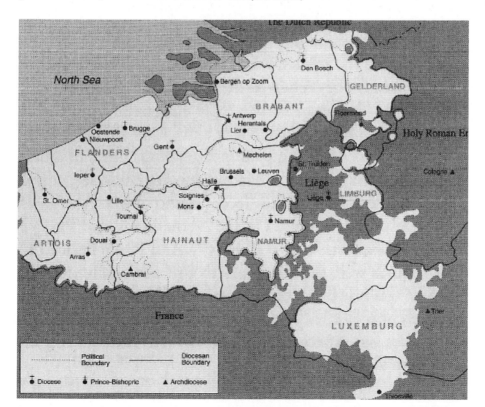

Plate V: The Southern Netherlands, 1606-29 (Craig Harline and Eddy Put, *A bishop's tale: Mathias Hovius among his flock in seventeenth-century Flanders* (New Haven: Yale University Press, 2000), p. 16, courtesy of the authors)

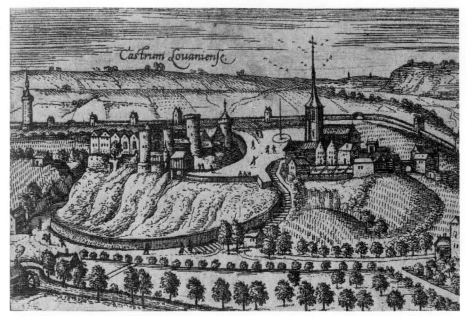

Plate VI: The City of Leuven (Ludovico Guicciardini, *Descrittione di tutti i Paesi Bassi* (Antwerp, 1567); John J. Murray, *Flanders and England: the influence of the Low Countries on Tudor-Stuart England* (Antwerp: Fonds Mercator, 1985), p. 65)

Plate VII: Chiesa di Santo Spirito, Rome (Giuseppe Vasi, *Delle Magnificenze di Roma Antica e Moderna,* (Roma, 1759), lib. 9, tav. 171), where Ó Maolchonaire was consecrated archbishop of Tuam in 1609; now the Sanctuary of Divine Mercy

Plate VIII: Ó Maolchonaire's Archiepiscopal seal of office, 1609-29, inscribed with the words *Florentius Conrius Archiepiscopus Tuamensis* (Archivo General de Simancas, Guerra Antigua-Servicios Militares, legajo 5, folio 78) courtesy of the Ministerio de Cultura, Madrid

Plate IX: Letter of Flaithrí Ó Maolchonaire to the guardian and friars at St Anthony's College, February 1613, with his seal beside his signature (UCD-OFM, MS. D.01, vol. 4, p. 791), courtesy of the UCD-OFM Foundation

Plate X: Title page of Ó Maolchonaire's *Sgáthán an Chrábhaidh*, reproduced by permission of the Librarian, National University of Ireland, Maynooth, from the collections of St Patrick's College, Maynooth

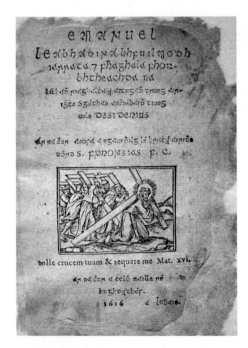

Plate XI: Title page of Ó Maolchonaire's first edition of *Tractatus de statu parvulorum sine Baptismo decedentium ex hac vita: iuxta sensum B. Augustini* (Lovanii: Henrici Hastenii, 1624); reproduced by permission of the Librarian, National University of Ireland, Maynooth, from the collections of St Patrick's College, Maynooth

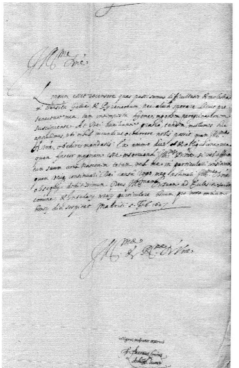

Plate XII: Letter of Flaithrí Ó Maolchonaire to Archbishop Jacob Boonen, Madrid, February 1627 (Mechelen Archief Aartsbisdom, Boonen-3) describing his journey from the Southern Netherlands to Madrid with Hugo de Burgo and pledging loyalty to Boonen

Plate XIII: Title page of Ó Maolchonaire's first edition of *Peregrinus ierichuntinus [...]* (Parisiis: apud Claudium Calleville, 1641); reproduced by permission of the Librarian, National University of Ireland, Maynooth, from the collections of St Patrick's College, Maynooth

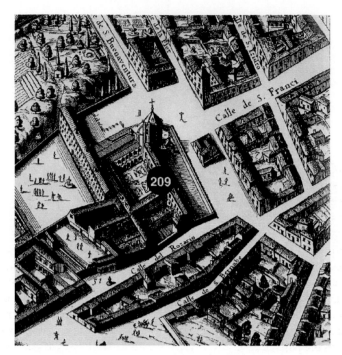

Plate XIV: The Convent of Jesus and Mary, and Basilica of San Francisco el Grande, Madrid, (marked 209), where Flaithrí Ó Maolchonaire died on Sunday, 18 November 1629 (Luis Miguel Aparisi Laporta, *El plano de Teixeira trescientos cincuenta años después* (Ayuntamiento de Madrid, 2008) p. 100)

Plate XV: College of St Anthony of Padua, Leuven, founded by Flaithrí Ó Maolchonaire (from an early eighteenth-century engraving by H. Otto, in Eduard Van Even, *Louvain monumental ou description historique et artistique de tous les édifices civils et religieux de la dite ville* (Louvain: Fonteyn, 1860), p. 158)

4

Realignment from Leuven, 1618–29

In 1618 Flaithrí Ó Maolchonaire returned to Spanish Flanders. That year represented a watershed in his career for a number of reasons. Politically, there were
great changes in Spain and further afield in Europe. Lerma's corrupt administration finally collapsed after concerted pressure exerted by factions at court.[1] The
defenestration of Prague marked the start of the Thirty Years War.[2] In Rome,
Spanish influence was increasingly under pressure from French competition.
Prompted by the need to bring his authority to bear at the papal court, Philip III
sent an embassy to the Holy See to defend the doctrine of the Immaculate
Conception.[3] Luke Wadding acted as theologian to the Spanish delegation and
thus began a long career in Rome. According to the Spanish secretary of state,
Antonio de Aroztegui, this embassy formed an integral part of Philip III's pres-
sure groups at the papal court.[4] It was led by Antonio de Trejo y Paniagua (†1635),
who was consecrated bishop of Cartagena on 16 September 1618. He, like Ó
Maolchonaire and Wadding, was a Franciscan of the province of Santiago at
Salamanca. The other members of the embassy were Benigno da Génova, minister-
general of the Friars Minor, and José Vásquez, commissary of the order.[5]

The doctrine of the Immaculate Conception – that Mary, as the mother of God,
was free from original sin from the moment of her conception – had grown in
importance during the Catholic Reformation. However, it was a contentious matter
and the source of intense theological debate between opposing factions, notably the
Franciscans, who supported papal definition of the doctrine and the Dominicans,
who did not.[6] Successive kings of Spain had championed the cause in the sixteenth
and seventeenth centuries. Philip III had a special devotion to the Blessed Virgin
and, like his father before him, wore a diadem of the Immaculate Conception on the
breastplate of his armour. Under the aegis of Spanish monarchy, artists such as El
Greco (†1615), Sánchez Cotán (†1627), Velázquez (†1660) and Murillo (†1682)
made the Immaculate Conception one of the most popular themes of Golden Age
painting in Spain and its empire.[7] In 1616, Philip III instituted a royal council to
see to the definition of the doctrine as a Catholic dogma by the pope.[8] The following year, on 12 September, he obtained a decree from Paul V that forbade
preaching or teaching, 'en el púlpito o en la cátedra', that Mary was not immaculate.[9]

According to Luke Wadding, he and Flaithrí Ó Maolchonaire had become
acquainted with one another in Madrid.[10] Ó Maolchonaire, Wadding recalled,
applied himself to the teachings of St Augustine in the Spanish capital, immersing
himself in the study of divine grace and predestination.[11] Wadding described him
as 'the best student of the Church Fathers' that he had met. Such was Ó

Maolchonaire's zeal for the subject, Wadding claimed, his confrère had read St Augustine's teachings seven times and those pertaining to Pelagianism, twenty times: 'When perplexed by a difficult passage or obscure terminology, he betook himself to prayer and fasts [...] until it seemed to him that he had grasped the true meaning.'[12] Ó Maolchonaire completed a number of writings on grace before he left Madrid and had had them read by the Salamanca professors.[13] As regards the Immaculate Conception, St Augustine refuted Pelagius declaring that all the just have truly known of sin 'except the Holy Virgin Mary, of whom, for the honour of the Lord, I will have no question whatever where sin is concerned'.[14] In 1619, the year after his return to Spanish Flanders, Ó Maolchonaire's *Tractatus de Augustini sensu circa beatae Mariae Virginis Conceptionem* was published in Antwerp by Jan van Keerberghen.[15]

After leaving the court of Philip III, Flaithrí Ó Maolchonaire and Wadding maintained correspondence and, according to Brendan Jennings, Ó Maolchonaire was first to nominate his confrère for the episcopacy.[16] Several years before, reflecting the great Marian devotion of the Franciscan order, Ó Maolchonaire had provided Monsignor Antonio Caetani (†1624), archbishop of Capua and nuncio to Spain, with a report of a 'recent miracle of the Blessed Virgin that has occurred' in Ireland. In reply to the nuncio, Secretary Porfirio Feliciani (†1634) told him that the matter would be 'examined and considered here before notifying you of what will be decided'.[17] Ó Maolchonaire's report of 1612 corresponds to an account of the unsuccessful attempt to burn 'an image of Our Lady renowned for its miracles' at Trim in County Meath which had hitherto been used to heal those afflicted with illness.[18]

Responding to repeated requests from Flaithrí Ó Maolchonaire, Wadding sent him a manuscript copy of his *Acta Legationis* from Rome.[19] This was a concise report of the proceedings and of the theological questions which needed to be resolved in the debate over the doctrine. Impressed with its contents, Flaithrí Ó Maolchonaire showed it to the Conde van Boxhorn, a member of the council of Brabant, who paid to have it published.[20] The Friars Minor had been in favour of a definition of the doctrine since the Marian writings of the Franciscan theologian Duns Scotus (†1308).[21] Despite Ó Maolchonaire's vocal opposition to the Spanish Match, such espousal of the Immaculate Conception was popular at the court of the archdukes and proved that he remained loyal to the political interests of Philip III. Such signs of allegiance helped him safeguard the Irish Franciscans' presence in Spanish Flanders.

Finding himself on the Counter-Reformation frontiers of northern Europe where the works of St Augustine were most popular, Ó Maolchonaire continued to study the live contemporary issues of grace and predestination. His interest in a rigorous interpretation of these subjects was almost certainly spurred on by the allegedly lax doctrine encouraged by some Jesuits. After a two-year delay, Ó Maolchonaire's amended *Tractatus de Statu Parvulorum*, a work on the fate of unbaptised infants, was accepted for publication in 1624 and printed under Philip IV's privilege.[22] According to Ceyssens, Ó Maolchonaire was wary of the decree 'forbidding the publication of anything relative to the questions of grace' without special permission from the papacy.[23] Before sending this work to Rome for approval in July 1623, therefore, Ó Maolchonaire had given it to his like-minded political ally in Brussels, Cardinal Alfonso de la Cueva.[24] In its opening pages, the names of those who provided approbations for the work reveal the extent of Ó Maolchonaire's contacts among theologians at Leuven and Douai.[25] The dedicatory epistle is written to Gabriel Cardinal de Trejo (†1630). He sat on the Inquisition council in Spain, had been a Lerma favourite, and was the brother of Antonio de Trejo who accompanied Luke Wadding to Rome on Philip III's theological embassy.[26] Two years later at St Isidore's Irish Franciscan college, the cardinal was consecrating prelate to the new archbishops of Armagh and Cashel, namely Aodh Mac Aingil and Thomas Walsh (†1654). Writing to Luke Wadding in Rome, Ó Maolchonaire confided that he had difficulty putting St Anthony's on a secure financial footing. As a result of this hardship, Ó Maolchonaire told Wadding, he did not have a published copy of *de Parvulis* for his own use and was unable to bring one with him to Madrid in 1627. It is worth bearing in mind, however, that Flaithrí Ó Maolchonaire may have expected Wadding to reciprocate the help he had given him by arranging the funds to publish the *Acta Legationis*.[27] Cornelius Jansen (†1638) referred to Ó Maolchonaire's *Tractatus* as 'son petit ouvrage' which was read at mealtimes in the refectory at St Anthony's.[28] Rather than being a book extracted from the teachings of Augustine, Ó Maolchonaire called it 'a mere prayer'.[29] According to a note in his own hand, Ó Maolchonaire gave a copy of his *Tractatus* to the archbishop of Compostela. This copy is now preserved at the Biblioteca Nacional in Madrid. In a letter to Wadding, he told his confrère he had written another more detailed treatise, *Peregrinus Jerichuntinus*.[30] Unable to make the necessary amendments to the text, Ó Maolchonaire had resigned himself to obtaining papal approbation for this work which set forth his ideas on humanity's fall from grace and redemption. Dedicated to Urban VIII, who had consecrated Ó Maolchonaire archbishop in 1609, the source for the title is the parable of the Good Samaritan.[31] Paradoxically, the *Peregrinus* had a greater impact after Ó Maolchonaire's death when, due to widespread interest in the works of Jansen, it was published posthumously at Paris in 1641 and approved by Sorbonne doctors including Jean Bourgeois.[32]

TACTICAL RETREAT TO ST ANTHONY'S, LEUVEN

As had been the case in 1607, Ó Maolchonaire made preparations for the move north to Leuven nearly two years prior to departure.[33] This was something of a tactical retreat. After the death of Aodh Ó Néill, Ó Maolchonaire, on learning that Spain would not jeopardise peace with England, made arrangements for the transfer of his income at the Madrid court to Brussels.[34] In Spanish Flanders, Ó Maolchonaire could provide for St Anthony's College which had become the overseas stronghold for the Irish Friars Minor and a hive of activity for the Irish community in exile. From there he worked to launch the Irish Franciscan mission to Scotland.[35] In addition, his presence in the Low Countries also allowed him to see to the needs of émigrés from Ireland by mediating on their behalf with the courts of Madrid, Rome and Brussels. He also had the chance now to devote more of his time to the neglected pastoral needs of his archdiocese while priming the next generation of Gaelic nobility, based in the Spanish Netherlands, for a return to Castile. Attempting, perhaps, to overcome his over-reliance upon Spain, Ó Maolchonaire spent eight years from 1618 to 1626 encouraging closer ties with the papacy *via* the nunciature at Brussels and the archbishop of Mechelen. When talks for the Spanish Match broke down Ó Maolchonaire and his coterie were ready with a military alternative which included the use of Irish troops assembled in the Low Countries.

The friars at St Anthony's had established themselves at Leuven from 1607. Nine years later a small site with a house attached, next to the river Dyle and just outside the old city walls, had been purchased on behalf of the Irish friars by the nobleman Jan Baptist de Spoelberch (†1627).[36] He, like the Conde van Boxhorn, represented the Irish Franciscans' interests in the Southern Netherlands.[37] The archdukes laid the foundation stone at St Anthony's in 1617 and the first phase of building began on the permanent college. It soon gained a good academic reputation: 'well-disciplined, learned and zealous for the salvation of souls in their *patria*'.[38] When two new edicts of persecution were published in Ireland against the clergy, it was to St Anthony's College that the new nuncio, Lucio Morra (†1623), turned for information.[39] With the building works underway on his return to Leuven, Flaithrí Ó Maolchonaire stayed elsewhere at first because, according to a contemporary record, he officially took up residence at St Anthony's in November 1623.[40] The Irish Franciscans' progress at the college needs to be understood in the wider experience of the University of Leuven. The archdukes' official visitation of the university in 1607 had been unprecedented in Spanish Flanders.[41] It eventually resulted in an official charter of reform agreed upon by the central government and university authorities. This, the Act of Visitation, saw the institution flourish. Soon there were more than thirty colleges and over 1,000 students. The standard of teaching improved with the implementation of new rules for the programme of studies and the conferring of degrees, the first of their type in the southern provinces. After enduring a difficult end to the previous century, professors of the highest repute were again attracted to Leuven and, from 1597 to 1631, the population of its religious houses rose more than 30 per cent.[42]

Many clergy attached to the university supported the Irish friars. Mattias Hovius, the archbishop of Mechelen, and Jacob Jansonius, professor of Holy Scripture, were both benefactors of St Anthony's College. Jansonius and fellow theologian Joannes Wiggers (†1639), close confidants of Hovius, were among Ó Maolchonaire's supporters within the faculty.[43] As part of his primatial see, Leuven had been within Hovius' sphere of influence since his consecration and the university was just a short journey from Mechelen. Hovius, like Ó Maolchonaire, was not a great ally of the Jesuits. He admired the Society of Jesus for its educational methods but, wishing to protect the interests of his diocesan seminary, he became wary of the order when they arrived in the cathedral city to establish a noviciate. Since the 1580s, the Society had endeavoured to make their presence felt in the Dutch provinces and by the middle of the 1620s, 1,574 Jesuits were based in the Netherlands.[44] The main target of the Leuven Jesuits was the Dutch mission, where, as was the case in Ulster, the diocesan system had collapsed. The Society's emphasis on episcopal exemption caused concern for Hovius and for the secular clergy in general. In 1615, Hovius warned his colleagues and old teachers at Leuven of his suspicions regarding the Jesuits.[45] After his arrival back in Leuven, Ó Maolchonaire was happy to support the university's attempts to maintain its monopoly in Leuven against the local Jesuits who were anxious to found their own college in the town.[46]

Jacob Jansonius' support for the Irish was especially significant. He was a Catholic from Amsterdam exiled in Leuven. He and Hovius were old classmates who had become fast friends at university and the archbishop often called on him to help resolve disputes within the archdiocese.[47] Known to his students as *Pater Severus*, Jansonius succeeded Michel Baius (†1589) at the College of Pope Adrian VI. As dean of St Peter's, Leuven, he supported Irish students before the emergence of an Irish Franciscan community at the university, maintaining his support for them into the 1620s.[48] He shared a keen interest in the works of St Augustine with Flaithrí Ó Maolchonaire and, like the Irish archbishop, was opposed to the allegedly lax doctrine of grace propagated by members of the Jesuit order. At Hovius' funeral, Jacob Jansonius delivered a baroque oration in his honour subsequently published as a thirty-page booklet.[49] The cathedral chapter of St Rombout, where Jacob Boonen (†1655), the next archbishop of Mechelen, had begun his career as Hovius' protégé, entrusted the *pontificalia* of Mechelen to Flaithrí Ó Maolchonaire, during the interregnum. This gave Ó Maolchonaire the opportunity to exercise his episcopal faculties abroad.[50] According to registers for the archdiocese of Mechelen, Ó Maolchonaire carried out ordinations in June and September 1621 and on 12 March 1622.[51] Among them was Edmund O'Reilly (†1669), the future Catholic archbishop of Armagh and primate of Ireland;[52] Fr Patrick Plunket OFM;[53] and Fr Robert Rochford OFM who subsequently served at Alcalá and was appointed superior of the Irish friars at Paris.[54] Ó Maolchonaire's involvement did not end there, however. On the first Sunday after Easter 1623, he assisted Jacob Boonen of Mechelen and Giovanni-Francesco Guidi di Bagno, papal nuncio in Brussels, in the consecration of William Terry (†1646), bishop of Cork and Cloyne.[55] By virtue of the mandate of Pope Urban VIII, the Franciscan Thomas Fleming (†1665) was raised to the see of Dublin in the church of St Anthony of Padua, Leuven, later that year. Once more, Flaithrí Ó Maolchonaire assisted Boonen in the consecration, along with Philip Rovenius (†1651), archbishop of Philippi and apostolic-vicar of the Netherlands.[56] The pastoral mission to Ireland needed to be provided for but Ó Maolchonaire's involvement in the ordination and consecration of priests and prelates who shared his viewpoint must have caused Peter Lombard further disquiet.

Stating that he hoped that the Holy See would provide a further subsidy for St Anthony's, the nuncio assigned Ó Maolchonaire 1,000 florins from the earl of Isenberg and Caroline, daughter of the duke of Aerschot, to mark the announcement of their nuptials.[57] Ó Maolchonaire and his confrère Fleming, both executors of Eóghan Mag Mathghamhna's will, helped to purchase a house for a new Irish pastoral college at Leuven which the friars at St Anthony's subsequently used to accommodate some of their novices.[58]

In 1616, the same year that St Anthony's moved to its permanent site, the Dutch college was founded nearby. Its first president, Cornelius Jansen, thus became Flaithrí Ó Maolchonaire's near neighbour.[59] Both were absorbed with the theology of St Augustine but, in letters to the Abbé de St-Cyran, Jean Duvergier de Hauranne (†1643), Jansen revealed his reticence about the disdain shown by Ó Maolchonaire for sharing his scholarly endeavours with the young Dutchman.[60] Jansen and Ó Maolchonaire did, however, liaise on some joint ventures. Five years after arrangements were made for Irish friars to attend university in Paris, Ó Maolchonaire sought the backing of Jansen and the Abbé de St-Cyran to obtain permission from Louis XIII for an Irish Franciscan residence in the city.[61] Jansen's indifference impeded such plans in Paris where a dim view was taken of Ó Maolchonaire's connections with the Spanish Habsburgs.[62]

These links remained strong following Flaithrí Ó Maolchonaire's return to the Low Countries. He and the Spanish ambassador in Brussels, Alfonso de la Cueva, marqués de Bedmar, knew one another.[63] After his alleged involvement in a plot to overthrow the government of Venice, Bedmar was reassigned to Brussels by Philip III a year after Ó Maolchonaire's return. The deaths of Philip III and Archduke Albert in 1621 effectively made Bedmar Spanish proconsul in Brussels where he formed a political triumvirate with Spínola and the Infanta Isabel, whose 'sovereign' status as governor was diluted.[64] That year Bedmar recommended that the council of state provide the discalced Carmelite convent at Leuven 'for the conversion of heretics' in England, Scotland and Ireland.[65] In 1622, this time wearing his cardinal's hat in Brussels, de la Cueva wrote to Rome in praise of the Irish archbishops of Dublin and Tuam.[66] Defending Ó Maolchonaire's absence from his see, Cardinal de la Cueva explained that his presence among 'his religious in the convent of his order in Leuven' was essential to their work.[67] As discussed in the previous chapter, de la Cueva and his collaborators, including Ó Maolchonaire, waited for an end to *Pax Hispánica* and a return to active military policies.[68] This casts light on the importance of Ó Maolchonaire's presence in the Southern Netherlands where he was able to exercise a modicum of influence at the vanguard of the Church militant. This was the immediate setting for his handling of Irish affairs at the courts of the Spanish Habsburgs in the early 1620s.

THE SCOTTISH MISSION IN ITS POLITICAL CONTEXT

The status enjoyed in the Low Countries by the Irish Franciscans during this period, dealt with earlier, was partly attributable to the support offered by the Infanta Isabel's confessor, Andrés de Soto OFM (†1625), and by successive archbishops of Mechelen.[69] For more than twenty-five years Andrés de Soto exercised considerable influence over decision making at the court of the archdukes which, under his guidance became known as an exemplum of Catholic devotion.[70] In 1616, Archbishop Mathias Hovius of Mechelen encouraged the archdukes in their devotion to several Flemish Franciscans martyred in the late sixteenth century. When Hovius died four years later, as he lay in state, two Friars Minor stayed near the body day and night to offer up prayers for the repose of his soul.[71]

   This favourable environment for the Irish friars gradually encouraged them to launch pastoral initiatives from St Anthony's. The Franciscan presence in Ulster and the start of the plantation provided the political context for Ó Maolchonaire's efforts to have his Irish confrères re-evangelise the Western Isles and Highlands of Scotland. As early as 1610, appeals had been made to Rome by beleaguered Scottish Catholics. Henry Fitzsimon SJ corresponded with the superior-general of the Society of Jesus about sending Irish Jesuits to Scotland and wrote in his hagiographical work that 'truly named Scots, now called Highlandmen, do profess themselves Irish, do consent and comply with Irish.'[72] Responding to instructions from Aquaviva, his Irish confrère Christopher Holywood subsequently sent a mission to the Western Isles.[73]

   In his devotional text, *Scáthán Shacraiminte na hAithridhe*, Aodh Mac Aingil, guardian at St Anthony's, expressed similar sentiments to Fitzsimon. Referring to Scotland as 'the faithful daughter' of Ireland, Mac Aingil implied that Christianity had first reached Scotland from Ireland.[74] The papal nuncio at Brussels, Guido Bentivoglio (†1644), made an official approach to St Anthony's in 1615 and a formal request for missionaries was issued three years later.[75] At first, however, Mac Aingil showed reticence towards the Scottish project.[76] This reflects, perhaps, what he saw as the potential for open conflict posed by James MacDonnell, kinsman and ally of the Uí Néill, whose escape from captivity in Edinburgh had made the local political situation uncertain. Ó Maolchonaire certainly knew of MacDonnell's activities and does not seem to have shared Mac Aingil's reservations.[77] MacDonnell was referred to as 'lord of Isla and Kintyre and of the Glens of Ireland' at the court of Philip III where he sought remuneration in either Italy or Spanish Flanders in 1616.[78] It would seem that Ó Maolchonaire regarded a mission to Scotland as part of wider military action in Ó Néill's interests which would have extended the friars' renewed activity in Ulster across the North Channel. Aodh Mac Aingil's worries that friars' lives would be placed at serious risk in Scotland led to the postponement of the Franciscan mission until after the rebellion had been put down.[79] The MacDonnell family of County Antrim grew wary of openly defying the authority of the Stuarts.[80] Randall MacDonnell the younger (†1683), for instance, was granted the title of marquis on the strength of his services to the royalist cause.[81]

   Initial efforts to gather information in Scotland for the proposed Franciscan mission identified the value of the Leuven friars' command of Gaelic for the work and reported a complete lack of clergy on the ground.[82] There was also the question of Anglican and Calvinist competitions. James I visited Edinburgh in 1617 to found a new chapel, at which point he instituted the Anglican liturgy, installed officials to carry out his orders regarding the Church of Scotland, dismissed three bishops and exiled another.[83] All this stirred up Calvinist hostility and made conditions for Scots Catholics more difficult. The Brussels nuncio reported to Rome 'the precarious situation for Catholicism in the country', highlighting the need for a pastoral mission to Scotland.[84] On Flaithrí Ó Maolchonaire's return to Leuven, Lucio Morra, the papal nuncio in Brussels, informed him that Paul V had approved the sending of Irish Franciscans to the Western Isles and Highlands. Ó Maolchonaire then acted on the nuncio's authority to try and persuade Mac Aingil to send missionaries from St Anthony's. This, in turn, reflected the advice offered by Andrés de Soto, the Infanta Isabel's confessor and commissary general of the order. A meeting was arranged at Antwerp between Morra and Mac Aingil but he 'remained adamant'.[85] According to Mac Aingil, similar calls made during Bentivoglio's nunciature had been discouraged.[86] He believed that there were not enough priests in his fledgling community to staff the mission and there was also a shortage of funds. As the Scottish seminaries at Rome and Douai were unable to provide enough priests fluent in Gaelic, Mac Aingil reasoned that they should at least contribute financially to a mission for their home country.[87] Paul V's expression of support offered the remote possibility of a foundation in Scotland to provide for such missionaries and, 'in deference to the wishes of the Holy See', Mac Aingil conceded.

Nuncio Morra wrote to Rome in October 1618 saying that, having 'availed himself of the help and information' given by Flaithrí Ó Maolchonaire, he had met with the guardian who agreed to send friars from Leuven. In reply, Cardinal Scipione Borghèse (†1633) sent the sum required for their expenses.[88] Two Irish priests, Edmund McCann and Patrick Brady, and a Scottish brother, John Stuart, set off in January 1619 and three months later Morra was notified of their safe arrival. Despite experiencing setbacks and hardship in Scotland, a second group was sent five years later and reported that several thousand Scots had been 'brought back to the practice of the Catholic religion'.[89] Extant manuscripts indicate that copies of Bonabhentura Ó hEoghasa's Gaelic catechism were used on the friars' mission.[90] Nevertheless, even though the standard literary language was still the same, at local spoken level the two languages were diverging quite rapidly from each other.[91]

Noble patronage and protection were essential to the success of the Irish Franciscans' Scottish mission, the progress of which was discussed on a regular basis at the general meetings of the Congregation of Propaganda Fide in Rome.[92] At Brussels, the Conde de Boxhorn was selected to take charge of financial transactions as procurator.[93] More importantly, perhaps, the earl of Antrim, Randall MacDonnell the elder, secretly provided the funds necessary to re-establish the friars at Bunamargy on the north Antrim coast, which became the headquarters of their mission.[94] His illegitimate son, Daniel, joined the order, taking the name Francis in religion, and had volunteered to go to Scotland by 1627.[95]According to Lord Lorne, in the event that Randall MacDonnell was allowed to buy back the Isle of Kintyre, he 'would bring in a number of priests, and so make the whole people turn Papistes'.[96] On their arrival, the friars were well received by certain local Scottish lairds whose followers subsequently returned to the sacraments. Among the most celebrated were: Iain Muideartach, twelfth lord of Clanranald, his father-in-law, Rury MacLeod of Harris, Sir John Campbell of Calder, who was won over after three days' argument by Fr Cornelius Ward, and Coll Ciotach MacDonald of Barbreck.[97] The mission to Scotland proved a lasting success for the Franciscans at Leuven. An estimated 6,000 Calvinists were converted to Catholicism and 3,000 baptisms conducted.[98] Flaithrí Ó Maolchonaire's direct involvement seems to have been limited to his role in launching the initiative. His interest in the welfare of Scottish Catholics continued, however. On his way to Madrid in the winter of 1627, he met with the nuncio in Paris to discuss 'the foundation of a Scots college at Bordeaux'.[99]

Missionary zeal was much in evidence at Leuven. In this context, the Irish friars' pastoral activities bear comparison with the Propaganda Fide mission launched in the northern Dutch provinces in the 1590s. As with parts of Ireland and Scotland, the diocesan system there had disintegrated. Cornelius Jansen, president of the Dutch college of St Pulcheria, opposite St Anthony's, endeavoured to supply priests to the Dutch mission. He supported its main advocate, Philip Rovenius, who had been appointed apostolic-vicar of Utrecht in 1614. Rovenius was made titular archbishop of Philippi six years later and 'did much to ensure the survival of Catholicism in the Netherlands', 'establishing an effective administration and a unified liturgy and catechetics'.[100] Like Ó Maolchonaire, Jansen and Rovenius clashed with members of the Society of Jesus who, in this case, sought overall control of the Dutch mission.[101] As stated above, Rovenius assisted at Thomas Fleming's consecration as archbishop of Dublin,[102] a sign, perhaps, that Irish and Dutch exiles in Spanish Flanders regarded their religious interests as a common cause.

PASTORAL PROBLEMS IN IRELAND AND Ó MAOLCHONAIRE'S RESPONSE FROM SPANISH FLANDERS

Ó Maolchonaire made arrangements to send a new vicar-general to the see of Tuam soon after arriving back at Leuven. Valentine Browne had been his vicar but his faculties had been questioned after he excommunicated the mother of one Thomas Lynch of Galway. Ó Maolchonaire overturned the decision and decided to replace Browne.[103] At this time, the Carmelite friar William Lynch suggested his nephew Francis Kirwan (†1661) for the post. The Kirwans were among 'the fourteen ancient families of Galway' and, until the seventeenth century, 'possessed the principal authority within the town'.[104] Francis Kirwan was at this time in Dieppe, where he taught philosophy.[105] Proceeding to Ireland in 1620, Kirwan diligently performed his duties:

> [...] making provision for older priests to be properly instructed in church ceremony, rusticating the sinful clergy, suspending the ignorant from pastoral duty, reducing the pluralists to a single parish, endlessly adjudicating the disputes of the laity and arranging to have adulterers publicly whipped.[106]

Kirwan helped Ó Maolchonaire assert his authority in the archdiocese of Tuam. He insisted that Ó Maolchonaire, as archbishop, had the controlling interest in the appointment of episcopal vicars of Galway according to the provision made by Pope Innocent VIII. Catholic members of Galway Corporation, fearing that the Protestants in the town might take over the position, 'had appointed James Fallon to the dignity', with Ó Maolchonaire's permission.[107] Fallon wrote to Ó Maolchonaire stating that Kirwan was refusing to sanction the corporation's decision without 'a general petition from the town; but this they refused for fear it would diminish in the least their privileges, and so go to the Protestant archbishop, and be lost.' The people of Galway remained constant in this matter, he asserted, and 'that for all the clergy in Ireland they would not lose one atom of privileges conceded to them by the Holy See.'[108] Despite Ó Maolchonaire's attempt to reassert his authority as archbishop, his absence from Ireland led to this dispute and, in the absence of a satisfactory solution, made it worse.

Entrenched ecclesiastical interests were widespread in Ireland at this time. For some years, the Franciscans and the vicar-general of Armagh, Balthazar Delahoyde, had been in dispute over ecclesiastical privileges in Drogheda. As part of the town lay in the diocese of Armagh, Delahoyde wanted to unite all of Drogheda 'under his own jurisdiction'. Led by Donnchadh Ó Maonaigh (†1624), the friars protested that the vicar-general recognised no superior and overlooked the rights of the ordinary clergy in favour of the Jesuits.[109]

The papal nuncio in Brussels from 1621 to 1627, Giovanni-Francesco Guidi di Bagno, soon became involved and requested information from Flaithrí Ó Maolchonaire, his nearest and best-placed Irish source. His reply defended the selection of Patrick Matthews as vicar-general to the diocese of Dromore, who Brian Jackson describes as 'the fence-sitter' in this row.[110] Though confirmed in office by Delahoyde,[111] Matthews was among the secular clergy who rejected the vice-primate's decree against the Franciscans and their celebration of the Mass.[112] Of the same family as the archbishop of Dublin, Ó Maolchonaire described Matthews as a learned man who spoke both English and Irish: '[…] serious, well-bred and widely respected'.[113] Although sensitive to episcopal authority, Ó Maolchonaire remained consistent in his support of the regular clergy, especially the Franciscans. Regardless of the needs of Irish exiles, his response on this occasion was, at best, non-committal and combined with the disorder in Galway, his absence from his archdiocese was seen by some as a dereliction of duty.[114]

Faced with increasing papal pressure to justify his presence in the Southern Netherlands in the early 1620s, Flaithrí Ó Maolchonaire ensured that he remained on good terms with both the Brussels nunciature and the archbishop of Mechelen. His use of contacts in Brussels was essential to ward off Roman demands for his return to Ireland. Three months after informing Ó Maolchonaire of a papal order that the nine Irish bishops found in Rome or in Spain were to return to their home country, Nuncio di Bagno made known 'Tuam's reasons for remaining in the Low Countries'. On hearing of his proscription by the civil authorities, Ó Maolchonaire was excused to the papacy in 1623.[115]

Ó MAOLCHONAIRE, THE YOUNG EARLS AND THEIR ALLIES

Despite his exile in the Low Countries, Ó Maolchonaire continued to represent the earls' interests to the Spanish council of state. After taking Archduke Albert's name in the sacrament of confirmation, Aodh Ó Domhnaill, 'el Conde de Tyrconel', served as a page to the Infanta in Brussels long enough 'to consider himself due for advancement'.[116] Prompted by Ó Maolchonaire, Aodh Ó Domhnaill obtained a recommendation from the archduke which was then submitted to Philip III.[117] The young earl had come of age. With followers to support and the welfare of his grandmother to consider he made this petition.[118] Following Gondomar's return to Madrid after his first embassy to James I, Ó Maolchonaire contacted him from Leuven. He asked Gondomar to remind the king of the importance of attending to the needs of Aodh. 'Seeing the business of the Conde de Tyrconel delayed for so long,' Ó Maolchonaire wrote 'to refresh the memory' of Gondomar, requesting an increase in Ó Domhnaill's salary, particularly because of his many followers and the dignity of his grandmother.[119] This formed part of Ó Maolchonaire's defence of the needs of the Irish élite. A further example of this approach occurred when James Fitzgerald applied for the office of Irish consul in Andalusia in 1620. He presented testimonials from the archbishop of Tuam, Diarmaid Ó Súilleabháin Béarra, and Walter de Burgo, both of the order of Santiago. Together they certified that they knew Fitzgerald to be 'the son of noble parents from one of the best families of the kingdom, a highly reputable man and a great Christian'.[120]

Further sources suggest that Ó Maolchonaire did not limit his sponsorship to the most prominent Irish families. On the strength of his deceased brother's bravery at the siege of Rhynberck and the confiscation of his family's lands in Ireland, one 'Don Terencio O'Melaghlin' received accreditation from the archbishop of Tuam in 1623. This valuable *certificación* was enclosed with five other documents, including Captain Nelano O'Melaghlin's patent from Archduke Albert, to raise an infantry company.[121] Colonel Seán Ó Néill, '*maestre de campo* of the Irish infantry for his Majesty in the states of Flanders', wrote in Terence O'Melaghlin's favour from Aarschot.[122] His letter, written after Ó Maolchonaire's, is an exact copy of the one drafted by the archbishop. This suggests that Ó Maolchonaire advised the young earl on the correct composition of such documents. It is worth noting also that Ó Néill was based in comparative safety at Aerschot and closer to Leuven than his comrades in arms at Rhynberck.[123] Evidence of Ó Maolchonaire's ongoing interest in the requirements of Irish military units based in Spanish Flanders occurred when he was consulted on the authenticity of 4 hundredweight of Irish butter for troops![124]

Flaithrí Ó Maolchonaire's role in coordinating Irish affairs after his consecration as archbishop of Tuam suggests that experience had taught him that blatantly overstretching his remit would not be countenanced in Rome.[125] In light of Ó Maolchonaire's refusal to return to his pastoral duties in Ireland, Urban VIII was unlikely to accept his *ultra vires* political activity. As discussed in Chapter 2, Ó Maolchonaire and his confrères at Salamanca had encouraged Éinrí Ó Néill, while still a student, to nominate Archbishop Mateo de Oviedo OFM as papal nuncio to Ireland.[126] In the same way, he appears to have encouraged Seán Ó Néill and Aodh Ó Domhnaill that it was in their best interests to make concerted appeals for the bishops in Ulster and Connacht, combined with protests against interference by Lombard. In an effort to explain his closeness to the earls' ambitions, Ó Maolchonaire told Luke Wadding that he regarded the Uí Néill and Uí Dhomhnaill as 'the means by which we hope to see the faith restored in our fatherland'.[127] In the 1620s this is apparent in the calls made by the young Ulster earls for influence over episcopal appointments. The demise of Aodh Ó Néill had helped Archbishop Peter Lombard implement his plans for Irish episcopal reform. After receiving permission from Paul V to ordain *alumni* of Irish colleges on testimonial of their superiors, Lombard petitioned for an increase in his authority.[128] These developments in Lombard's favour and the resistance which Ó Maolchonaire continued to show towards such moves caused further friction between them.

This contest began with news of Ó Maolchonaire's return to Spanish Flanders and was fought against internal forces which Ó Maolchonaire regarded as a threat to his Catholic integrity. From 1619, successive petitions from Ó Néill and Ó Domhnaill were lodged with the papal secretary of state and the nuncio to the Southern Netherlands. Blaming Peter Lombard for the lack of Irish bishops, they called for two episcopal appointments each for the archdioceses of Armagh and Tuam. Reliable advice on suitable candidates was always to be had from Flaithrí Ó Maolchonaire and his ally Eóghan Mag Mathghamhna, archbishop of Dublin, they said. Trusting that they would receive a sympathetic hearing from the papacy, the young earls recounted the exploits of their forebears advocating that with just a modicum of aid from outside they could reclaim their lost ancestral lands by force of arms.[129]

Such calls were not confined to the earls of Tyrone and Tyrconnell. They joined with the Ó Súilleabháin Béarra in asking that Irish nobles be consulted on nominations to the episcopacy for Ireland.[130] In response to their families' losses, sympathetic prelates, like Ó Maolchonaire and Mag Mathghamhna, sought to motivate their community by equating its experiences with those of the ancient Israelites in the Books of Maccabees.[131] In the words of Judas Maccabeus' father, who lamented their plight: 'Alas! Why was I born to see this, the ruin of my people, the ruin of the holy city [...] all of her adornments have been taken away [...] Why should we live any longer?'[132] According to this discourse, forbearance of adversity and distress offered the ultimate consolation of redemption. As shown earlier, Ó Maolchonaire had first expressed this view at court two decades before.[133] The Maccabean struggle also provided Gaelic political society with accounts of divinely inspired resistance to and liberation from tyranny.[134]

Despite his espousal of *tamquam redivivi Machabae* at the turn of the century, however, Archbishop Lombard reigned in these Gaelic ambitions as his renewal of the Irish episcopacy progressed. In 1618, the Catholic primate saw his vicar-general David Rothe promoted to the see of Ossory.[135] Even though the Dutch truce had ended, circumstances showed no signs of improvement for the Gaelic cause. Thus the supplications of Seán Ó Néill and Aodh Ó Domhnaill reflect the sense of despondency and disillusion felt in their political circle, interpreting exile, colonisation of their lands and the lack of help from Spain and Rome as reparation for their own sins.[136] In the contemporary opinion of Ross MacGeoghegan (†1644), this fall from grace and favour affected the young Ó Domhnaill more than Ó Néill.[137] According to Francis Harold (†1685), the high regard for Luke Wadding, Flaithrí Ó Maolchonaire and Seán Ó Néill in Rome, Spain and the Low Countries was such that, among the Irish, 'it seems impossible to overcome them [...] each one of them enjoys more influence and has greater credence given them than all the rest of their compatriots.'[138] Contrary to Seán Ó Néill's wishes, however, his family's long-standing ally, Roibeard Mac Artúir, resisted all efforts to raise him to the see of Armagh.[139] In a letter to Wadding, Flaithrí Ó Maolchonaire told his confrère:

The earl of Tyrone would have persisted in urging his first proposition for ever, but that Fr Robert, having smelt it by some channel, vowed that he would take himself to distant parts and never be seen again, unless they gave up discussing it.[140]

Ó Maolchonaire did not divulge his own views on this occasion but a report of Ireland submitted to Rome, possibly by Francis Nugent (†1635), compared Mac Artúir and Ó Maolchonaire.[141] It stated that the former was unable to go to Ireland,

[...] during the persecution after an indictment of *laesae majestatis* by the king of England, as with Ó Maolchonaire, because both assisted in the last war as comrades of Tyrone and Tyrconnell against the said king; whereby in the present position it would be useless to promote him.[142]

Before his death in 1625, Peter Lombard had made preparations for his return to Ireland, requesting an increase in his jurisdiction as Catholic primate to do so.[143] His demise, however, brought the programme of reform to an abrupt halt and, despite the increase of renewed pastoral activity in the early 1620s, internal Church relations deteriorated further. Spleen was vented on either side of the debate. Combined with worsening Anglo-Spanish relations, this culminated in several Gaelic promotions to the episcopacy which prevented the accession of Lombard's long-term understudy David Rothe to the see of Armagh.[144] Through the influence of Spain, Aodh Mac Aingil and his successor Hugh O'Reilly (†1653) were promoted to Armagh, along with Edmund Dungan (†1629) and Bonabhentura Mac Aonghusa (†1640) of Down and Connor.[145]

On the strength of precedent it is quite likely that, while avoiding direct involvement, Flaithrí Ó Maolchonaire influenced Seán Ó Néill's nomination of Aodh Mac Aingil for the primatial see of Armagh in 1626. Hence, the help Ó Maolchonaire gave the young Tyrone promoted the Gaelic cause in the interim while also providing for a cadre of future Irish leaders. In this particular case, having waited six months, Ó Néill argued that it was dangerous to raise anyone other than an Ulsterman to the primacy. He insisted that 'the magnates of the diocese' should now be heard, stating that candidates from other parts of Ireland were strangers ill-equipped to serve the people of Armagh. They would, he claimed, prove unpopular with the clergy there and in all likelihood 'be an absentee'.[146]

A letter by an unnamed Irishman was forwarded to Rome by the Brussels nuncio on the need to appoint an Ulsterman as primate in 1626.[147] Before setting out the case for promoting candidates from Connacht and Ulster, this source considers the arguments against appointing them, as opposed to contenders from anglicised parts of Ireland. This served as a riposte to a detailed description of Irish affairs prepared in 1625 by the recently appointed Catholic bishop of Ferns, John Roche.[148] The report of 1626 concludes by stating that, as the greater part of the population in Cashel and Armagh were Old Irish, it was fitting that Old Irishmen should be selected as their archbishops and, in the case of the Catholic primacy of Ireland, none better than Aodh Mac Aingil.[149] Of the names submitted for consideration, his was vigorously opposed by supporters of Rothe.[150]

Peter Lombard's eventual successor to Armagh, Mac Aingil was described in nominations as an Old Irish *lector theologiae* at the Ara Coeli friary, born in the diocese and educated in Spain.[151] As had been the case with Lombard, however, Mac Aingil's death in Rome prevented his return to Ireland.[152]

The content of the anonymous letter of 1626 bears a striking resemblance to two reports closely associated with Flaithrí Ó Maolchonaire's work in Castile.[153] The first of these was presented at court in Valladolid in 1605.[154] The second document was attributed to Philip O'Sullivan Beare at the end of the second decade of the seventeenth century.[155] Extant copies of this report are preserved among Luke Wadding's papers, and at Trinity College, Dublin.[156] It opens: 'The aunciente Irish descend from the Spaniards' who, until the coming of the Vikings 'governed it with just and holie lawes', before moving on to 'the wickednesse of Dermitius King of Leynster', his capture of O'Rourke's wife and the invitation to Henry II to invade Ireland in the late twelfth century. As was the case with Ó Maolchonaire's report of 1605, O'Sullivan Beare claimed that Ireland's Gaelic families 'beare great affection and love to the Spanish nation'.[157] The subsequent accusation that the 'Englished Irish follow the inclination of the English' was clearly aimed to foment enmity towards them in Madrid. It then provides a descriptive list of 'Ancient Irish', 'Myxt Irish', and 'English Irish' found in 'His Majesties dominions'. There, among the 'Ancient Irish ecclesiasticall', is 'Don Florence Conrio Archbishop' where he is described as 'entertained by his Majestie in the states of Flaunders'.[158] Such a source was of use to Luke Wadding who, since his arrival at Rome in 1618, had quickly emerged as a key figure in the appointment of candidates to the Irish episcopacy.

In the early 1620s, the militant hopes of Ó Néill and Ó Domhnaill for a Spanish descent on Ireland had been hindered by the Spanish administration's preference for peace with England. After 1624, however, the young earls' calls have received more recognition in Madrid and Brussels where relations with London had been weakened by Charles I's marriage to Princess Henrietta-Maria, the youngest daughter of Henry IV.[159] Ó Domhnaill, for instance, directed a new petition to Rome, asking the pope to intercede with the king of Spain 'to obtain a post which would permit him to live according to his true standing'.[160] That autumn, after receiving the habit of Alcántara and an expression of support from the Infanta, Ó Domhnaill was granted command of a new Irish *tercio* by Philip IV. This was in addition to his cavalry company, of which he served as captain.[161]

As stated above, Flaithrí Ó Maolchonaire maintained a network of contacts, secular and ecclesiastical, throughout Spanish Flanders who provided intellectual and financial support for his activities.[162] Reflecting, perhaps, a newfound sense of confidence and due to the numbers seeking admission to St Anthony's, he approached the papal nuncio in 1625, hoping to gain control of the Douai and Tournai Irish colleges for the education of the clergy.[163] Douai had been established by Christopher Cusack of Meath (†c.1624) in 1594.[164] By 1617, Ó Maolchonaire's foundation at Leuven had already received sixty-eight novices and needed more space.[165] The Douai college had important Franciscan links, as the publication of its student roll indicated. Fifty-two of Douai's *alumni* had joined the Friars Minor,[166] including the catechist and poet Bonabhentura Ó hEodhasa (†1614), the hagiographer Patrick Fleming (†1631) and Thomas Stronge, a cousin of Luke Wadding and Flaithrí Ó Maolchonaire's confessor.[167] As was the case with St Anthony's, the Douai Irish college was 'modelled on the Tridentine mission ideal of the diocesan seminary' in support of the Catholic mission for Ireland.[168] The Irish Jesuits maintained a presence at the Tournai foundation which was well situated near the Mildeberg winter quarters for Irish troops. The Irish military community there needed chaplains and offered stipends to their clergy.[169] Both Douai and Tournai were accused by Ó Néill's supporters of favouring entrants from Munster and Leinster, a charge already levelled by Ó Maolchonaire against Salamanca in the 1600s. Ó Maolchonaire still aimed 'to rid the seminaries of Jesuit superiors'.[170] The constant shortage of funds at Douai would not have escaped his attention. Its promised grant of 5,000 florins from Spain had to be supplemented with alms from Irish Catholics.[171] The cardinal protector of the Irish, Pompeo Arrigone, who supported Ó Maolchonaire's promotion to Tuam, had pleaded with the duke of Lerma for more reliable patronage for the college.[172] On their arrival in Spanish Flanders, Aodh Ó Néill and Rudhraighe Ó Domhnaill sent three consecutive appeals to Philip III for renewal of the college's annual subsidy.[173] Contrary to their wishes, however, nine Irish and English institutions, including the college at Douai, lost all or part of their allowance due to the reform of the army in the Southern Netherlands.[174] After Cusack's death, 'the [Douai] college was in immediate danger of being sold to meet its debts.'[175] Where exactly Ó Maolchonaire proposed to get the funding from is difficult to say, perhaps from his order's benefactors in Spanish Flanders. Fernández Navarrete (†1632) and his fellow *arbitristas* of Madrid identified a surfeit of such colleges as a burden which Spanish coffers could do without.[176] Despite their location, beyond his current sphere of influence in the archdiocese of Mechelen,[177] Ó Maolchonaire recognised the colleges' potential to educate a new cadre of Irish leaders.

Other Irish ecclesiastics held out hope, with an appeal 'deploring the languishing state of the Irish college at Douay, and praying his lordship [Ludovisi] to undertake its restoration'.[178] An official report for the year 1628 notified the papacy that Ó Maolchonaire continued to pursue his aim of combining the colleges at Douai and Tournai with St Anthony's, Leuven, where the best of candidates were said to be drawn to the religious life.[179] Meanwhile, Luke Wadding obtained papal sanction to acquire a small Spanish friary dedicated to St Isidore, making possible a new seat of Irish Franciscan learning at Rome.[180]

'THE MATCH IS BROKEN': Ó MAOLCHONAIRE'S RETURN TO MADRID

Gaelic interests at court in Madrid continued to make a case for military action in Ireland.[181] In parallel developments, Seán Ó Néill approached the Habsburgs, possibly at Flaithrí Ó Maolchonaire's instigation, to request that the Palatinate be restored to the Elector Frederick V only on the condition that the Uí Néill estates were restored also.[182] The young earl was supported in his claim by the Infanta Isabel, who wrote to Philip IV twice requesting that 'the king restore him to his estate in Ireland, which was confiscated from the earl his father'.[183] Talks for the

Spanish Match rumbled on into 1623. Accordingly, for his services with the Irish infantry *tercio* and the services of his forebears, Ó Néill called for the insertion 'in the articles which will be made in preparation for the marriage of the Infanta María with the Prince of Wales, the condition that the earl's estates be restored to him in full'.[184]

By the following year, however, it was declared that 'the match is broken'[185] and, after the death of James I, a renewed series of Irish and Scottish petitions for military aid were made to Philip IV.[186] The willingness shown by his chief minister, the Conde Duque Olivares (†1645), to reconsider martial policies may have made such plans seem well founded.[187]

Before the end of 1625, the newly crowned king of England, Charles I (†1649), declared war against Spain. This only confirmed the nagging doubts which had prevailed in Madrid. There, the council of state held that the English had been feigning support for peace while conspiring with the Protestant states of northern Europe to stir up discord.[188] Indeed, the futility of talks for a Spanish Match sum up the political inertia witnessed at court before the fall of Lerma. Disgruntled with years wasted on negotiations for a marriage that never happened, Charles I entered the Thirty Years War on the side of his sister's husband, Frederick V, Elector Palatine. Formal correspondence to Venice reported that there was 'every danger that the unsuccessful English attack on Cádiz would be followed by a Spanish diversion against Ireland'.[189] This change of climate suited Ó Maolchonaire and his allies in the Low Countries, or so they thought, and they prepared fresh plans for an assault on Connacht and Ulster.

Further evidence suggests that their hopes were raised by the worsening problems between Spain and England concerning the Palatinate.[190] The earls of Tyrone and Tyrconnell asked the pope to intercede with Spain on their behalf and for particular consideration to be shown to Ó Maolchonaire, who was ready to go to Madrid.[191] With the outbreak of war between England and Spain,[192] Urban VIII confirmed to the young earls that he had intervened with Philip IV to grant them funds via the archbishop of Tuam.[193] Nuncio di Bagno then endorsed Ó Maolchonaire's request for a passport to travel through Paris on his way to Madrid.[194] In a letter to Cardinal Barberini (†1646), the nuncio said that, although irreproachable Catholics, Ó Néill and Ó Domhnaill lacked the necessary experience and described their plans as poorly presented. Ó Maolchonaire, therefore, helped prepare a more detailed account to ensure that it would be well received at court. The Marqués Spínola and his military peers had to be convinced of its potential and, Ó Maolchonaire confided in the nuncio, despite praising such plans in the past nothing had been done to implement them.[195] The sharp contrast between Irish aspirations and Philip IV's insolvent administration in Madrid made the prospects bleak for Flaithrí Ó Maolchonaire and the Ulster earls.

Ó Maolchonaire approached the Infanta to tell her of his decision to travel back to Madrid, and she recommended him to her nephew Philip IV and to Don Diego Messía de Guzmán (†1655), marqués de Leganés, stating that it was 'thirty-four years since he was first employed and engaged by the nobles of Ireland to treat with his Majesty',[196] suggesting that Ó Maolchonaire was in the service of the Uí Dhomhnaill and Uí Néill at the beginning of his studies at the University of

Salamanca.[197] Eoghan Ruadh Ó Néill was then granted leave to accompany Ó Maolchonaire. As had been the case with his first cousin, Éinrí, in 1609, his role as military attaché in Madrid reflects the honour code of established diplomatic protocol.[198] As set out in the previous chapter, his twenty-five years' military service outweighed those of his younger cousin Seán Ó Néill, and of Aodh Ó Domhnaill who first sought preferment in Spanish Flanders. The Irish infantry *tercio* commanded by Eoghan Ruadh was based at Rhynberck, a fortress captured more often than any other during eighty years of war and strategically positioned on the left bank of the Rhine.[199] Eoghan Ruadh had held command of Rhynberck for eight years.[200]

Flaithrí Ó Maolchonaire had to contend with serious internal rivalries among young Irish nobles, within the Ó Néill family as well as between the Uí Néill and Uí Dhomhnaill. The previous year, Eoghan Ruadh countered moves made by his kinsman Phelim Ó Néill (†1653) to advance in the ranks, a situation which led Ó Maolchonaire to intervene, obtain a small salary for Phelim and support his return to England.[201]

After leaving St Anthony's for what would turn out to be his last time, Ó Maolchonaire made his way to Paris with Eoghan Ruadh and Hugh de Burgo (†1653). The latter had served as guardian at St Anthony's, Leuven, where he had been elected by the community.[202] Flaithrí Ó Maolchonaire realised de Burgo's potential and, from the early 1620s, he often acted as Ó Maolchonaire's secretary, attending his meetings with the archdukes and the papal nuncio in Brussels.[203] Letters signed by Ó Maolchonaire during this time are written in Hugh de Burgo's hand.[204] After his mentor's death in 1629, de Burgo and many others, such as the next archbishop of Tuam, Malachy Queely (†1645), remained resolute in their support of Flaithrí Ó Maolchonaire's political ideals.[205]

Ó Maolchonaire and de Burgo made their way across France and the Pyrenees, finally arriving in Madrid at the beginning of 1627. After settling in, the archbishop of Tuam wrote to Jacob Boonen, telling him 'of the difficulty and the troubles' that they experienced on their midwinter travels.[206] On account of his old age, Ó Maolchonaire said, the unexpectedly stormy weather only added to the burden of undertaking such a long journey.[207]

Sharply contrasting with the flourish of his hand in earlier years, Flaithrí Ó Maolchonaire's signature here is small and shaken. As a mark of his loyalty to the office of archbishop of Mechelen, Ó Maolchonaire referred to himself as Boonen's 'unworthy confrère and servant'.[208] Archbishops Hovius and Boonen of Mechelen had been an enduring presence during Ó Maolchonaire's second stay in Spanish Flanders. In comparison, successive papal nuncios to Brussels served short terms in the early 1620s and their jurisdiction, essentially, 'did not extend to the confines of the Catholic districts in the Low Countries'.[209] Boonen was also among the Jesuits' adversaries in the Low Countries.[210] On Ó Maolchonaire's return to Madrid in 1627, Cornelius Jansen was there on behalf of the University of Leuven seeking a formal sanction to prevent the Society of Jesus from conferring academic degrees in their colleges.[211] In a letter to the university authorities Jansen made known that, since his arrival, Ó Maolchonaire had expressed his support for such moves.[212]

A month earlier, Flaithrí Ó Maolchonaire had presented Olivares and Don Diego de Messía with two memorials on Irish affairs.[213] The first proposed launching an expeditionary force which would land in Killybegs, County Donegal, before seizing recently fortified Derry as a vantage point. From there, a combined force of Irish and Walloon troops could descend upon Connacht.[214] Exile had deprived the generation after Ó Maolchonaire of first-hand knowledge of conditions on the ground in the western and northern provinces of Ireland. Aside from his considerable understanding of papal and Habsburg diplomacy, Ó Maolchonaire could recall Elizabeth Tudor's first fortifications at Derry and the subsequent progress of the Nine Years War described in these documents. There are echoes of his writings from earlier years in these pages also, such as his calls for support to be included for western Scotland; the analogy from *Desidérius* of Irish sufferings to those of 'Christians who live under the Turks'; the lack of fortifications in Ireland; and 'the oppression inflicted on their trade and commerce'.[215] Bitter experience of treachery at regular intervals in his career led him to reiterate the need for total secrecy. This he accompanied with a request for the exclusion of English or Scots soldiers and senior ranking Palesmen from the expedition.[216] Such fears were real. The Irish Dominican William Talbot was alleged to have been colluding with the spy John Bathe. Ó Maolchonaire referred to the priest as *persona absurdissima* and warned the council of state that he too was spying for English interests. The hostility Talbot showed towards the Irish in Philip IV's service had raised suspicions among the exiles in Madrid who were saddened to see him favoured at court.[217]

Consideration was given to all matters in the plans. In the absence of Nuala Ní Dhomhnaill's nephew, whom she had tutored, Ó Maolchonaire called for the prompt payment of an allowance to her.[218] In an effort to defuse the enmity between them, Ó Maolchonaire called for command to be shared equally between the young earls, urging that 'the principal gentlemen of the other provinces [...] unite among themselves' in the same way as the Dutch who, 'in spite of their heresy, held out against the might of Spain'.[219]

Matters were held up by Spanish delaying tactics, however. The Infanta Isabel awaited the return of Eoghan Ruadh who was sent to present the plans in Brussels. After hearing them, she expressed the view that, in the event that such an undertaking was to occur, the disbanded *tercio* should sail to Ireland without banners. This, she said, would avoid damage to *Reputación* if the designs failed. Moreover, Ó Maolchonaire's idea that the two earls should be sent together was ill-advised as 'the two have never been able to tolerate each other'.[220] Taking this advice into account, Philip IV postponed any action in April of that year. He then delegated responsibility for arranging a fleet to Isabel and the Marqués Spínola, along with settling the dispute between Ó Neill and Ó Domhnaill.[221] The archbishop of Tuam reacted quickly, trying to maintain the political momentum, repeating his calls for Walloon troops to supplement Irish units.[222] In tandem with this, to overcome rivalry between the earls, he attempted to initiate an alliance of the two families with help from the Infanta Isabel. He arranged a dowry for a marriage between Mary Stuart O'Donnell (†c.1649), daughter of Rudhraighe and his wife Bridget Fitzgerald, daughter of Henry, earl of Kildare and Seán Ó

Neill, the third earl of Tyrone. Mary, however, rejected the idea of a politically motivated, arranged marriage.[223]

In October 1627, the Venetian ambassador to Rome reported that the papacy still regarded Ireland 'as a fief of the apostolic see' and was prepared 'to countenance any promising scheme which would bring about the re-establishment of Catholicism in the kingdoms of James I'. To this end, Olivares and Richelieu (†1642) were reported to have agreed in principle to invading Ireland and Scotland.[224] However promising this may have seemed to Irish and Scots petitioners at the court of Philip IV, the increasing level of competition between Madrid and Paris made a joint invasion highly unlikely. Nevertheless, Spain's representative in London, Don Carlos Coloma (†1637), promoted the view that 'we cause an uprising in Ireland [...] involving the Catholic princes and the pope in a certain secret league' for a combined attack against England. 'That is something that could be expected to have a very considerable effect,' he continued, 'and it is credible that Scotland would to some extent involve herself in this uprising.'[225]

Despite encouraging Spain and France against England, Urban VIII's caution about joining the league himself revealed his real attitude to such an idea.[226] In Madrid, meanwhile, the combined threat of Irish and Scottish claims against England was undone by increasing rivalry at court where Colonel William Semple (†1633) obtained Philip IV's patronage for a Scottish seminary.[227] Moreover, Spain's ambassador to London reported 'Diego Magdonel', as he was known in Spanish, 'reconciled in the good graces of James I' with an annual pension of 3,000 escudos.[228] As the Irish fell from favour, Scottish Catholics fared better. William Laing of Aberdeen, for instance, was employed as 'Agent in Scotland for the King of Spain'.[229]

Seán Ó Neill and his cousin Eoghan Ruadh joined Flaithrí Ó Maolchonaire to advocate their cause in person at the end of 1627. With the dispute between the young earls unresolved, it was proposed that the enterprise should be carried out 'in the name of the kingdom and republic of Ireland [...] in which the aristocracy shall govern'.[230] Provisions were included for 'one or two men assigned to them, who are of first-class judgment and able to give first-class advice in negotiation and government'.[231] This was a job description written for Ó Maolchonaire. He was already familiar with such arrangements elsewhere in Europe and during the flight of the earls he had visited the Swiss Confederation, and the Genoese republic.[232] He had then lived in the Southern Netherlands for almost a decade and would have been aware of the Dutch model of the *Staendestaat* republic further north in the United Provinces.[233] The Dutch, moreover, provided a successful example of political resistance.[234] The philosophy of social contract and divine right applied equally to monarchies and republics which rested upon social systems characterised by privilege in the seventeenth century. This was in keeping with the Aristotelian political system, where rule was not to be exercised for the sake of the ruler but for the sake of those ruled.[235] Crucially for Ó Maolchonaire, however, the Spanish monarchy's emphasis upon the virtue of obedience was, nevertheless, at odds with the idea of representative power and responsibility.

Faced with other events of greater importance to the prosperity of Spain and its dominions, such as the need to address rampant inflation in the economy,[236] the council of state announced that, rather than acquiring more territory, Philip IV wished 'only to preserve what he has'.[237] To this end, Isabel listened to Dutch political overtures on the possibility of an accord with Spain, England and Denmark.[238] Philip IV tried but failed to maintain the Spanish Habsburg legacy of what has been termed its 'messianic imperialism'.[239] His decision to send Peter Paul Rubens on a peace embassy to London in 1629 signalled the end of Flaithrí Ó Maolchonaire's last political mission. After three generations of almost constant warfare, the Habsburgs decided that ideological issues were irrelevant to international affairs.[240]

THE WANING INFLUENCE OF FLAITHRÍ Ó MAOLCHONAIRE AT COURT

At the end of July 1627, Ó Maolchonaire declared that he had arrived at court six months earlier, 'motivated only by zeal for the service of God, of your Majesty and that of his country'.[241] At that point, Olivares learned the reasons for his journey and ordered the president of finance to grant the archbishop 1,000 ducados *in lieu* of what he received annually in the Southern Netherlands.[242] Ó Maolchonaire felt that this was likely to be an isolated payment because he subsequently presented a memorial asking for his allowance to be continued and, moreover, for it to be paid in silver as it had been in Brussels.[243] Losing patience with him, the council of state at this point told Ó Maolchonaire to return to Spanish Flanders.[244]

Ó Maolchonaire turned again to Olivares. It was then that the Conde Duque deemed, as long as Anglo-Spanish hostilities continued, that it would be convenient to have at court someone acquainted with Irish politics, and Ó Maolchonaire seemed the obvious choice.[245] This was particularly the case in the absence of 'the other archbishop',[246] obviously a reference to David Kearney who had died in August 1624. A canon lawyer with a Gaelic background, he had served on the Junta of six advisers at court who deliberated on talks for a Spanish Match.[247] His more conciliatory attitude to Anglo-Spanish relations and his alliances with Peter Lombard's political circle meant that Kearney was ready to replace Flaithrí Ó Maolchonaire as adviser on Irish affairs after the Franciscan left Castile in early 1618. Kearney's death and Ó Maolchonaire's return to a consultative role in Madrid coincided with the transition towards the warlike policies pursued by Olivares in his early years as head of Philip IV's government.[248]

In their reply to Olivares on this occasion, the Spanish council of state realised that David Kearney's replacement should be someone the Irish would trust.[249] Their advice in Ó Maolchonaire's favour was seen by Philip IV, who scribbled underneath: 'Let the council tell me how I could pay him in such a way that it will not be drawn upon my treasury.' As a result of his hesitancy the request was sent back to the council of finance in August that year for further consideration.[250]

Of course, this wrangle over Ó Maolchonaire's payments went on throughout his attempts to convince Spain to consider invading Ireland. As observed by Enrique García Hernán, payments from Spanish state coffers to senior Irish clergymen were quite normal in the early seventeenth century. From 1606 onwards, Peter Lombard enjoyed an income of 400 ducados from Madrid.[251] David Kearney, 'guided by the fathers of the Societie', sought an annual pension of 1,000 ducados from Philip III.[252]

What mattered here was the realisation that Spain's financial exigencies did not match Ó Maolchonaire's ambitious political aims. The proviso that he should be employed as long as hostilities with England continued was crucial. Again, Ó Maolchonaire may not have been aware of this as, in his last months, he sought to recover what was due to him once more. A decade earlier, securing his own income strengthened Ó Maolchonaire's arm among Irish exiles,[253] enabling him to support his preferred causes, most notably St Anthony's, Leuven. He recounted how in 1610 and 1611 he had been granted *cédulas* by Philip IV's father entitling him to 1,000 ducados per annum from the *arcas de las tres llaves*.[254] This, a small enough income for the period, was equivalent to the annual alms promised to St Anthony's. On his subsequent departure for Spanish Flanders, the said allowance was paid to him from secret funds in Brussels until the end of August 1626.[255] This much was confirmed again in a letter written by Ó Maolchonaire's pugnacious old ally Cardinal Alfonso de la Cueva.[256] By September, though, de la Cueva was replaced as Philip IV's ambassador to Brussels and his influence at court was curtailed as a result.[257] According to the treasurer general's accountant, Don Mateo Ibañez de Segovia (†1645), apart from some expenses, the archbishop of Tuam had not been paid any more maravedís from the *arcas de las tres llaves* since the summer of 1626. Ó Maolchonaire, therefore, begged to be paid the 1,000 ducados outstanding, per year.[258] In answer to his plea, the treasurer general agreed to give him only 500 'which his Majesty granted him as a help with expenses'.[259] Unfortunately, though, Ó Maolchonaire appears to have lost the necessary *cédula* guaranteeing this sum.[260] As a result, he asked for a replacement.[261] Writing from his sick bed, 'very embarrassed not to have anything else to sustain himself' other than the said 500 ducados, Ó Maolchonaire called for his back pay to be allocated from the Flemish funds again.[262] His wishes were not complied with, however, and any support offered by local Franciscans in Madrid is unlikely to have stretched to the circle of political support which Ó Maolchonaire needed to maintain at court.

Hugh de Burgo stated that 900 ducados were owed to Flaithrí Ó Maolchonaire at the time of his death.[263] Three years later, de Burgo, named as the archbishop of Tuam's legatee, had recovered 500 ducados.[265] As explained earlier, faced with the chronic shortage of funds provided to the college, Ó Maolchonaire told Luke Wadding that he struggled to keep St Anthony's on a stable financial footing.[265] Taking this into account with the financial records of the college and de Burgo's statement that the money owed was for St Anthony's, it appears that Ó Maolchonaire used his own income for its upkeep and maintenance. The example offered by Christopher Cusack at the Irish college of Douai, which was threatened with closure after his death, indicates that such intervention was not unusual at this time.[266]

Throughout these difficulties, Ó Maolchonaire corresponded with his Roman confrère, Wadding. They discussed theological matters and current events for the

Irish abroad. An extant letter from this troubled period reveals much about Ó
Maolchonaire's character and offers new insights into his work among the
laity.[267] He accepted Wadding's view that, in light of the real and present danger
posed to the Viscount Mac Aonghusa, it would not, after all, be a good idea to
push for Bonabhentura Mac Aonghusa to be appointed archbishop of Armagh.
This was contrary to the wishes of Ó Neill and Ó Domhnaill who, from Spanish
Flanders, nominated their kinsman for the primacy on a repeated basis.[268]

In the same document, Ó Maolchonaire commented regarding the needs of
the O'Driscolls. He stated that he had 'no interest in [their] business other than
to do a good work of intercession on their part as they are poor, honourable gentlemen'.[269] At the close of his letter, Ó Maolchonaire reminded Wadding: 'I once
more commend to your paternity the business of the O'Driscolls, who have
asked me to do so.'[270] His work with the family in Spain had begun in 1604 when
Conor asked for his help to obtain a transfer from Galicia to the Low Countries.[271]
Conor was killed on board *El Rosario* in a sea battle with the Turks off the coast
of Algeria in 1623.[272] Those mentioned in dispatches for serving with distinction
were often rewarded for their valour.[273] In the absence of Conor O'Driscoll, a considerable number of his relatives based in Galicia subsequently called upon the
council of war for financial recognition of his services. Of these, Tadhg
O'Driscoll donated his pension in La Coruña towards his son Anthony's studies.[274]
Finding themselves in 'extreme necessity' two years later, O'Driscoll asked if he
could share his monthly payment of forty escudos between his son and his
daughter, Elena.[275] Two months after Ó Maolchonaire's death, Anthony O'Driscoll
submitted a new petition. In response, the secretary considered giving the young
O'Driscoll the 5,000 ducados that Ó Maolchonaire would otherwise have
enjoyed.[276]

Left without a patron to bankroll him in Castile, Ó Maolchonaire had been
unable to extend his influence further. This did not stop his work with other Irish,
though, and he dug in to hold ground. Thomas Walsh told Wadding that Ó
Maolchonaire was in Madrid for good, claiming the same income in the case
of being sent back to Spanish Flanders.[277] From the capital he combined his day-
to-day activity for the Irish community with attempts to fill the suffragan sees of
his archdiocese with appropriate candidates.[278] Since his return to Spain in 1609, Ó
Maolchonaire had identified the importance of operating within a specific sphere
of influence and may have felt uncomfortable in Rome where Peter Lombard held
sway for Irish exiles at the papal court, ably assisted by David Rothe.[279] An examination of the credentials of those Ó Maolchonaire nominated for bishoprics indicates the care that had to be taken in this sensitive matter. He avoided partisanship
towards his own order but consistently supported those who favoured Gaelic politics. When the see of Armagh fell vacant after the death of Lombard, for instance,
Ó Maolchonaire supported Ross MacGeoghegan OP for the position. In a further
example of Ó Maolchonaire's network of contacts and of the assimilation of the
Irish in the Low Countries, he was joined in his calls by Errijck de Put (†1646),
state counsel to Isabel and professor of history at Leuven.[280]

Otherwise known as Rocque de la Cruz, MacGeoghegan was from County
Westmeath and part of Ó Neill's extended family network.[281] His role as Irish

Dominican provincial marked him out for further promotion.[282] According to the newly appointed archbishop of Cashel, Thomas Walsh, Flaithrí Ó Maolchonaire wished to gain the support of the Dominicans.[283] Such moves by Ó Maolchonaire were indicative of a possible alliance between Ireland's regular clergy against the Irish secular clergy. With this in mind he repeatedly recommended John de Burgo as a suffragan bishop for his archdiocese. The brother of Oliver de Burgo OP and Hugh, Ó Maolchonaire's *socius*, John de Burgo was described as 'a priest and doctor of good parts', with whom Ó Maolchonaire could disarm the opposition.[284] In time, Ross MacGeoghegan and John de Burgo were both raised to the episcopacy, in Kildare and Clonfert respectively.[285] Others whose careers advanced with Ó Maolchonaire's backing included his successor as archbishop of Tuam, Malachy Queely.[286]

Finally, on this point, Flaithrí Ó Maolchonaire was among those who attested the suitability of John Moloney (†1670) for the see of Killaloe.[287]At Madrid on 17 November 1628, Ó Maolchonaire explained that Moloney was 'doctor in theology of the Sorbonne, abbot of Aran, and protonotary apostolic, born in lawful wedlock of noble parents'. Ó Maolchonaire's testimony, accompanied by almost an exact copy signed by Seán Ó Néill, described Moloney 'worthy of any ecclesiastical dignity in Ireland because of his holiness, zeal and learning, and because he was chosen *rector magnificus* of Paris university'.[288] Moloney owed much of the success of his nomination to French intervention. The queen of France put his name forward for Killaloe, Lemaistre, rector of the University of Paris, provided him with a testimonial and 'letters from the king of France spoke of Moloney with high esteem'.[289]

Taken together, these recommendations appear to have been part of a pastoral strategy to advance only those who accepted the political goals of the Uí Néill and Uí Dhomhnaill. In most instances this meant favouring clerics from a Gaelic background but as John de Burgo and his brothers demonstrate, this was not always the case. This, in turn, corresponds to the criticisms levelled at Ó Maolchonaire by Peter Lombard and his allies. Whether educated in France or Spain, whether of Old English stock or kinsmen of the young Ulster earls, acquiescence to their aims was essential for Ó Maolchonaire.

Inspired in part, perhaps, by his own decline in influence at court, Flaithrí Ó Maolchonaire kept up his work among the next generation of Irish exiles to ensure his political ambitions were entrusted to capable hands for the future. To this end, although deprived of an income himself, he endeavoured to secure Spanish financial support for a new cadre of Irish military leaders. He did this primarily by vouching for the religious orthodoxy and orthopraxis of exiled Irish nobles seeking preferment in Spanish military service.[290] A privileged few from the upper echelons of the Irish community received the habit from one of the four Spanish military orders.[291] Such documentation was highly valued by the recipient and applications often took several years to be processed. Future generations were also known to hold onto the papers credited to their forebears in order to remain eligible for emoluments.[292] Of the twenty Irishmen accepted into the military orders of Alcántara, Calatrava and Santiago throughout the seventeenth century, Ó Maolchonaire provided accreditation for 10 per cent of them. Both were with the order of Santiago – patron of Spain and its militant tradition.[293] Several of Ó Maolchonaire's political and religious associates in Madrid, such as his confessor, Thomas Stronge, and Francis Veahy, abbot of Cong, testified for others.[294]

Flaithrí Ó Maolchonaire and his allies also sponsored Fadrique Plunkett of Meath in his application to join the military order of Santiago.[295] In his testimony, Ó Maolchonaire stated that he was born at Figh in the province of Connacht.[296] According to the records for his studies at Salamanca in the early 1590s, Ó Maolchonaire was a native of county Roscommon and the diocese of Elphin in Connacht.[297] Close examination of the accompanying sources suggests that he omitted to mention that Plunkett's mother, Doña Ynes Biatax, had married twice, a point raised by Diarmaid Ó Súilleabháin Béarra.[298] This apparent discrepancy in Plunkett's background cast doubt on his claims of legitimate birth.

As a consequence, both Flaithrí Ó Maolchonaire and Hugh de Burgo were recalled to testify under oath, *in verbo sacerdotis*. Afterwards Ó Maolchonaire wrote 'to correct that which we said yesterday'.[299] Any suggestion that Plunkett's mother had married again during the lifetime of her first husband, MacWilliam de Burgo, was inadvertent on Ó Maolchonaire's part, he said.[300] MacWilliam de Burgo had died in Valladolid in 1604, the new marriage was *bona fidei* and Plunkett's mother was married two years before she had him. The process to prove Don Fadrique's eligibility for the military habit of Santiago was complete but the oversight on Ó Maolchonaire's part was a sign, perhaps, of his waning influence.

Similar cases reveal that the council of the orders would sometimes close their eyes to one or other of the prerequisites for admission: legitimacy and Catholic orthodoxy according to the Office of the Inquisition in Spain.[301] On receipt of the habit of Santiago and a salary of 200 ducados, Fadrique Plunkett was ordered to raise an Irish infantry company and provided with 'ayuda de costa por una vez' to travel to Flanders for this purpose.[302] This was not an isolated example for the Irish at that time. Aodh Ó Domhnaill's application for the knights of Alcántara was also called into question when it was found that his maternal great-grandfather, Admiral of England, 'lived and died a heretic'.[303] A year later, though, when he recommended his kinsman Bonabhentura Mac Aonghusa for the episcopacy, he entitled himself 'O'Donell, earl of Tirconell, baron of Lifford, Lord of the Province of Lower Connacht and Sligo, knight of the order of Alcántara'.[304]

Flaithrí Ó Maolchonaire continued to advance the interests of Irish officers in Madrid, supporting the claims of one Dionysius McGrath for preferment in 1628. According to Ó Maolchonaire, his service papers provided 'sufficient testimony of his virtues and good life'.[305] Three of his uncles were priests, including a bishop of Cork, and other members of his family had served in the Spanish fleet and in the Netherlands. Fluent in six languages, his studies in the arts and theology included several years of canon law. Reflecting the indivisible links between secular and religious at that time, this last point illustrates the parity identified among students in the universities of Castile.[306] Seven other testimonies accompanied that of Ó Maolchonaire, including those provided by the archbishop's allies at court – Seán Ó Néill, Balthazar de Burgo, the marqués de Mayo, and Eugene, abbot of Fermoy.[307] Using the surname de Castro, Dionisio McGrath subsequently served as an ensign in the Conde Duque Olivares' infantry company before being recommended for promotion to the rank of cavalry captain in 1642.[308]

Nevertheless, Flaithrí Ó Maolchonaire did not limit his political intervention to those in military service. When Matha Óg Ó Maoltuile died in Madrid, he left behind a wife and two daughters. As discussed in Chapter 3, Ó Maolchonaire successfully petitioned for Ó Maoltuile's widow, Elena Fitzgerald, to be granted a new *cédula* for thirty escudos per month in Galicia.[309] Seventeen years later, however, their daughters Ana and Juana were 'left defenceless, bereft of their parents or any other source of comfort'.[310] Ó Maolchonaire asserted that he had witnessed Ó Maoltuile's efforts for the Spanish monarchy,[311] stating that Ó Maoltuile 'had served many years with great satifaction in the last wars in Ireland, in the Spanish fleet and in the states of Flanders with a monthly salary of forty escudos'.[312] Furthermore, Philip III had such great confidence in Ó Maoltuile that he was also 'employed in England and Ireland where he stayed for several years by order of his Majesty on secret service of great importance'.[313] In return for this work, the king had ordered that Ó Maoltuile be paid all he was owed in his absence.[314] Recognising 'the services and losses of her father and brothers in the said wars in Ireland', Elena had been recompensed also.[315] The sisters placed their trust in the king's clemency. Ó Maolchonaire entreated him to show his great generosity and mercy by arranging for support in respect for their family's services to Spain, adding that 'they are coming of age.'[316] Such help would allow them to enter the convent or to marry, otherwise they would lose all hope and find themselves in a very difficult and embarrassing situation.[317] Nine other testimonies, carefully accumulated since 1606, were submitted by Ana and her sister from the people who had known their parents in person.[318] Following two *cédulas* issued by Philip IV, the auditor and financial inspector to military personnel based in Galicia announced that provisions would be made for Ó Maoltuile's daughters, 'in the interim'.[319]

Thomas Walsh met Ó Maolchonaire frequently in Madrid and reported to the bishop of Ferns, John Roche, that the Franciscan had told him he was 'set on by others' but who exactly, Walsh was unable to say.[320] Roche was an old ally of Peter Lombard and held the belief that Ireland's best interests lay in reaching accommodation with the government.[321] This view was shared by the Capuchin Francis Nugent, who regarded Flaithrí Ó Maolchonaire's direct involvement in political matters as an obstacle to addressing the real needs of Irish Catholicism.[322] According to Ó Maolchonaire, Nugent alleged that he and the earls were 'traitors to their *patria* and servile flatterers of Spain'.[323] The Capuchin mission to Ireland had been a cause for contention with the Friars Minor since the previous decade. Ó Maolchonaire leapt to defend himself against criticism from Nugent who was firmly on the side of Lombard and Rothe.[324]

In recommending Ross MacGeoghegan for higher office, Ó Maolchonaire may have expected the Ulster earls' kinsman to show them support but, as it turned out, he criticised the approach taken by Ó Maolchonaire and Seán Ó

Néill.[325] Writing from Leuven to a Dominican confrère in August 1627, MacGeoghegan argued,

> [...] that which Tyrone and the archbishop of Tuam represent as suitable to the service of the king of Spain [...] is the best neither for the said service, nor for the good of the [Irish] kingdom.[326]

Seemingly unaware that Ó Maolchonaire nominated candidates from orders other than the Franciscans and from the Irish secular clergy, MacGeoghegan continued:

> What moves them [...] is not the zeal of common good, not of this service principally, but the respect that they have for [Ó Néill's] flesh and blood, and for [Ó Maolchonaire's] order.[327]

The candid tone of Ó Maolchonaire's letter to Boonen from Madrid is apparent also in his final correspondence with Rome, suggesting the archbishop of Tuam's wish to settle his accounts. He compared the opposition of clergy in anglicised parts of Ireland to those who had preached against the Nine Years War, and who 'Primate Lombard, of blessed memory [had] so stoutly opposed'.[328] Ó Maolchonaire identified Nugent's tracts as part of a concerted campaign against the young earls' political objectives and their entitlement to nominate candidates for episcopal appointments in their parts of the country. He justified his continued support for them on the grounds that they represented the best means of restoring Catholicism in Ireland.[329]

On St Patrick's Day 1628, Ó Maolchonaire wrote to Ludovico Ludovisi, cardinal protector of the Irish, describing the condition of the Church in Connacht and nominated suffragans for his archdiocese.[330] He explained that, were he to return, it would place at grave risk those compelled to protect him in Ireland.[331] This line of reasoning was used on regular occasions for prominent Irish Catholic clergymen in the early seventeenth century.[332] In 1605, James Archer's fellow Jesuits claimed that he did not return after Kinsale for the same reason. It was said also that the Viscount Mac Aonghusa, 'a gentleman of such quality and Christianity, could not escape total ruin' if his nephew Fr Bonabhentura was raised to the Catholic primacy.[333] In Ó Maolchonaire's case, due to his allegiance to the exiled earls of Ulster, it is difficult to say whether there were nobles powerful enough or, indeed, willing to protect him were he to have returned to Tuam. On the grounds that he was impeded by old age and subject to a special edict of *laesae majestatis* against him in Ireland, Ó Maolchonaire was excused to the papacy three months before his demise.[334]

Although his nephew Daniel did serve as rector in due course,[335] there appears to be little original evidence to support the idea that, before his death, Ó Maolchonaire involved himself in efforts to open a new Irish college for secular clergy in the Spanish capital. The same can be said for recent claims that he intended to use the money owed to him at court for a new Irish Franciscan seminary in Madrid.[336] As described above, according to his secretary Hugh de Burgo and the college accounts at Leuven, this sum was for St Anthony's, which Ó Maolchonaire tried to keep on a firm financial footing.[337] The college also relied upon other sources of income. Notable examples include the money collected by

Irish soldiers at Oostende, fishermen from the North Sea ports of Flanders who contributed their catch in times of need and the recorded donations sent from dioceses and friaries in Ireland.[338]

Flaithrí Ó Maolchonaire became terminally ill six weeks after being excused to the papacy.[339] On 9 October 1629, he left the house and family where he had been staying in Madrid, accompanied by Hugh de Burgo, with 'a companion and an oblate, both attached to his lordship's service'.[340] This may be a reference to Daniel, the archbishop's nephew.[341] They made their way to the convent of Jesus and Mary in the south-east of Madrid, where the ailing archbishop's health improved slightly. To quote Manuel de Castro OFM: 'In that convent lived not only the heads of the Franciscan order in Spain but also the principal preachers.'[342] Ten days later, Ó Maolchonaire drafted his last will and testament.[343] Philip IV 'extended his kindness' by sending a physician from his chamber who soon advised that Ó Maolchonaire should receive the last rites.[344] Eight days afterwards, on Sunday 18 November 1629, he died 'of highe feaver' at 10.15 p.m., although he remained clear in his judgment and 'was helpinge the friars to say the litany for the dying'.[345] To enable the transfer of his remains to Leuven, de Burgo arranged their deposition, rather than complete burial, at La Real Basílica de San Francisco el Grande, Madrid. He commended the community there for their kindness and consideration. The patriarch of the Indies, Philip IV's own chaplain, Don Diego de Guzmán de Haros (†1631), was celebrant at Flaithrí Ó Maolchonaire's funeral Mass on Tuesday 20 November, along with 'all the royal choir' to solemnise the obsequies which were attended by 'many gentlemen and titled people' of the royal court.[346] Hugh de Burgo expressed a genuine sense of grief at the loss of his mentor as news of Flaithrí Ó Maolchonaire's death spread among Irish exiles in Spain, Rome and the Southern Netherlands.[347] Yet, even after his passing, informants continued to use Ó Maolchonaire's name to give weight to news of a fresh conspiracy to seize Ireland from the English king.[348]

NOTES

1. Davies, *The golden century of Spain 1501–1621*, pp. 256–9; Elliott, *Imperial Spain*, pp. 321–3.
2. Geoffrey Parker, *Europe in crisis, 1598–1648* (London: Fontana, 1979), Chapter 2.
3. Manuel de Castro, 'Wadding and the Iberian peninsula', in Franciscan Fathers (eds), *Father Luke Wadding: commemorative volume* (Dublin, 1957), pp. 119–70.
4. Silvano Giordano, *Istruzioni di Filippo III ai suoi ambasciatori a Roma, 1598–1621* (Rome: Dipartimento beni archivistici e librari-Direzione Gen.le per gli Archivi, 2006), pp. lxxviii–ix, 129.
5. Ibid.
6. Charles Balic, 'Wadding the Scotist', in *Father Luke Wadding: commemorative volume*, p. 475.
7. José María Pou y Martí, 'Embajadas de Felipe III a Roma, pidiendo la definición de la Inmaculada Concepción de María', *Archivo Ibero-americano*, 34 (1931), pp. 371–417, 508–34; 35 (1932), pp. 72–88, 424–34, 481–525; 36 (1933), pp. 5–48.
8. Juan Meseguer Fernández, 'La real junta de la Inmaculada Concepción', *Archivo Ibero-americano*, 15 (1955), pp. 621–866.
9. Julio Ricardo Castaño Rueda, *Nuestra Señora del Rosario de Chiquinquirá, historia de una tradición* (Bogotá: Fundación Editorial Epigrafe, 2005), p. 32.
10. Wadding's direct quote is: 'eum Madriti degentem cognovi'; see his *Scriptores Ordinis Minorum* (Rome: Nardecchia, 1906), pp. 75–6.
11. *Scriptores Ordinis Minorum*, p. 109; quoted by Heaney, *The theology of Florence Conry OFM*, p. 24.
12. Ibid.

13. Cornelius Jansen to Saint-Cyran, Leuven, 1 Jul. 1622 (Ceyssens, 'Florence Conry, Hugh de Burgo, Luke Wadding', pp. 318–19).
14. Augustine of Hippo, *Divi Aurelii Augustini De natura et gratia liber unus* (Venetijs: Per Ioannem Patauinum, & Venturinum de Ruffinellis, 1534), § 36.
15. Canice Mooney, 'The letters of Luke Wadding', *IER*, 88 (1959), p. 402.
16. To the Cardinal Protector in favour of Wadding, Leuven, 10 Oct. 1619 (*Wadding Papers*, ed. Jennings, p. 21).
17. Feliciani to Caetani, Rome, 20 Jun. 1612 (ASV, Borghèse, vol. 951, 87–8): 'É capitata con le lettere de VS di x di maggio la relatione che l'è stata data all' Arcivescovo Tuamense d'Irlanda sopra il Nuevo miraculo della Beata Virgine seguito in quest'isola, che si fara uedere et considerer qui et sene dara poi a lei quell poi che occorrera.'
18. Sept. 1611 (*Spic. Ossor.*, i, p. 120).
19. Francis Harold, *Vita Fratris Lucae Waddingi* (3rd ed. Quaracchi, 1931), pp. 19–21. Ó Maolchonaire was one among many clamouring for the manuscript and he appears to have been the sole recipient prior to its publication.
20. Luke Wadding, *Presbeia sive legatio Philippi III et IV Catholicorum regum hispaniarum ad Sanctissimos Paulum P. P. V, Gregorium XV et Urbanum VIII pro define controversia Conceptionis B. Virginis Mariae* (Louvain: Henrici Hastenii, 1624); Mooney, 'The letters of Luke Wadding', p. 402.
21. Balic, 'Wadding the Scotist', p. 475.
22. Benignus Millett, *The Irish Franciscans, 1651–1665* (Rome: Analecta Gregoriana, 1964), p. 185; see also Ruth Clark, *Strangers and sojourners at Port Royal* (Cambridge: Cambridge University Press, 1932), pp. 1–8.
23. Ceyssens, 'Florence Conry, Hugh de Burgo, Luke Wadding', pp. 313–14.
24. Ibid., pp. 320–1.
25. These were the archbishop of Dublin, Eóghan Mag Mathghamhna, and the following Leuven professors: William Fabry (†1634), the orator of the university, Jan van den Broeck (†1630), Giles de Baye, William Le Merchier, Cornelius Jansen (†1638), Joannes Wiggers (†1639), Henri Rampen, Jan Schinckels (†1646), Michael Paludanus (†1652), and of Douai: Francis Sylvius (†1649), Bartholomew Lintren, James Pollet and George Colveniers.
26. Florentius Conrius OFM, *Tractatus de statu parvulorum sine Baptismo decedentium ex hac vita: iuxta sensum B. Augustini* (Lovanii: Henrici Hastenii, 1624), pp. ii–vi.
27. Ceyssens, 'Florence Conry, Hugh de Burgo, Luke Wadding', p. 329.
28. Cornelius Jansen to Saint-Cyran, Leuven, 1 Jul. 1622; Jean Orcibal (ed.), *Correspondance de Jansénius* (Louvain & Paris: Bibliothèque de la Revue d'Histoire Ecclésiastique, 1947), p. 163.
29. 'Fray Florencio Conryo a Padre fray Luca', Madrid, 3 Aug. 1627: 'Huelgome mucho de la prosperidad del collegio. No es libro lo que vuestra paternidad piensa que yo saque de San Agustín, sino una oracion.'
30. Ibid: 'Verdad es que tengo un tratado muy intricado que he sacado del, lo que no acabe del todo aun, no tengo exemplo ninguno del *de Parvulis*, ni truxe ninguno a essa patria.'
31. Luc. 10: 30–7. *Homo quidam descendebat ab Ierusalem, in Iericho, &c. usque ad finem parabolae.*
32. Clark, *Strangers and sojourners at Port Royal*, pp. 2–4. See Thomas O'Connor, *Irish Jansenists, 1600–70: religion and politics in Flanders, France, Ireland and Rome* (Dublin: Four Courts Press, 2008).
33. 'A suplicacion de Don Fray Florencio Conrio Arçobispo Tuamense en Irlanda', Lerma, 1617 (AGS, CJH 549-27-8).
34. Ibid.
35. Cathaldus Giblin (ed.), *Irish Franciscan mission to Scotland, 1619–1646: documents from Roman archives* (Dublin: Assisi, 1964), pp. 1–21.
36. Edmond Reusens, *Documents à servir à l'histoire de l'ancienne université de Louvain, 1425–1797* (repr. Brussels, 1999), pp. 406–29.
37. Formerly chief-magistrate of Kampenhout, in recognition of the services of de Spoelberch's family to the Habsburgs since the reign of Charles V, he was made a knight of the Holy Roman Empire by Ferdinand II in Vienna on 30 June 1626. See Jean Charles Joseph de Vegiano, *Nobiliaire des Pays-Bas et du comté de Bourgogne, contenant les villes, terres et seigneuries érigées en titre de principauté, duché, marquisat, comté, vicomte et baronnie; les personnes qui ont étéde la dignité de chevalier, les familles nobles qui ont obtenu des ornements à leurs armes et le nom et les armes de ceux qui ont été anoblis [...] depuis le régne de Philippe le Bon jusqu'à la mort de l'empereur Charles VI* (Louvain, 1760), pp. 87, 163.
38. Jacob Jansonius, dean of the church of St Peter, Leuven, in commendation of the Irish Franciscans, 15 Apr. 1624 (*Louvain Papers*, ed. Jennings, pp. 73–4): 'Minoritae Hiberni bene disciplinati, docti, et in salutem animarum suae patriae zelosi et operosi.'

39. Lucio Morra to Cardinal Borghèse, Brussels, 5 Jul. 1618 (ASV, Borghèse II, 112, f. 321); Lucienne van Meerbeeck (ed.), *Correspondance des nonces Gesualdo, Morra, Sanseverino avec la Sécrétairerie d'État Pontificale, 1615–21* (Bruxelles & Rome: Analecta Vaticano-Belgica, 1937), p. 287.

40. 'Anno 1623, 3 Novembris, Guardianus Hugo de Burgo et discreti concluserunt ut Illmus Tuamensis cohabitaret eis in ipso conventu' – *Extracta ex monumentis asservatis in Collegio S. Antonii de Padua*; cited by Brendan Jennings, *Michael Ó Cléirigh, chief of the Four Masters* (Dublin: Talbot, 1936), p. 188.

41. Bruno Boute, 'Academics in action. Scholarly interests and policies in the early Counter Reformation: the reform of the University of Louvain 1607–1617', *History of Universities*, 17 (2003), pp. 34–89.

42. Henri Pirenne, *Histoire de Belgique* (Bruxelles: Lamertin, 1927), vol. 4, pp. 382, 452.

43. *Historia Universitatis Lovaniensis*, J. L. Bax, 1804–24 (BRB/KBB, MSS 22,172–3). I owe this reference to Jeroen Nilis.

44. Patricia Carson, *Het fraaie gelaat van Vlaanderen* (Tielt: Lannoo, 1968), pp. 190–1.

45. Harline and Put, *Mathias Hovius among his flock in seventeenth-century Flanders*, pp. 163–74.

46. *Testimonia Studii & Disciplinae Universitatis Lovaniensis & maximè Facultatis Artium*; Leuven, 17 May 1624 (UCD–OFM, MS C.11).

47. Ibid., Chapter 15.

48. Endorsed copy of certification to Edmond Dungan, later bishop of Down and Connor, to preach the Gospel, Leuven, 4 Jun. 1624 (UCD–OFM, D.03, pp. 289–90); see also Jacob Jansonius' commendation of the Irish Franciscans, Leuven, 15 Apr. 1624 (*Louvain Papers*, ed. Jennings, pp. 73–4).

49. Jacob Jansonius, *Oratio funebris in obitum Illustrissimi ac Reverendissimi Domini Matthiae Hovii, Archiepiscopi Mechliniensis* (Lovanii, 1620).

50. *Facultatem concedimus illustrissimo et reverendissimo Domino domino archiepiscopo Tuamensi pontificalia*, Brussels, 27 Feb. 1625 (*Archiv. Hib.*, 12, pp. 109–10); *Rogatus et a capitulo deputatus, qui pontificalia per diocesim exerceret reverendissimus Pater Florentius Conrius Thuamensis archiepiscopus, ex Hibernia pro fide exul. Hujus solicitudine Lovanii erectum est anno 1609 collegium S. Antonii a Padua, Archiducibus nostris prium fundamenti lapidem jacentibus.*

51. Brendan Jennings (ed.), 'Irish names in the Malines ordination registers', *IER*, 75 (1951), p. 149.

52. Tomás Ó Fiaich, 'Edmund O'Reilly, archbishop of Armagh, 1657–1669', in *Father Luke Wadding: commemorative volume*, p. 175.

53. Plunket later became definitor of the Irish Franciscans and guardian of their abbey at Multyfarnham. He was educated at St Anthony's, Louvain, 'receiving tonsure and minor orders there on 4 Jun. 1621, sub-diaconate on 5 Jun., and diaconate on 18 Sept. All three ceremonies were performed by Archbishop Florence Conry OFM.' See Terence O'Donnell, *The Franciscan abbey of Multyfarnham* (Multyfarnham: The Abbey, 1951), pp. 69–70. O'Donnell suggests that this is to be identified with the Patrick Plunket who passed from the Irish college at Douai to the Irish Franciscans; see *Exhibitio Consolatoria*, ed. John Brady, in *Archiv. Hib.*, 14 (1949), p. 80.

54. Ó Maolchonaire ordained Robert Rochford OFM to the priesthood in 1621. He took the name Robertus a Brigida in religion and, four years later, published at St Omer in Flanders a work in English on the lives of Sts Patrick, Brigid and Colmcille. By 1630 he had been sent to Spain, perhaps to teach. His confrère Patrick Fleming, the noted hagiographer, wrote to him at Alcalá. See Brendan Jennings (ed.), *An. Hib.*, 6 (1934), pp. 126–7. See also 'Liber constitutionem ac ordinationum quae ab initio hucusque pro felici regimine hujus colegii S. Antonii de Padua facta sunt, pp. 36–8; Extracta ex monumentis asservatis in Collegio S. Antonii'; cited by Canice Mooney, *Irish Franciscan relations with France, 1224–1850* (Dublin: Assisi, 1951), pp. 37–45.

55. 'Notes on a short manuscript life of the prelate William Terry', ed. Patrick Moran, *JCHAS*, 3 (1893), pp. 142–3. This consecration occurred in Brussels, 23 Apr. 1623.

56. Certified copy of testimonium to the consecration of Thomas Fleming, 1 Oct. 1624 (UCD–OFM, D.03, p. 405, HMC *Franciscan MSS*, p. 77).

57. Bagno to Ó Maolchonaire, Brussels, 10 Nov. 1624 (de Meester (ed.), *Correspondance du Nonce Giovanni-Francesco Guidi di Bagno: 1621–27* (Bruxelles & Rome: Analecta Vaticano-Belgica, 1938), p. 520).

58. Jeroen Nilis, 'Irish students at Leuven University, 1548–1797', *Archiv. Hib.*, 60 (2007), p. 4.

59. Louis Antheunis, 'Some Irish prelates who lived or died in Belgium in the seventeenth century', *IER*, 84 (1955), pp. 316–22: 321. See also *Archiv. Hib.*, 12, pp. 88–9.

60. As this aspect of his life has been dealt with elsewhere, I will not dwell upon it here. See Lucien Ceyssens, 'Florence Conry, Hugh de Burgo, Luke Wadding, and Jansenism', in *Father Luke Wadding: commemorative volume*, pp. 310–15. For recent work see Thomas O'Connor, *An Irish Jansenist in seventeenth-century France: John Callaghan, 1605–54: the 32nd O'Donnell Lecture*

(Dublin: National University of Ireland, 2004).

61. Clark, *Strangers and sojourners at Port Royal*, p. 2; Canice Mooney, 'St Anthony's College, Louvain', *Donegal Annual*, 8 (1969), p. 25.

62. Ceyssens, 'Florence Conry, Hugh de Burgo, Luke Wadding, and Jansenism', in *Father Luke Wadding: commemorative volume*, p. 315; *cf.* Mooney, *Irish Franciscan relations with France*, pp. 37–45.

63. Downey, 'A Salamancan who evaded the Inquisition', p. 96.

64. Carter, *The secret diplomacy of the Habsburgs*, p. 283.

65. Marqués de Bedmar to the council of state, Brussels, 19 Sept. 1621 (AGS, Estado, Flandes, l. 2310).

66. Cardinal de la Cueva to the Cardinal Protector of the Irish, Ludovico Ludovisi, Brussels, 15 Sept. 1622 (BAV, Barberini Latini 6802, pp. 1–4).

67. Ibid., pp. 3–4.

68. John H. Elliott, *El conde duque de Olivares: el político en una epoca de decadencia* (Barcelona: Crítica, 2004), pp. 83–93.

69. Andrés de Soto, Franciscan commissary, to the friars at St Anthony's College, Brussels, 16 Aug. 1617 (UCD–OFM, D.01, p. 791).

70. Cordula van Wyhe, 'Court and convent: the Infanta Isabella and her Franciscan confessor Andrés de Soto', *Sixteenth Century Journal*, 35 (2004), pp. 411–45.

71. Craig Harline and Eddy Put, *Mathias Hovius among his flock in seventeenth-century Flanders*, pp. 268–9, 285.

72. Edmund Hogan, *Distinguished Irishmen of the sixteenth century* (London: Burns & Oates, 1894), pp. 267, 284–5.

73. Ibid., pp. 493–5.

74. Mac Aingil, *Scáthán Shacraiminte na hAithridhe*, eag. Cainneach Ó Maonaigh (Lobháin: S. Antoine, 1618; Baile Átha Cliath: Institiúid Árd-Léinn Bhaile Átha Cliath, 1952), p. 190: 'Éire agus a hinghean ionmhuin Alba'.

75. Cathaldus Giblin, 'Hugh McCaghwell OFM: aspects of his life', in Benignus Millett and Anthony Lynch (eds), *Dún Mhuire, Killiney: 1945–95* (Dublin: The Lilliput Press, 1995), p. 77.

76. See Raymond Gillespie, 'Destabilizing Ulster, 1641–2', in Brian Mac Cuarta (ed.), *Ulster 1641: aspects of the rising* (Belfast: Institute of Irish Studies, 1993), p. 116.

77. Council of state to Philip III, Madrid, 10 Jan. 1616 (AGS, Estado, Inglaterra, libro 372, p. 4): 'La guerra a los rebeldes de las montañas del Scocia y de las Islas'.

78. Macdonel Sr. de los estados de Ila y Kintire en Escoçia y de los Glinnes de Irlanda [...] pide sueldo en Italia o Flandes', 10 Oct. 1616 (AGS, E., Inglaterra, l. 845, f. 72).

79. See Jan-Baptiste van Male to Archduke Albert, London, 30 Oct. 1620 (AGR/ARA, Vienne, 56/394–5); Carter, *The secret diplomacy of the Habsburgs*, pp. 150, 295.

80. Hector MacDonnell, 'Surviving Kinsale Scottish-style: the MacDonnells of Antrim', in Morgan (ed.), *The Battle of Kinsale*, pp. 265–77; idem, 'Responses of the MacDonnell clan to change in early seventeenth-century Ulster', in O'Connor and Lyons (eds), *Irish migrants in Europe after Kinsale, 1602–1820*, pp. 64–87.

81. Jane Ohlmeyer, *Civil war and restoration in the three Stuart kingdoms: the political career of Randall MacDonnell, first marquis of Antrim, 1609–83* (Cambridge: Cambridge University Press, 1993).

82. Giblin, *Irish Franciscan mission to Scotland*, pp. 1–11. Mícheál Mac Craith, 'The Gaelic reaction to the Reformation', in Steven Ellis and Sarah Barber (eds), *Conquest and union: fashioning a British state, 1485–1725* (London: Longman, 1995), pp. 139–61.

83. Silvano Giordano, *Le istruzioni di Paolo V ai diplomatici pontifici 1605–21* (3 vols, Rome: Dipartimento beni archivistici e librari-Direzione Gen.le per gli Archivi, 2003), pp. 1077–8.

84. Morra to Borghèse, Brussels, 9 Sept. 1617 (ASV, Borghèse II, 137, ff 64–5); van Meerbeeck (ed.), *Correspondance*, pp. 175–6.

85. Giblin, 'Hugh McCaghwell OFM', p. 79.

86. Giblin, *Irish Franciscan mission to Scotland*, pp. 14–18.

87. Ibid., p. viii.

88. Ibid., pp. 18–21.

89. Giblin, 'Hugh McCaghwell OFM', p. 80.

90. Mícheál Mac Craith, 'Literature in Irish, c. 1560–1690: from the Elizabethan settlement to the Battle of the Boyne', in Margaret Kelleher and Philip O'Leary (eds), *The Cambridge History of Irish Literature* (2 vols, Cambridge: Cambridge University Press, 2006), vol. 1, pp. 191–231.

91. Aonghas MacCoinnich, 'Where and how was Gaelic written in late medieval and early modern Scotland? Orthographic practices and cultural identities', *Scottish Gaelic Studies*, 24 (2008), pp. 309–56.

92. Cathaldus Giblin, 'The *Acta* of Propaganda Archives and the Scottish mission, 1623–1670', *The Innes Review*, 5/1 (1954), pp. 39–76.

93. Cathaldus Giblin, 'Francis MacDonnell OFM, son of the first earl of Antrim, (d. 1636)', *Seanchas*

Ard Mhacha, 8 (1975–6), p. 50.
94. MacDonnell, 'Responses of the MacDonnell clan to change in early seventeenth-century Ulster', in O'Connor and Lyons (eds), *Irish migrants in Europe after Kinsale, 1602–1820*, pp. 64–87.
95. Giblin, 'Francis MacDonnell OFM, son of the first earl of Antrim', pp. 45–6.
96. Ibid., p. 52.
97. John Lorne Campbell, 'Irish mission to Scotland', *The Innes Review*, 5/2 (1954), p. 5.
98. Jason Harris, 'The Irish Franciscan mission to the Highlands and Islands', in David Edwards and Mícheál Ó Siochrú (eds), *The Scots in Stuart and Commonwealth Ireland* (Manchester: Manchester University Press, forthcoming). On the political and cultural factors which motivated religious alignment, see Fiona McDonald, *Missions to the Gaels: Reformation and Counter-reformation in Ulster and the Highlands and Islands of Scotland, 1560–1760* (Edinburgh: John Donald, 2006).
99. Ceyssens, 'Florence Conry, Hugh de Burgo, Luke Wadding', p. 334.
100. By 1617, Rovenius reported that 'priests were, almost without exception, pure in their doctrine, without reproach in their conduct, self-sacrificing and full of zeal for the welfare of the Church and the propagation of the faith'. See Herman Bakvis, *Catholic power in the Netherlands* (Montréal: McGill-Queen's University Press, 1981), p. 22; G. H. Anderson, *Biographical dictionary of Christian missions* (New York: Macmillan, 1998), pp. 580–1.
101. Willem Frijhoff and Marijke Spies, *Dutch culture in a European perspective: hard-won unity* (Assen: Royal van Gorcum, 2004), p. 373.
102. Certified copy of testimonium to the consecration of Thomas Fleming, 1 Oct. 1624 (UCD–OFM, D.03, p. 405, HMC *Franciscan MSS*, p. 77).
103. Lawrence Renehan, *Collections on Irish church history*, ed. Daniel McCarthy (2 vols, Dublin: Warren, 1861–73), vol. 1.
104. Hardiman, *History of the town and county of Galway*, pp. 8–9, 18–20.
105. John Lynch, *Pii Antistitis Icon*, ed. and trans. Charles Meehan (Dublin: James Duffy, 1884), pp. 33–7.
106. Aidan Clarke, 'Colonial identity in early seventeenth-century Ireland', in T. W. Moody (ed.), *Nationality and the pursuit of national independence* (Belfast: Appletree Press, 1978), p. 63.
107. Burke, *The history of the Catholic archbishops of Tuam*, pp. 113–14.
108. Ibid.
109. For full details, see Brian Jackson, 'Sectarianism: division and dissent in Irish Catholicism', in Alan Ford and John McCafferty (eds), *The origins of sectarianism in early-modern Ireland* (Cambridge: Cambridge University Press, 2005), pp. 203–15.
110. Ibid. For another view of the Drogheda dispute, see Mac Cuarta, *Catholic revival in the north of Ireland*, pp. 77–8.
111. 'Florentius Conrius à Bagno' (Paris, BN, MSS Latins, 5174, f. 126; 5175a, p. 421; de Meester (ed.), *Correspondance du Nonce Giovanni-Francesco Guidi di Bagno: 1621–27*, vol. 1 (Bruxelles & Rome: Analecta Vaticano-Belgica, 1938), p. 163).
112. Jackson, 'Sectarianism: division and dissent in Irish Catholicism', p. 212.
113. 'Conrius à Bagno' (Paris, BN, MSS Latins, 5174, f. 126; 5175a, p. 421).
114. To David Rothe, who refused to be *accusator fratrum meorum*, this was a vicious circle where, it seemed, 'no sooner one debate is either ordered or abated, then an other sproutly arose'. See his letter to Peter Lombard, 17 Sept. 1625 (*Wadding Papers*, ed. Jennings, pp. 101–5: 104).
115. Bagno to Ó Maolchonaire, Brussels, 8 Mar. 1623; same to same, 8 Jun. 1623 (de Meester, (ed.), *Correspondance du Nonce Giovanni-Francesco Guidi di Bagno*, p. 297).
116. Brendan Jennings, 'The career of Hugh, son of Rory O'Donnell, earl of Tirconnel, in the Low Countries, 1607–1642', *Studies*, 30 (1941), p. 227.
117. Archduke Albert to Philip III, Brussels, 2 May 1619 (AGR/ARA, État/State, c1.937).
118. Flaithrí Ó Maolchonaire to Diego Sarmiento de Acuña, Conde de Gondomar, Louvain, 5 Nov. 1619 (RBPM, MS II-2132, 191, f. 325).
119. Ó Maolchonaire to Gondomar, Louvain, 5 Nov. 1619 (RBPM, MS II-2132, 191, f. 325): 'Por veer que la resolucion del negocio del Señor Conde de Tyrconel tarde tanto, me aparecido refrescar la memoria de Vsa.'
120. Memorial for James Fitzgerald, Madrid, 11 Nov. 1620 (AGS, Estado, legajo 2867); Karin Schüller, *Die beziehungen zwischen Spanien und Irland im 16. und 17. Jahrhundert* (Münster: Aschendorf, 2001), pp. 212–13.
121. 'Don Terencio Omelaglin, soldado yrlandes […] Lobayna a 2 de março de 1623' (AGS, Guerra Antigua, Servicios Militares, legajo 81, f. 12).
122. Ibid: 'O Neyl conde de Tyron, maestre de campo de la infanteria yrlandessa por su Magestad en estos estados de Flandes.'
123. The fortress changed hands so often that it was known as *La Puta*. See Julio Albi de la Cuesta, *De*

Pavía a Rocroi: los Tercios de Infantería española en los siglos XVI y XVII (Madrid, 1999), p. 196; Enrique de Tapia Ozcariz, *Eugenio O'Neill: capitán de los tercios de Flandes* (Madrid: IMNASA, 1969), pp. 104–6.

124. Jennings (ed.), *Wild Geese in Spanish Flanders*, p. 209.
125. For the complaint made against Ó Maolchonaire see Cardinal Pompeo Arrigone to Cardinal Barberini, Rome, 22 Jan. 1610 (BAV, Barb. Lat., 8676, 236).
126. Éinrí Ó Néill to the papal secretary of state, Valladolid, Jan. 1601 (ASV, Particolare 1, pp. 391–2).
127. 'Fray Florencio Conryo a Padre fray Luca', Madrid, 3 Aug. 1627 (UCD–OFM, D.03, pp. 857–9).
128. Lombard to Cardinal Fabrizio Verallo, Rome, 1617 (Archivio della Congregazione per la Dottrina della Fede (Rome), Sanctum Officium, Stanza storica (ACDF, S.O., St st.), 1-e, f. 794r.; I am grateful to Dr Thomas O'Connor for this reference. See also Letter Apostolic of Paul V upon petition of Archbishop Peter Lombard, Rome, 27 Jan. 1615 (HMC *Franciscan MSS*, p. 69).
129. See *Archiv. Hib.*, 3 (1914), pp. 302–10 and *Archiv. Hib.*, 4 (1915), pp. 292–9; 302–9.
130. 'Favorecer la súplica de los condes de Tirón y Birhaven sobre proveer los obispados de Irlanda con parecer la nobleza', 23 Oct. (AAEE, FSS, Estado, legajo 57, f. 231).
131. Casway, 'Gaelic Maccabeanism: the politics of reconciliation', pp. 176–88.
132. I Maccabees II.1–14; cited by Casway, 'Gaelic Maccabeanism: the politics of reconciliation', p. 177.
133. Ó Maolchonaire to Philip III, 1603 (AGS, E., Inglaterra, l. 840, ff 200–1): 'por mis pecados y por los de Yrlanda y de España, el socorro y todos estamos aqui aun, porque quando fue esso resuelto nos respondian los ministros que era menester haçer otro acuerdo a Vuestra Magestad'.
134. Casway, 'Gaelic Maccabeanism: the politics of reconciliation', pp. 178–88.
135. Silke, 'Later relations between Primate Peter Lombard and Hugh O'Neill', *Ir. Theol. Quart.*, 22 (1955), pp. 15–30: 28; Donal Cregan, 'The social and cultural background of a counter-reformation episcopate', in idem (ed.), *Studies in Irish History presented to R. Dudley Edwards*, pp. 85–117.
136. See the following petitions to the Sacred Congregation and to Urban VIII: *Spic. Ossor.*, i, pp. 136–7; *Archiv. Hib.*, 2 (1913), pp. 106–7.
137. 'Fray Rocque de la Cruz al padre fray Miguel de Espiritú Santo', Louvain (*Wadding Papers*, ed. Jennings, pp. 211–13): 'Tirconel ha caydo mucho de su predicamento [...] y assi Tiron solo gozo todo el favor.'
138. *Epitome Annalium*, vol. i, p. 64; cited by Felim O'Brien in 'Florence Conry, archbishop of Tuam', *Irish Rosary*, 32 (1928), p. 459.
139. Ó Maolchonaire to Wadding, Madrid, 3 Aug. 1627 (UCD–OFM, D.03, pp. 857–9).
140. Ibid: 'El conde de Tiron proseguiria siempre la primera proposicion que hizo, sino es que el Padre fray Roberto, que lo olio por algun camino, juro que avia de ir en partes remotas donde nunca le viessen sino desistiessen de hablar del.' (*Wadding Papers*, ed. Jennings, p. 252).
141. *Brevis et exacta relation seu description regni Hiberniae in praesenti statu*, 1627 (*Wadding Papers*, ed. Jennings, p. 213). This may have been among Friar Nugent's broadsides against Ó Maolchonaire and his allies.
142. Ibid: 'frater Robertus durante persecutione nullo modo in Hyberniam proficisi potest, quia a rege Angliae banditus, et crimine laesae majestatis reus est, sicut Tuamensis, quia ambo astiterunt in ultimo bello cum comitibus de Tiron et Tyrconell contra dicta regem; quare in praesenti statu inutilis esset ejus promotio.'
143. Peter Lombard to Paul V, Rome, 13 Mar. 1622 (Patrick Moran (ed.), *Memoir of the most reverend Peter Lombard* (Dublin: James Duffy, 1868), pp. lxviii–lxix).
144. Cregan, 'The social and cultural background', pp. 85–117.
145. *Wadding Papers*, ed. Jennings, p. x.
146. Ó Néill to the Propaganda Fide, Brussels, 23 Oct. 1626 (HMC *Franciscan MSS*, pp. 96–7); Meehan, pp. 542–5.
147. The nuncio of Flanders on the election of the archbishops of Armagh and Cashel, Brussels, 21 Feb. 1626 (HMC *Franciscan MSS*, pp. 87–92).
148. Patrick Corish, (ed.), 'Two reports on the Catholic Church in Ireland in the early seventeenth century', *Archiv. Hib.*, 22 (1959), pp. 140–52.
149. Brussels, 21 Feb. 1626 (HMC *Franciscan MSS*, pp. 87–92).
150. A summary of the objections to the appointment of Hugh Mac Aingil, OFM, to Armagh, with answers, 1626 (*Wadding Papers*, ed. Jennings, pp. 149–56).
151. *Nomina et origines ecclesiasticorum Hibernorum pro quibus nunc Romae episcopatus postulantur* (1626); *Wadding Papers*, ed. Jennings, pp. 174–8.
152. Before he died, on 22 September 1626, he bequeathed 1,000 apostolic blessings from Urban VIII to his friend Flaithrí Ó Maolchonaire and four others. See 'Apostolic blessings between MacCaghwell and Conry', 26 Feb. 1627, Rome (*Archiv. Hib.*, 12, pp. 130–1).

153. *Cf.* Special report on the kingdom of Ireland, Valladolid, 7 Nov. 1605 (AHL, FH/Lerma t. I/c. 27); 'Breviate of Ireland', *c.* 1618 (TCD, MS E.3.8 (580), ff. 22, 49–52).
154. Valladolid, 7 Nov. 1605 (AHL, FH/Lerma t. I/c. 27).
155. Declan Downey, 'Irish–European integration: the legacy of Charles V', p. 101.
156. 'Briefe relation of Irland and diversity of Irish in the same', *c.* 1618 (UCD–OFM, D.01, vol. 1, pp. 15–26). Ciarán O'Scea is completing a detailed analysis of this source and its Spanish cognates.
157. Ibid.
158. Ibid.
159. *Cf.* Robin Briggs, *Early-modern France: 1560–1715* (Oxford: Oxford University Press, 1998), p. 96.
160. de Meester (ed.), *Correspondance du Nonce Giovanni-Francesco Guidi di Bagno (1621–27)*, p. 784.
161. Jennings, 'The career of Hugh, son of Rory O'Donnell, earl of Tirconnel, in the Low Countries, 1607–1642', p. 230.
162. See above, both for the approbations from Louvain and Douai for his *Tractatus de statu parvulorum*, and the funding he received to publish works at Antwerp in 1619 and 1624.
163. Spada to Mellini, Paris, 5 Dec. 1625: *Tuamensis vero, manens extra patriam, et non contentus uno cleri seminario Lovanii, duo alia, Duaci ac Tornaci posita, fratrum syndico tradi fecit* (*Wadding Papers*, ed. Jennings, pp. 122–5, 227).
164. Patrick Corish, 'The beginnings of the Irish college, Rome', in *Father Luke Wadding: commemorative volume*, pp. 284–94: 285. See also John Brady, 'Father Christopher Cusack and the Irish college of Douai, 1594–1624', in Sylvester O'Brien (ed.), *Measgra Mhichíl Uí Chléirigh: miscellany of historical and linguistic studies in honour of Brother Michael Ó Cléirigh, chief of the Four Masters, 1643–1943* (Dublin: Assisi Press, 1944), pp. 98–107.
165. Novices received at the college since 1607, Louvain, 1617 (*Louvain Papers*, ed. Jennings, pp. 54–8).
166. Canice Mooney, *Irish Franciscan relations with France, 1224–1850* (Killiney: Four Masters Press, 1951), pp. 22–3, 86–7.
167. Stronge, a lector of theology at both Santander and Medina de Pomar, was once taken captive at sea by the Turks. See Canice Mooney, 'The Franciscans in Waterford', *Jn. of the Cork Historical and Archaeological Society*, 69 (1964), p. 89.
168. Gráinne Henry, *The Irish military community*, pp. 99–102.
169. Ibid.
170. Thomas, archbishop of Cashel, to John Roche, Madrid, 14 Mar. 1627 (UCD–OFM, MS D.03, p. 814).
171. Silvano Giordano, *Le istruzioni di Paolo V ai diplomatici pontifici 1605–21*, p. 999. Governed by Jesuits, the nearby English college was provided for by the archdukes and the papacy.
172. Arrigone to Lerma, Rome, 27 Oct. 1605 (ADM, legajo 51-ramo 5).
173. Kerney Walsh, *Destruction by peace*, pp. 200, 219.
174. Gráinne Henry, *The Irish military community*, p. 104.
175. Corish, 'The beginnings of the Irish college, Rome', in *Father Luke Wadding: commemorative volume*, p. 287.
176. Elliott, *Imperial Spain, 1469–1716*, pp. 316–17.
177. See the accompanying map of the Spanish Netherlands.
178. Thomas Fleming, archbishop of Dublin, David Rothe, bishop of Ossory, and William Terry, bishop of Cork, to Cardinal Ludovisi, Brussels, Apr. 1627 (HMC *Franciscan MSS*, p. 103).
179. 'Ristretto delle scritture spettanti all'elletione dell'Arcivescovo Armacano, primate d'Hibernia', 1628 (*Wadding Papers*, ed. Jennings, pp. 221–9: 227). '[...] e il vescovo Tuamense ha unito i seminarii di Lovanio, Duaco, e Turnaci, ai Reformati, et sottopostoli alla loro cura, da che succeed che tutti i migliori sogetti di quelli si fanno religiosi.'
180. Patrick Corish, 'The beginnings of the Irish college, Rome', pp. 284–94.
181. Igor Pérez Tostado, 'Tu, felix Austria, nube: la actividad política bicéfala de la comunidad exiliada irlandesa', in *Tiempos modernos: revista de historia moderna* (2006/1).
182. Captain Lombard's memorial, London, *circa* 1622 (TNA, Foreign Office Papers, 94/124, 353).
183. Seán Ó Néill to the Infanta, Brussels, 12 Jun. 1622 (Jennings (ed.), *Wild Geese in Spanish Flanders*, p. 181).
184. Infanta Isabel to Philip IV, 4 Feb. 1623 (Jennings (ed.), *Wild Geese in Spanish Flanders*, p. 188).
185. Report to the lord deputy, 17 Jun. 1624 (*Cal. S. P. Ire. 1615–25*, p. 504).
186. For instance: 'Advertimiento dado a 6 de mayo en Aranjuez 1625 años sobre la empresa de Irlanda e Escocia contra Inglaterra' (BNE, MS 2357, ff 9–14).
187. J. H. Elliott, *The count-duke of Olivares: The statesman in an age of decline* (New Haven, CT: Yale

University Press, 1986), pp. 25–53.
188. García Oro, *Don Diego Sarmiento de Acuña, Conde de Gondomar y embajador de Espana*, pp. 307–8. For opposing views, see Redworth, *The Prince and the Infanta: the cultural politics of the Spanish match*, and Brennan Pursell, 'The end of the Spanish Match', *The Historical Journal*, 45 (2002), pp. 699–726.
189. Venetian ambassador at Madrid to the Doge and Senate, 10 Nov. 1625 (*Cal. S. P. Venetian, 1625–6*, p. 209).
190. Sir Francis Annesley to Sir Edward Conway, Dublin, 27 Mar. 1624 (*Cal. S. P. Ire., 1615–25*, pp. 473–4); Jennings (ed.), *Wild Geese in Spanish Flanders*, pp. 52, 191–2, 561.
191. *Archiv. Hib.*, 2 (1913), p. 106–7.
192. Spanish policymakers expressed the view that England had been opposed to the crown of Castile since the times of Henry VIII: 'Discurso sobre la constante enemistad de Inglaterra', Madrid, 1625 (BNE, MS 2357, ff 19–24).
193. Urban VIII to Seán Ó Néill and Aodh Ó Domhnaill, Rome, 8 Oct. 1625 and 6 Sept. 1626 (ASV, *Epistolae ad Principes*, 40, ff 271v-3r).
194. Guidi di Bagno to Spada, Brussels, 23 Oct., 1626 (ASV, Nunziatura di Fiandra, 21, ff 440r-64r).
195. Guidi di Bagno to the papal secretariate, Brussels, 24 Oct. 1626 (ASV, Nunziatura di Fiandra, 15, f. 225; *Collectanea Hibernica*, 1 (1958), pp. 61, 63).
196. Jennings (ed.), *Wild Geese in Spanish Flanders*, pp. 209–10.
197. See, for example, 'Lo que pide el Conde de Puñonrostro', Madrid, 25 Jan. 1610 (AGS, E. NP, l. 2745).
198. *Cf.* Mattingly, *Renaissance diplomacy*, pp. 104–5.
199. Under the command of Éinrí Ó Néill, Irish troops served at the 1606 Rhynberck siege; see Enrique de Tapia Ozcariz, *Eugenio O'Neill: capitán de los tercios de Flandes*, pp. 104–5.
200. Jennings (ed.), *Wild Geese in Spanish Flanders*, pp. 210–11.
201. Casway, *Owen Roe O'Neill and the struggle for Catholic Ireland*, p. 30.
202. Andrés de Soto to Hugh de Burgo, Brussels, 11 Mar. 1622 (Cathaldus Giblin (ed.), *Liber Lovaniensis, c. 1629–1717* (Dublin: Clonmore Reynolds, 1956). He was subsequently designated commissary general of the Irish Friars Minor in 1623 at which point he travelled to Dublin. In May 1625, he was in Rome to attend the Franciscans' general chapter before being directed to reform the order's province of Aquitaine. See Ceyssens, 'Florence Conry, Hugh de Burgo, Luke Wadding', pp. 332–3.
203. Lucienne de Meester (ed.), *Correspondance du Nonce Giovanni-Francesco Guidi di Bagno: 1621–27*, vol. 1, p. 317; O'Brien in 'Florence Conry, archbishop of Tuam', *Irish Rosary*, 32, p. 459.
204. See, for instance, *Wadding Papers*, ed. Jennings, pp. 252–4.
205. Ceyssens, 'Florence Conry, Hugh de Burgo, Luke Wadding', pp. 331–55. After succeeding Ó Maolchonaire, Malachy of Tuam continued to use the Red Hand of Ulster insignia to seal his letters.
206. Flaithrí Ó Maolchonaire to Archbishop Jacob Boonen, Madrid, 5 Feb. 1627 (Archief Aartsbisdom Mechelen-Brussel, Boonen-3).
207. Ibid., 'Longum esset recensere quas passi sumus difficultates et molestias in transitu Galliae et Pyreneorum; nec aliud sperare licuit pro senectute mea, tam intempesta hyeme, ingentem peregrinationem suscipiente.'
208. Ibid., 'indignus confrater et servus fray Florentius'.
209. Cathaldus Giblin, 'Catalogue of material of Irish interest in the Collection *Nunziatura di Fiandra*, Vatican archives: part 1, vols 1–50', *Collectanea Hibernica*, 1 (1958), pp. 14–15, 38.
210. Pirenne, *Histoire de Belgique*, vol. 4, p. 376.
211. Ibid.
212. Orcibal, *Correspondance de Jansénius*, p. 363.
213. Olivares to the Infanta Isabel, Madrid, 19 Jan. 1627 (AGR/ARA, SEG, correspondence, 301), cited by Jennings (ed.), *Wild Geese in Spanish Flanders*, p. 212; Don Diego de Messía to the Infanta Isabel, Madrid, 30 Jan. 1627 (AGR/ARA, SEG, correspondence, 301), cited by Jennings (ed.), *Wild Geese in Spanish Flanders*, p. 214.
214. Brendan Jennings, 'The career of Hugh, son of Rory O'Donnell, earl of Tirconnel, in the Low Countries, 1607–1642', pp. 219–34; idem (ed.), *Wild Geese in Spanish Flanders*, pp. 212–15, 217–18; Recio Morales, 'Florence Conry's memorandum for a military assault on Ulster', *Archiv. Hib.*, 56 (2002), pp. 65–72.
215. Jennings (ed.), *Wild Geese in Spanish Flanders*, p. 212.
216. Ibid., p. 228.
217. Ó Maolchonaire to the Spanish council of state, Madrid, 28 Sept. 1627 (AGS, Estado, l. 2041); cited by Thomas Flynn, *The Irish Dominicans 1536–1641* (Dublin: Four Courts Press, 1993), pp. 116–17.

218. Nuala was Aodh Ruadh's sister. See Jerrold Casway, 'Heroines or victims? The women of the flight of the earls', *New Hibernia Review*, 7 (2003), pp. 69–74.
219. Jennings (ed.), *Wild Geese in Spanish Flanders*, p. 234.
220. Ibid., pp. 215–17.
221. Ibid.
222. Ibid., pp. 217–18.
223. Ibid., p. 567. See also Tomás Ó Fiaich, 'Republicanism and separatism in the seventeenth century', *Léachtaí Cholm Cille*, 2 (1971), pp. 74–87.
224. Venetian ambassador at Rome to the Doge and Senate, 23 Oct. 1627 (*Cal. S. P. Venetian, 1626–8*, pp. 429–30, 437).
225. Coloma to Olivares (AGS Estado, Inglaterra, l. 2519, f. 78): 'a Irlanda por otro camino […] y metiendo en alguna liga secreta a los principes cattolicos y al Papa y contribuyendo nosotros en ella […] cosa que se puede esperar que haga efecto muy considerable y que Escocia en alguna parte se podria creer que se yncluyria en esta solebacion'.
226. R. Dudley Edwards, 'Church and state in the Ireland of Mícheál Ó Cléirigh, 1626–41', in O'Brien (ed.), *Measgra i gCuimhne Mhíchíl Uí Chléirigh*, pp. 1–20.
227. For Semple's petitions from 1623 to 1625 see AGS, Estado, Inglaterra, l. 2516, f. 114. The Scots' college deed of foundation was executed in Madrid on 10 May 1627.
228. 'Sucesos del año', Madrid, 1625 (BNE, MS 2357, ff 11–4).
229. Olga Turner, 'A Spanish ambassador's half-yearly account', *Bulletin of Hispanic Studies*, 31 (1954), pp. 98–108: Don Carlos Coloma paid Laing 2,800 reales in August 1624.
230. *Cf.* Casway, 'Gaelic Maccabeanism: the politics of reconciliation', pp. 180–1.
231. Jennings (ed.), *Wild Geese in Spanish Flanders*, pp. 230–6.
232. Genoa was consecrated to the Virgin Mary, under protection from Spain. See Silvano Giordano (ed.), *Le istruzioni di Paolo V ai diplomatici pontifici 1605–21*, vol. 1, p. 55.
233. In recent decades, political historians have defined these power aggregates, along with Florence and Siena, as 'the great work of art' of Renaissance politics. See David L. Hicks, 'The Sienese oligarchy and the rise of Pandolfo Petrucci', *La Toscana al tempo di Lorenzo il Magnifico: politica, economia, cultura, arte* (3 vols, Pisa: Pacini, 1996), vol. 3, pp. 1051–72. *Cf.* Mattingly, *Renaissance diplomacy*, pp. 110–25.
234. Casway, 'Gaelic Maccabeanism: the politics of reconciliation', p. 185.
235. Herbert Rowan, 'Kingship and republicanism in the seventeenth century: some reconsiderations', in Carter (ed.), *From the Renaissance to the Counter-Reformation*, pp. 420–31.
236. Elliott, *Imperial Spain*, p. 334. This reflects the conclusions drawn by Antonio Domínguez Ortiz, *Política y hacienda de Felipe IV* (Madrid: Editorial de Derecho Financiero, 1960), pp. 11–36.
237. Jennings (ed.), *Wild Geese in Spanish Flanders*, pp. 235–6.
238. 'Correspondence of the Infanta and the duke of Mirabel on proposals by the Dutch', 16 Sept. 1627 (AGS Estado, Inglaterra, l. 2517, ff 60–6).
239. Geoffrey Parker, 'The making of strategy in Habsburg Spain: Philip II's "bid for mastery", 1556–1598', in W. Murray, K. MacGregor and A. Bernstein (eds), *The making of strategy: rulers, states, and war* (Cambridge: Cambridge University Press, 1994), p. 127.
240. Carter, *The secret diplomacy of the Habsburgs, 1598–1625*, pp. 268–70.
241. Flaithrí Ó Maolchonaire to Don Juan de Villeda, Madrid, 28 Jul. 1627 (AGS, E, Es. NP, l. 2646, f. 18): 'que llego a esta corte el mes de enero passado movido solo por el zelo del servicio de Dios de Vuestra Magestad y el de su patria.'
242. Ibid: 'Y entendiendo entonzes el Conde Duque de San Lucar la causa de su benida se ordeno al Pressidente de Hazienda que detubiese aqui de las provisiones que se hazen al Exto de Flandes los mill ducados al año que alla se le pagan por gastos secretos al Arzobispo para poderse sustentar mientras asistiese a los dichos negocios.'
243. Ibid: 'Que despues dio un memorial en este conssejo pidiendo la continuacion de los meses corridos y que fuesen corriendo y que la paga fuese en plata pues las provisiones dichas se hazian en esta moneda.'
244. Ibid: 'A que se le respondio que se bolbiese a Flandes'.
245. Ibid: 'durante el tipo de la rotura'.
246. Ibid: 'de que dio quenta al Conde Duque el qual le respondio dijese a Don Juan Villela le hablase en su negocio y haviendolo hecho Don Juan le respondio el Conde Duque que desde el rompimiento con Inglaterra avia parecido conveniente tener aqui persona ynteligente en las cosas de Irlanda particularmente aviendo faltado el otro arzobispo que estava aca'.
247. 'Junta de los teologos [con] fray Ponze de Leon OP, fray Francisco Araijo OP', 1621 (AGS, E., Inglaterra, l. 2518, ff. 48–56).
248. *Cf.* Elliott, *Imperial Spain*, pp. 324–5.

249. Ó Maolchonaire to Don Juan de Villeda, Madrid, 28 Jul. 1627 (AGS, E, Es. NP, l. 2646, f. 18): 'que sea persona de quien los mismos irlandeses hagan confianza'.
250. Ibid.
251. Enrique García Hernán, 'El Colegio de San Patricio de los irlandeses de Madrid', *Madrid: revista de arte, geografía, e historia*, 8 (2006), pp. 219–46.
252. 'Breviate of Ireland', *c.* 1618.
253. 'Las dichas consignaciones', Aug. 1613, Madrid (AGS, Contaduría Mayor de Cuentas, 3a epoca, l. 3,159, sección 23, ff 23v–24v); 'A suplicacion de Don Fray Florencio Conrio Arçobispo Tuamense en Irlanda', 7 Oct. 1617, Lerma (AGS, CJH 549-27–8, Particulares).
254. Ó Maolchonaire to the council of finance, Madrid, 7 Mar. 1629 (AGS, CJH, l. 661).
255. Testimony of Secretary Jorge Lendinez, Brussels, 27 Apr. 1629 (AGS, CJH, l. 661).
256. Ó Maolchonaire to the council of finance, 7 Mar. 1629 (AGS, CJH, l. 661).
257. Cardinal Alfonso de la Cueva to Philip IV, Brussels, 9 and 18 September 1629 (AGS, E., l. 2322); cited by Jonathan Irvine Israel, *Empires and entrepots: the Dutch, the Spanish monarchy and the Jews, 1585–1713* (London: Continuum, 1990), pp. 174–6.
258. Ó Maolchonaire to the council of finance, Madrid, 7 Mar. 1629 (AGS, CJH, l. 661).
259. 'Don Juan Ibañez de Segovia', Madrid, 19 Jul. 1629 (AGS, CJH, l. 661).
260. Ibid: '[…] pago el año pasado de 628 quinientos ducados al arçobispo de Tuamense de que vuestra Magestad le hiço merced de ayuda de costa y andando despachando la cedula que sele dio para su descargo sea perdido.'
261. Ibid: 'Suplica a vuestra Magestad le haga merced de mandar sele de otra en que reçivira merced.'
262. Ó Maolchonaire to Philip IV, Madrid, 20 Sept. 1629 (AGS, CJH, l. 661): 'Y porque esta enfermo en la cama y muy empañado para no tener otra cosa de que se poder sustentar mas que la dicha merced y no se le haver pagado […] Con advertencia que a de ser la paga de las provisiones de Flandes.'
263. Hugh de Burgo to Wadding, Madrid, 29 Nov. 1629 (*Wadding Papers*, ed. Jennings, p. 327): 'No tenia cosa que dexarme ordenar más de cerca novicientos ducados que le deve su Magestad, que dexo para el colegio de Lovayna.'
264. St Anthony's College statement of accounts, Louvain, 16 Apr. 1632 (*Louvain Papers*, ed. Jennings, pp. 98–9).
265. 'Fray Florencio Conryo a Padre fray Luca', Madrid, 3 Aug. 1627 (*Wadding Papers*, ed. Jennings, pp. 252–4).
266. *Cf.* Corish, 'The beginnings of the Irish college, Rome', pp. 284–94.
267. 'A padre Luca', Madrid, 3 Aug. 1627 (*Wadding Papers*, ed. Jennings, pp. 252–4).
268. For the years 1625–7, see HMC *Franciscan MSS*, pp. 83, 97 (2), 103 (6). The Countess Caitríona, wife of Aodh Ó Néill, was related to Fr Bonabhentura Mac Aonghusa OFM.
269. 'A padre Luca', Madrid, 3 Aug. 1627: 'Yo no tengo en esso negocio de los Driscoles sino hazerle buena obra de intercession por ver que son cavalleros pobres y honrrados' (UCD–OFM, D.03, pp. 857–9).
270. Ibid: 'Encomiendo a vuestra paternidad otra vez esse negocio de los Driscoles, que me rogaron lo hiziesse.'
271. Conor O'Driscoll to Ó Maolchonaire, 26 Aug. 1605 (AGS, E. In., l. 843, f. 57).
272. 'El Capitan Don Cornelio Odriscol' (AGS, GM, Libros de Registro, Mar (1616–18) 121, p. 192; (1621–3), 131, pp. 163, 338).
273. Parker, *The army of Flanders and the Spanish road*, p. 110.
274. 'Don Tadeo Odriscol', 30 Apr. 1627 (AGS, GM, Libro de Registro 148 (1626) pp. 67, 141).
275. 'Don Tadeo Odriscol […] en estrema necessidad', 8 and 19 Jun. 1629 (AGS, GM, Libro de Registro 158 Galicia y Portugal, p. 167).
276. 'Don Antonio Odriscol' (AGS, GM, Libro de Registro, Decretos del Consejo, Secretaría de Tierra, 156 (1629–32), p. 50).
277. Thomas Walsh to Luke Wadding, Madrid, 14 Mar. 1627 (*Wadding Papers*, ed. Jennings, pp. 243–6).
278. Ibid.
279. Matha Óg Ó Maoltuile represented Ó Néill's case in Madrid up to the return of the archbishop, whereupon he applied to leave for Galicia. See Chapter 2 for details.
280. Encomium on MacGeoghegan written by Hendrik Put, Louvain, 12 Sept. 1626; Flaithrí Ó Maolchonaire, archbishop of Tuam, attesting the suitability of MacGeoghegan, minister provincial of the Irish Dominicans, for the highest preferment, Brussels, 25 Oct. 1626 (HMC *Franciscan MSS*, pp. 94, 97).
281. For a description of his family's history, see John O'Donovan (ed.), 'Covenant between MacGeoghegan and the Fox, with brief historical notices of the two families', *The Miscellany of the Irish Archaeological Society*, 1 (Dublin: Irish Archaeological Society, 1846), pp. 179–84.

282. 'ultra hoc suam trahit originem ex nobilissima familia comitis de Tyron' (*Wadding Papers*, ed. Jennings, p. 210). Attempts to promote MacGeoghegan to Armagh fell foul of prejudice against those from Meath, who, it was said, 'ever stood on the side of the heretics and against the Catholics'. Compare this with 'To the Cardinals of the Congregation on behalf of the Ulster earls', 1626 (HMC *Franciscan MSS*, p. 95); and, on the same grounds, *Wadding Papers*, ed. Jennings, p. 225: 'Da monsignor Nuntio di Fiandra, il che però stima non esser bene d'ellegerlo.'

283. Walsh to Luke Wadding, Madrid, 20 Feb. 1628 (*Wadding Papers*, ed. Jennings, pp. 257–60: 258).

284. Ibid: 'Trató el Tuamense conmigo aver otro obispo suffraganeo, y quiere sea el hermano de fray Hugo sacerdote y doctor de buenas partes.'

285. Ross MacGeoghegan OP, bishop of Kildare, in favour of John de Burgo for the see of Clonfert, 10 Oct. 1629, Louvain (HMC *Franciscan MSS*, p. 15).

286. Flaithrí Ó Maolchonaire's recommendation of Queely, de Burgo and Plunkett, 17 Mar. 1626 (UCD–OFM, D.02, f. 5; HMC *Franciscan MSS*, p. 2); Queely to Wadding, Limerick, 26 Jun. 1630 (HMC *Franciscan MSS*, pp. 26–8: 27): 'God knoweth I was brought uppon the stage in this matter unknowne to meselfe by Mr. Florence Conry.'

287. Giblin, 'The *Processus Datariae* and the appointments of Irish bishops in the seventeenth century', in *Father Luke Wadding: commemorative volume*, pp. 560–2.

288. Ibid.

289. *Wadding Papers*, ed. Jennings, pp. 338, 352.

290. Benjamin Hazard, '"A new company of crusaders like that of St John Capistran" – interaction between Irish military units and Franciscan chaplains: 1579–1654', in Óscar Recio Morales y Enrique García Hernán (eds), *La nación irlandesa en el ejército y la sociedad española, 1580–1818* (Madrid: Ministerio de Defensa, 2007), pp. 181–97.

291. Micheline Kerney Walsh (ed.), *Spanish knights of Irish origin: documents from the Archivo Histórico Nacional, Madrid and the Archivo General de Simancas* (4 vols, Dublin: Irish Manuscripts Commission, 1960–70).

292. Elena Postigo Castellanos, *Honor y privilegio en la corona de Castilla*, p. 205; Domínguez Ortiz, *The golden age of Spain*, Chapter 8: 'The privileged estates of nobles and clergy'.

293. Pope Alexander III confirmed the status of the military order of Santiago in 1175. A chapel consecrated to the order is to be found at the church of San Francisco el Grande in Madrid; see Cándido Rial, *Saint François le Grand: description historique et artistique* (Madrid: Editorial Cisneros, 1966).

294. See, for instance, the sworn testimonies for Diarmaid Ó Súilleabháin Béarra, Madrid, 1613 (AHN, Madrid, OO. MM. Pruebas de Caballeros de Santiago, expediente 7957, p. 2). Of all those Ó Maolchonaire vouched for, 75 per cent of those were with the order of Santiago.

295. 'Fadrique Plunqueto. Balgid, Irlanda', Madrid, 1626 (AHN, Madrid, OO.MM., Pruebas de Caballeros de Santiago, expediente 6536).

296. 'Fadrique Plunqueto' (AHN, Madrid, OO.MM., Pruebas de Caballeros de Santiago, exp. 6536), p. 2.

297. 'Matriculacion: artistas y filosofos. Florencio Conrio, ne de Roscoman, Diec. de Olfin de al 3 año', Salamanca, 10 Dec. 1594 (Ranson Papers, Cuaderno v, 29).

298. Fadrique Plunqueto' (AHN, Madrid, OO.MM., Pruebas de Caballeros de Santiago, exp. 6536).

299. Flaithrí Ó Maolchonaire to the council of military orders, Madrid, 18 Jul. 1627 (AHN, Madrid, OO. MM., Pruebas de Caballeros de Santiago, exp. 6536).

300. Ibid: '[…] su primer marido, el qual salio de Irlanda el año de 1603 y murio en Valladolid el año de 604 […] su madre era solamente dos años casada antes que el dicho Don Fadrique naciesse'.

301. Castellanos, *Honor y privilegio en la corona de Castilla*, pp. 255–66. Applicants were also expected to be above the age of infancy with a genealogy free from Jewish or Moorish blood, a good name and an unblemished record of service.

302. Cédula of Philip IV, Madrid, 1 Feb. 1630 (AGS, Guerra y Marina, Libro de Registro 154 (1629–30), p. 89): 'ya que le he mandado lebantar una compañia de yfanteria yrlandezesses'.

303. 'Don Alberto Hugo O Donell', Madrid, 30 May 1625 (AAEE, FSS, Caballeros de Alcántara, legajo 134, f. 28).

304. Aodh Ó Domhnaill's recommendation for Mac Aonghusa, Brussels, 26 Dec. 1626 (HMC *Franciscan MSS*, p. 99). His cousin Seán Ó Néill was admitted to the order of Calatrava in 1632.

305. Ó Maolchonaire's recommendation of Dionisius Mac Craith, Madrid, 20 Jul. 1628 (AGS, GA, Servicios Militares, l. 15, f. 94): 'Como consta por sus papeles que dan tambien sufficiente testimonio de sus virtudes y buena vida.'

306. Kagan, *Students and society in early-modern Spain*, pp. 30–61.

307. 'Don Dionisio de Castro' (AGS, GA, Servicios Militares, l. 15, f. 94).

308. Ibid. See also, AGS, GA, Servicios Militares, l. 15, f. 90, where it states that his military career started

in Captain Daniel MacCarthy's troop company. I am grateful to Ciarán O'Scea for this reference.
309. Flaithrí Ó Maolchonaire to Alonso Nuñez de Valdiva, 5 Jul. 1610 (AGS, CJH, l. 499-20, ff 44–5); Cédula from Philip III to Doña Elena Geraldine, Madrid, 20 Oct. 1611 (AGS, GA-Serv. Mil., legajo 51, f. 53).
310. Ó Maolchonaire to Philip IV, Madrid, 16 Nov. 1627 (AGS, GA-Serv. Mil., legajo 42, f. 36): 'las dichas hijas quedan ya desamparadas sin padre y madre y sin otro genero de consuelto'.
311. Ibid: 'soy yo testigo de vista'.
312. Ibid: 'el qual sirvio con mucha satisfacion a su Magestad muchos años en las ultimas guerras de Irlanda, en la Armada Rreal del Mar Oceano y en los estados de Flandes con quarenta escudos de entretenimiento al mes'.
313. Ibid: 'su Magestad de Don Phelippe tercero de gloriosa memoria le estimava mucho, haziendo tanta confiança del que le empleava con orden secreta en Inglaterra y Irlanda, donde quedava algunos años por orden de su Magestad haziendole servicios secretos en cosas de mucha importancia'.
314. Ibid: 'y embiano le muy buenos avisos de que su Magestad quedava tan satisfecho, que le mandava pagar lo que corria de su sueldo los años que quedava ausente, serviendo en los dichos reynos'.
315. Ibid: 'una señora […] muy noble de la casa de los Geraldinos con la qual era casado que tambien por los servicios y perdidas de su padre y hermanos en las dichas guerras en Irlanda tenia 30 escudos de entretenimiento al mes'.
316. Ibid: 'sera obra dignisima de la liberalidad y misericordia de real pecho de su Catolica Magestad que mande dar algun sustento a las dichas dos doncellas en consideracion de los servicios de su padre, servicios y perdidas de su abuelo y tyos (ya que son de edad para tomar estado)'.
317. Ibid: 'puedan meterse monjas, o casarse, antes que lleguen a desesperar de todo remedio'.
318. These were Archduke Albert; the Conde de Villamediana, Spanish ambassador to London from 1603 to 1605; Thomas Walsh, archbishop of Cashel; Colonel Éinrí Ó Néill; Hugh de Burgo OFM, Flaithrí Ó Maolchonaire's secretary; Captain Richard de Burgo; Don Balthazar de Burgo, Marqués de Mayo; Eugene MacCarthy, abbot of Fermoy and former rector of the Irish college in Santiago; and Captain Alonso Vásquez (AGS, GA, Servicios Militares, legajo 42).
319. 'Don Diego Portillo': 'en el ynterim' (AGS, GA, Servicios Militares, legajo 42, f. 36).
320. Walsh to Wadding, Madrid, 14 Mar. 1627 (*Wadding Papers*, ed. Jennings, p. 242); Walsh to John Roche, bishop of Ferns, Madrid, 14 Mar. 1627 (*Wadding Papers*, ed. Jennings, p. 244).
321. F. X. Martin, *Friar Francis Lavalin Nugent: agent of the Counter Reformation* (London: Methuen, 1962), p. 249.
322. Ibid., p. 251.
323. Ó Maolchonaire to Wadding, 3 Aug. 1627 (*Wadding Papers*, ed. Jennings, pp. 252–4): 'proditores patriae y adulatores Hispaniae'.
324. Nugent nominated Rothe for the see of Armagh after the Catholic primate's death in September 1625. See 'Sogetti proposti per la Chiesa Armacana', Rome, 1625 (UCD–OFM MSS, D.03/441).
325. 'Fray Rocque de la Cruz al padre fray Miguel de Espiritú Santo', 6 Aug. 1627 (*Wadding Papers*, ed. Jennings, p. 213).
326. Ibid: '[…] que lo que Tiron y Tuamense representan como cosa conveniente para el servicio del rey de España […] no es el mejor para el dicho servicio, ni para el bien comun del reyno'.
327. Ibid: 'y lo que ellos mueve […] agora no es el zelo del bien comun, ni deste servicio principalmente, sino el respecto que tienen a su carne y sangre, y su orden.'
328. 'Florencio Conryo a Padre fray Luca', Madrid, 3 Aug. 1627 (UCD–OFM, D.03, pp. 857–9).
329. Ibid.
330. 'Florentius Conrius, Archiepiscopus Tuamensis. Madriti, 17 Martii, 1628' (*Spic. Ossor.*, i, pp. 162–3).
331. Ibid: 'non potendo egli trasferirsi alla sua residenza senza grandissimi pericoli, per imputatione data gli che nell'ultima guerra tra gli Inglesi et Ibernesi habia trattato col re di Spagna'.
332. See Thomas Morrissey's entry in *Diccionario histórico de la Compañia de Jesús* (Rome: Institutum Historicum Societatis Iesu, 2001), vol. 1, p. 220.
333. 'Padre fray Luca', Madrid, 3 Aug. 1627 (UCD–OFM, D.03, pp. 857–9).
334. 'Senectute impeditus et speciali edicto Regio sub poena criminis laesae Majestatis exclusus'; Memorandum to the Sacred Congregation, Rome, 7 Aug. 1629 (*Spic. Ossor.*, i, pp. 161–2; George O'Brien, *The economic history of Ireland* (Dublin: Maunsel, 1919), p. 839).
335. García Hernán, 'El Colegio de San Patricio de los irlandeses de Madrid', pp. 219–46.
336. Micheline Kerney Walsh, 'The Irish College of Madrid', *Seanchas Ard Mhacha*, 15 (1993), pp. 39–50; Schüller, *Die beziehungen zwischen Spanien und Irland im XVI und XVII Jahrhundert*, pp. 162–3.
337. Hugh de Burgo to Luke Wadding, Madrid, 29 Nov. 1629 (*Wadding Papers*, ed. Jennings, p. 327).
338. For the period 1619–29, see *Louvain Papers*, pp. 59–61, 88. See also Edel Bhreathnach, 'Permission to receive fish from Sant Vliet', in Edel Bhreathnach and Bernadette Cunningham

(eds), *Writing Irish history: the Four Masters and their world*, pp. 114–15. I am grateful to John McCafferty for making this point.

339. Flaithrí Ó Maolchonaire to Philip IV, Madrid, 20 Sept. 1629 (AGS, CJH, l. 661).

340. Hugh de Burgo to Wadding, 29 Nov. 1629; cited by Brendan Jennings, 'Florence Conry, archbishop of Tuam: his death, and the transfer of his remains', *JGHAS*, 23 (1949), pp. 83–92; St Anthony's statement of accounts, Louvain, 16 Apr. 1632 (*Louvain Papers*, ed. Jennings, pp. 98–9).

341. Enrique García Hernán, 'Irish clerics in Madrid, 1598–1665', pp. 279–80. See also Denis O'Doherty, 'Students of the Irish college, Salamanca (1595–1619)', *Archiv. Hib.*, 2 (1913), pp. 32–3.

342. Manuel de Castro, 'Wadding and the Iberian peninsula', p. 142. See also, Luis Miguel Aparisi Laporta, El plano de Teixeira, trescientos cincuenta años despiués (Ayuntamiento de Madrid, 2000), p. 100.

343. Notario Miguel Claro, Madrid, 19 Oct. 1629 (AGS, CMC, 3ª; Dirección General del Tesoro); *Rexistro Protocolo de Escripturas que se han otorgado por ante Miguel Claros de Pazos SSno. de Rentas de la Casa y Estados de el Ynfantado en Madrid desde el Año de 1619 á el de 1645* (Archivo Histórico de Protocolos, Madrid, 5398/877).

344. Hugh de Burgo to Wadding, 29 Nov. 1629 (*Wadding Papers*, ed. Jennings, pp. 326–8).

345. Boetius McEgan to Brian McEgan, 5 Jun. 1630, Louvain (Ignatius Fennessy (ed.), 'Two letters from Boethius (Augustine) MacEgan, OFM, on the death of Archbishop Florence Conry, OFM, 1629', *Collectanea Hibernica*, 43 (2001), pp. 7–12).

346. Hugh de Burgo to Wadding, Madrid, 29 Nov. 1629. On the office of 'Capellan Mayor del Real Palacio': Archivo General de Palacio, Madrid, caja 85-expediente 1. In 1660, Philip IV sent his chaplain, Don Alfonso Pérez de Guzmán el Bueno, Patriarch of the Indies, to comfort the court painter Diego Velázquez on his deathbed and to give him the last rites (Julián Gállego, *Diego Velázquez* (Barcelona: Anthropos, 1983), p. 141).

347. Patrick Comerford, bishop of Waterford, to Luke Wadding, 24 Feb. 1629 [o. s.] (*Wadding Papers*, ed. Jennings, p. 346); Valentine Browne to same, 11 Mar. 1629 [o. s.] (*Wadding Papers*, ed. Jennings, p. 349); Francis Matthews to same, 14 Nov. 1630 (*Wadding Papers*, ed. Jennings, p. 436).

348. George Watts (Daniel McCarthy) to Lord Dorchester, concerning the Irish plotters, 19 Nov. 1631 (*Cal. S. P. Ire., Charles I, 1625–1632*, p. 634). 'My information was taken from one Condon, an Irishman, in a town called Burbrook, in Flanders. The plotters intend to seize, burn, and sack the new plantations in Munster, and to seize and fortify Limerick, which is in a good position for communicating with the disaffected parts of the country and with Spain, for the winds serve from it to Spain [...] As well as I can remember, my informant named the following [...] Flahrty [*Flaithrí*], archbishop of Tuam, since dead in Spain.'

Conclusion

Following his return to Leuven in the final years of Philip III's reign, Flaithrí Ó Maolchonaire commented on the contention between the poets of the northern and southern halves of Ireland. Refusing to take sides, he described their dispute as 'wrangling over an empty dish'.[1] Although raised among the scholarly families of Connacht and Ulster, Ó Maolchonaire had absorbed new thinking in Spain, Rome and Flanders. Using his continental contacts, both religious and political, he looked forward, serving Gaelic interests and modernising Irish religious and cultural institutions within the Spanish political system. Ó Maolchonaire and his contemporaries were at the heart of the significant developments that shook early-modern Ireland and Europe: religious change, political turmoil, economic expansion and contraction. In the world of technological change, Ó Maolchonaire and his entourage were active also: the printing press they inaugurated at St Anthony's, Leuven helped transform how religious knowledge was understood and transmitted in Ireland and among the Irish military diaspora.

Ó Maolchonaire's career illustrates the vicissitudes of Anglo-Spanish relations for the period and reveals the level of interaction between Ireland, Spain and the papacy. He provides a particularly useful example of the continuities and discontinuities between patronage networks developed in Ireland and their continental manifestations, as the Irish political and religious elites gained a foothold in the Southern Netherlands, Spain and later France. Diplomatic activity during this period was characterised by the pursuit of stability, typified by the succession of negotiations between ambassadors for marriage alliances between ruling houses.[2] Ó Maolchonaire's repeated calls for a renewal of conflict, however, indicate that he used diplomacy as 'another arm of the military'.[3] Though well acquainted with life at court, he placed himself firmly on the side of the nobility of the sword rather than that of the robe. Despite the regular inclusion of memorials favouring the Old English among his papers,[4] the social cohesiveness of Ó Maolchonaire's work was diluted by a greater determination on his part to defend the Ulster earls' aims and, in doing so, he articulated the political views of many among the Irish community in exile. After Ó Maolchonaire's death, his successor to the Catholic archbishopric of Tuam, Malachy Queely, continued to use the Red Hand of Ulster to seal his correspondence,[5] and later emerged as a leader of the Supreme Council at Kilkenny in the 1640s.

From the 1590s to the late 1620s, Ó Maolchonaire identified a role for Ireland in Habsburg geo-politics.[6] For the Ulster earls, this was designed to preserve and later to restore their hegemony.[7] Although Ó Maolchonaire adopted this as a priority and supported the integration of Irish interests into the early-modern

Habsburg *imperium*,[8] he was aware of how this contradicted the religious aims of many of his own co-religionists, particularly the Irish Jesuits and their patronage networks. For them religious renewal did not involve the restoration of the Ulster earls or the transferral of Irish sovereignty to the Habsburgs. Yet, Ó Maolchonaire, in linking the restoration of Catholicism in Ireland with the reinstatement of the Ulster earls, influenced the politico-religious future of the whole country and its migrant offshoots on the continent.

NOTES

1. 'Flaithrí Ó Maoil Chonaire cecinit' *circa* 1618–24 (RIA, Stowe MS E.iv.3, p. 264); cited by T. F. O'Rahilly, *Dánfhocail: Irish Epigrams in Verse* (Dublin: Talbot Press, 1921), p. 31; Eleanor Knott, *Irish Classical Poetry* (Dublin: Three Candles, 1960) pp. 90–1. See also Lambert McKenna (ed.), *Iomarbhágh na bhFileadh* (2 vols, Baile Átha Cliath: Irish Texts Society, 1918–20).

2. Charles Howard Carter, *The Secret Diplomacy of the Habsburgs*, p. 98. See also Jonathan Wright, *The Ambassadors: From Ancient Greece to the Nation State*, pp. 170–262.

3. *Cf.* Brendan Bradshaw, 'Robe and sword in the conquest of Ireland', in J. J. Scarisbrick et al. (eds), *Law and Government under the Tudors: Essays Presented to Sir Geoffrey Elton on his Retirement* (Cambridge: Cambridge University Press, 1988), pp. 139–62. See also Hugh Kearney, 'The Irish parliament in the early seventeenth century', in Brian Farrell (ed.), *The Irish Parliamentary Tradition* (Dublin: Gill & Macmillan, 1973), pp. 93–5.

4. See, for instance, Ó Maolchonaire's mediation on behalf of Anthony de Burgo: 'Pide Entretenimiento para la Armada. Don Antonio de Burgo cavallero yrlandes', Madrid, 1610 (AGS, Guerra Antigua (Servicios de Militares), l. 5, f. 78). The previous year Ó Maolchonaire wrote a *certificación* for Gerald Fitzmaurice: 'Don Geraldo Mauricio caballero irlandes' (AGS, E. NP, l. 1746); see also 'Florin O Mulchonor and James Geraldine', 12 Oct. 1609 (HMC *Downshire*, vol. 2 (1605–10) p. 154).

5. 'Malachy of Tuam and Boetius of Elphin to Fr Luke Wadding', Galway, 12 Apr. 1631 (o.s.) (UCD–OFM, D.02, ff. 303r, 305r; pp. 849, 851).

6. Declan Downey, 'Irish–European integration: the legacy of Charles V', p. 101.

7. Hiram Morgan, *Tyrone's Rebellion*, pp. 214–15.

8. Ó Maolchonaire to Lerma, La Coruña, 21 Mar. 1602 (AGS, Estado, España, l. 188): 'La obligacion que tengo de servir à nuestro Señor Jesu Xpo y el deseo grande de ver à nuestro Rei Catolico Señor de Irlanda.'

Appendix I
Biographical Chronology

1560/1:	Born at Figh, civil parish of Tibohine, barony of Frenchpark, County Roscommon
1590, 10 Jul:	Named in an Elizabethan *fiant*
1592:	Among the first students at the new Irish college, Salamanca
1593:	Translates into Irish Jerónimo de Ripalda's catechism
1594, 10 Dec:	In his third year of arts and philosophy at the Irish college
1595, 20 Nov:	In his first year of studies in theology
1598, Apr:	Sails from Lisbon to Ireland at the height of the Nine Years War, where he works as chaplain to Aodh Ruadh Ó Domhnaill
1600, Mar–Apr:	Drafts letters in Latin for the leaders of the Catholic league
1601, 14 Jan:	Nominated for the vacant see of Tuam by Ó Néill and Ó Domhnaill
1601:Dec:	With the Ulster earls and Don Alonso del Campo at Kinsale
1602:Feast of the Epiphany:	Sails with Aodh Ruadh, Raymond de Burgo, Hugh Mostian and nine others from Castlehaven on board a Scottish ship commanded by General Pedro de Zubiaur. They land in Asturias and travel over land to Galicia
1602, 21 Jan:	They arrive at La Coruña and are warmly welcomed by the governor. Soon afterwards Aodh Ruadh travels south with Ó Maolchonaire to meet Philip III in person at court in Zamora. They then return to La Coruña
1602, 22 May:	Ó Maolchonaire at court in Valladolid where he lodges a letter of protest against the Irish college, Salamanca
1602, Jun:	Ó Domhnaill sends Ó Maolchonaire to intercede for him at the Escorial palace, near Madrid
1602, Sept:	Attends to the dying Aodh Ruadh Ó Domhnaill at Simancas castle
1603, Jun:	Sails to Ireland with Don Martín de la Cerdá, Roibeard Mac Artúir and Matha Óg Ó Maoltuile. Returns to Valladolid as Mac Uilliam de Burgo's translator
1603–4:	Assists Fray Gaspar de Cordova OP in dealing with Irish arrivals at court
1604, Mar:	Appointed as adviser on Irish affairs to the Conde de Puñonrostro, protector of the Irish at court in Valladolid

1606: Feast of the Ascension, May:	Elected Irish minister-provincial by the Franciscan General Chapter at San Juan de los Reyes, Toledo
1606, Jun:	Prevails upon Philip III to establish St Anthony's College, Leuven
1606, Dec:	Travels to Flanders with Richard and David de Burgo, and Matha Óg Ó Maoltuile. Obtains access to the court of the Archdukes at Brussels
1607, Mon. 22 Oct:	Travels through Flanders to meet the Ulster earls at Douai and take them to Leuven
1607, Sun. 25 Nov:	Leaves for Spain with the earls and thirty horsemen
1607, Mon. 26 Nov:	They are forced to turn back at Namur, a day into their journey
1607, Dec. to Jan. 1608:	Ó Maolchonaire visits the papal nuncio, Guido Bentivoglio, in Brussels
1608, Thurs. 28 Feb:	Leaves Leuven with the earls on their way to Rome
1608, St Patrick's Day:	They reach the St Gothard Pass to the Alps
1608, Sun. 23 Mar:	Arrives at Milan and stays for three weeks
1608, Sat. 12 Apr:	Leaves Milan with Ó Néill, Ó Domhnaill and their followers
1608, Tues. 15 Apr:	They arrive at Bologna
1608, Tues. 29 Apr:	Accompanies the earls to Rome
1609, Mon. 30 Mar:	Cardinal Arrigone, protector of the Irish, submits a request from Ó Néill to nominate Ó Maolchonaire for the archiepiscopal see of Tuam
1609, 23 Apr:	Pope Paul V accedes to the nomination sent to the papal chancellery at San Lorenzo in Damaso, Rome
1609, Sun. 3 May:	Consecrated archbishop of Tuam by Cardinal Barberini at Chiesa di Santo Spirito in Sassia, Rome
1609, Jul:	Returns to Madrid, staying with the papal nuncio Decio Carafa
1610, Jan:	Presents Ó Néill's proposals for his return to Ireland
1611–12:	Acts to protect the Irish *tercio* in Flanders and helps to clear the court of Irish petitioners
1613:	Receives confirmation of his financial entitlements at court
1614, Jul–Aug:	Seeks to have Nicholas Wise made Irish consul in Andalusia
1615, Mar:	Writes from the convent of St Francis, Valladolid, remonstrating with Irish Catholic members of parliament
1615, Sept:	Renews Aodh Ó Néill's appeals for military intervention at court in Madrid

1616, Aug:	Travels from Alcalá de Henares to the Escorial palace to meet Philip III after Ó Néill's death. *Sgáthán an Chrábhaidh* published the same year
1617:	Recommends Domhnall Ó Súillebháin Béarra for the military order of Santiago
1618, Late spring:	Returns to Leuven from Madrid after completing his writings on grace and giving them to the Salamanca professors to read
1619:	*De Augustini sensu circa b. Mariae Virginis Conceptionem* published at Antwerp by Jan van Keerberghen
1619, Oct:	Recommends Luke Wadding for the Irish episcopacy
1620, Nov:	Supports James Fitzgerald's application for the office of Irish consul in Andalucφia
1621, 4, 5, 21 Jun. & 17 Sept:	Exercises the *pontificalia* after the death of Mathias Hovius (20 May 1620) by carrying out ordinations in Mechelen archdiocese
1622:	As an executor of Eóghan Mag Mathghamhna's will, Ó Maolchonaire helps to purchase a house for a new Irish pastoral college at Leuven which the friars at St Anthony's subsequently used to accommodate some of their novices
1622, Jan:	Cornelius Jansen appeals to the abbot of St Cyran on behalf of Ó Maolchonaire for the foundation of a college for Irish Franciscans in Paris
1622, 12 Mar:	Carries out more ordinations to the priesthood
1623:	Assists at the consecrations of Thomas Fleming and William Terry in Brussels
1624:	*Tractatus de statu parvulorum sine Baptismo decedentium ex hac vita* published at Leuven
1625, 27 Feb:	Granted pontifical rights by Archbishop Jacob Boonen of Mechelen
1625, Dec:	Tries to gain control of the Irish colleges at Douai and Tournai
1626, Sept:	Attending to Irish affairs at the court of Archduchess Isabel in Brussels
1626, Oct:	Travels back to Madrid via Paris and the Pyrenees
1627, Jan:	Proposes a marine invasion of Ireland by Spanish forces
1627, 18 Jul:	Recommends Fadrique Plunkett for the military order of Santiago
1627, 20 Jul:	Supports Dionysius McGrath's claims for preferment at court in Madrid

1627, Aug–Nov:	Nominates Ross MacGeoghegan OP for the Irish episcopacy
1627, 16 Nov:	Appeals to Philip IV on behalf of Matha Óg Ó Maoltuile's daughters
1628, St Patrick's Day:	Writes to Cardinal Protector Ludovisi in Rome, explaining his absence from Ireland
1629, 7 Aug:	Memorandum on Ó Maolchonaire presented to the Sacred Congregation in Rome, excuses him to the papacy since he was subject to 'a special edict' in Ireland
1629, Feast of the Assumption:	Nominates John de Burgo as his suffragan bishop
1629, 19 Oct:	Drafts his last will and testament
1629, 18 Nov:	Dies at La Real Basílica de San Francisco el Grande, Madrid
1629, 20 Nov:	Laid to rest at San Francisco el Grande after funeral Mass there.

Appendix II[1]
Selected Transcripts of Documents

1

1601, 14 Jan., Donegal. Letter from Hugh O'Neill and Red Hugh O'Donnell to Philip III of Spain, nominating Flaithrí Ó Maolchonaire for the vacant archiepiscopal see of Tuam (AGS, E., Neg. de España, l. 236)

S. C. R. M.[2]

Inter alia plura incommoda, quae propter nostra peccata, his multis retroactis annis petimur, supremum locum habet, quod pleraeque nostrae ecclesiae cathedrales orbatae propriis et catholicis pastoribus iacent; in quibus, si zelosi et exemplaris vitae prelati existent, mirum in modum nostrum in spiritualibus et temporalibus profectum augerent. Hinc est quod duos, e paucis, qui nobis et nostris in hac tempestate, ecclesiastica sacramenta et salutaria vitae precepta indefesse administrant, universi cleri et populi iudicio approbatos, illis non petentibus, ultro elegimus, quos propter generis nobilitatem (claris enim et catholicis legitime orti sunt parentibus) vitae et morum probitatem, divinarum litterarum sufficientem cognitionem et maximum animarum lucrandarum zelum, ad dignitates episcopales commendandos duximus: quarum unum, nomine Florencium Conrium quondam seminarii invictissimi patris vestri, regia liberalitate nostris Hybernis Salmant.ca erecti, alumnum, ac nunc instituti sancti Francesci de observantia consummatum theologum et predicatorem ad Archiepiscopatum Tuamensem, vel episcopatum Elfenensem, utrumque in provincia Connacia, ex qua ipse cste oriundus, (mallemus tamen ad primum propter universalis bonum ab illo dependens). Alterum vero, nomine Bernardum Oferail, sacerdotem theologum qui per septem continuos annos, in Academia Valesoletana in Hispaniis literarum studiis incumbebat, ac in eadem quatuor ab hinc annis in sacra theologia gradum susceperat ad Episcopatum Midensem, plurimum in modum commendamus rogamus que humiliter V.am M.am C.am ut illis promotionem ad dictas ecclesias, a Sua Sanctitate impatrari facere dignetur in prioribus namque omnino residere et multum fructum facere poterunt, in posteriori vero magna ex parte hoc enim Deo, propter animarum salutem (cui per dictam provisionem satis consultum fore non dubitamus) nimis acceptum erit, nobis autem et universis huius regni Catholicis gratissimum. Deos Op. Max. tuam catholicam Maiestatem universae Reipublicae christianae diu incolumem conservet. Datum Dungallia quarto decimo Januarii 1601.

Tuae Ma.tis. fidelissimi subditi
Oneill & Odonnell

Potentissimo Philippo Hispaniarum ac Indiarum regni Catholico
Dunigal A su Magestad 1601
Oneyll & Odonail

2

1602, 21 Mar., La Coruña. Letter from Flaithrí Ó Maolchonaire to the Duke of Lerma pledging his allegiance to Philip III and appeals to Lerma on behalf of Aodh Ruadh Ó Domhnaill for arms and reinforcements after the battle of Kinsale (AGS, E., España, l. 188)

La obligacion que tengo de servir à nuestro Señor Jesu Xpo y el deseo grande de ver à nuestro Rei catholico Señor de Irlanda y de todo el mundo me a mobido à dar parte à Vuestra Exçelençia que no pareçe cosa conveniente que el Señor O'Donel se vaia agora con un solo navio a su tierra, parte por el peligro grande en que en la mar corre su persona tan importante al servicio de Dios y nuestro reyno, parte por el peligro en que se puede ver en tierra con 20 personas que llegaba de compaña no sabiendo quien es Señor agora de sus puertos: y lo que es peor que todo por no aver en Irlanda una persona mas principal y mas noble y que a hecho maiores servicios a su Magestad que el Señor, si le vean apportando sin gente perderan en todo esperanzas antes el mesmo Señor O'Donel no tendra esperanzas de socorro porque con las mesma facilidad que mudaron en lo que en Zamora an determinado que estubiese en La Coruña hasta llevar la Armada en fin deste mes, pensara que han de mudar qualquier otra determinacion aunque agora tengan mas y mas voluntad de ir a Irlanda. Yo seguro a Vuestra Excellencia que la ida del Señor alla de aquella manera a de haçer mas daño que provecho, que si quisiesen embiarle accompañado de 2 o 3 mil soldados el servicio que pudiese haçer seria mui famoso y mas que de piensa y esto pareçe mas açertado por que sin duda si vee que el socorro se dilate mas de Pasqua de Flores (que es un poco mas tiempo asseñalado) tomara su viage por su tierra aunque no halla mejor comodidad para este camino sino ir a pie disfraçado por el camino de Escoçia hasta morir lastimosamente en el camino, o hasta ponerse con sus vasallos: esta sin duda con alguna paena que se enformen de las cosas de Yrlanda de gente no platicada en ellas estando el presente aqui en España – Supplico a Vuestra Excellencia que me perdone este attrebimiento que no me metiera en esso, sino pensara ser servicio de Dios y nuestro Rei. De La Coruña. 21 de março de 602.

Pobre capellan y criado de Vuestra Excellencia.
.F. Florentio Conrio

Carta del Confessor del Señor Odonel. La Coruña + Al Duque 1602. Fray Florençio Conrio a 21 de março.

3

1602, 12 Aug., La Coruña. Letter of General Pedro de Zubiaur to fray Gaspar de Cordova OP, confessor to Philip III, vouching for Denis O'Driscoll, lord of Castlehaven, after the loss of his castle (ADM, legajo 50, ramo 4)

El Portador es Dionisio O Driscol dueno y Señor de castillo de Castel Aben en Yrlanda muy buen caballero y muy catolico quien nos reçevio en nombre de Su Magestad y nos entrego su castillo con mucha voluntad y con su gente travajo en lo que se ofreçio muy honrradamente como su castillo y tierrae conforme el conçierto que hizo Don Juan del Aguilla. Se entregarron a los enemigos yngleses hubo de Retiroye[?] con su muger y familia a las Montomal donde dexandoles ha venido con un barro en compañia de otros – en todo el Xpo que alli estubimos tubo clerigos y frailes en su cassa y nos dezian missa y nos regalava – ba a Su Magestad Paraque le Ampare y le faboresca como padre de todos los catolicos de aquel Reyno. Guarde Dios A Vuestra Paternidad Reverendissima como yo su servidor deseo de la Corunna 12 de agosto 1602 Pedro de Çubiaur.

4

1602, 14 Aug., La Coruña. Letter from the Conde de Caracena, governor of Galicia, to fray Gaspar de Cordova, asking for the O'Driscolls to be shown every mercy (ADM, legajo 50, ramo 4)

Don Dionysio Odriscol Señor de Castelhaben y Cornelio Odriscol hijo mayor del Señor de Valentimor ban a dar quenta a su Magestad del estado en que se allan las cosas de Irlanda y otras que ynporta que las tenga su Magestad entendidas aviendo sido nombrados pa[ellos] por los demas cavalleros catolicos. Supplico a Vuestra Paternidad Reverendissima los oyga y aga toda merced en consideracion de sus servicios y del deseo que tienen de emplearse en el de su Magestad como lo an mostrado las occasiones que se han offrezdo. La brevedad en su despacho paraque con ella de la buelta a aquel Reyno por la falta que hazen ynporta mucho, el Padre Archero va en su companya aquien particularmente oiga Vuestra Paternidad Reverendissima por estar tan alcavo de todo que aunque para hazer esta jornada a guardava orden ynporta tanto que de luego la buelta aquel Reyno con estos cavalleros que me ha parezdo que cada ora que lo dilate es de muy consideracion. Guarde Dios a Vuestra Paternidad Reverendissima como deseo en la Coruña 14 de agosto 1602.

5

1602, 11 Sept., San Pablo. Letter from fray Gaspar de Cordova to the Duke of Lerma, San Pablo, asking Lerma to meet Denis O'Driscoll, lord of Castlehaven and Conor O'Driscoll, eldest son of the lord of Baltimore (ADM, legajo 50, ramo 4)

[Dorso:] Papeles del Padre Confessor Fray Gaspar de Cordova, Para Su Excelençia. El Padre Confesor para Vuestra Excelençia y Su Respuesta. Pide Audiencia para el Señor de Castelhaben, y para el hijo mayor del Señor de Balentimor y Vuestra Excelençia los despache con brevedad. 11 de sete 1602.

Aqui esta seis o siete dias a El Señor de Castilhaben que fue el primero que rrezibio los vanderos de Su Magestad en su castillo como vera Vuestra Excelençia por esa carta de Çubiaure quando vino aqui el hermano sele hizo mucha honrra y mrd y le ordeno a bustamente que los hospedaje tanbien esta aqui el hijo maior del Señor de Valentimor. Suplico a Vuestra Excelençia sea ser vido de [c]i[r]los y mandarlos despachar con brevedad. En San Pablo a 11 de Sete 1602 Fr Gaspar de Cordova.

[Lerma's marginalia:] Aun papel de la Junta en que se halla Vuestra Paternidad Reverendissima madara Su Mt. Responder sobre esto lo que sea servido y luego. En Palacio a 15 de Sete 1602.

6

1602 [later than 9 Sept.] Flaithrí Ó Maolchonaire's report on Irish matters, written after the death of Aodh Ruadh Ó Domhnaill. Ó Maolchonaire proposes a military expedition to Galway to assist Hugh O'Neill against Elizabeth's forces
(Archivo Histórico de Loyola, FH, caja 27, no. 26/9)

Relacion del P. Fr. Florencio Conrio sobre las cosas de Irlanda – 1602 – El P. Fr. Florencio Conrio dice que al cabo de nueve años que sustentan los Católicos guerra contra el enemigo ingles mas con milagros que con poder humano, hallabanse tan gastados y cansados con las promesas no cumplidas de España, que para salir de estas dudas, enviaron á España al mejor mensajero que tenian (que era el Conde de O'Donell) para que representase á su Magestad la necesidad de los Irlandeses y pidiese socorro. Cuando agora sepan la muerte del Conde, y que sus ruegos no han aprovechado, y que no va allá socorro de gente sino algun dinero y otras cartas; haran por precision conciertos de algun modo con sus enemigos. Si tienen aún fuerzas haran convenios generales: si carecen de ellas y estan en mucho aprieto, á cada señor en particular ofrecera el enemigo de buena voluntad excelentes partidos.

De esta suerte dejará aislados á los principales y sin poder resistir - Es gran lastima - que deste modo se pierda para España la nacion Irlandesa despues de los infinitos trabajos que se ha impuesto para servir a su Rey! Se ha de seguir de aqui que viendo las demas naciones este lastimoso suceso y miserable espectáculo de la destrucion de Irlanda por falta de este auxilio de España, nadie querrá ponerse jamas en peligro fiado en las promesas de esta nacion. Por otra parte los Irlandeses que desde hace 1300 años conservan la fe católica, tendran por fuerza y necesidad que sujetarse á los herejes y renegar de sus antiguas y ver-daderas creencias. Nadie los socorre y la Reina de Inglaterra enviara contra ellos los 18000 soldados que tiene sobre las armas, sin contar los que envia á Flandes, y contra las costas de España y las flotas de las Indias.

Todo pudiera deshuirse enviando sin dilacion socorros á Irlanda de la manera que lo pidió el Conde de O'Donell. Si el socorro, decia este, fuese de diez ó doce mil hombres ir á Corque ó á Lumbr.; y si fuera de dos mil ó mil quinientos ir á su tierra y ponerlos en los presidios de Dunigall y Sligo, y no llevarlos á pelear sin fortificar aquellos puntos con los peones de la tierra.- Si tres ó cuatro mil ir á Galvay y tomar la dicha villa, donde el Conde O'Neill y su hermano pudieran unirseles sin que el enemigo pudiera estorbarles el paso. Por esto trajo el Conde de O'Donell en su compañia al Baron de Letrym de quien es todo aquel pais, tiranizado hoy por su enemigo. Puesto sitio á Galvay se rendirá á los pocos dias por no poder ser socorrido por el Virrey ni por mar ni por tierra. Y siendo casi una isla con gran facilidad se puede hacer inespugnable haciendo una trinchera en la lengua que le une con la tierra, y levantando un baluarte por la parte del rio y colocando en él dos piezas de artilleria, se impide que puedan entrar en el puerto barcos enemigos.-

Si S.M. fuese servido de enviar ahora á Galvay tres mil hombres, el dicho Baron que esta aqui, los conducirá y promete apoderarse de Galvay si el Virrey no está dentro. En caso contrario los llevaria dos leguas de allí donde podrian estar apresar del enemigo. El se encarga de abastecerles de pan y carne por seis mes, y en caso de no cumplirlo como él ahora lo asegura, es contento de que le corten la cabeza.

Esta provincia de Conacia donde esta Galvay está rodeada por un gran rio llamado Sinon que viene de la tierra de los Condes. No hay sino dos entradas, uno por Lumbrique y otra por Alóen. Por las diez y seis millas de bosque que cierra la primera no pueden pasar caballos ni artilleria. Por la otra hay cuatro millas de bosque y dos de pantanos con un camino de piedra y maderos que en destruyendole no es posible pasar, por lo que los de la tierra partan para defender estas dos entradas.
Se verá cuan facil es esta empresa de Galvay, por el adjunto plano.

7

1604, 12 Jan., Valencia. Letter of Fray Gaspar to Philip III. The king's confessor writes of the papers that MacWilliam de Burgo and Ó Maolchonaire his translator have brought from Aodh Ó Néill and Rudhraighe Ó Domhnaill, pledging their loyalty and asking for help (ADM, legajo 50, ramo 4)

[Dorso:] El Padre Confessor a Su Magestad, Valencia, 12 de enero 1604. Dize lo que se le ofresce sobre unos papeles del Conde Marwillano Burk. Despachado.

E visto com[o] Vuestra Magestad me manda estos papeles de Mac William Burk. Y por ser materias tan grandes los que en ellos a puesta y que de certamente pertenezen al consejo de estado no me atrevo a rrepresentar a Vuestra Magestad lo que siento en esta parte y asi suplico a Vuestra Magestad sea servido de mandar que le vean luego en el consejo de estado que viene sirviendo a Vuestra Magestad en este camino para que sea despachado este cavallero con toda brevedad.

Juntamente suplico a Vuestra Magestad sea servido de mandar que le vea en el mismo Consejo de Estado lo que suplican el Conde O Nell y el Conde O Donell ambos han escrito a Vuesta Magestad y yo embie una carta que me escrivio O Nell para que Vuestra Magestad fuese servido de mandarla ver y agora van con esta carta que escrive O Donel. Son materias muy de Estado las que ambos Condes p[ro]ponen y es nezesario que se le vea si conviene al servicio de Vuestra Magestad que sean sustentados en la protecion y dependencia de Vuestra Magestad como ellos pretenden si oferan desengañados y desamparados. Si se le dara a O Nell su hijo que esta en Salamanca y lo pide con instancia y tiene aqui persona para llevarlo. Estas y otras materias que tartan los Condes rrequieren presta y madura rresolucion.
Guarde Nuestro Señor La Catholica persona de Vuestra Magestad tantos siglos como el mundo a menester. En Valencia 12 de enero 1604 Fray Gaspar de Cordova.

[Lerma's marginalia:] Su Mt ha mandado al Consejo de Estado de Valladolid que con mucha diligencia y brevedad le sufuime[?] sobre esto que Vuestra Paternidad Reverendissima en Denia 17 de enero 1604. El Duq.

8

1604, 17 Jan., Denia. Letter from Lerma to the Spanish secretary of state, Denia, on the subject of MacWilliam de Burgo's news from Hugh O'Neill (ADM, legajo 50, ramo 4)

[Dorso:] El Duque al Señor Secretario Andres de Prada. Denia, 17 de enero 1604. Su Mt manda se vean en Consejo de Estado con mucha brevedad y diligencia los papeles inclusos del Conde Macvillano Burc y se le consulte lo que paresca. Tambien manda se vea lo que suplican el Conde Onel y el Conde Odonel en considerando si convidea Su Mt. desengañaran y si a Onel sale dare a su hijo aqui pide constancia y tiene aqui que lo solicita. Dios guarde a VM en Denia 17 de enero 1604.   El Duq.

9

1605, 27 Oct. 1605, Rome. Letter from Cardinal Pompeo Arrigone, protector of the Irish, to the duke of Lerma, appealing for funds for Irish colleges (ADM, l. 51, ramo 5, carpeta 6)

Por los seminarios Irlandeses.
All'Illustrissimo et Eccellentissimo Signore Il Duca di Lerma del' Cons.o di Stato di S. M.ta Catt.ca Suo Cavallerillo Magg., et Suo miglioro di Corps [et General della Cavalleria di Spagna.]
Essendo io protettore della natione Iberna, mi e'stato mandato l'accluso Memoriale; perch'io lo raccomandi a Vostra Eccellenza il che certo faccio di

cuore pregandola a degnassi di tener mano, che quei Collegii d'Ibernia habbiano il loro assignamento onde possano sostentarsi. che oltre al far opera di molta charita', ne fara' a' me favor particulare, et li ne vistero con l'obligo, che conviemi. In tanto mi raccomando nella sua buona gratia, et li prego dal Signore ogni maggior contento. Di Roma li xv di ottubre 1605. Di Vostra Eccellenza

Affetionatissimo Servitore
P. Cardinale Arrigone

Sr Duca di Lerma

10

1605, Rome. Memorial of Cardinal Pompeo Arrigone to Lerma on behalf of Irish students in Antwerp and Douai
(ADM, l. 51, ramo 5, carpeta 6)

Illme et Rme Dñe. Cum in Universitate Duaceñ in Belgio erectum sit ab aliquot annis Collegium studiosorum Hibernorum, pro quo manutenendo Rex Catholicus concessit bis mille ducados annuos, renovandos de duobus in duos annos; et cum insuper in Civitate Antuerpieñ uniores studiosi Hiberni aliud habeant Collegium a paucis hinc annis inchoatum, pro fundatione cuius Collegii stabilienda, qui in exercitu Catholico in Belgio militant diversarum nationum stipendiarii, praecipue vero Hispani et Itali de stipendiis sibi debetis liberalem concesserunt eleemosynam quam et Archiduces libenter approbarunt et pro ulteriore eiusdem confirmatione proprias dant l[itte]rãs ad Regem Catholicum per eorundem Collegium Superiorem deferendas; etiam Smus D N mittit iam particulare Breve ad eandem Catholica [Il]tem comendando ut et pentio tam liberaliter concessia semel, et itero renovata pro sustentatione Collegii Duaceñ imposterum continetur, et pro recipienda eleemosyna tam religiosè concessa in fundationem Collegii Antuerpieñ, certa aliqua et secura ratio assignetur. Itaq supplicatur humiliter Ill.mor[?] DV ut tamquam Protector nationis Hibernorum dignetur suas etiam l[itte]rãs adiungere ad Ducem Lermae, comendando ei ut eandem causam euisq exequitionem commedatam habeat quod faciendo.

11

1607, 29 Jan. Letter from Flaithrí Ó Maolchonaire to the Spanish secretary of state, requesting that the archdukes, the viceroy to Portugal and governor of Galicia recognise the equality of students from all the four provinces of Ireland
(AGS, E., NP, l. 1748)

Fray Florencio Conryo, Provincial de Yrlanda al Secretario Andres de Prada

Señor,

Fray Florencio Conryo Provincial de los frayles menores de Yrlanda dice que

Vuestra Magestad conforme a su acostumbrada piedad y liberalidad da limosna a ciertas casas de sacerdotes y estudiantes yrlandeses para ayuda de su sustento para que en acabando sus estudios vuelvan a predicar el santo evangelio a su patria para conservar en ella la fee catholica que los herejes quitando que no aya estudios en todo el reyno y con otras mil persecuciones quieren extinguir, y para que este gran beneficia que Vuestra Magestad hace a la dicha naçion redonde en comun provecho a todos las provinçias sin admetir parçialidad, se suplica muy humilmente a V Magestad se sirva mandar escrivir una carta a Su Alteza ordenandole que en las casas o seminarios yrlandeses que ay en los estados de Flandes haga guardar la dicha ygualidad admettiendo los estudiantes ygualmente de todas las provincias de Yrlanda en los dichos seminarios y otras dos cartas al Virey de Portugal y al gobernador de Galicia paraque hagan guardar la dicha ygualidad en las dos casas se yrlandeses que ay en Lisboa y Santiago y en esto hara V Mgd gran merced a todo el reyno de Yrlanda.

12

1608, 13 Aug., Genova, Letter of Don Juan Vivas to the Marqués de Aytona, reporting the final illness and death of both Cúconnacht Maguire and Séamus McMahon on their way to Spain with their confessor, possibly Flaithrí Ó Maolchonaire (ADM, l. 56, ramo 2)

Recibida a 21 del mismo
Respondida a 22 del mismo

Al Marques de Aytona del Conssejo de Su Magestad y su Embaxador en Roma. Beso las manos de Vuestra Excelençia por la merced que me haze en su carta de 8 deste y de nuevo lo que puedo dezir à Vuestra Excelençia de acà es que havrà 4 dias que murieron aquel cavallero irlandes primo de los condes de Tiron y a si-mismo otro pariente suyo que vino de ay en su compañia. Su mal à sido de calentura continua nacida del mal ayre de hazia Çivitavieja donde se detuvieron. Su viaje hera à España embiados de los condes y con la enfermedad gastaron quanto tenian y faltandoles de otra parte me pareçio hazellos enterrar onrradamente y pagar otros gastillos como se hizo pareçiendome que Su Magestad lo tendria por bien pues me mandó socorriese à los condes si pasavan por aqui. A me hecho mucha lastima la muerte destos cavalleros por ser quien heran y la que han padeçido solo por la fèe. Han dexado solo algunos vestidos viejos los quales ha tomado un criado dellos que se entretiene aqui hasta que el conde de Tiron le embie a mandar lo que deva hazer aquien escrive largamente de quanto à pasado aqui y el testamento por no estar sacado de los registros del escribano no va con esta pero yra con el ordinario que viene Vuestra Excelençia podra mandar dar parte desto al Conde de Tiron pues esta ay y consolarle de la perdida que a hecho destos cavalleros los quales murieron con tanta demostraçion de buenos christianos, que como dize su confesor, sin duda estan gozando de Dios.

13

1609, 30 Mar., Quirinale Palace, Rome. Memorial of the submission of Ó Maolchonaire's nomination for the archbishopric of Tuam by Cardinal Pompeo Arrigone (ASV, Protocollo Consecration. Episcoporum et Alia, 129/62)

Roma in Monte Quirinali Die Lune 30 Martii 1609 fuit Consistorium Secretum, In Quo Ecca. Thuam in Hibernia

Referente Rmo Cardinale Arigonio providit Eccliae Tuamen in Regno Hybernie vacan[t] titul[um] obitum bo: me: Jacobi ultimi Archiepi de Persona R. F. Florentiis Ordinis Sti Francisci de Observantia omnia res iusta haben[s], eumque Stas Sua Ecclie Tuamen in Archiepum prefecit, et Pastorem, curam committam, cum condonat[io]ne Jurium, et cum aetis opportunis.

14

1609, 23 Apr.–3 May, San Lorenzo in Damaso, Rome. Record of the acceptance of the nomination to make Ó Maolchonaire archbishop of Tuam (ASV, Protocollo Consecration. Episcoporum et Alia, 157, 125/126)[3]

Die 23 menti Aprilis 1609 fer.a 3a indictione septima Pontificatus SDN Domini Paul divina providentia Papa quinti anno 4o admitti Illustrisimus et Reverendisimus dominus frater Florentius Conrius ordinis minor observantii S. Francesco Archiepiscopus Tuamen' in Ibernia praestitit. […] et debitum fidelitatis iuramentum in manibus Ilustrissimi et Reverendissimi Domini Domini Alexandri Pereti tituli St Laurentii in Damaso Sancti Roma Ecclesiae Diaconi Cardinalis De Monte nuncupati & presentibus ibidem Illustrissimo Domino Plinio Boniovanae Romano, M.D. Iulio Vicomanno cammerinen testibus.

Die Dominica 3a mensis Maii indictione septima Pontificatus SDN Domini Paul divina providentia Papa quinti anno 4o Illustrisimus et Reverendisimus in Xpo Reverendisimus' et Dominus Dominus Maffeus tituli S. Petri in mo[n]te aureo Santo Romano Ecclesia Praesbiter Cardinalis Barberinus nuncapatus viva vocis oraculo in Ecclesia Sti Spiritus in Saxia consecravit in Archiepiscopum, et Pastorem Ecclesiae Tuamen in Ibernia admodum Illustrissimum. et Reverendissimum Dominum frater Florentius Conrium ordinis minor observantii Sti Francisci adhibitis, et Assistentibus, sibi admodum Illmis et Reverendissimis Dominis Octavio Acorambono episcopo Forosempronien, et Andrea Sorbolengo episcopo Eugubinen et presentinus ibidem Reverendissimus Reverendissimus Dominus Dominus Carolo Antonio Vaccario Praesbitero. Bononien et Antonio Maroccho praesbiter diocesis Tridentinae testibus.

15

1609, Friday 1 May, Rome. Letter of Flaithrí Ó Maolchonaire to Philip III relating to the decision by James I to plant the Ulster earls' lands (AGS, E., Roma, l. 992)

Despues de aver despachado el correo y escrito por el a Vuestra Magestad llegò a mis manos un librillo ingles impresso en Londres poco meses ha que contiene unos articulos del Rey de Inglaterra en los quales declara confiscados para si las tierras de los condes de Tiron y Tirconel hasta seis condados, sin declarar la causa por que, y offresce las dichas tierras perpetuamente (para si y para sus herederos) a todos los Ingleses y Escoceses que quisieren yr a habitar las con tal que paguen un tanto al Rey cada año y no pueda una persona tener quanta tierra quisiere sino cierta cantidad que alli prescribe para cada uno, y que primero jure que el Rey es cabeça de la Iglesia. Item que no puedan arrendar las dichas tierras a ningun Irlandez que sea de la antigua stirpe de Irlanda. Que en cada condado aya escuelas para instruir a los mancebos en la Religion de Calvino. Y que en todas las Iglesias parrochiales en lugar de sacerdotes aya ministros herejes que comen la renta de la Iglesia. [Abbrev.] euj.a

Esta es la substancia de lo contenido en el librillo lo que quise escrivir a Vuestra Magestad para que echasse de ver quan[ta razon] tenia el conde de dar priessa a Su Magestad Catholica todo este año passado para que le bolviesse a sus Estados por alguna via, o a lo menos le embiasse alguna resolucion antcs que se hiziesse esta confiscacion la qual (como entiende el conde) se atrevieron a hacer por ver que sus cosas van tan por el suelo y que Su Magestad Catholica no los favoreze tanto como al principio se esperava. A mi me pone alguna culpa por no le aver dexado dar mas priessa a Su Magestad de la que dio, que siempre le yva yo a la mano en no dar priessa por parezerme que bastava la que se dava que Su Magestad yva disponiendo las cosas del conde bien como agora espero que las compondra y que aquellos iniquos articulos del Rey de Inglaterra se resolverán en ayre con la ayuda de Dios y el auxilio de Su Catholica Magestad que no consentira tan extraordinaria y nueva extirpacion y opression de los Catholicos y de la Santa Fee. Por el primer correo embiare a V Magestad el librillo traducido en español por el qual y por la carta que el conde escrivirà a Su Magestad verà Vuestra Magestad quanta razon tienen y todos los Catholicos de quexar y entristezerse y cuan poco se puede esperar de aquellos Herejes. Guarde Dios a Vuestra Magestad como desseo. De Roma y Mayo a primero de 1609.

Fr Florencio Conryo
Arçobispo Tuamen.

16

1610, 25 Feb. Report of council of state to Philip III relating to the Conde de Puñonrostro's memorial for Ó Maolchonaire (AGS, E., España, NP, l. 2745)

De parte. El Conssejo destado a 25 de Hebrero 1610
Sobre lo que pide El Conde de Puñoenrostro por el Arcobispo de Tuamense

[In Lerma's hand:] quedo advertido desto

Señor. Vuestra Magestad mando remitir al Conssejo un memorial que el Conde de Puñoenrostro dio antes su muerte en refiere que ha 6 meses que vino a esta Corte Fray Florencio Conrrio Arcobispo Tuamense por orden de Su Santidad y del Conde de Tiron a tratar los negocios del dicho Conde y de los Catholicos de Yrlanda con Vuestra Magestad que ha 12 años sirve a Vuestra Magestad el dicho Arcobispo en Yrlanda en las guerras que alli se han offrecido asistiendo a los Catholicos particularmente a los Condes Oneill y Odonnell y siempre les persuadio que quedasen firmes en el servicio de Dios y de Vuestra Magestad como lo han hecho que lo mismo ha hecho en España y Vuestra Magestad le embio con despachos de importançia a los dichos Catholicos y despues desto Vuestra Magestad le empleo en negocios de Su Real servicio algunos años en La Corte y por que […] es persona que se puede ser de mucho servicio en las cossas de Yrlanda y para conservar los catholicos de aquel Reyno en su devoçion y informarles desde alla de las Cossas que se offreçieren y de los animos y secretos de los dichos Catholicos y para moverles a qual quiera buena resoluçion porque todos ellos le respectan que aqui padeçe mucha neçesidad y se alla empeñado y no puede andar en la deçençia que requiere su persona por no tener sustento de su tierra supplica a Vuestra Magestad le haga merced de un entretenimiento en esta corte para poderse sustentar mientras acude a los dichos negocios.

Al Conssejo pareze que seran muy bien empleados en su persona quatroçientos ducados de pension eclesiastica porque le consta ser assi todo lo que se refiere. Vuestra Magestad lo que mas fuere servido. En Madrid a 25 de hebrero 1610.

17

1610, 5 Jul., Madrid. Letter of Flaithrí Ó Maolchonaire to the council of finance on behalf of Matthew Tully, his wife and children (AGS, CJH 499-20, ff 44-5)

Matheo Tulio irlandes. Al Presidente de Hazienda. Presidente Hazienda.

A Alonso Nuñez de Valdiva del Consejo de Su Magestad y Su Secretario en el Hazienda. [Archepiscopal seal: Florentius Conrius Archiepiscopus Tuamensis] Matheo Tulio que solicita aqui los negocios del Conde de Tiron y esta dará a Vuestr. merced [a] el y su muger sesenta ducados de entretenimiento al mes en las arcas, ha mas de un año que su muger no recibe blanca y a el se le deven mas de diez y seis meses. Tienen cargo de hijos y familia y andan muy necessitados de manera que sus acreedores le molestan por via de justicia y porque se que su necesidad es muy grande y anda empeñado supplico a Vuestr. merced procure con el Señor Presidente que de orden al Thesorero para que le pague lo que se resta deviendo para lo qual tiene cedula de Su Magestad y yo recibire muy particular merced en que se le hagen Vuestra Magestad. A quien guarde Nuestro Señor como desseo. De casa a 5 de julio de 1610.

Fr Florencio Conryo
Arçobispo Tuamen.

18

1610, 30 Oct., Madrid. Letter from Flaithrí Ó Maolchonaire to the Spanish secretary of state, relating to the transfer of Irish troop units to Flanders, proposing that Eoghan Ruadh Ó Néill and Aodh Mac Aingil OFM be placed in charge of administering the pay of Irish soldiers (AGS, E., Flandes, l. 2292)

Aqui embio a Vuestra Magestad la carta de Su Magestad que trata de las vacantias, y para que VM pueda enformar y dar luz a essos señores de todo este negocio de las vacantias, y que fue la causa que movio su Magestad à tomar esta resolucion le advierto[,] que siendo al principio su Magestad enformado de lo que an perdido los yrlandeses en su real serbicio, y de lo que an serbido a la causa cattholica en la ultima guerra de Yrlanda, movido de compassion, y tambien de equidad para recompensarles en alguna manera sus serbicios y perdidas les mando dar gran golpe de entretenimientos y ventajas, y como corrio la fama desta liberalidad que su Magestad uso con los irlandeses an acudido tantos, que en breve tiempo se juntaron dellos en Flandes un tercio de mil y 500 soldados y estando yo entonçes en la corte por orden de Su Magestad, y viendo lo mucho que importaba al serbicio de Su Magestad y a la quietud de sus ministros buscar algun remedio para que no viniessen mas yrlandeses a la corte propuse Sr Conde de Puñorostro (que esta en gloria) que el unico medio seria haçelles mas merçedes en esta corte, sino que fuessen todos remittidos al Sr Archiduque y que de los mesmos entretenimientos y ventajas que estaban ya dadas a los yrlandeses por Su Magestad, quando fuessen vacando se fuessen proveiendo en adelante en otros yrlandeses benemeritos conforme la relacion que diesse Don Henrique O Nel a Su Alteza de los meritos y qualidades de cada uno, y que desta manera no irian las merçedes creçiendo cada dia, y se limpiaria la corte aqui, porque no vendrian a ella viendo que cessaran las merçedes accudirian todos a serbir en el tercio por las esperanças que tendrian de alcançar alguna vacantia, y que assi se conserbaria bien el tercio. Todo esto propusimos en consejo de estado, lo qual approbaron aquellos señores de buena gana y en conformidad dello escrivio Su Magestad despues la carta que va con esta à Su Alteza para distribuir 500 ducados que vacaron en España en cierto yrlandeses que acudieron a esta corte lo qual no se effectuo hasta agora. Yo entonces y agora no veo mejor medio para los sobre dichos effectos, que mandar que se executa la dicha orden en los entretenimientos y ventajas que vacaron desde entonces en el tercio solamente y lo mesmo se haga en los que vacaren en adelante, y que se ordene al Sr Archiduque quando proveiere estos entretenimientos dar credito a la relacion que le dieren el Capitan Don Eugenio O Nel sobrino del Conde O Nel y el Padre fray Hugo Cavello Guardian del Collegio Yrlandes de Lovayna y Capellan Mayor del dicho Tercio Yrlandes de cuyas virtud y buenas partes Su Alteza tiene harta satisfaction, y haciendo esso no se vera yrlandes aqui, ni sera menester hacer alguna relacion dellos, y si los primeros messes por no saber esta orden vinieran algunos, ia son despachados con decilles que accudan a Su Alteza, y si son pobres que no pueden serbir que los Alcaldes tengan orden general para echarlos que no esten en la corte mas que tres dias. Guarde Dios a VM como desseo de nuestra casa a 30 de octubr.

Fr Florencio Conryo
Arçobispo Tuamen.

19

1611, 10 Jul., Madrid. *Certificación* **of Flaithrí Ó Maolchonaire in support of Anthony de Burgo's application to serve with the Spanish naval forces (AGS, Guerra Antigua, Servicios Militares 5, f.78)**

Don Fray Florencio Conryo por la Gracia de Dios y de la Santa Sede Apostolica, Arçobispo Tuamense en Irlanda

Hago fe que conosco a Don Antonio de Burgo ser hijo de un cavallero de la familia de los Burgos, primo de Mac Villiam Burc, y que el y sus parientes han servido en la ultima guerra de Irlanda, y perdido mucha gente y haçienda en servicio de Su Magestad por los quales serviçios de sus padres y parientes, me parece que el dicho Antonio es digno de la merced que Su Magestad catholica fuere servido haçelle, y a Su pedimiento le di esta fe, firmada y sellada con mi sello; en Madrid a 10 de Julio de 1611.

Fr. Florencio Conryo
Arçobispo Tuamen.

20

1614, 2 Aug., Madrid. Report of the Spanish council of state to Philip III, relating to Flaithrí Ó Maolchonaire's appeal for an Irish consul for the ports of southern Spain (AGS, Estado, España y Norte, l. 4191)

De Officio y Parte
El Conssejo Destado a 2 de agosto 1614
Sobre lo que ha pedido la nacion irlandesa acerca de tener consul de su nacion en el Andaluzía. Esta Bien [Lerma's hand]

Señor
Don fray Florencio Conrrio Arzobispo Tuamensi en Irlanda refirio los dias passados en un memorial que se vio en el Consejo que cada año bienen muchos navios y mercaderias de irlandeses a San Lucar de Barrameda, puerto de Sta Maria y Cadiz[,] y los que ban a San Lucar suelen visitados por un ingles llamado Thomas Jaimes Morador alli con quien no se entienden los dichos irlandeses y les haze muchas molestias y agravios por ser de naçion enemiga y diferente en la lengua, y suplico a VMD en nombre de toda la naçion irlandessa fuesse servido de mandar al Duque de Medina, que reciviesse por consul de todos los irlandeses que aportasen a aquella costa a un Nicolas Vis de su naçion vecino de San Lucar y

casado con española persona de muy buenas partes.

VMD ordene al Duque de Medina que avisase en esto lo que se le offreçia con su pareçer y ha respondido que haciendose informado si tendria incombeniente en nombrar en el dicho officio al dicho Nicolas Vis teniendole VMD proveydo en persona muy benemerita que es el dicho Thomas Jaimes ingles con entretenimiento de VMD y muy catolico y fiel y es consul de la Gran Bretaña en quese incluye Irlanda y Escocia por ser toda de la Corona de Inglaterra. Ha hallado y le pareçe que seria novedad yntroducir el dicho officio de consul de irlandeses desmembrandole de lo demas, que aunque el Nicolas Vis es hombre de bien y catolico es ostalero y da de comer y camas y el ingles es muy inteligente y confidente pero que si toda dia paresquesse otra cossa bastaria que el dicho Nicolas Vis fuesse consul de los irlandeses de San Lucar sin darle mas mano y jurisdicion y haviendolo visto el Consejo (como VMD lo mando) se boto como se sigue.

El comendador mayor de Leon que los consules suelen serlo de todas las naciones de Su Rei sin dividirse aunque ellas sean diferentes y assi le pareçe que sea consul que lo es agora.
El Duque del Infantado que se mobio esto por las quexas y enemistad que ay entre irlandeses y ingleses y el Thomas Jaimes es ingles y assi le paresce que este se quede con los de su naçion y el propuesto lo sea de irlandeses por ser justo que tengan de quien fiarse siendo como son catolicos, y deste pareçer fueron el Marques de Villafranca y Don Agustin Messia. VMD proveera lo que demas fuere servido en Madrid a 2 de agosto 1614.

21

circa 1615, Madrid. Ó Maolchonaire's objections to the negotiations for a marriage agreement between Spain and England. Due to a perceived threat to the Indies and to Catholic orthodoxy, he proposed an alternative involving Spanish accord with France and closer union with Ireland to protect the Indies and undermine the ruling houses of England and the United Provinces
(AGS, E., Inglaterra, libro 369, pp. 72–4)

[Dorso:] Don Fr. Florencio Conrrio arçobispo de Tuemia en Yrlanda. Prueva con raçones ebidentes lo poco que España puede fiar de Ingalatierra por mas union que tenga con ella y lo mal que le estaria para todo travar alli casamiento [recto, p. 72] Fr. Florencio Conrrio arçobispo de Tuemia en Yrlanda. Raçones que apunta Don Fr. Florencio Conrrio arçobispo de Tuemia en Yrlanda que no esta bien a Su Cathca Magestad fiarse en amistad de los Yngleses. Por mas union que aja entre las dos naçiones Española y Ynglesa &c.

Primeramente no se puede pensar que por bia de casamientos se pudiera granxera la voluntad del Rey de Yngalatierra por esperiencia pues se vee que por esta bia apenas. Se puede oj dia ganar la voluntad de un Principe Xptiano como

Françia. Que es çierto que todos los principes de la christianidad estan tan temerosos de ver tanta potencia como la de España y tan ymbidiosos de ber que toda la Riqueza de este mundo que es lo que viene cada año de las Yndias entra en una Volssa como los herejes suelen deçir. Y assi mientras Su Magestad no les da a los Yngleses sus Yndias no se puede fiar dellos por mas uniones que haga con ellos. Que con semejante union asegura el Rey de España al Yngles sus estados que estando en union con España no se atreveran sus Vasallos a haçer cossa contraer y el Rey de España tendra sus estados menos seguros por la dicha union por que el fruto que se sacare della sera tener el Rey de Yngalatierra mas comodidad para las dos cossas que mas desea en el mundo que son pegar mas y mas cada dia su herejia en España secretamente [so] capa de amistad y trato e yr ganando mas tierra en el Camino de las Yndias asta que bea su coyuntura de acometer a todas. Que tantas coyunturas se ofreçen que no seria milagro ver semejante ocasion especialmente estando los [verso, p. 72] Yndianos tan cansados y deseosos de ber otro genero de govierno y los Españoles que naçen y tienen haçienda alla bulliçiosos y sujetos a levantarse con todo allando a Su Magestad una vez muy ocupado por aca por berse tan distante y lejos de sus fuerças.

Lo segundo se piensa que Su Magestad haçe mucho bien a los catholicos del septentercion obligando al yngles a que diese livertad de conciençia a sus Vasallos dejando ap[ar]te quando viniese en ello el yngles que es la palabra de hereje que no la cumplia mañana no pareçe sino lo contrario que no se haçe bien en ello a los catholicos sino mal por que estando el yngles seguro de España per Raçon de Casamiento o otra buscara mill caminos debajo de otro pretextos civiles para extinguir los catholicos y privarlos de sus tierras y haçiendas sin que aja quien les tenga lastima pues se podria deçir entonces que no sufririan por la fee sino por rebelliones y otras mill mentiras que los ministros del Rey de Yngalatierra les levantarian cada momento como los levantan oy dia a los ob[is]pos y sacerdotes que mentiriçan significando que no lo hacen por ser ellos catholicos sino por crimen de lesa Magestad que cometiesen. Quanto y mas que quando les diese de coraçon Livertad de Conçiençia y les guardase bien su palabra no estaria esso bien al servicio de Su Catholica Magestad per que en tal cassio sus Vasallos del Yngles le querrian mas que a ningun otro principe y le servirian de beras contrato el mundo y en la conquista de las Yndias que nunca dexara el Yngles de proseguir por mas union que tenga con España.

Lo tercero como los enemigos ven que en España son tan amigos de la paz que por mas tiros que ellos hagarian desimulando en España por el mesmo casa que España con menos reputaçion obligada a conservar [recto, p. 73] y aun a mendigar las voluntades de los enemigos con dadivas disimilaçiones. Y subjeciones muy endignas de tanta monarquia y queda echado por tie[rra] aquel espanto y temor que en tiempos pasados todo el mundo tenia a España y quedan los enemigos muy ufanos y arrogantes espantando Y atemoriçando con deçir que romperan las paçes que como saven el umor de aca esta es su primera palabra. Y por la mesma Raçon queda España en perpetuo peligro porque queda en paz con sus enemigos y los enemigos en guerra, con ella como se echa deber en todas las ocassiones que se ofreçe contra el serviçio de Su Catholica Magestad que ninguna de han pasar no obstante la paz como se vio en lo que hiçieron ultimamente en ayuda del Saboyano embiandole ocultamente doçientos mill ducados para pagar la cavalleria. Y en la conquista de la Virginia y Bermudas cosas que puedan ser de mucho peligro a España. Y quien les quitara que armen una fuerte armada de Yngleses y Olandeses quando vean su ocassion Y tomen alguna vez la flota de Yndias con que despues por muchos años podran dar travajo a España. Y pone la en gran riesgo pues saven que por tentarlo salgan o no salgan con ello no an de Romper las paçes por aca que por tener conoçida esta demasiada paçiençia de España se an atrevido despues de las paçes a conquistar la Virginia y Bermudas en quien no gano España mucha reputaçion. Y ellos dieron exemplo a otros principes a que hagan otra conquista contra España pues sufre todo por conservar las paçes. Ademas que cada dia sea provechan los enemigos de las paces portificandose en la Virginia y Bermudas de tal manera que lo que gastara Su Magestad ahora con echarlos por ventura le costaria seis veçes tanto si tarda mucho [verso, p. 73] Que si el Rey ahorrara muchos millones con la paz y los amontonaria para dar despues sobre sus enemigos su paçiençia Y silençio mas tolerable pero temese que no ahorra. Y tenban los enemigos desarragando y aniguilando Los Catholicos de Yrlanda que son amigos de España y el unico puesto por donde el Yngles teme la Reyna de sus estados que presto acavaran con ellos si Dios no les socorre de que es indiçio bastante la confiscaçion que hiçieron ahora de las tierras de los condes de Tiron y Tirconel que contenienen cassi la quinta parte del Reyno y teniendo el Rey de Yngalatierra sus tres Reynos una bez seguros Y plantados de hereges como pretende por lo que haçe agora se puede conjeturar que toros hara entonces a España y las ligas que hara con Principes enemigos. De lo suso se saca quan ymportante es a la conservaçion de la monarquia de España poner algo remedio a los dichos yncombinientes. Que haora es el tiempo mientras el Rey de Françia tiene neçessidad de las amistades de España y antes que venga a [la] edad de Ombre que entonçes podr[a] ser que sea del umor de Su padre.

Y el Remedio es poner a Yrlanda en livertad que se del bando de España cossa que no tiene mas dificultad que empeçarlo bien Y con secreto por los muchos señores que ay de aquella tierra desterrados Y por el tercio que ay en Flandes en qual ay cavalleros de cada familia del Reyno Y por la disposiçion de los cavalleros que en el estan oprimidos y tiraniçados de los herejes yngleses Y por otros medios que se daran mas en particular quando fuese menester. [recto, p. 74] Y echo esto una bez fuera de la grande gloria que se sigue dello al serviçio de Dios Y de su Yglesia Y de cumplir con la obligacion que tiene Su Magestad a los dichos Catholicos por que se perdieron por haverle serbido se ebitan todos los peligros y desbenturas que los enemigos y la adbersa fortuna amenaçan a España. Que como Lombardia y Flandes sirven a Su Catholica Magestad por freno contra el fraces para detenerle a [que] no haga contra España todo lo que dessea. Y como Su Magestad alço al Duque de Neoburgo y le ayuda para tenerle por contrapresso contra los Olandeses assi es necessario tener otro contrapreso contra el Ingles que de otra manera estando metido en Sus Islas y tiros que quisiere pero teniendo Su Catholica Magestad a Yrlanda le ata las manos de manera que no se atreviera a haçer nada contra España ni aun en secreto que daran las Yndias muy seguras del sepentrion. Y si el Rey de Yngalatierra muere presto y su hijo que entre ambos [so] enfermiçios en tal caso teniendo Su Magestad Catholica gente de Yrlanda los Catolicos de Yngalatierra viendo el socorro tan cerca nunca admitiran al Palatino que es hereje y estrangero por Su Rey que no seria poco serviçio a España pues siendo el sobrino del Conde Mauriçio si biniese a ser Rey de Yngalatierra claro esta que ayudaria a los Olandeses con todas sus fuerças. Y que tentaria salir por Emperador con ayuda de los Olandeses y de los demas herejes de Alemania y Francia y proveraria haçer todo quanto pudiese contra España. Y no solo el Remedio desto y de lo demas referido [verso, p. 74] se puede esperar sino toda probabilidad que teniendo Su Magestad a Yrlanda quedaran los Catholicos de Yngalatierra, Escoçia tan animados que no tendra el Rey herege que les hiço tantos agravios un dia de quietud por los lebantamientos que harian contra el demanera que bendria el gobierno de Yngalatierra a caer presto Y Su Magestad a ser Rey de ella y absoluto monarcha Y a sujetar con facilidad a los olandeses no gastando con todo ello lo que gasto con obstende porque ni en Yrlanda ni en Escoçia ni en Yngalatierra ay Plaças fuertes en que el que fue Señor de la Campaña lo sera luego de todo Y en cada tres leguas de Flandes ay un Ostende y dexaran de ser Ostendes el dia que les faltara la ayuda de estos otros Reynos que bendrian de Rodillas los Reveldes a dar la obedençia a Su Cattholica Magestad viendo que les faltarian las espaldas.

22

1617, 7 Oct., Lerma. Letter of the duke of Lerma to the president of finance, advising him that Philip III has resolved to transfer Ó Maolchonaire's annual income of 1,000 ducados to Flanders, where the archbishop of Tuam will reside
(AGS, CJH 549-27-8, Particulares)

A suplicacion de Don Fray Florencio Corrio Arçobispo Tuamense en Irlanda ha resuelto su Magestad que se le acuda en Flandes (donde ba a residir) desde primero de setiembre en adelante con los mill ducados de sueldo al año que gozava en las arcas de tres llaves. Y manda su Magestad que lo que importa el dicho sueldo se añada a las provissiones del exercito para que esto no haga falta a la gente de guerra y assi mismo manda su Magestad que lo que se le deviere al dicho arçobispo hasta fin de agosto passado[,] que el desde quando le ha de cesar en las arcas este sueldo[,] de le pague sin dilacion para que pueda hazer su viaje - de que aviso a VS para que assi lo ordene nuestro Señor guarde a VS. en Lerma a 7 de otubre 1617.

Señor Pressidente de Hazienda

Señor Duq.   +   7 de ottubre 1617
                                   El arçobispo Tuamense

En Madrid a 26 de octtubre 1617
Que sele de el despacho necessario
como Su Magestad manda.

23

1629, 7 Mar., Madrid. Ó Maolchonaire to the Spanish president of finance requesting the payment of his pension at court in Madrid to the same value he received in Flanders before his departure from there in 1626

Don fray Florencio Conrrio Arçobispo Tuamense dize que vuestra Magestad le hizo merced de mill ducados cada un año consigos en las arcas de las tres llaves donde se le pagaron hasta que sele ordeno fuese a los estados de Flandes a donde se le mandaron pagar de los gastos de aquella embaxada como se hizo hasta fin de agosto de 626 que por mandamiento de vuestra Magestad vino a esta corte a donde sele an pagado por quenta de lo que se le deve de los dichos mill ducados cada año quinientos mill marevedis y se le restan desde primero de setiembre del dicho año de 626 hasta fin de diziembre de 628[,] 375,000 marevedis que como consta de las certificaciones que presento de Flandes no se le han pagado alla. Y porque esta enfermo en la cama y muy empañado para no tener otra cosa de que se poder sustentar mas que la dicha merced y no se le haver pagado. Supplica a vuestra Magestad mande al Contador Mayor se libre[n] y haga pagar los dichos 1,000 ducados que en ello recibira merced. Con advertencia que a de ser la paga de las provisiones de Flandes.

24

1627, 5 Feb., Letter from Ó Maolchonaire to Jacob Boonen, archbishop of Mechelen, describing his arduous journey through France and the Pyrenees with Hugh de Burgo OFM, their safe arrival in Madrid and a pledge of their continued loyalty to Boonen (Archief Aartsbisdom Mechelen-Brussel, Boonen-3)

Illme Dne
Longum esset recensere quas passi sumus difficultatis & molestias in transitu Galliae & Pyreneorum; nec aliud sperare licuit pro senectute mea, tam intempesta hyeme, ingentem peregrinationem suscipiente.

At Dei auxiliante gratiâ, tandem, incolumis hic appulimus, ubi nihil iucundius occurrere nobis possit, quam Illme Dne, obedire mandatis: Ex animo dico, & obligatione mea quam fateor magnam esse inserviendi Illme Dne, si vel affectum suum circa nationem totam, vel me in particulari considerem quem utrique continuali Dei causâ rogo, me que aestima Illme Dne obsequiis deditissimum

Deus Illme Dne suam ad Ecclesiae sanctae comune, & Insularis maris particulare bonum, pro voto omnium bonos diu sospitet. Madriti 5 Feb. 1627

Illme et Rme Dne

indignus confrater et servus
Florentius Conrius
Archieps Tuamen.

NOTES

1. I have retained the original documents' orthography and contractions. Square brackets are used to mark uncertain readings. The spelling of words in early-modern Castilian differed from the standardised forms used today. A few examples will suffice here. The letter 'y' is often interchangeable with the letter 'i'; e.g. yrlandes, vaia; the letter 'x' instead of the letter 'j' in modern spelling; e.g. embaxador; and 'ç' is sometimes used in place of the letter 'z'; e.g. 'março' instead of 'marzo'.
2. In Castilian, this abbreviation stands for: 'Sacra, Catolica, Real Magestad'.
3. I am grateful to Fr Ermenegildo Camozzi da Bergamo of the Archivum Secretum Vaticanum for his help in deciphering the abbreviations in this document.

Bibliography

GUIDES

Almirante, José, *Bibliografía militar de España* (Madrid, 1876)

Alzina, José Pablo, *Embajadores de España en Londres: una guía de retratos de la embajada de España* (Madrid, 2001)

Burrieza Sánchez, José María, *Guía del Investigador a los fondos de la Sección Guerra Antigua, Servicios de Militares* (Archivo General de Simancas, 2000)

Cappelli, Adriano, *Dizionario di abbreviature latine ed italiane* (repr. Milan, 1990)

Cuvelier, Joseph, Henri Lonchay and Joseph Lefèvre (eds), *Correspondance de la cour d'Espagne sur les affaires des Pays–Bas au XVIIe siècle* (6 vols, Brussels, 1923–37)

De Gayangos, Pascual (ed.), *Catalogue of the manuscripts in the Spanish language at the British Library [formerly the British Museum]*, vol. 1 (London, 1875)

Diccionario de la lengua española, Real Academia Espanola (Madrid, 1956)

Foulché-Delbosc and L. Barraudihigo, *Manuel de l'hispanisant* (2 vols, New York, 1920–5)

Giblin, Cathaldus (ed.), 'Barberini Latini: guide to material of Irish interest', in *Archiv. Hib.*, 18 (1955), pp. 73–124

Giordano, Silvano (ed.), *Le istruzioni di Paolo V ai diplomatici pontifici: 1605–21* (3 vols, Rome, 2003)

Giordano, Silvano, *Istruzioni di Filippo III ai suoi Ambasciatori a Roma: 1598–1621* (Rome, 2006)

Guía del Archivo de Simancas. Dirección General de Archivos y Bibliotecas (Madrid, 1958)

Hayes, R. J., *The manuscript sources for the study of Irish civilisation* (11 vols, Boston, 1965), Supplement (3 vols, Boston, 1979)

Jennings, Brendan (ed.), 'Irish preachers and confessors in the archdiocese of Malines, 1607–1794', in *Archiv. Hib.*, 23 (1960), pp. 148–66

Kerney-Walsh, Micheline (ed.), *Spanish knights of Irish origin: documents from the Archivo Histórico Nacional, Madrid and the Archivo General de Simancas* (4 vols, Dublin, 1960)

Lewis, C. T. and Charles Short, *A Latin dictionary founded on Ethan Allen Andrews' edition of William Freund's Latin dictionary* (Oxford, 1966)

MacCurtain, Margaret (ed.), 'Irish material in Fondo Santa Sede, Madrid', in *Archiv. Hib.*, 26 (1963), pp. 40–50

Mooney, Canice, et al. (eds), *Catalogue of Irish manuscripts in the Franciscan Library, Killiney* (Dublin, 1969) *New Dictionary of National Biography* (Oxford, 2005)

O'Neill, Charles and Joaquín María Domínguez (eds), *Diccionario histórico de la Compañia de Jesús* (4 vols, Rome, 2001)

Parker, Geoffrey, *Guide to the archives of the Spanish institutions in or concerned with the Netherlands, 1556–1706* (Brussels, 1971)

Pou y Marti, José María, *Guía del Archivo de la Embajada de España cerca de la Santa Sede* (Rome, 1919)

PRIMARY SOURCES

Belgium

Archives Générales du Royaume, Brussels/Algemeen Rijksarchief, Brussel
- Sécrétairerie d'État et de Guerre/Secretarie van State en Oorlog,
179–80, 181, 195, 301

Bibliothèque Royale Bruxelles/Koninklijke Bibliotheek van België, Brussel
- *Historia Universitatis Lovaniensis*, J. L. Bax, 1804–24; Mss 22,172–3

Ireland

National Archives, Dublin
- Repertories to Inquisitions (Exchequer), County Roscommon, Elizabeth
- Repertories to Inquisitions (Exchequer), County Roscommon, James I
National Library of Ireland, Dublin
- Genealogical Ms. 155
Royal Irish Academy, Dublin
- *Linea Antigua*, Ms. E.44
Russell Library, Maynooth
- Salamanca Archives, S52, S59
Trinity College, Dublin
- *Collectanea Historica*, Ms. 580 (E.3.8)
University College, Dublin
- UCD–OFM, Mss 'C' 11, 12
- UCD–OFM, Mss 'D', volumes D.01, D.02, D.03

Italy

Archivum Romanum Societate Iesu, Rome
- Anglia 9.II
- *De Rebus Hibernicis* (1576–1698)
Archivio Segreto Vaticano, Rome
- *Epistulae ad Principes*, 40
- Fondo Borghèse, Ser. I, vol. 269–72
- Fondo Borghèse, Ser. II, volumes 100, 112, 115, 137, 204–6, 429
- Fondo Borghèse, Ser. III, volumes 124c, 126a
- Inghilterra, volume 19
- Lettere di Particolari, volume I
- Nunziatura di Fiandra, volumes 12, 15, 21a, 138
- Protocollo, volumes xlv, cxxix
- Protocollo, *Episcoporum et Alia*, xiii, 33
Biblioteca Apostolica Vaticana, Rome

–   Barberini Latini, volumes 1575, 5919, 6206, 6802, 6808, 6810, 8286, 8581, 8618–19, 8676, 8928

Spain

Archivo de Asuntos Exteriores de España, Madrid
–   Fondo Santa Sede, legajos 55–7
–   Fondo Santa Sede, Ordenes Militares, legajos 131, 134

Archivo General de las Indias, Seville
–   Indiferente 427–8

Archivo General de Simancas
–   Consejo y Juntas de Hacienda, legajos 385–663, 1714–30
–   Consejo y Juntas de Hacienda, libros 363–5, 376–81
–   Contadurías Generales, 271
–   Contaduría Mayor de Cuentas, 3a epoca, legajo 3159
–   Corona de Castilla, legajos 188–9, 191, 194, 199, 202, 205, 228, 236
–   Dirección General del Tesoro, legajo 1288; inventario 24
–   Estado, España, legajos 1797, 2637, 2640, 2643, 2646, 2651
–   Estado, Indiferente de España y Norte, legajos 4126, 2852, 2858, 2863
–   Estado, Negociación de Flandes, legajos 620, 621–2, 628–9, 2023, 2025, 2030, 2034, 2041, 2044, 2139, 2146, 2226–7, 2229, 2235, 2289
–   Estado, Negociación de Inglaterra, legajos 839–45, 2511, 2513, 2516, 2519, 2527, 2557, 2577, 2587, 2598
–   Estado, Negocios de 'Partes', legajos 1745, 1748–52, 1754, 1771, 1802, 2744–6, 2749, 2752, 2768, 2797
–   Estado, Roma, legajos 992, 994, 997–9, 1001, 1002, 1856, 1863
–   Guerra Antigua, legajos 582, 587, 589–90, 596, 640, 3143–5
–   Guerra Antigua, Servicios de Militares, 5, 15, 42, 51, 81
–   Guerra y Marina, Libros de Registro 109, 121, 129, 145, 148, 151, 154, 158
–   Guerra y Marina, Decretos del Consejo, Secretaría de Tierra, 156
–   Secretaría de Estado, libros 366–9, 1444
–   Tribunal Mayor de Cuentas, 912/24

Archivo Histórico de Loyola
–   Fondo Histórico, Lerma, caja 27

Archivo Histórico Nacional, Madrid
–   Ordenes Militares; Pruebas de Caballeros, Calatrava, expedientes 980, 1832–3
–   Ordenes Militares; Pruebas de Caballeros, Santiago, expedientillo 71,
–   Ordenes Militares; Pruebas de Religiosas, Calatrava, expediente 233 bis.
–   Ordenes Militares; Pruebas de Caballeros, Santiago, expedientes 1280, 1282, 2830, 3089, 3146, 3387, 3388, 5808, 5852, 6536, 7957
–   Ordenes Militares; Pruebas de Caballeros, Santiago, expedientillos, 171–2, 15402

Archivo Histórico Nacional, Nobleza
- Frias, cajas 66–7

Archivo Histórico de Protocolos, Comunidad de Madrid
- *Rexistro Protocolo de Escripturas que se han otorgado por ante Miguel Claros de Pazos SSno. de Rentas de la Casa y Estados de el Ynfantado en Madrid desde el Año de 1619 á el de 1645* [5398/877]

Archivo Municipal de Valladolid
- Libros de Actas, 1602–6

Biblioteca del Colegio de Santa Cruz, Valladolid
- *Historia de Valladolid*, Juan Antolínez de Burgos (1722), Manuscrito 324
- *Historia de la insigne ciudad de Segovia y compendio de las historias de Castilla*, Diego de Colmenares (1637), Manuscrito 3,769

Biblioteca Nacional de España, Madrid
- Manuscritos, 2348, 2357 (AD 1625)
- Frai Matías de Sobremonte, *Noticias chronographicas y topographicas del Real y Religiosissimo Convento de los frailes menores observantes de San Francisco de Valladolid* (20.XII.1660), Manuscrito 19,351

Real Biblioteca del Palacio Real de Madrid
- Manuscritos, volumes II–2108; II–2115; II–2132, II–2168; II–2191; II–2221

United Kingdom
National Archives, Kew
- Foreign Office Papers, 94/23–94/124

PRINTED EDITIONS

[Published documents and correspondence]

Annála Connacht: The Annals of Connacht, ed. and tr. A. Martin Freeman (Dublin, 1944)

Annals of Loch Cé, ed. and tr. W. M. Hennessy (2 vols, London, 1871)

Annals of Tigernach, ed. and tr. Whitley Stokes (2 vols, repr. Felinfach, 1993)

Annala Rioghachta Éireann: Annals of the kingdom of Ireland by the Four Masters, ed. and tr. John O'Donovan, 7 vols (Dublin, 1848–51; repr. 1990)

Augustine of Hippo, *On Christian teaching*, ed. and tr. R. P. H. Green (Oxford, 1997)

Beatha Aodha Ruaidh Uí Dhomhnaill: the life of Hugh Roe O'Donnell by Lughaidh O'Clery, ed. and tr. Denis Murphy SJ (Dublin, 1893)

Beatha Aodha Ruaidh Uí Dhomhnaill, transcribed from the book of Lughaidh Ó Cléirigh, ed. and tr. Paul Walsh (2 vols, Dublin, 1948–57)

Best, R. I. (ed.), *Ms. 23 N 10 (formerly Betham 145) in the Library of the Royal Irish Academy, facsimiles in collotype of Irish manuscript*, 6 (Dublin, 1954)

Boate, Gerard, *A natural history of Ireland* (London, 1652)

Bordoni, Francesco, *Historia tertii Ordinis Regularis S. Francisci* (Parma, 1658)

Calendar of State Papers, Ireland, ed. H. C. Hamilton, E. G. Atkinson and R. P. Mahaffy (24 vols, London, 1860–1912)

Calendar of the State Papers, Spanish, ed. M. A. S. Hume (4 vols, London, 1892–9)

*Calendar of the Carew manuscripts preserved in the Archiepiscopal Library at Lambeth,
1515–1624*, ed. J. S. Brewer and William Bullen (6 vols, London, 1867–73)

Calendar of Fiants, Henry VIII to Elizabeth (Dublin, 1875–90)

Calendar of the Irish Patent Rolls of James I, ed. Margaret Griffith (Dublin, 1966) *The
Compossicion booke of Conought*, ed. A. M. Freeman (Dublin, 1936)

Creswell, Joseph, *Carta escrita al embaxador de Inglaterra* (1606) ed. Albert Loomie
(New York: Fordham University Press, 1963)

Curtis, Edmund and R. B. McDowell (eds), *Irish historical documents: 1172–1922*
(London, 1943)

Dán Na mBráthar Mionúr, eag. Cuthbert Mhág Craith (Baile Átha Cliath, 1967)

Davies, John, *A discoverie of the true causes why Ireland was never entirely subdued, nor
brought under obedience of the crowne of England, until the beginning of his
Majestie's happie raigne* (London, 1612; repr. 1969)

Foppens, J. F., *Biblioteca Belgica, sive virorum in Belgio vita, scriptisque illustrium cat-
alogues, librorumque, nomenclatura continens scriptores à clariff. viris [...]*
(Bruxelles, 1739)

Gonzaga, Francesco, *De origine Seraphicae Religionis Franciscanae* (Rome, 1587)

Gonçales da Costa, M., *Fontes inéditas portuguesas para a história de Irlanda* (Braga, 1981)

Hagan, John (ed.), 'Miscellanea Vaticano-Hibernia: Borghese collection, Vatican
Archives', in *Archiv. Hib.*, 2–4 (1913–15)

Harold, Francis, *Vita Fratris Lucae Waddingi* (repr. Dublin, 1931)

Historical Manuscripts Commission reports:
  Buccleuch Mss (London, 1897–1926)
  Downshire Mss (London, 1924–96)
  Egmont Mss (London, 1905–9)
  Franciscan Mss (Dublin, 1906)
  Salisbury Mss (London, 1883–1976)
  Tenth report, appendix v (London, 1885)

Hogan, Edmund, *Ibernia Ignatiana* (London, 1880)

Jennings, Brendan (ed.), 'Brussels MS. 3947: Donatus Moneyus, De Provincia Hiberniae
S. Francisci', in *An. Hib.*, 6 (1934), pp. 12–121

Jennings, Brendan (ed.), 'Brevis synopsis provinciae Hiberniae FF. Minorum', in *An.
Hib.*, 6 (1934), pp. 143–86

Jennings, Brendan (ed.), *Wadding Papers: 1614–1638* (Dublin, 1953)

Jennings, Brendan (ed.), *Wild Geese in Spanish Flanders, 1582–1700: Documents relating chiefly to Irish regiments, from the Archives Générales du Royaume, Bruxelles,
and other sources* (Dublin, 1964)

Jennings, Brendan (ed.), *Louvain Papers: 1606–1827* (Dublin, 1968)

Jones, Frederick, 'Correspondence of Father Ludovico Mansoni SJ, papal nuncio to
Ireland', *Archiv. Hib.*, 17 (1953), pp. 1–51

Liber Lovaniensis, c. 1629–1717, ed. Cathaldus Giblin (Dublin, 1956)

Lombard, Peter, *De regno Hiberniae, sanctorum insula, commentarius* (Lovanii, 1632;
Dublin, 1868)

Lynch, John, *De praesulibus Hiberniae [...]* vol. 2, Cashel and Tuam (Dublin, 1944)

Lynch, John, *Pii Antistitis Icon, or, the life of Francis Kirwan, bishop of Killala* (Saint-
Malo, 1669; Dublin, 1951)

Medina, Pedro de, *Libro de grandezas y cosas memorables en España* (Alcalá de Henares, 1548)

Memorials of affairs of state in the reigns of Q. Elizabeth and K. James I., collected (chiefly) from the original papers of the right honourable Sir Ralph Winwood, Kt. sometime one of the principal secretaries of state, ed. Edmund Sawyer (3 vols, London, 1725)

Moran, Patrick (ed.), *Spicilegium Ossoriense [...] being a collection of original letters and papers* (3 vols, Dublin, 1884)

Ó Cianáin, Tadhg, *The flight of the earls*, edited from the author's manuscript with translation and notes by Paul Walsh (Dublin, 1916)

Ó Cléirigh, Micheál, *Genealogiae regum et sanctorum Hibernia*, ed. Paul Walsh and Colm Ó Lochlainn (Maynooth, 1918)

Ó Cuív, Brian (ed.), 'Flaithrí Ó Maolchonaire's catechism of Christian doctrine', *Celtica*, 1 (1950), pp. 161–206

Olivares, Conde Duque de, *Memoriales y cartas (1621–27)*, ed. J. H. Elliott and José F. de la Peña (2 vols, Madrid, 1978–81)

Ó Maolchonaire, Flaithrí, *Desiderius: Sgáthán an Chrábhaidh* (Louvain, 1616; ed. with an Introduction by T. F. O'Rahilly, Dublin Institute for Advanced Studies, 1941)

Ó Maolchonaire, Flaithrí, *Tractatus de statu parvulorum sine baptismo decedentium: juxta sensum B. Augustini* (Lovanii: Henrici Hastenii, 1624)

Ó Maolchonaire, Flaithrí, *Perigrinus Jerichuntinus, hoc est, de natura humana feliciter instituta, infeliciter lapsa, miserabiliter vulnerata, misericorditer restaurata* (Paris, 1641)

Ó Muraíle, Nollaig (éag.), *Turas na dTaoiseach nUltach tar Sáile: from Ráth Maoláin to Rome – Tadhg Ó Cianáin's contemporary narrative of the journey into exile of the Ulster chieftains and their followers, 1607–8* (Rome, 2007)

O'Rahilly, Thomas, F. (ed.), 'Irish poets, historians, and judges in English documents, 1538–1615' in *R.I.A. Proc.* (C.), 36 (1921–24), pp. 86–163

Ó Raithbheartaigh, Toirdhealbhach, *Genealogical Tracts A* (Dublin, 1932), pp. 1–106

Orcibal, Jean (ed.), *Correspondance de Jansénius* (Louvain and Paris, 1947)

Orrego, Santiago (ed.), *Pedro de Ledesma: La perfección del acto de ser creado* (Pamplona 2001)

O'Sullivan Beare, Philip, *Historiae Catholicae Iberniae compendium* (Lisbon, 1621; Dublin 1850)

Pender, Seamus (ed.), 'The O'Clery Book of Genealogies', *An. Hib.*, 18 (1951), pp. 1–194

Reusens, E. H. (ed.), *Documents relatifs à servir à l'histoire de l'ancienne université de Louvain, 1425–1797* (5 vols, 1881–1903; repr. Brussels, 1999)

Ribadeneira, Pedro de, *Historia ecclesiastica del scisma del reyno de Inglaterra* (2 vols, Madrid, 1588, Alcalá, 1593)

Rich, Barnaby, 'Remembrances of the state of Ireland, 1612', ed. C. Litton Falkiner, in *Proc. RIA*, vol. 26, section C (1907), pp. 125–42

Salazar, Pedro, *Crónica e historia de la provincia de Castilla* (Madrid, 1612)

Scott, Thomas, *Certaine reasons and arguments of policie, why the king of England should hereafter enter into warre with the Spaniard* (London, 1624)

Simmington, Robert (ed.), *Bks survey & Dist., Roscommon* (Dublin, 1944)

Spenser, Edmund, *A Veue of The Present State of Ireland*, ed. Alexander Grosart (London, 1894)

Stafford, Thomas, *Pacata Hibernica: Ireland appeased and reduced, or a historie of the late warres of Ireland [...]* (London, 1633; repr. 2 vols, 1896)

Velde, Jan Frans van de, *Synopsis Monumentorum Collectionis proxime edendae conciliorum omnium Archiepiscopatus Mechliniensis [...] notis*, Tomus I–Tomus III (Gandavi, 1821)

Vita Tripartita, ed. Whitley Stokes, Rolls Ser. 8vo (London, 1887)

Wadding, Luke, *Presbeia sive legatio Philippi III et IV Catholicorum regum hispaniarum ad Sanctissimos Paulum P. P. V, Gregorium XV et Urbanum VIII pro define controversia Conceptionis B. Virginis Mariae* (Louvain, 1624)

Wadding, Luke, *Scriptores Ordinis Minorum* (repr. Rome, 1906)

Walsh, Paul (ed.), *Gleanings from Irish manuscripts* (Dublin, 1918)

Ware, James, *The history of the writers of Ireland in two books*, tr. and rev. by Walter Harris (2 vols, Dublin, 1746)

Waterworth, James (ed. and trans.), *The canons and decrees of the sacred and œcumenical Council of Trent* (London, 1848)

White, Stephen, *Apologia pro Hibernia adversus Cambri Calumnias: sive fabularum et famosorum libellorum Silvestri Giraldi Cambrensis* (repr. Dublin, 1849)

Zubiaur, Pedro de, *Epistolario del General Zubiaur: 1568–1605*, ed. Conde de Polentinos (Madrid, 1946)

SECONDARY SOURCES

Albi de la Cuesta, Julio, *De Pavía a Rocroi. Los tercios de infantería española en los siglos XVI y XVII* (Madrid, 1999)

Allen, Paul, *Philip III and the Pax Hispanica, 1598–1621: The failure of grand strategy* (New Haven, 2000)

Alvarez Villar, Julián, *La Universidad de Salamanca: arte y tradición* (Salamanca, 1972)

Anderson, Benedict, *Imagined communities: reflections on the origin and spread of nationalism* (London, 1983; repr. 1990)

Andrews, K. R., 'Caribbean rivalry and the Anglo-Spanish treaty of 1604', *History*, 59 (1974), pp. 1–17

Andrews, K. R., *Trade, plunder and settlement* (Cambridge, 1991)

Andrews, K. R., Nicholas Canny and P. E. H. Hair (eds), *The westward enterprise: English activities in Ireland, the Atlantic and America 1480–1650* (Detroit, 1979)

Bagwell, Richard, *Ireland under the Stuarts* (3 vols, London, 1909–16)

Bakvis, Herman, *Catholic power in the Netherlands* (Montréal, 1981)

Balic, Charles, 'Wadding the Scotist', in Franciscan Fathers (eds), *Father Luke Wadding: commemorative volume* (Dublin, 1957), pp. 463–507

Barry, John, 'Richard Stanihurst's *De Rebus in Hibernia Gestis*', *Renaissance Studies*, 18 (2004), pp. 1–18

Bartlett, Thomas and Keith Jeffrey (eds), *A military history of Ireland* (Cambridge, 1996)

Bécquer, Gustavo Adolfo, *Historia de los templos de España: Toledo* (repr. Toledo, 2005)

Bellenger, Dom Aidan et al. (eds), *Body and soul: hospitality through the ages on the road to Compostela* (London, 2001)

Bennassar, Bartolomé, *Valladolid au siècle d'or: une ville et sa campagne au XVIe siècle* (Paris, 1967)

Bergin, Osborn (ed.), *Irish Bardic Poetry* (Dublin, 1970)

Binchy, Daniel, 'An Irish ambassador at the Spanish court, 1569–74', *Studies*, 10–14 (1921–5)

Black, J. B., 'The reign of Elizabeth, 1558–1603', in G. N. Clark (ed.), *The Oxford history of England*, vol. 8 (Oxford, 1936)

Black, Jeremy, *A Military Revolution? Military change and European society 1550–1800* (London, 1991)

Black, Jeremy, *European warfare 1494–1660* (London, 2002)

Blom, J. C. H. and Emiel Lamberts (eds), *Geschiedenis van de Nederlanden* (Rijswijk, 1993)

Bonney, Richard, *The European dynastic States: 1494–1660* (Oxford, 1991)

Bossy, John, 'The Counter Reformation and the people of Catholic Ireland, 1596–1641', *Historical Studies* 8 (1971), pp. 155–69

Bottigheimer Karl, S., 'The failure of the Reformation in Ireland: *une question bien posée*', *Journal of Ecclesiastical History*, 36 (1985), pp. 196–207

Boute, Bruno, 'Academics in action. Scholarly interests and policies in the early Counter Reformation: the reform of the University of Louvain 1607–1617', *History of Universities*, 17 (2003), pp. 34–89

Bover i Font, August, 'Notes sobre les traduccions no castellanes de l'Spill de la vida religiosa', *Estudis de la llengua i literatura catalanes*, 3 (1981), pp. 129–38

Boyce, D. G., Robert Eccleshall and Vincent Geoghegan (eds), *Political thought in Ireland since the seventeenth century* (London, 1990)

Bradley, John, 'Sir Henry Sidney's bridge at Athlone, 1566–7', in Thomas Herron and Michael Potterton (eds), *Ireland and the Renaissance, c. 1540–1660* (Dublin, 2007), pp. 173–94

Bradshaw, Brendan, 'Robe and sword in the conquest of Ireland', in C. Cross, D. Loades and J. J. Scarisbrick (eds), *Law and government under the Tudors: essays presented to Sir Geoffrey Elton on his retirement* (Cambridge, 1988), pp. 139–62

Bradshaw, Brendan and Peter Roberts (eds), *British consciousness and identity: the making of Britain, 1533–1707* (Cambridge, 1998)

Brady, Ciarán, *The chief governors: the rise and fall of reform government in Tudor Ireland, 1536–1588* (Cambridge, 1994)

Brady, Ciarán 'The end of the O'Reilly lordship, 1584–1610', in David Edwards (ed.), *Regions and rulers in Ireland, 1100–1650* (Dublin, 2004), pp. 174–200

Brady, Ciarán and Raymond Gillespie (eds), *Natives and newcomers: the makings of Irish colonial society* (Dublin, 1986)

Brady, John, 'Father Christopher Cusack and the Irish college of Douai, 1594–1624', in Sylvester O'Brien (ed.), *Measgra Mhichíl Uí Chléirigh: miscellany of historical and linguistic studies in honour of Brother Michael Ó Cléirigh, chief of the Four Masters, 1643–1943* (Dublin, 1944), pp. 98–107

Brady, John, 'Some Irish scholars of the sixteenth century', *Studies*, 37 (1948), pp. 226–31

Braudel, Fernand, *The Mediterranean and the Mediterranean world in the age of Philip II* (2 vols, Berkeley, 1995)

Breatnach, Pádraig, *Téamaí taighde nua-Ghaeilge* (Maigh Nuad, 1997)

Breathnach, R. A., '*Desiderius* (Ó Maolchonaire) (O'Rahilly)', Léirmheas in *Éigse*, 4 (1945), pp. 72–7

Briggs, Robin, *Early-modern France: 1560–1715* (Oxford, 1998)

Brightwell, Peter, 'The Spanish system and the Twelve Years Truce', *English Historical Review*, 89 (1974), pp. 270–92

Brown, Alexander, *The Genesis of the United States* (New York, 1890)

Burke, Francis, *Loch Cé and its annals: north Roscommon and the diocese of Elphin in times of old* (Dublin, 1895)

Burke, Oliver, *The history of the Catholic archbishops of Tuam, from the foundation of the See* (Dublin, 1882)

Caball, Marc, 'Providence and exile in early seventeenth-century Ireland', *IHS*, 29 (1994), pp. 174–88

Cánovas del Castillo, Antonio, *Historia de la decadencia de España desde el advenimiento de Felipe III al trono, hasta la muerte de Carlos II* (Málaga, 1992)

Canny, Nicholas, 'Hugh O'Neill and the changing face of Gaelic Ulster', *Studia Hibernica*, 10 (1970), pp. 7–35

Canny, Nicholas, 'Why the Reformation failed in Ireland: *une question mal posée*', *Journal of Ecclesiastical History*, 30 (1979), pp. 423–50

Canny, Nicholas, 'The formation of the Irish mind: religion, politics, and Gaelic Irish literature, 1580–1750', *Past & Present*, 95 (1982), pp. 91–116

Canny, Nicholas and Anthony Pagden (eds), *Colonial identity in the Atlantic world, 1500–1800* (Princeton, 1987)

Canny, Nicholas, *Making Ireland British: 1580–1650* (Oxford, 2002)

Canny, Nicholas, 'Writing early-modern history: Ireland, Britain, and the wider world', *The Historical Journal*, 46 (2003), pp. 723–47

Carroll, Clare, 'Irish and Spanish cultural and political relations in the work of O'Sullivan Beare', in Hiram Morgan (ed.), *Political ideology in Ireland, 1541–1641* (Dublin, 1999), pp. 229–53

Carroll, Clare, *Circe's cup: cultural transformations in early modern Ireland* (Cork, 2001)

Carter, Charles, *The secret diplomacy of the Habsburgs, 1598–1625* (New York, 1964)

Carter, Charles (ed.), *From the Renaissance to the Counter Reformation: essays in honour of Garrett Mattingly* (London, 1966)

Castaño Rueda and Julio Ricardo, *Nuestra Señora del Rosario de Chiquinquirá, historia de una tradición* (Bogotá, 2005)

Castro y Castro, Manuel de, 'Wadding and the Iberian peninsula', in Franciscan Fathers (eds), *Father Luke Wadding: commemorative volume* (Dubli, 1957), PP. 119–70

Casway, Jerrold, 'Henry O'Neill and the formation of the Irish regiment in the Netherlands, 1605', *IHS* (1973), pp. 481–8

Casway, Jerrold, *Owen Roe O'Neill and the struggle for Catholic Ireland* (Philadelphia, 1984)

Casway, Jerrold, 'Gaelic Maccabeanism: the politics of reconciliation', in Jane H. Ohlmeyer (ed.), *Political thought in seventeenth century Ireland: kingdom or colony* (Cambridge, 2000), pp. 179–81

Casway, Jerrold, 'Heroines or victims? The women of the flight of the earls', *New Hibernia Review*, 7 (2003), pp. 69–74

Ceyssens, Lucian, 'Florence Conry, Hugh de Burgo, Luke Wadding, and Jansenism', in Franciscan Fathers (eds), *Father Luke Wadding: commemorative volume* (Dublin, 1957), pp. 295–404

Chambers, Liam, 'A displaced intelligentsia: aspects of Irish Catholic thought in *ancien régime* France', in Thomas O'Connor (ed.), *The Irish in Europe, 1580–1815* (Dublin, 2001), pp. 157–74

Chambers, Liam, *Michael Moore c.1639–1726: provost of Trinity, rector of Paris* (Dublin, 2005)

Chambers, Liam, 'The library of an Irish Catholic *émigré*: Michael Moore's *bibliothèque*', *Archiv. Hib.*, 58 (2004), pp. 210–42

Clark, Ruth, *Strangers and sojourners at Port Royal: being an account of the connections between the British Isles and the Jansenists of France and Holland* (Cambridge, 1932)

Clarke, Aidan, 'Colonial identity in early seventeenth-century Ireland', in T. W. Moody (ed.), *Nationality and the pursuit of national independence* (Belfast, 1978), pp. 57–71

Cleary, Gregory, *Father Luke Wadding and Saint Isidore's College, Rome* (Rome, 1925)

Comerford, R. V., Mary Cullen, Jacqueline R. Hill and Colm Lennon, *Religion, conflict and co-existence in Ireland: essays presented to Monsignor Patrick J. Corish* (Dublin, 1989)

Conlan, Patrick, *St Anthony's College of the Irish Franciscans, Louvain* (Dublin, 1978)

Connellan, M. J., 'Ballymulconry and the Mulconrys', *IER*, 90 (1958), pp. 322–30

Connors, T. G., 'Surviving the Reformation in Ireland (1534–80): Christopher Bodkin, archbishop of Tuam, and Roland Burke, bishop of Clonfert', *Sixteenth Century Journal*, 32 (2001), pp. 335–55

Coppens, Christian, '"Steadfast I hasten": the Louvain printer Henrick van Ha(e)stens', *Quaerendo*, 17 (1987), pp. 185–204

Corcoran, R. P., *Studies in the history of classical teaching, Irish and continental: 1500–1700* (Dublin, 1911)

Corcoran, R. P., 'The Irish Franciscans at Rome and Louvain in the seventeenth century', in Gregory Cleary (ed.), *Ireland's tribute to Saint Francis: seven lectures on Franciscan subjects* (Dublin, 1928), pp. 1–10

Corish, Patrick, *The Catholic community in the seventeenth and eighteenth centuries* (Dublin, 1981)

Corish, Patrick, *The Irish Catholic experience: a historical survey* (Dublin, 1985)

Cotter, Francis, *The friars minor in Ireland from their arrival to 1400* (New York, 1994)

Cregan, Donal F., 'The social and cultural background of a Counter Reformation episcopate, 1618–1680', in Art Cosgrove and Donal McCartney (eds), *Studies in Irish history presented to R. Dudley Edwards* (Naas, 1979)

Cubero Garrote, José (ed.), *Valladolid: todo los pueblos de la provincia* (Valladolid, 2006)

Cunningham, Bernadette, 'The composition of Connacht in the lordships of Clanricard and Thomond, 1577–1641', *IHS*, 24 (1984), pp. 1–14

Cunningham, Bernadette, 'Seventeenth century interpretation of the past: the case of Geoffrey Keating', *IHS*, 25 (1986), pp. 116–28

Cunningham, Bernadette, 'Native culture and political change', in Raymond Gillespie and Ciarán Brady (eds), *Natives and newcomers: the makings of Irish colonial society, 1534–1641* (Dublin, 1986), pp. 148–70

Cunningham, Bernadette, 'The culture and ideology of Irish Franciscan historians at Louvain', in Ciarán Brady and Raymond Gillespie (eds), *Ideology and the historians* (Dublin, 1991), pp. 11–30

Dandelet, Thomas, *Spanish Rome: 1500–1700* (New Haven, 2001)

Daniel-Rops, Henri, *The Catholic Reformation* (London, 1963)

Davies, Godfrey, 'The early Stuarts, 1603–1660', in G. N. Clark (ed.), *The Oxford history of England*, vol. 8 (Oxford, 1937)

Davies, R. T., *The golden century of Spain, 1501–1621* (London, 1939)

Davies, R. T., *Spain in decline 1621–1700* (London, 1957)

de Castro y Castro, Manuel, 'Wadding and the Iberian peninsula', in Franciscan Fathers (eds), *Father Luke Wadding: commemorative volume* (Dublin, 1957), pp. 119–70

Delumeau, Jean, *Catholicisme entre Luther et Voltaire* (Paris, 1971)

de Tapia Ozcariz, Enrique, *Eugenio O'Neill: caudillo de la independencia de Irlanda* (Madrid, 1969)

de Vinck, José (ed. and trans.), *St Bonaventure: Apologia Pauperum* (Paris, 1966)

Devlin, Kieran, 'The beatified martyrs of Ireland', *Ir. Theol. Quart.*, 65 (2000), pp. 266–80

Dillon, Myles (ed.), 'Laud Misc. 610', in *Celtica*, 5 (1960), pp. 64–76

Dillon, Myles (ed.), 'The Inauguration of O'Conor', *Med. studies presented to A. Gwynn* (Dublin, 1961), pp. 186–202

Domínguez Ortiz, Antonio, *Política y hacienda de Felipe IV* (Madrid, 1960)

Domínguez Ortiz, Antonio, *The golden age of Spain, 1516–1659* (London, 1971)

Downey, Declan, 'The Irish contribution to Counter Reformation theology in continental Europe', in Brendan Bradshaw and Daire Keogh (eds), *Christianity in Ireland: revisiting the story* (Dublin, 2002), pp. 96–108

Duffy, Patrick, 'The territorial organisation of Gaelic landownership and its transformation in County Monaghan, 1591–1640', *Ir. Geography*, 14 (1981), pp. 1–26

Duffy, Patrick, David Edwards and Katherine Fitzpatrick (eds), *Gaelic Ireland c. 1250–1650: land, lordship and settlement* (Dublin, 2001)

Echevarría Baciagalupe, Miguel Ángel, *La diplomacia secreta en Flandes, 1598–1643* (Bilbao, 1984)

Echevarría Baciagalupe, Miguel Ángel, *Flandes y la Monarquía Hispánica, 1500–1713* (Madrid, 1998)

Edwards, R. Dudley, 'Church and state in the Ireland of Micheál Ó Cléirigh, 1626–41', in Sylvester O'Brien (ed.), *Measgra i gCuimhne Mhíchíl Uí Chléirigh: miscellany of historical and linguistic studies in honour of Brother Micheál Ó Cléirigh, chief of the Four Masters* (Dublin, 1944), pp. 1–20

Eisenstein, Elizabeth, *The printing press as an agent of change: communications and transformations in early-modern Europe* (2 vols, Cambridge, 1979)

Elliott, John H., 'Self-perception and decline in early seventeenth-century Spain', *Past & Present*, 74 (1977), pp. 41–61

Elliott, John H., 'Foreign policy and domestic crisis: Spain, 1598–1659', in idem (ed.), *Spain and its world, 1500–1700* (New Haven, 1989), pp. 114–36

Elliott, John H., *Imperial Spain, 1469–1716* (repr. London, 2002)

Elliott, John H., *The revolt of the Catalans: a study in the decline of Spain, 1598–1640* (repr. Cambridge, 2001)

Elliott, John H., *El conde duque de Olivares: el político en una epoca de decadencia* (Barcelona, 2004)

Ellis, Steven, *Tudor Ireland: crown, community and the conflict of cultures, 1470–1603* (London, 1985)

Espino López, Antonio, *Guerra y cultura en la época moderna* (Madrid, 2001)

Esteban Estríngana, Alicia, *Guerra y finanzas en los Países Bajos Católicos de Farnesio a Spínola: 1592–1630* (Madrid, 2002)

Esteban Estríngana, Alicia, *Madrid y Bruselas. Relaciones de gobierno en la etapa postarchiducal: 1621–1634* (Leuven, 2005)

Falkiner, C. Litton, 'His Majesty's Castle of Dublin', in idem (ed.), *Illustrations of Irish history and topography, mainly of the seventeenth century* (London, 1904)

Fennessy, Ignatius, 'Guardians and staff of St Anthony's college', *Coll. Hib.*, 42 (2000), pp. 215–41

Fennessy, Ignatius (ed.), 'Two letters from Boethius (Augustine) MacEgan, OFM, on the death of Archbishop Florence Conry, OFM, 1629', *Collectanea Hibernica*, 43 (2001), pp. 7–12

Fernández Álvarez, Manuel and Luis Enrique Rodríguez-San Pedro, *The University of Salamanca: eight centuries of scholarship* (Salamanca, 1992)

Fernández Armesto, Felipe, 'The improbable empire', in Raymond Carr (ed.), *Spain: a history* (Oxford, 2000), pp. 116–51

Fernández del Hoyo, María Antonia, *Patrimonio perdido: Conventos desparecidos de Valladolid* (Valladolid, 1998)

Feros, Antonio, *El duque de Lerma. Realeza y privanza en la España de Felipe III* (Madrid, 2002)

Fitzgerald, Brendan, *Seventeenth-century Ireland: the war of religions* (Dublin, 1995)

Fletcher, George (ed.), *Connaught* (Cambridge, 1922)

Flynn, Thomas, *The Irish Dominicans 1536–1641* (Dublin, 1993)

Ford, Alan, *The Protestant Reformation in Ireland, 1590–1641* (Dublin, 1995)

Ford, Alan and John McCafferty (eds), *The origins of sectarianism in early-modern Ireland* (Cambridge, 2005)

Foster, R. F., *Modern Ireland: 1600–1972* (London, 1988)

Fraser, John, Paul Grosjean and J. G. O'Keefe (eds), *Irish Texts*, 4 (London, 1934)

Frijhoff, Willem and Marijke Spies, *Dutch culture in a European perspective: hard-won unity* (Assen, 2004)

García García, Bernardo, 'El confesor Fray Luis Aliaga y la consciencia del rey', in Flavio Rurale (ed.), *I religiosi a corte: teologia, politica e diplomazia in Antico Regime* (1995), pp. 159–94

García García, Bernardo, *La Pax Hispanica. Política exterior del duque de Lerma: 1598–1621* (Leuven, 1996)

García García, Bernardo (ed.), *El final de la guerra de Flandes (1621–1648). 350 aniversario de la paz de Münster* (Madrid, 1998)

García Guerra, Elena María, 'Las acuñaciones de moneda de vellón durante el reinado de Felipe III', *Banco de España: estudios de historia económica*, 38 (1999) pp. 1–155

García Hernán, Enrique, *Francisco de Borja, grande de España* (Valencia, 1994)

García Hernán, Enrique, *Irlanda y el rey prudente* (2 vols, Madrid, 2000)

García Hernán, Enrique, Óscar Recio Morales et al. (eds), *Irlanda y la monarquía hispánica:*

Kinsale 1601–2001. Guerra, política, exilio y religion (Madrid, 2002)

García Hernán, Enrique, 'Obispos irlandeses y la Monarquía hispánica durante el siglo XVI', in Alvar, Contreras and Ruíz (eds), *Política y cultura en la época moderna: cambios dinásticos, milenarismos, mesianismos y utopías* (Madrid, 2004)

García Hernán, Enrique, 'Capellanes Militares y Reforma Católica', in idem and David Maffi (eds), *Guerra y sociedad en la Monarquía hispánica: política, estrategia y cultura en la Europa moderna* (2 vols, Madrid, 2006), vol. 2, *Ejército, economía, sociedad y cultura*, pp. 709–42

García Hernán, Enrique and Óscar Recio Morales (eds), *Extranjeros en el ejército. Militares irlandeses en la sociedad española, 1580–1818* (Madrid, 2007)

García Hernán, Enrique, *Ireland and Spain in the reign of Phillip II* (Dublin, 2009)

García Oro, José, *Don Diego Sarmiento de Acuña, Conde de Gondomar y embajador de España (1567–1626): estudio biográfico* (Xunta de Galicia, 1997)

Gardiner, David, '"These are not the thinges men live by now a days": Sir John Harington's visit to the O'Neill, 1599', *Cahiers Élisabéthains*, 55 (1999), pp. 1–17

Geyl, Pieter, *The revolt of the Netherlands, 1555–1609* (London, 1962)

Giblin, Cathaldus, 'Aspects of Franciscan life in Ireland in the seventeenth century', *The Franciscan College Annual* (1948), pp. 67–72

Giblin, Cathaldus, '*Processus Datariae* and the appointments of Irish bishops in the seventeenth century', in Franciscan Fathers (eds), *Father Luke Wadding: commemorative volume* (Dublin, 1957), pp. 508–616

Giblin, Cathaldus (ed.), *The Irish Franciscan mission to Scotland: 1619–1646* (Dublin, 1964)

Giblin, Cathaldus, 'Francis MacDonnell OFM, son of the first earl of Antrim (d. 1636)', *Seanchas Ard Mhacha*, 8 (1975–6), pp. 44–54

Giblin, Cathaldus, 'The contribution of Irish Franciscans on the continent in the seventeenth century', in Michael Maher (ed.), *Irish spirituality* (Dublin, 1981), pp. 88–104

Giblin, Cathaldus, 'Hugh McCaghwell OFM: aspects of his life', in Benignus Millett and Anthony Lynch (eds), *Dún Mhuire, Killiney: 1945–95* (Dublin, 1995), pp. 63–94

Gillespie, Raymond, 'Destabilizing Ulster, 1641–2', in Brian Mac Cuarta (ed.), *Ulster 1641: aspects of the rising* (Belfast, 1993), pp. 107–21 Giménez Martín, Juan, *Tercios de Flandes* (Madrid, 1999)

González Castrillo, Ricardo, *El arte militar en la España del siglo XVI* (Madrid, 2000)

Hammerstein, Helga, 'Aspects of the continental education of Irish students in the reign of Elizabeth', *Historical Studies*, 8 (1971), pp. 137–53

Hardiman, James, *History of the town and county of Galway* (London, 1820)

Hardiman, James, *Irish minstrelsy: bardic remains of Ireland* (2 vols, London, 1831)

Harline, Craig and Eddy Put, *A bishop's tale: Mathias Hovius among his flock in seventeenth-century Flanders* (New Haven, 2000)

Havely, Nicholas, *Dante and the Franciscans: poverty and the papacy in the 'Commedia'* (Cambridge, 2004)

Hayes-McCoy, G. A., 'The Renaissance and the Irish wars', *Iris Hibernia*, 3 (1957), pp. 43–51

Hayes-McCoy, G. A., *Irish battles* (Dublin, 1980)

Hazard, Benjamin, '"A new company of crusaders like that of St John Capistran" – interaction between Irish military units and Franciscan chaplains: 1579–1654', in

Óscar Recio Morales y Enrique García Hernán (eds), *La nación irlandesa en el ejército y la sociedad española, 1580–1818* (Madrid, 2007), pp. 181–97

Hazard, Benjamin, 'Gaelic political scripture: Uí Mhaoil Chonaire scribes and the *Book of Mac Murchadha Caomhánach*', *Proceedings of the Harvard Celtic Colloquium, 2003* (Harvard, 2009), pp. 149–64

Hazard, Paul, *La Crise de la conscience européene* (2 vols. Paris, 1935)

Heaney, C., *The theology of Florence Conry OFM* (Drogheda, 1935)

Henry, Gráinne, *The Irish military community in Spanish Flanders: 1586–1621* (Dublin, 1992)

Hernández Martín, Ramón, 'El teólogo Pedro de Herrera en los claustros salmantinos, 1593–1598', *Revista Española de Teología*, 34 (1974), pp. 373–92

Hoeven, Marco van der (ed.), *Exercise of arms: warfare in the Netherlands, 1568–1648* (Leiden, 1997)

Hogan, Edmund, *Distinguished Irishmen of the sixteenth century* (London, 1894)

Hogan, Edmund, *Onomasticon Goedelicum: locorum et tribuum Hiberniae et Scotiae* (repr. Dublin, 2000)

Hyde, Douglas, *A literary history of Ireland: from earliest times to the present day* (New York, 1901)

Israel, Jonathan Irvine, *Empires and entrepots: the Dutch, the Spanish monarchy and the Jews, 1585–1713* (London, 1990)

Israel, Jonathan Irvine, *Conflicts of empires: Spain, the Low Countries and the struggle for world supremacy, 1585–1713* (London, 1997)

Israel, Jonathan Irvine, *The Dutch Republic, its rise, greatness and fall: 1477–1806* (Oxford, 1998)

Jackson, Brian, 'Sectarianism: division and dissent in Irish Catholicism', in Alan Ford and John McCafferty (eds), *The origins of sectarianism in early-modern Ireland* (Cambridge, 2005), pp. 203–15

Jedin, Hubert, *The Council of Trent, 1545–63* (2 vols, Edinburgh, 1961)

Jefferies, Henry, 'Erenaghs in pre-plantation Ulster: an early seventeenth-century account', *Archiv. Hib.*, 53 (1999), pp. 16–19

Jennings, Brendan (ed.), *Michael Ó Cléirigh, chief of the Four Masters* (Dublin, 1936)

Jennings, Brendan, 'The career of Hugh, son of Rory O'Donnell, earl of Tirconnel, in the Low Countries, 1607–1642', *Studies*, 30 (1941), pp. 219–34

Jennings, Brendan, 'Irish students in the university of Louvain', in Sylvester O'Brien (ed.), *Measgra i gcuimhne Mhichíl Uí Chléirigh* (Dublin, 1944) pp. 74–97

Jennings, Brendan, 'Florence Conry, archbishop of Tuam: his death and the transfer of his remains', *JGHAS*, 3–4 (1949), pp. 83–92

Jensen, Delamar, *Diplomacy and dogmatism: Bernardino de Mendoza and the French Catholic League* (Harvard, 1964)

Jones, Frederick, 'James Blake and a projected Spanish invasion of Galway in 1602', *JGAHS*, 24 (1950–1951) pp. 1–18

Jones, Frederick, 'The Counter Reformation', in Patrick Corish (ed.), *A history of Irish Catholicism*, 3, 2 (Dublin, 1967)

Jong, Michiel de, *'Staat van oorlog': wapenbedrijf en militaire hervorming in de Republiek der Verenigde Nederlanden, 1585–1621* (Hilversum, 2005)

Kagan, Richard, *Students and society in early modern Spain* (Baltimore, 1974)

Kagan, Richard (ed.), *Spain, Europe and the Atlantic world: essays in honour of John H. Elliott* (Cambridge, 1995)

Kamen, Henry, *The Spanish inquisition: a historical revision* (New Haven, 1997)

Kamen, Henry, 'Vicissitudes of a world power, 1500–1700', in Raymond Carr (ed.), *Spain: a history* (Oxford, 2000), pp. 152–72

Kearney, Hugh, 'Ecclesiastical politics and the Counter Reformation in Ireland: 1618–1648', *Journal of Ecclesiastical History*, 11 (1960), pp. 202–12

Kearney, Hugh, 'The Irish parliament in the early seventeenth century', in Brian Farrell (ed.), *The Irish parliamentary tradition* (Dublin, 1973), pp. 88–101

Kelly, Fergus, *Early Irish Farming* (Dublin, 1998)

Kerney Walsh, Micheline, *The O'Neills in Spain* (Dublin, 1957)

Kerney Walsh, Micheline, *Destruction by peace* (Monaghan, 1986)

Kerney Walsh, Micheline, 'O'Sullivan Beare in Spain: some unpublished documents', *Archiv. Hib.*, 45 (1990), pp. 46–63

Kerney Walsh, Micheline, 'The Irish College of Madrid', *Seanchas Ard Mhacha*, 15 (1993), pp. 39–50

Kerney Walsh, Micheline, *An exile of Ireland: Hugh O'Neill* (Dublin, 1996)

Kesselring, K. J., *Mercy and authority in the Tudor state* (Cambridge, 2003)

Kléber Monod, Paul, *The power of kings: monarchy and religion in Europe, 1589–1715* (New Haven, 1999)

Knott, Eleanor, *Irish classical poetry* (Dublin, 1960)

Knox, Hubert, *Notes on the early history of the dioceses of Tuam, Killala and Achonry* (Dublin, 1904)

Königsberger, H. G., *The Hapsburgs and Europe: 1516–1660* (Ithaca, 1971)

Lamberts, Emile and Jan Roegiers (eds), *Leuven University, 1425–1985* (Leuven, 1990)

Lefèvre, Joseph, *Le ministère espagnol de l'Archiduc Albert, 1598–1621* (Antwerp, 1925)

Lennon, Colm, *Richard Stanihurst the Dubliner* (Dublin, 1981)

Lennon, Colm, *Sixteenth-century Ireland: the incomplete conquest* (Dublin, 1994)

Lines, David A., 'Moral philosophy in the universities of medieval and renaissance Europe', *History of Universities*, 20 (2005) pp. 38–77

Loomie, Albert, *English polemics at the Spanish court* (New York, 1993)

Loomie, Albert, 'Spanish secret diplomacy at the court of James I', *Sixteenth-Century Journal*, 27 (1994), pp. 230–44

Loomie, Albert, *Spain and the early Stuarts, 1585–1655* (Brookfield, 1996)

Lozano Navarro, Julián José, *La Compañía de Jesús y el poder en la España de los Austrias* (Madrid, 2005)

Lynch, John, *The Hispanic world in crisis and change* (Oxford, 1994)

Mac Cana, Proinsias, 'The rise of the later schools of *filidheacht*', *Ériu*, 25 (1984), pp. 126–46

Mac Craith, Mícheál, 'The political and religious thought of Florence Conry and Hugh McCaughwell', in Alan Ford and John McCafferty (eds), *The origins of sectarianism in early-modern Ireland* (Cambridge, 2005), pp. 183–202

Mac Cuarta, Brian, 'Conchubhar Mac Bruaideadha and Sir Matthew De Renzy', *Éigse*, 27 (1993), pp. 122–6

Mac Cuarta, Brian, 'The plantation of Leitrim, 1620–41', *IHS*, 32 (2001), pp. 297–320

Mac Cuarta, Brian, *Catholic revival in the north of Ireland, 1603–41* (Dublin, 2007)

Mac Culloch, Diarmaid, *Reformation: Europe's house divided, 1490–1700* (London, 2003)

MacCurtain, Margaret, *Tudor and Stuart Ireland* (Dublin, 1972)

MacDonnell, Hector, 'Surviving Kinsale Scottish-style – the MacDonnells of Antrim', in Hiram Morgan (ed.), *The Battle of Kinsale* (Dublin, 2004), pp. 265–77

MacDonnell, Hector, 'Responses of the MacDonnell clan to change in early seventeenth-century Ulster', in Thomas O'Connor and Mary Ann Lyons (eds), *Irish migrants in Europe after Kinsale, 1602–1820* (Dublin, 2003), pp. 64–87

Mac Niocaill, Gearóid, *The medieval Irish annals* (Dublin, 1975)

Marrou, Henri, *St Augustin et l'augustinisme* (Paris, 1957)

Martin, F. X., *Friar Nugent: an agent of the Counter Reformation, 1569–1635* (Rome, 1962)

Martin, F. X., 'Ireland, the Renaissance and Counter Reformation', *Topic*, 13 (1967), pp. 10–16

Martin, F. X., 'Confusion abounding: Bernard O'Higgin, bishop of Elphin, 1542–1561', in Art Cosgrove and Donal McCartney (eds), *Studies in Irish History presented to R. Dudley Edwards* (Dublin, 1979), pp. 38–84

Martín Melquiades, Andrés (ed.), *Historia de la teología española* (Madrid, 1983)

Martínez Millán, José, *La Monarquía de Felipe III* (4 vols, Madrid, 2008)

Mattimoe, Cyril, *North Roscommon: its people and past* (Boyle, 1992)

Mattingly, Garrett, *Renaissance diplomacy* (London, 1955)

McAdoo, H. R., 'Three poems by Peadar Ó Maolchonaire', *Éigse*, 1 (1939), pp. 160–6

McBride, Patrick, 'Some unpublished letters of Mateo de Oviedo, archbishop of Dublin', *Repertorium Novum*, 1 (1955–6)

McCavitt, John, 'The flight of the earls', *IHS*, 29 (1994), pp. 154–73

McCoog, Thomas, *The Society of Jesus in Ireland, Scotland and England, 1541–1588* (Leiden, 1996)

McCoog, Thomas, 'Jesuit nuncios to Tudor Ireland', in Enrique García Hernán et al. (eds), *Irlanda y la monarquía hispánica* (Madrid, 2002), pp. 23–38

McCotter, Paul, *Medieval Ireland: territorial, political and economic divisions* (Dublin, 2008)

McGettigan, Darren, *Red Hugh O'Donnell and the Nine Years War* (Dublin, 2005)

McGurk, John, *The Elizabethan conquest of Ireland* (Manchester, 1997)

McGurk, John, 'The Kinsale campaign: siege, battle and rout', *Seanchas Ard Mhacha*, 19 (2002), pp. 59–65

McKenna, Lambert (ed.), *Iomarbhágh na bhFileadh: the Contention of the Bards* (2 vols, Dublin, 1918–20)

Meehan, Charles, *The rise and fall of the Irish Franciscan monasteries, and memoirs of the Irish hierarchy in the seventeenth century* (Dublin, 1870)

Meehan, Charles, *The fate and fortunes of Hugh O'Neill, earl of Tyrone, and Rory O'Donel, earl of Tyrconnell* (Dublin, 1886)

Merino Peral, Esther, *El arte militar en la época: los tratados de 're militari' en el Renacimiento, 1536–1671. Aspectos de un arte español* (Madrid, 2002)

Meseguer Fernández, Juan, 'La real junta de la Inmaculada Concepción', *Archivo Ibero–americano*, 15 (1955), pp. 621–866

Millett, Benignus, *The Irish Franciscans: 1651–1665* (Rome, 1964)

Millett, Benignus and Anthony Lynch (eds), *Dún Mhuire, Killiney, 1945–95: leann agus seanchas* (Dublin, 1995)

Moody T. W., Martin F. X. and Byrne F. J. (eds), *A New History of Ireland*, vol. 3 (Oxford, 1976)

Mooney, Canice, 'Irish Franciscan libraries of the past', *IER*, 60 (1942), pp. 214–28

Mooney, Canice, 'The Irish sword and the Franciscan cowl', *The Irish Sword*, 1 (1949), pp. 80–8

Mooney, Canice, *Irish Franciscan relations with France, 1224–1850* (Dublin, 1951)

Mooney, Canice, *Devotional writings of the Irish Franciscans: 1224–1950* (Dublin, 1952)

Mooney, Canice, 'The death of Red Hugh O'Donnell', *IER*, 81 (1954), pp. 328–45

Mooney, Canice, 'The letters of Luke Wadding', *IER*, 88 (1957), pp. 396–410

Mooney, Canice, 'Father John Colgan OFM: his work and times and literary milieu', in Terence O'Donnell (ed.), *Father John Colgan OFM, 1592–1658: essays in commemoration of the third centenary of his death* (Dublin, 1959), pp. 7–40

Mooney, Canice, 'Scríbhneoirí Gaeilge an Seachtú hAois Déag', *Studia Hibernica*, 2 (1962), pp. 182–208

Mooney, Canice, 'Elphin', *Dictionnaire d'histoire et de geographie ecclésiastiques*, 15 (1963), pp. 269–92

Mooney, Canice, 'The Franciscans in Waterford', *JCHAS*, 69 (1964), pp. 73–93

Mooney, Canice, 'The first impact of the Reformation', in Patrick Corish (ed.), *A history of Irish Catholicism* (Dublin, 1967), vol. 3, part 1

Mooney, Canice, 'St Anthony's College, Louvain', *Donegal Annual*, 8 (1969), pp. 18–48

Morgan, Hiram, *James Archer: Kilkenny Jesuit* (Dublin, 1979)

Morgan, Hiram, 'Extradition and treason-trial of a Gaelic lord: the case of Brian O'Rourke', *Irish Jurist*, 22 (1987), pp. 285–301

Morgan, Hiram, 'Writing up early-modern Ireland', *The Historical Journal*, 31 (1988), pp. 701–11

Morgan, Hiram, 'The end of Gaelic Ulster: a thematic interpretation of events between 1534 and 1610', *IHS*, 26 (1989), pp. 8–32

Morgan, Hiram, 'Hugh O'Neill and the Nine Years War in Tudor Ireland', *The Historical Journal*, 36 (1993), pp. 21–37

Morgan, Hiram, *Tyrone's Rebellion: The outbreak of the Nine Years War in Tudor Ireland* (Woodbridge, 1993)

Morgan, Hiram, 'A booke of questions and answers concerning the wars or rebellions of the kingdome of Ireland', *An. Hib.*, 36 (1994), pp. 93–156

Morgan, Hiram, 'Faith and fatherland or queen and country? an unpublished exchange between O'Neill and the state at the height of the Nine Years War', *Dúiche Néill*, 9 (1994), pp. 9–65

Morgan, Hiram, 'The 1597 ceasefire documents', *Dúiche Néill*, 11 (1997), pp. 8–33

Morgan, Hiram (ed.), *Political ideology in Ireland: 1541–1641* (Dublin, 1998)

Morgan, Hiram, 'Beyond Spenser? A historiographical introduction to the study of political ideas in early-modern Ireland', in idem (ed.), *Political ideology in Ireland, 1541–1641* (Dublin, 1999), pp. 9–21

Morgan, Hiram, '"Over-mighty officers": the early-modern Irish lord deputyship', *History Ireland*, 7 (1999), pp. 17–21

Morgan, Hiram (ed.), 'Information, media and power through the ages', *Historical Studies*, 22 (Dublin, 2001)

Morgan, Hiram, 'Spanish armadas and Ireland', in Luc François and Ann Katherine Isaacs (eds), *The sea in European history* (Pisa, 2001), pp. 219–28

Morgan, Hiram, 'The real Red Hugh', in Pádraig Ó Riain (ed.), *Beatha Aodha Ruaidh: the life of Red Hugh O'Donnell: historical and literary contexts* (London, 2002), pp. 1–35

Morgan, Hiram, 'Calendars in conflict: dating the battle of Kinsale', *History Ireland*, 10 (2002), pp. 16–20

Morgan, Hiram (ed.), *The Battle of Kinsale* (Wicklow, 2004)

Morgan, Hiram, '"Never any realm worse governed": Queen Elizabeth and Ireland', *Transactions of the Royal Historical Society*, 6th ser., 14 (2004), pp. 295–308

Morrissey, Thomas, 'The Irish student diaspora in the sixteenth century and the early years of the Irish college at Salamanca', *Recusant History*, 14 (1978) pp. 242–60

Motley, John, *History of the United Netherlands from the death of William 'the Silent' to the Twelve Years Truce – 1609* (4 vols, New York, 1867)

Murray, A. E., *A history of the commercial and financial relations* (London, 1907)

Neary, J., 'Florence Conry, archbishop of Tuam: 1608–1629', in *JGHAS*, 7 (1912), pp. 193–204

Netzloff, Mark, 'Forgetting the Ulster plantation: John Speed's *The theatre of the empire of Great Britain* (1611) and the colonial archive', *Journal of Medieval and Early-Modern Studies*, 31 (2001), pp. 313–48

Nicholas, David, *The transformation of Europe: 1300–1600* (London, 1999)

Nicholls, K. W. (ed.), 'Some documents on Irish law and custom in the sixteenth century', *An. Hib.*, 26 (1970), pp. 105–29

Nicholls, K. W. (ed.), 'Visitations of the dioceses of Clonfert, Tuam and Kilmacduagh, c. 1565–7', *An. Hib.*, 26 (1970), pp. 144–58

Nicholls, K. W. 'Rectory, vicarage, and parish in the western Irish dioceses', *Jn. Royal Soc. Antiq. Ire.*, 101 (1971), pp. 53–84

Nicholls, K. W., *Gaelic and gaelicised Ireland* (Dublin, 1972; repr. 2003)

Nicholls, K. W., 'A list of the monasteries in Connacht, 1577', *JGHAS*, 33 (1972–3), pp. 28–43

Nicholls, K. W., 'Some patrician sites of eastern Connacht', *Dinnseanchas*, 5 (1973), pp. 114–18

Nicholls, K. W., 'The Irish genealogies: their value and defects', *Irish Genealogist*, 5 (1974–9), pp. 256–61

Nicholls, K. W., *Land, law and society in sixteenth-century Ireland* (Dublin, 1976)

Nicholls, K. W., 'Towards a new *Monasticon Hibericum*', *Peritia*, 3 (1984), pp. 330–3

Nicholls, K. W., 'Gaelic landownership in Tipperary from the surviving Irish deeds', in William Nolan and T. G. McGrath (eds), *Tipperary: history and society* (Dublin, 1985), pp. 92–103

Nicholls, K. W., 'Gaelic society and economy in the high middle ages', in Art Cosgrove (ed.), *A New History of Ireland, vol. 2: Medieval Ireland 1169–1534* (Oxford, 1987), pp. 397–438

Nicholls, K. W., 'Irishwomen and property in the sixteenth century', in Margaret MacCurtain and Mary O'Dowd (eds), *Women in early-modern Ireland* (Edinburgh, 1991), pp. 17–31

Nicholls, K. W., 'Review of R. R. Davies, 'Domination and conquest: the experience of Ireland, Scotland and Wales', *Scottish Economic and Social History*, 12 (1992), pp. 82–3

Nicholls, K. W., 'Woodland cover in pre-modern Ireland', in Patrick Duffy, David Edwards and Elizabeth Fitzpatrick (eds), *Gaelic Ireland, c.1250–c.1650: land, lordship and settlement* (Dublin, 2001), pp. 181–206

Nilis, Jeroen, 'Irish students at Leuven University, 1548–1797', *Archiv. Hib.*, 60 (2007), pp. 1–304

Nilis, Jeroen, 'Irish names in the ordination registers of the diocese of Ghent, 1559–1802', *Archiv. Hib.*, 60 (2007), pp. 305–19

O'Brien, Felim, 'Florence Conry, archbishop of Tuam', *Irish Rosary*, 31–2 (1927–8) pp. 843–7, 896–904, 346–51, 454–60, 839–46

O'Brien, George, *The economic history of Ireland* (Dublin, 1919)

O'Brien, Sylvester (ed.), *Measgra i gCuimhne Mhíchíl Uí Cléirigh* (Dublin, 1944)

Ó Buachalla, Breandán, 'Na Stíobhartaigh agus an t-aos léinn: Cing Séamas', *Proc. RIA*, 83, (1983) section C., pp. 81–134

Ó Buachalla, Breandán, *Aisling ghéar: na Stíobhartaigh agus an taos léinn, 1603–1788* (Baile Átha Cliath, 1996)

Ó Ciardha, Éamonn, *Staidéar Bunfhoinsí Imeacht na nIarlaí* (Dún na nGall, 2007)

Ó Ciosáin, Éamon, 'A hundred years of Irish migration to France, 1590–1688', in Thomas O'Connor (ed.), *The Irish in Europe 1580–1815* (Dublin, 2001), pp. 93–106

Ó Clabaigh, Colmán, *The Franciscans in Ireland, 1400–1534: from Reform to Reformation* (Dublin, 2002)

Ó Cléirigh, Tomás, *Aodh Mac Aingil agus scoil Nua-Ghaedhilge i Lobháin* (Dublin, 1935)

Ó Cléirigh, Tomás, 'A poembook of the O'Donnells', *Éigse*, 1 (1939) pp. 51–61

O'Connor, Thomas, 'Towards the invention of the Irish Catholic *natio*: Thomas Messingham's *Florilegium* (1624)', *Ir. Theol. Quart.*, 64/2 (1999), pp. 157–77

O'Connor, Thomas, 'Custom, authority and tolerance in Irish political thought: David Rothe's *Analecta Sacra et Mira* (1616)', *Ir. Theol. Quart.*, 65/2 (2000), pp. 133–56

O'Connor, Thomas, 'Thomas Messingham (c. 1575–1638?) and the seventeenth-century Church', *Ríocht na Midhe*, 11 (2000), pp. 88–105

O'Connor, Thomas, 'Irish migration to Spain and the formation of an Irish college network, 1589–1800', in Luc François and Ann Katherine Isaacs (eds), *The sea in European history* (Pisa, 2001), pp. 109–23

O'Connor, Thomas (ed.), *The Irish in Europe: 1580–1815* (Dublin, 2001)

O'Connor, Thomas, 'The ideology of state building in early-modern Europe', in Gudmundur Hálfdanarson and Ann Katherine Isaacs (eds), *Nations and nationalities in historical perspective* (Pisa, 2001), pp. 245–56

O'Connor, Thomas, 'Diplomatic preparations for Kinsale: Lombard's *Commentarius* (1600)', in Enrique García Hernán et al. (eds), *Irlanda y la monarquía hispánica: Kinsale 1601–2001. Guerra, política, exilio y religion* (Madrid, 2002), pp. 137–50

O'Connor, Thomas, 'Perfidious machiavellian friar: Florence Conry's campaign for a

Catholic restoration in Ireland', *Seanchas Ard Mhacha*, 19 (2002), pp. 91–105

O'Connor, Thomas, 'The Irish College, Rome, in the age of religious reform', in Albert MacDonnell et al. (eds), *The Irish College, Rome 1628–78: an early manuscript account of the foundation and development of the Ludovisian College of the Irish in Rome* (Rome, 2003), pp. 13–26

O'Connor, Thomas and Mary Ann Lyons (eds), *Irish migrants in Europe after Kinsale, 1602–1820* (Dublin, 2003)

O'Connor, Thomas, 'Hugh O'Neill: free spirit, religious chameleon or ardent Catholic?', in Hiram Morgan (ed.), *The Battle of Kinsale* (Wicklow, 2004), pp. 59–72

O'Connor, Thomas, *An Irish Jansenist in seventeenth-century France: John Callaghan, 1605–54: the 32nd O'Donnell Lecture* (Dublin, 2004)

O'Connor, Thomas and Mary Ann Lyons (eds), *Irish communities in early-modern Europe* (Dublin, 2006)

O'Connor, Thomas, *Irish Jansenists, 1600–70: religion and politics in Flanders, France, Ireland and Rome* (Dublin, 2008)

O'Conor Don, Charles Owen, *The O'Conors of Connaught* (Dublin, 1891)

Ó Corráin, Donnchadh, 'Irish origin legends and genealogy: recurrent aetiologies', in Tore Nyberg (ed.), *History and heroic tale: a symposium* (Odense, 1985), pp. 51–96

O'Curry, Eugene, *Lectures on the manuscript materials of ancient Irish history* (Dublin, 1861)

O'Doherty, Denis, 'Students of the Irish college, Salamanca', *Archiv. Hib.*, 2 (1913), pp. 1–12

O'Dowd, Mary, *Power, politics and land: early-modern Sligo, 1568–1688* (Belfast, 1991)

Ó Dúshláine, Tadhg, *An Eoraip agus litríocht na Gaeilge, 1600–1650: gnéithe den bharócachas Eorpach i litríocht na Gaeilge* (Baile Átha Cliath, 1987)

Ó Fiaich, Tomás, 'Edmund O'Reilly, archbishop of Armagh, 1657–1669', in Franciscan Fathers (eds), *Father Luke Wadding: commemorative volume* (Dublin, 1957), pp. 171–227

Ó Háinle, Cathal, 'The Pater Noster in Irish', *Celtica*, 22 (1991), pp. 145–64

Ó Háinle, Cathal, 'An Phaidir: Ó Maolchonaire agus Ó hEodhasa', *Celtica*, 24 (2003), pp. 239–51

Ó hAnnracháin, Tadhg, 'Though hereticks and politicians should misinterpret their good zeal: political ideology and Catholicism in early-modern Ireland', in Jane Ohlmeyer (ed.), *Political thought in seventeenth-century Ireland: kingdom or colony* (Cambridge, 2000), pp. 155–75

Ohlmeyer, Jane (ed.), *Civil war and restoration in the three Stuart kingdoms: the political career of Randall MacDonnell, first marquis of Antrim, 1609–83* (Cambridge, 1993)

Ohlmeyer, Jane, *Political thought in seventeenth-century Ireland* (Cambridge, 2000)

O'Leary, Joseph, 'The Irish and Jansenism in the seventeenth century', in Liam Swords (ed.), *The Irish–French connection: 1578–1978* (Paris, 1979), pp. 21–43

Ó Macháin, Pádraig, 'Poems of Fearghal Óg Mac An Bhaird', *Celtica*, 24 (2003), pp. 252–63

Ó Muraíle, Nollaig, *The celebrated antiquary: life, lineage and learning* (Maynooth, 1996)

O'Neill, Timothy, *The Irish hand: scribes and their manuscripts from the earliest times to the seventeenth century, with an exemplar of Irish scripts* (Dublin, 1984)

O'Rahilly, T. F., *Dánfhocail: Irish epigrams in verse* (Dublin, 1921)

Ó Riain, Pádraig (ed.), *Beatha Aodha Ruadh: historical and literary contexts* (Dublin, 2002)

O'Riordan, Michelle, *The Gaelic mind and the collapse of the Gaelic world* (Cork, 1990)

O'Scea, Ciarán, 'En busca de papeles: la transformación de la cultura oral de los inmigrantes irlandeses', in Enrique García Hernán, Oscar Recio Morales et al. (eds), *Irlanda y la Monarquía Hispánica, Kinsale 1601–2001: Guerra, política, exilio y religión* (Madrid, 2001), pp. 359–80

O'Scea, Ciarán, 'Irish wills from Galicia, 1592–1666', *Archiv. Hib.*, 56 (2002), pp. 73–131

O'Scea, Ciarán, 'The devotional world of the Irish Catholic exile in early-modern Galicia, 1598–1666', in Thomas O'Connor (ed.), *The Irish in Europe: 1580–1815* (Dublin, 2001), pp. 27–48

O'Scea, Ciarán, 'The significance and legacy of Spanish intervention in west Munster during the battle of Kinsale', in Thomas O'Connor and Mary Ann Lyons (eds), *Irish migrants in Europe after Kinsale, 1602–1820* (Dublin, 2003) pp. 32–63

O'Scea, Ciarán, 'Irish emigration to Castile in the opening years of the seventeenth century', in Patrick Duffy (ed.), *To and from Ireland: planned migration schemes c. 1600–2000* (Dublin, 2004), pp. 17–38

O'Scea, Ciarán, 'Caracena: champion of the Irish, hunter of the Moriscos', in Hiram Morgan (ed.), *The battle of Kinsale* (Wicklow, 2004), pp. 229–39

O'Scea, Ciarán, 'The role of Castilian royal bureaucracy in the formation of early-modern Irish literacy', in Thomas O'Connor and Mary Ann Lyons (eds), *Irish communities in early modern Europe* (Dublin, 2006), pp. 200–39

Ó Súilleabháin, Seán, 'Údar *Sgáthán an Chrábhaidh*', *The Maynooth Review* (1989), pp. 42–50

Ó Súilleabháin, Seán, '*Sgáthán an Chrábhaidh*: Foinsí an Aistriúcháin', *Éigse*, 24 (1990), pp. 26–36

Palmer, Patricia, *Language and conquest in early modern Ireland: English Renaissance literature and Elizabethan imperial expansion* (Cambridge, 2001)

Palmer, William, *The problem of Ireland in Tudor foreign policy, 1485–1603* (Woodbridge, 1994)

Paquot, Jean-Noël, *Mémoires pour servir à l'histoire littéraire des dix-sept provinces des Pays-Bas* (Louvain, 1769)

Parker, Geoffrey, *The military revolution* (Cambridge, 1967)

Parker, Geoffrey, *The army of Flanders and the Spanish road, 1567–1659: the logistics of Spanish victory and defeat in the Low Countries' wars* (Cambridge, 1972)

Parker, Geoffrey, 'Mutiny and discontent in the Spanish army of Flanders, 1572–1607', *Past & Present*, 58 (1973), pp. 38–52

Parker, Geoffrey, *Europe in crisis, 1598–1648* (London, 1979)

Parker, Geoffrey, *Spain and the Netherlands, 1559–1659* (London, 1979)

Parker, Geoffrey, 'The making of strategy in Habsburg Spain: Philip II's "bid for mastery", 1556–1598', in W. Murray, K. MacGregor and A. Bernstein (eds), *The making of strategy: rulers, states, and war* (Cambridge, 1994)

Pérez Bustamante, Ciriaco, *La España de Felipe III*, Ramón Menéndez Pidal (ed.), *Historia de España*, vol. 14 (Madrid, 1983)

Pérez Tostado, Igor, '"Fiarse cautamente": The circulation of information and the Irish pressure group in the court of Spain', in Enrique García Hernán, Óscar Recio Morales et al. (eds), *Irlanda y la monarquía hispánica: Kinsale 1601–2001: Guerra, política, exilio y religion* (Madrid, 2002)

Pérez Tostado, Igor, 'Irish political activity in the Spanish monarchy during the Restoration', in Thomas O'Connor (ed.), *Irish communities in early-modern Europe* (Dublin, 2006)

Peristiany, J. G. (ed.), *Honour and shame: the values of Mediterranean society* (London, 1965)

Pirenne, Henri, *Histoire de Belgique* (8 vols, Brussels, 1911–48), vol. 4: *Le régime espagnol*

Pizarro Llorente, Henar, 'El control de la consciencia regia. El confesor real fray Bernardo de Fresnada', in José Martínez Millán (ed.), *La corte de Felipe II* (Madrid, 1995), pp. 149–88

Postigo Castellanos, Elena, *Honor y privilegio en la corona de Castilla. El consejo de las ordenes y los caballeros de hábito en el siglo XVII* (Soria, 1988)

Pou y Martí, José María, 'Embajadas de Felipe III a Roma, pidiendo la definición de la Inmaculada Concepción de María', *Archivo Ibero-americano*, 34 (1931), pp. 371–417, 508–34; 35 (1932), pp. 72–88, 424–34, 481–525; 36 (1933), pp. 5–48

Pulido Bueno, Ildefonso, *La Real Hacienda de Felipe III* (Huelva, 1996)

Puype, Jan Piet and Anton Wiekart, *Van Maurits naar Munster, tactiek en triomf van het Staatse leger* (Delft, 1998)

Recio Morales, Óscar, 'Not only seminaries: the political role of the Irish colleges in seventeenth-century Spain', *History Ireland*, 9 (2001), pp. 48–52

Recio Morales, Óscar, *El socorro de Irlanda en 1601 y la contribución del ejército a la integración social de los irlandeses en España* (Madrid, 2002)

Recio Morales, Óscar, 'De nación irlandés: percepciones socio-culturales y respuestas políticas sobre Irlanda y la comunidad irlandesa en la España del XVII', in Enrique García Hernán et al. (eds), *Irlanda y la monarquía hispánica* (Madrid, 2002) pp. 315–40

Recio Morales, Óscar, 'Florence Conry's memorandum for a military assault on Ulster, 1627', *Archiv. Hib.*, 56 (2002), pp. 65–72.

Recio Morales, Óscar, *Irlanda en Alcalá: la comunidad irlandesa en la Universidad de Alcalá, 1579–1785* (Alcalá, 2003)

Recio Morales, Óscar, 'Irish émigré group strategies of survival, adaptation and integration in seventeenth- and eighteenth-century Spain', in Thomas O'Connor and Mary Ann Lyons (eds), *Irish communities in early-modern Europe* (Dublin, 2006), pp. 240–66

Recio Morales, Óscar, *Ireland and the Spanish Empire, 1600–1815* (Dublin, forthcoming)

Redworth, Glyn, 'Beyond Faith and Fatherland: the appeal of the Catholics of Ireland, c. 1623', *Archiv. Hib.*, 52 (1998), pp. 3–23

Redworth, Glyn, *The Prince and the Infanta: the cultural politics of the Spanish match* (New Haven, 2003)

Reusens, Edmond (ed.), *Documents relatifs á l'histoire de l'Université de Louvain, 1425–1797* (5 vols, 1881–1903; repr. Brussels, 1999)

Revilla González, Fidel and Rosalía Ramos Guarido, *Madrid de los Austrias: recorridos didácticos* (Madrid, 2003)

Richardson, Regina Whelan (ed.), *Salamanca letters: a catalogue of the Irish college of Salamanca correspondence between 1619–1870, from the archives of the Irish colleges in Spain in the library of St Patrick's College* (Maynooth, 1994)

Rodríguez Pazos, Manuel, 'Cofradías piadosas y capellanías castrenses en el convento de San Francisco de La Coruña (siglos XVI–XVII)', *Boletín de la Real Academia Gallega* (1945), pp. 423–37

Rodríguez Villa, Antonio, *Ambrosio Spínola, primer marqués de los Balbases. Ensayo biográfico* (Madrid, 1905)

Saavedra Vázquez, María del Carmen, 'Algunos rasgos del comportamiento religioso de los militares españoles en época austriaca: el ejemplo de La Coruña', *Historia Moderna*, 7 (1994), pp. 271–86

Schüller, K., *Die Beziehungen zwischen Spanien und Irland im XVI und XVII jahrhundert: Diplomatie, Handle und die Soziale Integration Katholischer exulanten* (Münster, 1999)

Schurhammer, Georg, 'Ein christlicher japanischer Prunkschirm des 17. Jahrhunderts', *Artibus Asiae*, 2 (1927), pp. 94–123

Silke, J. J., 'Later relations between Primate Peter Lombard and Hugh O'Neill', *Ir. Theol. Quart.*, 22 (1955), pp. 15–30

Silke, J. J., 'The Irish appeal of 1593 to Spain: some light on the genesis of the Nine Years' War', *IER*, 92 (1959), pp. 279–90, 362–71

Silke, J. J., *Ireland and Europe, 1559–1607* (Dundalk, 1966)

Silke, J. J., *Kinsale: the Spanish intervention in Ireland at the end of the Elizabethan wars* (Liverpool, 1970)

Silke, J. J., 'Irish scholarship and the Renaissance, 1580–1675', *Studies in the Renaissance*, 21 (1973), pp. 169–205

Silke, J. J., 'The last will of Red Hugh O'Donnell', *Studia Hibernica*, 24 (1988), pp. 51–60

Silke, J. J., 'Outward bound from Portnamurray', in Enrique García Hernán et al. (eds), *Irlanda y la monarquía hispánica: Kinsale 1601–2001. Guerra, política, exilio y religion* (Madrid, 2002), pp. 423–45

Simms, Katherine, 'Guesting and feasting in Gaelic Ireland', *Journal of the Royal Society of Antiquaries of Ireland*, 108 (1978), pp. 67–100

Simms, Katherine, *From kings to warlords: the changing political structure of Gaelic Ireland in the late middle ages* (Woodbridge, 1987)

Simms, Katherine, 'The poetic Brehon lawyers of early sixteenth-century Ireland', *Ériu*, 57 (2007), pp. 121–32

Stone, M. W. F., 'Scholastic schools and early-modern philosophy', in Donald Rutherford (ed.), *The Cambridge companion to early-modern philosophy* (Cambridge, 2006), pp. 299–327

Stradling, R. A., *Europe and the decline of Spain* (London, 1981)

Stradling, R. A., *The Spanish monarchy and Irish mercenaries: the Wild Geese in Spain, 1618–1668* (Dublin, 1986)

Stradling, R. A., *Spain's struggle for Europe, 1598–1668* (London, 1994)

Tapia Ozcariz, Enrique de, *Eugenio O'Neill: caudillo de la independencia de Irlanda* (Madrid, 1969)

Thomas, Werner (ed.), *De val van het Nieuwe Troje: het beleg van Oostende 1601–1604* (Leuven, 2004)

Thompson, I. A. A., *War and government in Habsburg Spain: 1560–1620* (London, 1976)

Treadwell, Victor, 'Sir John Perrott and the Irish parliament of 1585–6', *PRIA*, section C, 85/10 (1985)

Trevor-Roper, H. R., 'The general crisis of the seventeenth century', *Past & Present*, 16 (1959), pp. 31–64

Turner, Olga, 'A Spanish ambassador's half-yearly account', *Bulletin of Hispanic Studies*, 31 (1954), pp. 98–108

Vergara, Alejandro et al. (eds), *El Arte en la Corte de los Archiduques Alberto de Austria e Isabel Clara Eugenia (1598–1633): Un reino imaginado* (Madrid, 1999)

Vicens Vives, J., *Aproximación a la historia de España* (Barcelona, 1952)

Vinck, José de (ed. and trans.). *St Bonaventure: Apologia Pauperum* (Paris, 1966)

Wall, Tomás, 'Seventeenth-century Irish theologians in exile', *IER*, 53 (1939), pp. 501–15

Wall, Tomás, 'The catechism in Irish', *IER*, 59 (1942), pp. 36–48

Walsh, Paul, 'The O'Clerys of Tirconnell', *Studies* (1929), pp. 247–53

Walsh, Paul, 'James Blake of Galway', *IER*, 50 (1937), pp. 382–97

Walsh, Paul, *Irish men of learning* (Dublin, 1947)

Walsh, T. J., *The Irish continental college movement* (Cork, 1973)

Watson, Robert, *The history of the reign of Philip the Third, king of Spain* (London, 1839)

Willaert, P. L., 'Négociations politico-religieuses entre l'Angleterre et le Pays-Bas catholiques', *Revue d'histoire ecclésiastiques*, 6 (1905), pp. 47, 566, 811; 7 (1906), p. 585; 8 (1907), p. 81

Williams, Patrick, 'Lerma, Old Castile and the travels of Philip III of Spain', *History*, 73 (1988), pp. 379–97

Wilson, Margaret, *Spanish drama of the golden age* (London, 1969)

Wright, Jonathan, *The Jesuits: missions, myths and histories* (London, 2004)

Wright, Jonathan, *The Ambassadors: from ancient Greece to the nation state* (London, 2006)

Index